Custom Edition for Metropolitan State University of Denver

SPE 1010 Public Speaking

The Speaker's Handbook 10e

Jo Sprague | Douglas Stuart | David Bodary

Australia • Brazil • Japan • Korea • Mexico • Singapore • Spain • United Kingdom • United States

CENGAGE
Learning®

Custom Edition for Metropolitan State University of Denver: SPE 1010 Public Speaking, The Speaker's Handbook 10e

The Speaker's Handbook, 10th Edition
Jo Sprague | Douglas Stuart | David Bodary

© 2013, 2010, 2008 Wadsworth, Cengage Learning. All rights reserved.

Executive Editors:

Maureen Staudt
Michael Stranz

Senior Project Development Manager:

Linda deStefano

Marketing Specialist:

Courtney Sheldon

Senior Production/
Manufacturing Manager:

Donna M. Brown

Production Editorial Manager:
Kim Fry

Sr. Rights Acquisition
Account Manager:

Todd Osborne

For product information and technology assistance, contact us at
Cengage Learning Customer & Sales Support, 1-800-354-9706

For permission to use material from this text or product,
submit all requests online at **cengage.com/permissions**
Further permissions questions can be emailed to
permissionrequest@cengage.com

This book contains select works from existing Cengage Learning resources and was produced by Cengage Learning Custom Solutions for collegiate use. As such, those adopting and/or contributing to this work are responsible for editorial content accuracy, continuity and completeness.

Compilation © 2012 Cengage Learning

ISBN-13:   978-1-285-10343-3

ISBN-10:   1-285-10343-2

Cengage Learning
5191 Natorp Boulevard
Mason, Ohio 45040
USA

Cengage Learning is a leading provider of customized learning solutions with office locations around the globe, including Singapore, the United Kingdom, Australia, Mexico, Brazil, and Japan. Locate your local office at:
international.cengage.com/region.

Cengage Learning products are represented in Canada by Nelson Education, Ltd.

For your lifelong learning solutions, visit **www.cengage.com/custom.**
Visit our corporate website at **www.cengage.com.**

Printed in the United States
of America

Speaker's *Quick Start* Guide

The Quick Start Guide on the next page is designed to help you find the specific public speaking information you're looking for as quickly as possible.

Basic Content Information, Color-Coded

This Guide provides only the most basic information about the **handbook's contents**:

▶ Part numbers and titles

▶ Chapter numbers and titles within each part

▶ Page range for each part (identifying first and last pages)

The handiest feature of this guide is that it is **color-coded**: The color applied to each part in the guide corresponds to the color used for the actual part's tabbed section divider and introductory pages as well as the thumb tabs you'll find at the top of each page.

Where You'll Find More Detailed Content Information

The handbook's **full table of contents** begins on page vii. Additionally, each part's **tabbed section divider** includes a detailed listing of each chapter and the chapter's subsections within the part. At the back of the book, on its last pages and inside back cover, you'll find **listings of the handbook's boxes, tables, and figures**. A detailed **index** begins on page 495.

Mapping Your Skill Development Plan

To help orient you so that this book is as useful as possible, we offer these key suggestions:

▶ **Read Chapter 1.** This chapter introduces the five steps of public speaking that will help you prepare and deliver an effective speech. It will also help you diagnose your skill level and give you an approach to mapping out a skill-development plan for yourself.

▶ **Prepare a skill-development plan.** There are many steps to preparing an effective speech, but if you try to master every step simultaneously, you'll become frustrated and find it harder to build skills. That's why the secret of public speaking success lies in having a clear idea of what your priorities are and in deciding on a limited number of goals to pursue at any one time. This text's handbook format lets you pick one or two important skills to work on and, when those are mastered, move to other skills. Take the time to write down a skill-development plan and refer back to it. Even if you revise it as you go, we guarantee that it will help you succeed.

Online Resources for *The Speaker's Handbook*, Tenth Edition

This text comes with a rich array of **online resources** to enhance and extend your learning. If your instructor did not request that these resources be packaged with the text, you can purchase them separately. Available resources include flashcards, self-quizzing, sample speech videos, the Speech Builder Express™ 3.0 program for coaching through the speechmaking process, downloadable Audio Study Tools, the InfoTrac® College Edition periodicals database, and an interactive eBook.

For more information and to access this book's online resources, visit www.cengagebrain.com.

THE
Speaker's
HANDBOOK

Custom Edition for
Metropolitian State University of Denver

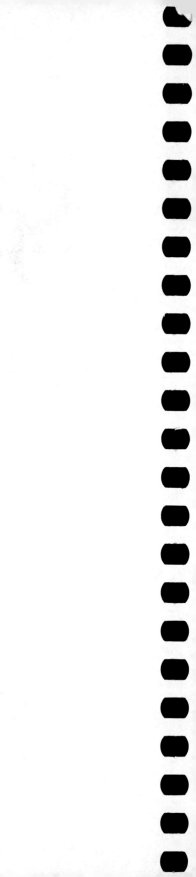

Contents

(1)))) Foundation

4: Overcoming Fear of Speaking 46

(2))) Preparation

5: Planning 58

6: Topic Selection and Analysis 65

(3)))) Organization

(4)))) Development

(5))) Presentation

24: Practice Sessions   316

25: Vocal Delivery   328

26: Physical Delivery   340

8   Additional Resources

Guide to Common Pronunciation and Usage Errors   481

Preface

As a flexible compendium of principles and examples that cover the entire process of preparing and delivering a speech, the tenth edition of *The Speaker's Handbook* is, like its earlier editions, both a reference guide for individual speakers and a textbook for use in public speaking courses. What distinguishes *The Speaker's Handbook* from other books on public speaking, though, is not just that it was the first handbook of public speaking, but that it was originally conceived and written as one too. From the start, each of its chapters was designed to stand by itself so that speakers may directly consult only those sections of the book that present the specific help they need. This text's origins are still evident, offering the greatest flexibility and ease of use for all kinds of public speakers.

Why We Wrote *The Speaker's Handbook*

In a sense, a book about public speaking is a contradiction. Public speaking is a lived, performed, embodied event that draws its special qualities from the immediate context, the personality of a particular speaker, and the response of a certain audience. Is there really any useful general advice about so specific an act?

Apparently so. For as long as people have felt the need to speak in public, they have turned to others for advice on how to do so more effectively. Early evidence from Egyptian tombs shows that leaders gave serious thought to the choices they faced in speaking to their followers. The oral tradition captured in Homeric legend hints that the giving and taking of this advice predated the written word. The increasing supply of information about the ancient cultures of China, India, and the Americas shows that these peoples had culturally distinctive ways of speaking, which some analyzed and discussed. These observers then formulated advice for others in their culture. Such advice usually came in two forms: Those who had vast experience as speakers told stories about what worked for them; others looked beyond what worked and theorized about why it worked.

Both forms of guidance are still present. Leading platform speakers write books about their experiences. The popularity of such books year after year suggests that people find benefits in the personal and experiential approach. At the same time, university libraries continue to accumulate academic treatises on rhetoric and communication. Here, too, the vitality of these lines of research after thousands of years suggests that much is left to be said and investigated.

There is a third form of guidance, one that we differentiate from both those kinds of books and place within another venerable tradition that is over two thousand years old. This form is neither a narrative account of personal success stories nor a scholarly theoretical tome. It is the handbook. The first written handbooks for speakers were probably produced by the Sophists in the Greece of 200 BCE. In any field, a handbook represents a particular blending of theory and practice displayed in a concise format. There are scouting handbooks, birding handbooks, management handbooks, and meditation handbooks. In all these cases, a handbook is a distillation of the experience and theory of many people and many eras. The particular usefulness of handbooks can be found in their distinctive characteristics, and the value of this handbook can be found in its unique features.

Handbooks Are Brief

In *The Speaker's Handbook* we have tried to distill the most meaningful advice, provide the most useful examples, and avoid bulking out the book. However, sample speeches abound: This edition includes an updated Part 7 that presents annotated sample speeches by both student speakers and public figures, many accompanied by speech videos and interactive activities available among the book's online resources. We refer to these sample outlines, transcripts, manuscripts, and videos throughout the text in both examples and exercises. Interspersing sample speeches throughout the body of the book, as is usual in standard textbooks, would defeat the advantages offered by the handbook format. Cartoons and photographs would likewise have taken up too much space.

Handbooks Are Reference Books

Long before the "information superhighway," people liked to learn things as they needed them. *The Speaker's Handbook* proceeds from the premise that people like to focus first on the area of greatest concern and then design their own learning experience outward from that point. Jo Sprague, Doug Stuart, and David Bodary agree that there are and ought to be many "right ways" to approach a course in public speaking. As such, the contents of a handbook are meant to be used in any order. The progression of this handbook's chapters is not random, but a reader or teacher does not necessarily have to follow that order. We have written the chapters to be as self-contained as possible so that the book is adaptable to the differing needs of its various users.

As a reference, this book seeks to meet the needs of adult learners. Adult learners have their own way of designing their learning programs, whether they are playing with their new smartphone or understanding a new job. People don't expect to need a course in how to use their smartphone. Instead they try a few things, glance at the manual, ask a friend and work until they get into trouble. Then they seek assistance again, but only for the specific information they need to get beyond the current problem. In effect, they don't worry about the things they don't have to worry about, and they often don't know that a thing to worry about exists until it becomes a problem for them. Public speaking is like that. Until people start speaking, they cannot be sure of all the areas in which they may need improvement. Therefore, students and individual users should take what they need from this book in the order they need it.

Likewise, teachers—who bring to the classroom different experience and an understanding of the values, needs, and capabilities of their specific students—may choose to assign chapters in any order that fits their perceptions of the best way to increase the skills of their students. There's some benefit for everyone in every chapter of this handbook; by using it you will find the order that suits you best.

Handbooks Are Handy

When people open the documentation that comes with their smartphone, they want to find the section on storing phone numbers, not read about taking photographs or how to clear the screen. A good user guide compartmentalizes related information and then makes that information as accessible as possible through a variety of pointers and references, using design tools to make things easy to find: the hallmark of handiness. We have included aids to help users get to where they want to be as quickly as possible, from elements such as the Quick Start Guide on the inside front cover to the tabbed part openers that include directories of each part's content, and from the checklists to the tables, figures, and straightforward cross-references provided throughout the book.

With this compartmentalization, users do not have to read everything at once. A student may be preparing to give an informative speech for a class and is thinking of including some humor. The student could jump ahead and read the section in Chapter 18 on using appropriate humor. A businessperson may be giving a presentation to the board on the introduction of a new product but may feel uncertain about whether he or she has covered everything and in the most effective order. That person could read Chapter 9 on transforming ideas into speech points and Chapters 21 and 22 on informative and persuasive strategies.

About the Tenth Edition

We have been gratified by the response to the first nine editions of *The Speaker's Handbook*, and we are pleased that the handbook format has worked for so many students and their instructors as well as for people who give presentations in their business or community. In this edition, we have once again responded to user suggestions on how to make the information even more timely and accessible.

▶ **Co-author David Bodary, an award-winning teacher and scholar,** continues to contribute to this latest edition, preserving the tradition and strength of *The Speaker's Handbook* while infusing it with contemporary contexts and community connections. His love of teaching and his experience at the community college level comes through in every chapter via his practical tips and advice for students. In addition, his focus on civic engagement highlights the importance of effective public speaking skills in many contexts, including the workplace and the community.

▶ **New For Your Benefit boxes** replace the Key Point boxes in previous editions, continuing to provide practical speech advice while also offering insights for speaking in the classroom and in the boardroom. These tips address common challenges encountered by many speakers in school, in the workplace, and in volunteer contexts. New and updated content provides students with tips for

- ✓ Estimating preparation time.
- ✓ Tailoring main points to an audience and speaking situation.
- ✓ Understanding how the six universal human values affect audience analysis.
- ✓ Learning to utilize research resources in speaking situations and beyond.
- ✓ Applying organizational patterns not only to speeches but also to workplace documents and presentations.

▶ **New Putting It into Practice activities** replace the Speaking Beyond the Classroom activities at the end of each chapter, continuing to emphasize that speaking is a lifelong skill and to provide students with opportunities to analyze and practice public speaking skills in various contexts.

▶ **New and updated content** includes a new section on avoiding presenting opinion as fact (Chapter 3), updated research on managing public speaking anxiety (Chapter 4), and advice on adapting to generational differences in terms of generational groups: Traditionalists, Boomers, Gen Xers, and Millennials (Chapter 7).

▶ **Fresh, updated examples** have been incorporated throughout the book, providing readers with relatable references to popular culture and current events. Many new examples touch on topics students are interested in and can identify with, including social media, gaming, and current concerns such as the environment. In addition, updated samples from recent public speeches are incorporated throughout the text.

▶ **Part 7, Speeches by Student Speakers**, continues to provide speech models and opportunities for analysis, and this edition features a fully updated collection of annotated outlines and transcripts of student speeches. Many of the speeches include visual aids, and all include video captures of the speakers with captions focusing on aspects of their delivery. Brand new student speeches include

- ✓ "Understanding Hurricanes" (informative)
- ✓ "Four-Day School Week" (invitational)
- ✓ "No More Sugar!" (persuasive)
- ✓ "Bite Back" (persuasive speech about malaria prevention)
- ✓ "Together, We Can Stop Cyber-Bullying" (persuasive)

As in previous editions, video for all student speeches are provided online along with critical-thinking questions, transcripts, full-sentence and keyword outlines, and speaking notes.

▶ **Part 7, Speeches by Public Figures,** have been chosen to reflect the diversity and disparity of voices that define the current age. Included in this section are five speeches, all brand new, that are sure to provide meaningful illustration and considerable debate:

- ✓ Entrepreneur and author Julian Treasure's "The Four Ways Sound Affects Us" (informative)
- ✓ President Barack Obama's "Remarks on a Historic Day in Egypt" (commemorative)
- ✓ Artist and activist Dianna Cohen's "Tough Truths about Plastic Pollution" (persuasive)
- ✓ Author and activist Feisal Abdul Rauf's "There Is Everything Right with Being an American Muslim" (persuasive)
- ✓ Former Massachusetts governor and Republican presidential candidate Mitt Romney's "Speech to Conservative Political Action Conference (CPAC), February 2011" (special occasion)

All speeches by public figures are accompanied by transcripts and critical-thinking questions.

▶ The Speech Communication **CourseMate for *The Speaker's Handbook*** provides one-stop access to the book's updated online resources, including a fully interactive electronic version of the text and Wadsworth Cengage Learning's online speech upload and critique tool, Speech Studio™. You'll find more information about CourseMate and many other resources on pages xxix–xxxiv.

▶ To accommodate new content while still keeping the handbook to a manageable length, the guidelines for employment and other interviews have been removed from Chapter 32. However, custom material on employment interviews is available through Wadsworth Cengage Learning's Flex-Text Customization Program. See page xxxiv for more information about this program.

Hallmarks of *The Speaker's Handbook*

The great strength of oral communication is that its many dimensions offer people ways to seek out connections in the midst of differences; its immediacy allows for on-the-spot adjustments. The following features of the text have therefore been retained:

▶ **Skill-building pedagogy and study tools.** Checklist boxes help readers better understand—and apply—chapter concepts. Speaker's Workshop boxes provide activities that help students prepare effective, well-structured speeches. In addition, Part 8 provides resources that speakers and users of the handbook will find practical and helpful: a guide to common pronunciation and usage errors for native and nonnative speakers of English, and a glossary of key terms.

▶ **Communicative approach.** Public speaking is consistently presented as a blend of communicative resources: writing, performance, and conversation.

▶ **Distinctive coverage of audience analysis.** Not just audience members' traits and characteristics are analyzed, but also the processes by which they make sense of messages (Chapter 7).

▶ **Extensive coverage of reasoning.** Reasoning (Chapter 16) is discussed through an examination of the links people draw between data and conclusions. The text discusses how people can logically reach opposite conclusions from the same evidence, emphasizing the need to spell out and justify the links in one's reasoning.

▶ **Emphasis on language.** Language (Chapter 17) is presented as a primary communicative process and style as an essential communicative element (rather than an adornment or frill) in order to emphasize the need for sensitive and appropriate use of words and symbols.

▶ **Full chapter on ethics.** "Speaking Ethics" (Chapter 3) draws together key points and provides guidelines for responsible speaking. The ethical decisions speakers make are treated as a series of careful compromises, not as clear-cut do's and don'ts.

▶ **Full chapter on practicing speeches.** Chapter 24 provides detailed guidelines for practicing speech presentations, including concrete suggestions and timetables for this important dimension of speech preparation.

▶ **Consistent attention paid to social and cultural diversity.** We strive to continue attuning the handbook to the diversity of contemporary life. In our treatment of language, reasoning, and vocal and physical delivery, we attempt to show how social forces shape—and are shaped by—speech. What is appropriate or clear or persuasive constantly changes as society changes, and we emphasize that effective speakers are open to the subtle cultural variations in speech situations. If there were no differences between people, communication would be unnecessary. If there were no similarities, it would be impossible.

Resources for Students and Instructors

Accompanying this book is an integrated suite of resources to support both students and instructors.

Student Resources

Students and other individuals have the option of utilizing a rich array of resources to enhance and extend their learning while using *The Speaker's Handbook*. **Note to instructors:** If you want your students to have access to the online resources for *The Speaker's Handbook,* please be sure to order them for your course—if you do not order them, your students will not have access to them on the first day of class. These resources can be bundled with every new copy of the text or ordered separately. Students whose instructors do not order these resources as a package with the text may purchase them or access them at **www.cengagebrain.com**. *Contact your local Wadsworth Cengage Learning sales representative for more details.*

▶ **Speech Communication CourseMate for *The Speaker's Handbook*.** Provides students with easy access to the integrated technology resources that accompany the book. These resources include learning, study, and exam preparation tools such as the handbook's interactive eBook, Audio Study Tools, flashcards, and activities. Watch comprehension soar as your class works with the printed textbook and the textbook-specific website. In addition, CourseMate's Engagement Tracker tracking tools allow instructors to monitor the progress of the class as a whole or of individual students. Engagement Tracker helps you identify students at risk early in the course, uncover which concepts are most difficult for your class, monitor time on task, and keep your students engaged. The CourseMate for the handbook goes beyond the book to deliver what you need!

▶ **Interactive Video Activities.** Presented within Wadsworth Cengage Learning's unique interactive user interface, the speech videos help students gain experience evaluating and critiquing introductory, informative, invitational, persuasive, and special occasion speeches so that they can more effectively provide feedback to their peers and improve their own speeches and delivery. This highly praised resource includes the following features:

✓ Transcripts for all speech videos.

✓ Preparation outlines, speaking outlines, and note cards for full-length student speech videos so students can recognize the connection between creating an effective speech outline and delivering a speech.

✓ A "scroll" function that students may choose to turn on or off for full-length speech videos. When the scroll feature is on, synchronized highlighting tracks each speaker's progress through an outline or transcript of the speech as the video of the speaker's delivery plays alongside.

✓ A "notes" function that lets students insert written comments while watching the video. At a student's command, the program pauses, enters a timestamp that indicates where the video was paused, and offers students the ability to write their own critiques of the video or choose from a set of prewritten rubrics that teach students how to effectively evaluate speeches.

✓ Assignable analysis questions with responses written by the text's authors, available when students answer the questions themselves and submit them to their instructor.

▸ **Audio Study Tools.** This text's Audio Study Tools provide a fun and easy way for students to download audio files and review chapter content whenever and wherever. For each chapter of the text, students will have access to a chapter review consisting of the learning objectives for the chapter, a brief summary of the main points in the text, audio of a sample student speech, and five to seven critical thinking questions. Students can go to the CourseMate for *The Speaker's Handbook* to listen to or download the Audio Study Tools.

▸ **Speech Studio 2.0™.** With Speech Studio, students can upload video files of practice speeches or final performances, comment on their peer's speeches, and review their grades and instructor feedback. By popular demand, Speech Studio 2.0 includes enhancements such as adding, deleting, and resetting assignments on the fly, uploading additional assignment elements such as outlines and Microsoft PowerPoint® slides, enhanced peer review functionality, grading with weighed rubric criteria, and a rubric editor! Speech Studio's flexibility lends itself to use in traditional, hybrid, and online courses. It allows instructors to save valuable in-class time by conducting practice sessions and peer review work virtually; combine the ease of a course management tool with a convenient way to capture, grade, and review videos of live, in-class performances; and simulate an in-class experience for online courses.

▶ **Speech Builder Express 3.0.** Many of the book's activities can be completed with this interactive Web-based tool that coaches students through the speech organization and outlining process. By completing interactive sessions, students can prepare and save their outlines, formatted according to the principles presented in the text. Text models of speech elements reinforce students' interactive practice.

▶ **InfoTrac College Edition™.** This virtual library's more than 18 million reliable, full-length articles from 5,000 academic and popular periodicals allow students to retrieve results almost instantly. They also have access to InfoMarks—stable URLs that can be linked to articles, journals, and searches to save valuable time when doing research—and to the InfoWrite online resource center, where students can access grammar help, critical-thinking guidelines, guides to writing research papers, and much more.

▶ **CengageBrain Online Store.** CengageBrain.com is a single destination for more than 15,000 new print textbooks, textbook rentals, eBooks, single eChapters, and print, digital, and audio study tools. CengageBrain.com provides the freedom to purchase Cengage Learning products à-la-carte—exactly what you need, when you need it. Visit **www.cengagebrain.com** for details.

▶ *The Art and Strategy of Service-Learning Presentations,* **Second Edition.** Authored by Rick Isaacson and Jeff Saperstein of San Francisco State University, this handbook provides guidelines for connecting service-learning work with classroom concepts and advice for working effectively with agencies and organizations.

▶ *A Guide to the Basic Course for ESL Students.* Specifically for communicators whose first language is not English, it features FAQs, helpful URLs, and strategies for managing communication anxiety.

Instructor Resources

Instructors who adopt this book may request a number of resources to support their teaching. These resources are available to qualified adopters, and ordering options for supplements are flexible. *Please consult your local Wadsworth Cengage Learning sales representative* for more information, to evaluate examination copies of any of these instructor or student resources, or to request product demonstrations.

▶ **Instructor's Resource Manual.** Written by Tina Lim of San José State University, this manual offers guidelines for setting up your course, sample syllabi, chapter-by-chapter outlines of content, suggested topics for lectures and discussion, and a wealth of class-tested exercises and assignments. It also includes a test bank with questions marked according to varying levels of difficulty.

▶ **Instructor's Website.** The password-protected site allows you to view all the assets your students can view, helps you determine what you can assign and encourage your students to use, and includes electronic access to the Instructor's Resource Manual, downloadable versions of the book's Microsoft PowerPoint presentations, and more. Visit the Instructor's Website by accessing **http://login.cengage.com** or by contacting your local sales representative.

▶ **PowerLecture CD-ROM.** This CD-ROM contains an electronic version of the Instructor's Resource Manual, ExamView computerized testing, and ready-to-use Microsoft PowerPoint presentations. The PowerPoint slides contain text, images, and cued videos of the sample speech videos, and they can be used as they are or customized to suit your course needs. This all-in-one lecture tool makes it easy for you to assemble, edit, publish, and present custom lectures for your course.

▶ **ExamView® Computerized Testing.** This enables you to create, deliver, and customize tests and study guides (both print and online) in minutes using the test bank questions from the Instructor's Resource Manual. ExamView offers both a Quick Test Wizard and an Online Test Wizard that guide you step-by-step through the process of creating tests, while its "what you see is what you get" interface allows you to see the test you are creating on-screen exactly as it will print or display online. You can build tests of up to 250 questions using up to twelve question types. Using the complete word processing capabilities of ExamView, you can also enter an unlimited number of new questions or edit existing ones.

▶ **JoinIn™ on TurningPoint®.** "Clicker" content for Response Systems is tailored to *The Speaker's Handbook*, allowing you to transform your classroom and assess your students' progress with instant in-class quizzes and polls. TurningPoint software lets you pose book-specific questions and display students' answers seamlessly within the Microsoft PowerPoint slides of your own lecture and in conjunction with the "clicker" hardware of your choice. Enhance how your students interact with you, your lecture, and one another.

▶ *The Teaching Assistant's Guide to the Basic Course.* Katherine G. Hendrix, who is on the faculty at the University of Memphis, prepared this resource specifically for new instructors. Based on leading communication teacher training programs, this guide discusses some of the general issues that accompany a teaching role and offers specific strategies for managing the first week of classes, leading productive discussions, managing sensitive topics in the classroom, and grading students' written and oral work.

▶ **Instructor Workbooks: Public Speaking: An Online Approach, Public Speaking: A Problem Based Learning Approach, and Public Speaking: A Service-Learning Approach for Instructors.** Written by Deanna Sellnow, University of Kentucky, these instructor workbooks include a course-syllabus and icebreakers;

public speaking basics such as coping with anxiety, learning cycle, and learning styles; outlining; ethics; and informative, persuasive, and ceremonial (special occasion) speeches.

▶ ***Guide to Teaching Public Speaking Online.*** Written by Todd Brand of Meridian Community College, this helpful online guide provides instructors who teach public speaking online with tips for establishing "classroom" norms with students, utilizing course management software and other eResources, managing logistics such as delivering and submitting speeches and making up work, discussing how peer feedback is different online, strategies for assessment, and tools such as sample syllabi and critique and evaluation forms tailored to the online course.

▶ ***Service Learning in Communication Studies: A Handbook.*** Written by Rick Isaacson and Jeff Saperstein, this is an invaluable resource for students in the basic course that integrates or will soon integrate a service learning component. This handbook provides guidelines for connecting service learning work with classroom concepts and advice for working effectively with agencies and organizations. It also provides model forms and reports and a directory of online resources.

▶ **Wadsworth Cengage Learning Communication Video and DVD Library.** Wadsworth's video and DVD series for Speech Communication includes Student Speeches for Critique and Analysis, and Communication Scenarios for Critique and Analysis.

▶ **Videos for Speech Communication 2011: Public Speaking, Human Communication, and Interpersonal Communication.** This DVD provides footage of news stories from BBC and CBS that relate to current topics in communication, such as teamwork and how to interview for jobs, as well as news clips about speaking anxiety and speeches from contemporary public speakers such as Michelle Obama and Senator Hillary Clinton.

▶ **ABC News DVD: Speeches by Barack Obama.** This DVD includes nine famous speeches by President Barack Obama, including his speech at the 2004 Democratic National Convention; his 2008 speech on race, "A More Perfect Union"; and his 2009 inaugural address. Speeches are divided into short video segments for easy, time-efficient viewing. This instructor supplement also features critical thinking questions and answers for each speech, designed to spark class discussion.

▶ **CourseCare Training and Support.** Get trained, get connected, and get the support you need for the seamless integration of digital resources into your course. This unparalleled technology service and training program provides robust online resources, peer-to-peer instruction, personalized training, and a customizable program you can count on. Visit **www.cengage.com/coursecare/** to sign up for online seminars, first days of class services, technical support, or personalized, face-to-face training. Our online and onsite trainings are frequently led by one of our Lead Teachers, faculty members who are experts in using Wadsworth Cengage Learning technology and can provide best practices and teaching tips.

▶ **Custom Chapters for *The Speaker's Handbook.*** Customize your chapter coverage with bonus chapters on conquering speech anxiety, impromptu speaking, group presentations, civic engagement, or service learning. You can access these chapters online within the Instructor's Website, or you can order print versions of the student text that include the extra chapter of your choice. Contact your local sales representative for ordering details.

▶ **Flex-Text Customization Program.** With this program you can create a text as unique as your course—quickly, simply, and affordably. As part of our flex-text program, you can add your personal touch to *The Speaker's Handbook* with course-specific coverage and up to thirty-two pages of your own content—at no additional cost. Use this program to add content on topics such as rhetoric and employment interviewing.

Acknowledgments

Many thanks to the team at Wadsworth who accommodated us, challenged us, and ultimately made us better—true synergy. Instrumental in the transition from ninth to tenth edition were Monica Eckman, publisher for Communication Studies, Greer Lleuad, senior development editor, and Kassi Radomski, development editor—who have been huge supporters of the handbook approach and invaluable partners in this project. Also invaluable are Wadsworth Cengage Learning colleagues, immediate and extended, who brought their expertise to this edition: Rebekah Matthews, senior assistant editor; Colin Solan, editorial assistant; Jessica Badiner, media editor; Amy Whitaker, senior marketing manager; Brittany Blais, marketing coordinator; Courtney Morris, marketing communications manager; Michael Lepera, senior content production manager; Mandy Groszko, rights specialist; Linda Helcher, art director; Lisa Jelly Smith, photo researcher; and Karyn Morrison, text permissions researcher. Edward Dionne, project manager at Macmillan Publishing Solutions, and copyeditor Catherine Albano provided expert production guidance. As always, we want to mention and thank Peter Dougherty, who initially approached us with the idea for *The Speaker's Handbook.* Likewise, we owe special thanks to the students who have granted us permission to use their speeches as examples, particularly David's student, Kayla Strickland, who provided a new speech to this edition.

We are grateful to the reviewers who took the time to help us further improve this text:

Jeffrey Brand, Millikin University;

Monette Callaway-Ezell, Hinds Community College;

Jim Conway, California Polytechnic State University;

Stephen Eckstone, San José State University;

Andra Hansen, Brigham Young University, Idaho;

Mike Hostetler, St. John's University;

and Lynn Perkins, University of San Francisco.

We remain grateful to the reviewers of previous editions for their thoughtful recommendations. We are indebted to the many loyal users of *The Speaker's Handbook* who have generously shared their comments with us and who, along with our reviewers, ensure that we continually consider how the text is best used in our classrooms and conference rooms.

Family and friends provide the love and support that serve as the foundation of completing a writing project. That they have continued with that love and support through ten editions without "revision fatigue" leaves us thankful and appreciative. David, in particular, is appreciative to his family for understanding when "just five more minutes" turns into forty-five.

Jo Sprague
Douglas Stuart
David Bodary

Table of Contents

Dear Metro Students,

Welcome to SPE 1010 at Metropolitan State University of Denver. My name is Mike Monsour, and I am the SPE 1010 Coordinator of Public Speaking for the department of Communication Arts and Sciences. We teach about 70 sections of this class every semester for a total of almost 2,000 students each academic year! So you are one of thousands who take this course each year, but a very important one!

I wanted to take this opportunity to welcome all of you into the class and inform you about some of the basics. Before doing so, you will find listed below some information about the field of Communication and the Speech Communication part of our department. Throughout this section of the book we will use the acronym "CAS" when referring to the department of Communication Arts and Sciences (CAS). The fact that our department is titled "Communication *Arts and Sciences*" is no accident. Communication departments across the country are an elegant and intellectual interweaving of "science" and "art." Communication is a combination of practical skills, the science part, but also the more intuitive and heartfelt aspects of communicating, the "art" part. Aristotle, as you will learn in your SPE 1010 class, referred to this duality as "logos" and "pathos."

The Field of Communication

The study of communication, which can be traced back to the days of Aristotle and Plato, is a rapidly growing discipline within colleges and universities across the United States. Why? Search the "help-wanted" ads! Communication is a skill that is in high demand and CAS can help you achieve the communication skills necessary to succeed in today's international world of business and politics. Businesses and organizations in today's society often have the view that they can teach new employees the nuts and bolts of their business, BUT they readily admit and understand that they cannot teach employees basic communication skills. They expect you to already have those skills when you enter the marketplace and apply for a job in their organization. A degree in Communication, or at least some training in the art and science of communicating, is the most commonly listed "desired characteristic" of businesses and industries seeking good employees. The speech program at Metro is designed to provide students with the practical skills and theoretical knowledge that will enable students to succeed both within and beyond the classroom.

The CAS Department

CAS has the honored distinction of being the ONLY department on the Metropolitan campus responsible for teaching public speaking to 2,000 students a year. CAS is a very large department, comprised of Speech Communication, Speech, Language and Hearing Sciences, and Journalism. We have a combined total of over 800 majors. The part of the department responsible for the public speaking class is Speech Communication. Within the Speech Communication component of the department there are four subcategories: Rhetoric and Public Address, Communication Theory, Organizational Communication, and Broadcast Journalism. If you take a few minutes to read the following descriptions of each part of CAS you will have a better idea of how public speaking fits into the larger field of communication and, more importantly, how the field of communication can prepare you for a vast array of potential jobs and careers once you leave the university.

Rhetoric and Public Address

Career Options:

A graduate of Speech Communication with an emphasis in Rhetoric and Public Address will be prepared for a wide range of employment opportunities in law, industrial and organizational communication, educational administration, speech writing for political figures, teaching, and theology. From Aristotle to Martin Luther King Jr., students will learn the art of rhetoric and the skills of persuasion that will make them successful in the modern world of politics, law, and administration. Rhetoric and Public Address is an emphasis in Speech Communication that meets the needs of students preparing for law school, pursuing a career in politics, planning to study Communication at a Master's level, or pursuing a career in education, administration, or business.

Primary Communication Core Requirements: (each course is a 3-credit hour class: total of 24 hours). Note, the first four classes are required of all Speech Communication Majors.

SPE 1301 Communication Inquiry

SPE 2301 Communication Theory

SPE 3301 Rhetorical Foundations of Communication

SPE 4301 Communication Ethics

SPE 3090 Argumentation and Advocacy

SPE 4080 Rhetorical Criticism of Public Address

SPE 4090 Classical Rhetoric

SPE 4100 Techniques of Persuasion

Elective Courses: (each course is a 3-credit hour class: total of 18 hours). Students select six courses from all SPE offerings. Courses are selected with the help of an advisor. Listed below are examples of five of the 30 classes students get to select from.

SPE 3010 Advanced Public Speaking

SPE 3050 Intercollegiate Forensics

SPE 3080 Great American Speakers

SPE 3160 Communication in Politics

SPE 4120 Freedom of Speech

The total number of hours required for the major with an emphasis in Rhetoric and Public Address is 42. Please consult with one of the Faculty listed below for more information.

Faculty:

Dr. Katia Campbell kcampb28@mscd.edu

Dr. Virginia McCarver vsanprie@mscd.edu

Communication Theory

Career Options:

A graduate of Speech Communication with an emphasis in Communication Theory is prepared for employment success in communication consulting on relationship topics, human resources, management, consulting/training, and career planning. Careers are available in education, government, politics, business, industry, and private practice as a consultant. In addition, this is an excellent program to prepare students for graduate degrees in the social services and social science research programs.

Requirements: (each course is a 3-credit hour class: total of 24 hours). Note, the first four classes are required of all Speech Communication Majors.

SPE 1301 Communication Inquiry

SPE 2301 Communication Theory

SPE 3301 Rhetorical Foundations of Communication

SPE 4301 Communication Ethics

SPE 1710 Interpersonal Communication

SPE 2720 Nonverbal Communication

SPE 3740 Foundations of Speech and Thought

SPE 4790 Communication Theory Building & Research Methods

Elective Courses: (each course is a 3-credit hour class: total of 18 hours). Students select six courses from all SPE offerings. Courses are selected with the help of an advisor. Listed below are examples of five of the 30 classes students get to select from.

SPE 1730 Listening and Interviewing Communication Skills

SPE 2730 Communication Conflict

SPE 3170 Interpersonal Negotiation

SPE 3710 High Performance Teams

SPE 4700 Communication and the Trainer

The total number of hours required for the major with an emphasis in Communication Theory is 42. Please consult with one of the Faculty listed below for more information.

Faculty:

Mr. David Kottenstette kottensd@mscd.edu

Dr. Karen Lollar lollar@mscd.edu

Dr. Mike Monsour wmonsour@mscd.edu

Organizational Communication

Career Options:

A graduate of Speech Communication with an emphasis in Organizational Communication might aspire to a lucrative and satisfying career in organizational consulting/training, conference planning, workplace communication, and public relations. Careers are open in government , business (including not-for-profit), industry, and private consulting.

Requirements: (each course is a 3-credit hour class: total of 24 hours). Note, the first four classes are required of all Speech Communication Majors.

SPE 1301 Communication Inquiry

SPE 2301 Communication Theory

SPE 3301 Rhetorical Foundations of Communication

SPE 4301 Communication Ethics

SPE 2160 Organizational Communication Theory

SPE 3165 Organizational Identity

SPE 4160 Advanced Organizational Communication

SPE 4790 Communication Theory Building and Research Methods

Elective Courses: (each course is a 3-credit hour class: total of 18 hours). Students select six courses from all SPE offerings. Courses are selected with the help of an advisor. Listed below are examples of five of the 30 classes students get to select from.

SPE 3110 Organizational Leadership

SPE 3130 Conference Leadership

SPE 3170 Interpersonal Negotiations

SPE 4700 Communication and the Trainer

SPE 4755 Consulting and Organizational Development

The total number of hours required for the major with an emphasis in Organizational Communication is 42. Please consult with one of the Faculty listed below for more information.

Faculty:

Dr. Susan Cook   cooks@mscd.edu

Dr. Christine Cooper ccoope42@mscd.edu

Dr. Karen Krupar krupark@mscd.edu

Broadcast Journalism

Careers Options:

A graduate of Speech Communication with an emphasis in Broadcast Journalism might aspire to careers in radio, television, cable and film as talent, writer, producer, director, or a specialist in promotion, public affairs, sales and marketing, management, production engineering, advertising, public information in business, industry and government.

Requirements: (each course is a 3-credit hour class: total of 24 hours). Note, the first four classes are required of all Speech Communication Majors.

SPE 1301 Communication Inquiry

SPE 2301 Communication Theory

SPE 3301 Rhetorical Foundations of Communication

SPE 4301 Communication Ethics

The Broadcast Journalism component of the Department of Communication Arts and Sciences has three different concentrations, and a student selects one of the three: Broadcast Journalism, Broadcast Performance, and Broadcast Production. Each of these three concentrations requires a different set of courses in addition to the four listed above. All three concentrations require the student to take SPE 2400 Electronic Media and Society.

 The total number of hours required for the major is 42. Please consult with one of the Faculty listed below for more information and a list of possible elective courses.

Faculty:

Dr. Larry Collette lcollett@mscd.edu

Mr. Jim Furrer jfurrer@mscd.edu

SPE 1010 Public Speaking Goals

Now that you know a little bit about CAS , let's get down to business! **We have two goals for our students who enroll in public speaking here at Metro: Competence and Confidence.** Your instructor for the class is in charge of making sure that you reach that first goal. There's a lot of material to cover in a short amount of time, but I know that your instructors will be able to guide you through the course and put each and every one of you into a position where you can be successful this semester. Whether your instructor has a Ph.D. in communication and has been teaching public speaking for 20 years, or whether your instructor has just received his or her masters, I have faith in our dedicated professionals here at Metro. They will all do their best to help you learn how to be a competent public speaker!The second goal, confidence, is up to you. Like any class, you're going to get back what you put in. Each time you step in front of the class to give a speech, you're going to have an opportunity to become a more confident public speaker. Communication is a highly valued expertise out there in the "real world," and SPE 1010 is a great opportunity for you to develop your own style and voice as a speaker. The more opportunities you have to develop that style and voice, the more marketable you will be after you graduate. Embrace this opportunity and you will become a more confident public speaker!

SPE 1010 Textbook

Let's take just a minute to talk about your textbook. Public speaking textbooks come in all shapes and sizes. There are dozens of available textbooks on the market and they all have their own special strengths and weaknesses. There has been a movement in the last decade towards developing what are known as "customized textbooks." A customized textbook is textbook that has been changed from its original form to one that is customized to fit the particular set of students served by the textbook. For a number of years we have been using *The Speakers Handbook*, written by Sprague and two of his colleagues. It is an excellent text, but we thought it could be improved with the deletion of a number of chapters and the addition of some new material. Each year we are going to re-customize the book in an attempt to make it better. If you have ideas about how the current textbook could be improved for next year, please share them with me! In the next few pages you will see a description of: 1) the standardized syllabus that we use for the class, 2) the class attendance policy, 3) grievance procedures, and 4) a template for the preparation outline that you will use in preparing your speech. After those four things, you will find a fairly detailed description of the oratory contest that CAS sponsors each April.

I wish you the very best this semester as you begin your SPE 1010 journey. If you ever need help with the course or have a concern about your instructor (which is highly unlikely!) please give me a call at 303-352-7043 or email me at wmonsour@mscd.edu. You can also stop by my office for a visit. I am located in the Central Classroom Building on the first floor.

Mike Monsour

SPE 1010 Coordinator

Standardized Syllabus

All instructors for this class, often as many as 40 different teachers, use the same standardized syllabus for the 1010 class, with some minor changes. This means that about 75% of the syllabus in your class will be identical to the ones used in other classes. For example, we all use the same attendance policy and the same grievance procedure. The "Student Learning Objectives" are the same in every class. The "Evaluation of Student Performance" is very similar in the sense that all instructors require between four and six graded speeches and give the same standardized final exam. All syllabi also have a list of "Academic Deadlines" supplied by the college that we are all required to include in our syllabi. Every syllabus also includes a weekly breakdown of activities and speech assignments. The syllabi in all the classes are very similar in order to provide a consistent and high level experience from one class to the next. Although this part is optional, most of our instructors include as the last page of the syllabus an informal "contract" between you and the instructor. The contract essentially says, "I have read and understood the syllabus and will perform to the best of my ability to abide by its policies." Your instructor may request that you sign it and turn it in. It is your choice whether you want to do so or not. However, the "informal contract" works both ways. It not only obliges you to follow the policies, but it also prevents the instructor from changing fundamental student expectations such as the number of speeches given or the grading policies used.

Class Attendance Policy

As an SPE 1010 class member you have two basic responsibilities: To give speeches and to regularly show up as an audience member to hear the speeches of your fellow classmates. Public speaking is pointless without an audience. Each of you will work hard preparing your speech AND will be totally invested and engaged when delivering your speech. You will appreciate having an audience full of your peers who can offer both constructive feedback and moral support. Each of you needs to show your support for one another by being an audience member and that means showing up to class. Because of the vitally important role of attendance in a performance class, the Department of Communication Arts and Sciences (CAS) has adopted the following policy regarding class attendance. Please note that this attendance policy is in line with the expectations for the majority of other classes on the Metropolitan State University campus.

1. There are NO excused absences EXCEPT for military duty, jury duty, and religious holidays. As noted in the box below, you are allowed a certain number of absences before your grade is lowered. Absences for military duty, jury duty, and religious holiday observances DO NOT count towards the number of absences you are allowed as long as you can provide documentation on the authenticity of your reason for missing class. If you are going to miss a class for a religious holiday you need to inform your instructor the first week of class. In your syllabus there is a link that you can access which lists the religious holidays recognized by Metropolitan State University of Denver.
   We were very careful in deciding how many absences you are allowed. Please do not use your allowed absences for trivial reasons. Any one of you might get sick at some point in the semester or

have a work or personal emergency you must attend to. That is why we allow a certain number of absences. For example, in a class that meets twice a week for 16 weeks, a student is allowed four absences. If you don't use up your absences for reasons like sleeping in, or going to the mountains, or just skipping classes, then IF you do get sick or have a work or family emergency, you would have four absences at your disposal. If you waste your allotted absences and then need to miss a fifth or sixth class your instructor will not be able to help you. Four absences is the equivalent of missing two full weeks of class. If you have a true medical or family emergency, four absences should be enough to get you over the hump, IF YOU DON'T WASTE YOUR ABSENCES ON TRIVIAL MATTERS.

2. Final grades will be reduced for absences from the initial grade earned as follows:

Classes Per Week			Action
Three	**Two**	**One**	
Classes Missed	*Classes Missed*	*Classes Missed*	
6	4	2	No Grade Reduction
7	5	3	One Letter Grade Reduction
11	9	5	Two Letter Grade Reduction
15	13	7	Three Letter Grade Reduction
19	16	8	Failure to Complete Course

Grievance Procedures

The CAS SPE 1010 instructors are all carefully screened and interviewed before being hired. Metropolitan State University of Denver, in addition to CAS, has additional screening procedures. They even conduct a background check. Each instructor is highly qualified to teach the SPE 1010 Public Speaking class. CAS also knows that individual instructors are careful and fair when conducting class and assigning grades to speeches and exams. However, if in the unlikely event that you do have a problem with your instructor during the course of the semester, CAS has a policy in place that you must follow. Here are the steps of the policy.

1. You should send an email to your instructor and request a private meeting on campus in the CAS department office. He or she will say yes. It is imperative that you first try and work out your grievance with your instructor.

2. You should try to work out your differences with the instructor. Clearly communicate your concerns. Listen to your instructor with respect. Make sure you have carefully read his or her syllabus before the meeting.

3. If you are unable to work out a satisfactory resolution to your problem, inform your instructor that you are going to talk to the Coordinator of Public Speaking (me, Mike Monsour) about your concern (if you decide that is what you want to do).

4. Send the Coordinator of Public Speaking (me, Mike Monsour) an email requesting a meeting, and I will meet with you. Before we meet I will have a separate meeting with your instructor. If you and I are unable to reach a satisfactory resolution to the problem, as a student you have the option of taking your concern to the chair of CAS, Dr. Karen Lollar. If you tell me you are going to pursue this option, I will inform Dr. Lollar and your instructor of your decision.

5. Dr. Lollar will listen to your concerns. By this point in the process she has probably spoken to me and the instructor about the situation.

6. After meeting with you and a separate meeting with me and the instructor, Dr.Lollar makes the final decision about your concerns.

The Preparation Outline

Preparation outlines are necessary to insure that your speech is clearly organized and easy to follow. Studies have conclusively shown that well organized speakers have more credibility with the audience than poorly organized speakers. Well organized speeches also increase retention by audience members. It is easier to remember important points from speeches that are clearly and effectively organized.

For every speech you give this semester you will need to turn in a "Preparation Outline." Your instructor may or may not assign a grade to the outline. A preparation outline is a **full sentence outline**. The preparation outline is used to help you develop your speaking notes (which are key words that you place on two or three index size note cards that you use during your speech). Some speakers use the preparation outline to practice their speech until they are comfortable moving on to the use of just note cards.

Listed below is the SKELETON for the organizational structure of your Preparation Outline. When developing a specific outline for a specific speech, such as a speech to inform an audience about acid rain, follow this organizational structure. Your instructor may have you deviate somewhat from the pattern I describe, but this is a good one and has worked for hundreds of thousands of speakers.

Your outline should have all the key parts to it (such as Topic, General Purpose, Specific Purpose, Thesis Statement, Introduction, Attention Getter, Thesis Statement, Preview Statement, Transition, First Main Point, First Subpoint, Second Subpoint, Transition, Second Main Point, First Subpoint, Second Subpoint, Transition, Conclusion, First Main Point (which may be establishing psychological closure), Second Main Point (which may be establishing psychological closure), and finally, a Closing Clincher.

The bold faced part of the outline is the structure you need to follow. Have each bold faced part in your outline and then complete the outline with your own content as I have done below with my example of acid rain. For instance, the first seven parts of your skeleton outline should read: **Title of the Speech, Topic, General Purpose, Specific Purpose, Thesis Statement, Introduction, and Attention Getting Device**

Your individual instructor may require you to have a title to your speech, as I have below in my sample.

Title of the Speech: Acid Rain: No, It's Not a Jimmy Hendrix Song

Topic (in a full sentence state your topic, e.g., "My topic is acid rain")

General Purpose (in a full sentence state your general purpose, e.g., "My purpose is to inform" or persuade, demonstrate, or advocate)

Specific Purpose (in a full sentence state your specific purpose, e.g., "I am going to inform the audience about acid rain.")

Thesis Statement: (in a full sentence state your thesis statement ((the central idea)) of your speech, e.g., "My central idea is that acid rain causes significant damage resulting in billions of dollars.")

I. Introduction

      a. Attention Getting Device (in a full sentence state what your attention getting device will be,)

e.g., "I will get the attention of the audience by giving the following startling statistic about acid rain....."

e.g., "I will get the attention of the audience by telling a story about acid rain."

e.g., "I will get the attention of the audience with an interesting quotation on acid rain."

b. Thesis (in a full sentence state your central idea, e.g., "Acid rain causes significant damage to existing structures.")

c. Preview Statement (in a full sentence OR two state your preview statement, e.g., "In the next few minutes I will be covering three major points about acid rain. Point one is the definition of acid rain. My second point describes the places where acid rain is most likely to fall. My third point gives statistics about the financial cost of acid rain."

d. Transition (in a full sentence state your transition, e.g., "Now let's move on to my first point.")

II. Body

a. First main point (in a full sentence state your first main point, e.g.," The first thing I will do is define acid rain. According to the Environmental Protection Agency, acid rain is defined as…)

      1. First subpoint (your subpoint develops your first main point)

      2. Second subpoint (your subpoint develops your first main point)

Transition: (in a full sentence state the transition you will use to move from your first main point to your second main point, for example, "Now that I have defined acid rain, let's move on to my second main point.")

b. Second main point (in a full sentence state your second main point, e.g., "Acid rain falls in three primary types of locations.")

      1. First subpoint (your subpoint develops your first main point)

      2. Second subpoint (your subpoint develops your first main point)

      3. Third subpoint (your subpoint develops your first main point)

Transition: (in a full sentence state the transition you will use to move from your second main point to your third main point, for example, "Now that I have defined acid rain and described where it is most likely to fall, let's move on to my third and last main point.")

c. Third main point (in a full sentence state your third main point, e.g., "Acid rain causes significant financial damage")

      1. First subpoint (your subpoint develops your first main point)

      2. Second subpoint (your subpoint develops your first main point)

Transition: (in a full sentence state the transition you will use to move from your third main point to the conclusion of your speech, for example, "Ok, there you have it. I have defined acid rain, described where it is most likely to fall, and given you some statistics about the tremendous amount of damage that acid rain can cause"). Please note that sometime the transition in the conclusion of your speech can sometimes be something as simple as saying, "In conclusion..."

III. Conclusion

a. Logical Closure (in a full sentence state how you will provide logical closure, e.g. I will provide logical closure by stating something similar to the following, "In the last few minutes I have done what I said I would do: I have defined acid rain, I have identified where it is most likely to occur, and I have given you some statistics about the financial damage caused by acid rain.")

b. Psychological Closure (in a full sentence state how you will provide psychological closure, e.g., I will provide psychological closure by making a statement similar to the following, "I hope the information I have provided you has been useful in helping you to fill in any gaps in the knowledge that you had concerning acid harm and its harmful effects.")

c. Clincher (in a full sentence explain what your clincher will be, e.g., "I will finish telling the story I began in the introduction" or "I will give an even more startling statistic than I began my speech with.")

The Spectacular Vernacular: An Oratory Contest With Cash Prizes

Every year in April the Department of Communication Arts and Sciences organizes an oratory contest on this campus. An oratory is a certain kind of speech that you may or may not present in your SPE 1010 class. The student intern responsible for coming up with a name for the event dubbed it the "Spectacular Vernacular." We all know what "spectacular" means, but what about the much less commonly used word, "vernacular?" That word is commonly defined, and I am paraphrasing Mr. Webster here, as the spoken language used by a particular group, profession, or region of the country. For example, doctors and lawyers have their own vernacular (language) that we sometimes have difficulty understanding. Professors in a particular content area, such as communication, chemistry, or computer software design, have their own vernacular as well. Young adults who are college students, like yourselves, also have your own special language and way of communicating.

 Last year was our inaugural kickoff of the Spectacular Vernacular event. We plan on hosting the event every April. We do the event for three reasons. Perhaps the most important reason is to highlight what we in CAS believe is a fundamental ingredient of all successful democracies: Freedom of Speech. Constitutional scholars, political scientists, and communication scholars and practitioners all believe that the constitutional right to speak openly and honestly without fear of repercussions is vitally important for a democracy to flourish. Contestants in the oratory contest are FREE to select ANY topic they believe is worth speaking about. In connection to Freedom of Speech, you will hear your instructor make frequent references to what we in CAS call "civic engagement." Civic engagement occurs when citizens communicate with one another in order to discover common ground and ways of solving problems that affect them all. Civic engagement works best when individuals have the communication tools to not only present their own thoughts and views in a coherent and compelling fashion, but to analyze the communication of others. A second reason for the contest is to further a sense of community among Metropolitan State University students. As you probably know, the Auraria campus is home to 40,000 students representing three institutions: Metropolitan State University with 24,000 students, the University of Colorado at Denver with about 11,000 students, and the Community College of Denver with about 5,000 students. Our campus is also a commuter campus so most students just drive in for class and then go back home. Our hope is that an oratory contest will help to foster more of a feeling of our campus having some of the more traditional and fun aspects of a residential campus, such as a number of exciting events occurring all the time. A third reason for the contest is to give our students a chance to showcase their skills and perhaps make a little money in the process! The first place winner receives a cash prize of $200.00 and the second place winner takes home a respectable $100.00. The third place prize is $50.00. Along with the cash prizes come very nice plaques from "Golden Awards and Engraving" here in town. Winners will be able to state in their resume that they won in an event that highlights excellent communication skills.

The Spectacular Vernacular Fact Sheet for the April 2013 Contest

The information below gives the key facts for the next Spectacular Vernacular to be help in April of 2013. This is similar to the flyer that was distributed for the contest last year. Please note that the dates of the contest may change, but it will take place in April.

What:	It is a public speaking contest (an oratory contest).
When:	Friday April 12th and Saturday April 13th (spring semester 2013)
Where:	Tivoli Room 320 (The Tivoli is the Student Union on campus)
Times:	Preliminary rounds take place on Friday; the semi-final and final round takes place on Saturday.
Cost:	Free
First Prize:	$200.00 and a first place plaque
Second Prize:	$100.00 and a second place plaque
Third Prize:	$50.00 and a third place plaque
Eligibility:	Contestant must be a registered Metro student during Spring 2013 and must have already taken SPE 1010 Public Speaking or currently taking it.
Registration:	Registration is during the month of March and is accomplished in one simple phone call or email to the contact person. Registration is FREE
Sponsored By:	This event is financially sponsored by CENGAGE Publishing, the publishers of our textbook. The event is also sponsored by Lambda Pi Eta, the communication honor society.
Judges:	All rounds are judged by faculty who teach our public speaking classes.
Contact Person:	Mike Monsour, Public Speaking Coordinator, office number: 303-352-7043. wmonsour@mscd.edu
Registration:	Just send Mike an email and let him know that you want to be registered for the contest. He will register you once you send him the following information: Your Name, Your Metro email, Your Student 900 number, Your Phone Number, and an indication of when you took SPE 1010. Please note that Metro students who

had a public speaking class transferred in from a different school, such as a community college or university, ARE eligible to compete.

The Speech:

Although "oratory" sometimes has a fairly restrictive definition, for this event we have broadened its defining characteristics. Competitors may present speeches that are designed to do one or more of the following: advocate, persuade, convince, inspire, evoke, motivate, commemorate, celebrate, eulogize, or entertain. Often, an oratory might do many of these things simultaneously. A speaker need not restrict her or his goals to just "persuading" or just "inspiring." Although competitors select their own topic, they are encouraged to focus on topics such as embracing diversity, freedom of speech, war and peace, civility in communication, civic engagement, multi-cultural sensitivity, social justice, and personal space in an age of digital discourse. The speech MUST BE the speaker's ORIGINAL WORK.

The speaker's first speech will be given sometime Friday (to be determined during registration). If he or she does well, that person will move on to the second round, also on Friday. The best speakers will move on to the semi-final and final rounds on Saturday. Visual aids and power points are not allowed. Use of notes is highly discouraged. Speakers must use the same speech throughout the tournament. The speech should be 8 to 10 minutes long.

All contestants must provide the contact person, Mike Monsour, with a written (typed) transcript of their speech on the first day of the tournament in order to be eligible to place first, second, or third in the event.

The Spectacular Vernacular Oratory Ballot for Judges

All competitive speaking events have judges who watch the various speeches and make a decision on who the best speakers are. In order to insure fairness and consistency in evaluating the many speakers, organizers of the event construct a "ballot." A ballot is simply a standardized evaluation sheet where judges rate the speaker on various components of delivery and content. The judges also rank order the speakers. For example, if a judge listens to 5 speakers in the same oratory round, he or she would decide who ranked highest and lowest, and everywhere in between. Here is a sample ballot so you can get an idea of what speakers, perhaps yourself, will be evaluated on in the upcoming event in April of 2013.

Sample Spectacular Vernacular Judging Ballot

Contestant's Name: Please print _____   **Date:** _____

Round: (e.g., Round 1, Semi-Final Round, Final Round): _____

Speaker's Rotation Number: (first, second, third speaker, etc): _____

Judge's Instructions: Judge the speaker on content and delivery. Remember, the category of "oratory" is broadly defined as a speech designed to do one or more of the following: persuade, inspire, motivate, actuate, commemorate, celebrate, eulogize or entertain. You may even have speakers who incorporate a bit of poetry or dramatic interpretation into their speech. Contestants are free to use any topic they like. We encouraged them to speak on topics such as embracing diversity, freedom of speech, civility in communication, war and peace, civic engagement, multi-cultural sensitivity, social justice, and maintaining personal space in an age of digital discourse, but those were just suggestions.

Criteria for Evaluation:

Content: (consider the following questions)

> Was the speech well organized and easy to follow?

> Did the speaker have an interesting and provocative topic?

> Did the speech reflect careful language use for the situation?

> Logos, was the speech logical and reasonable?

Were sources for the speech identified and sound?

Pathos, did the speaker effectively utilize appropriate emotional appeals?

Delivery: (consider the following aspects of delivery)

Eye Contact

Proxemics

Vocal Variety

Vocalized Pauses

Knew the speech well

Poise and Posture

Rank the Speaker: Circle one

1st 2nd 3rd 4th 5th

Judge's Signature: _____

The Winning Speeches

Students: The last part of this section includes transcriptions of the first and second place speeches in the inaugural Spectacular Vernacular oratory contest. Although they are both excellent speeches and competitively selected from the 36 contestants, they are by no means perfect. Both winners were basically beginning speakers, although powerful ones. Under the instructor's guidance, critique both speeches based on the kinds of things you are learning in your public speaking class. The speeches are available for viewing on the SPE 1010 home page.

First Place Speech by Connor Cordova

Personal Space in an Age of Digital Discourse

One Hundred Billion... according to their statistics page, that's the number of times Facebook is visited every single day. 100 Billion! This number is staggering, and is truly a testament to how interlocked we are with our social media in todays' day and age. Now even though these innovations are new and exciting, it's my contention that there are unforeseen consequences that we could have never imagined that will come to pass in the near future.

Hello, my name is Conner Cordova, and today I am going to be speaking to you all about the ever changing norms that define personal space in the digital age we live in. First, we examine the counterculture that has developed due to our personality types online. And secondly, truly grasping the scope of our actions in the cyber space that is the internet.

By my understanding, we occupy one or two different personalities online. Those who show

everything... and those who show nothing. Now if someone I hardly knew, walked up to

me on the street and was able to tell me: who may family was, what my interests were, my

telephone number, and where I lived... honestly I would think I have a stalker on me hands! But

really, this information is really not that hard to come by, and odds are, you're giving it away.

Never before in the history of our nation have we had that kind of information so readily

available to us. Whether it's on your iPhone, Droid, laptop, or iPad, we are constantly connected.

Now giving this kind of information face to face is unheard of, but online, it's normal. It's

routine. Never before has the line of where our personal lives begins or ends has been so blurred.

What we once considered to be intimate information about ourselves is now simply labeled as

"basic information". This phenomenon is remarkable, but really we are still not quite synced up

with the technology we are ourselves have created. There is still a disconnect to the realization

that what we do or say as our online selves, can and most often times will have consequences in

real time. You hear about people getting fired all the time on the news because they called in sick

from work, and then posted pictures of themselves partying on Facebook. There is still a

disconnect to where we on a psychological level, we still can't comprehend our actions online as

relevant and having concrete effects.

No let's flip that coin, to the personality type that shows nothing online. Those people

who are just a user name, a pseudonym, a pen name. Online you can hide your true identity from everyone. You can say anything and everything you could possibly want, no matter how horrible, inappropriate or vulgar it may be, and never be called on it. In essence, we have created a morality free zone, where you can say whatever you want, and never be held accountable. Think about it, this has taken the right of free speech to a place where we could have never imagined. Before, the norm was that your right to swing your hand ended at another man's nose. Not anymore. At this point, we are like a kid who has a brand new toy. We aren't thinking of the harm that could accidentally be done, we are just trying to see what the sucker can do! If we're not careful, this new form of communication can and will bleed over and effect the way in which we communicate in our day to day lives. Which brings me to my next point, understanding, and truly grasping the effect of our habits online, and how they will affect us all in the future.

We as people need to start making a conscious effort to maintain the way we communicate in our country. Because eventually, we will end up living in a time where tact is dead, where civility in communication comes second, and where there is no difference between public and privileged information. The way we view our personal boundaries in changing every day due to the amount of technology we use just walking around. So it's up to us to make the decision, that just because you can post it, doesn't necessarily mean you should. Now I'm not saying that Facebook is the devil or, twitter will lead to the apocalypse. Honestly, I checked into Facebook right before I started giving this speech. What I am saying is, don't let the negative traits of your communications be enhanced due to your online identities. Because it doesn't matter how many passwords you have or how many fire walls you put up, until we make the psychological change within ourselves... we will continue down this path we have laid for ourselves. Only when we treat the two entities of real world and cyber communication exactly the same, can we maintain the norms of our communications and personal space that were hundreds of years in the making.

In conclusion, I want to leave you all with a quote, from a man, much wiser than I am. From a time where the internet wasn't even a twinkle is someone's eye. And the craziest part about this, in my opinion, this statement is more true today then the day he said it. Benjamin Franklin once stated : "He that would live in peace and at ease, must not speak all he knows, or judge all he sees"

Thank you so much for your time.

Second Place Speech

Savannah Sanburg

Separate But Equal

Imagine, you are 17 years old. You have just finished playing basketball and just had a long hard day at school. As you are preparing to pack your bags from basketball practice, you think about what is going on at home. You eagerly anticipate going home to see your family. After all, your mom has just finishing making your favorite meal. You quickly finish packing your gym bag, and put on your hooded sweatshirt and start preparing to head home. As you begin to walk from school through the neighborhood, you noticed that there is someone following you. You become fearful and, as a result, you start walking faster and faster. Next thing you know, you are shot in cold blood, and your life has ended. No warning. No explanation. No justice.

The Trayvon Martin story has hit a huge nerve in America. According to Bonnie Goldstein of the Washington Post, "Hoodies, like the one he was wearing and Skittles, the candy found in his pocket, have become emblems of the last terrible moments of the young man's life when he was chased and killed." In other words, what he wore and what he was carrying (even the iced tea, though not mentioned in the Washington Post story) has become symbols of racial prejudice that still exists in this country.

I can relate to the family of Trayvon Martin, because I have undergone something similar to what they are going through. Today, April 20th, is the eighth anniversary of my twin-brother's murder. Jeremy Phillips was gunned down in Northeast Denver. The pain still haunts my family today. The question that runs through my mind is how much value do we place on an individual human being's life? Furthermore, how does race play a role in deciding whose life has more value?

In the United States, we have an inherent problem with racial stratification and self-segregation. As you can see, this prohibits the creation of a truly cohesive and shared American identity and shows America not to be the great melting pot that we self-stylize ourselves as, or a salad bowl like other Westernized nations, but as a microwavable meal with the communities somewhat separated, like the meat & vegetables.

In this speech, we are going to touch on the history of racial self-segregation and discrimination. Then we will address current barriers to unity though process and practices. Finally, we will help bring awareness to and fight these corrosive stereotypes which compromise our national polity. This will help to create a much more racially conscious society and help to encourage national unity. The entire public is engaged in a continual discussion on race and it is important that we make significant changes to the body politic. We need to honestly discuss racism, stereotypes and how they still have a significant impact on the lives of minority Americans today, if we have any hope of creating national unity.

First, let us examine the history of racial self-segregation and discrimination. In the 1890s, *Plessy v. Ferguson*, which was a case put before the Supreme Court, established a clear precedent that allowed railroad companies to carry whites and minorities; however, they were required to ride in separate carriages. This same law carried over to schools, parks, restaurants, and more for decades to come. This is where the legal precedent for "Separate but Equal" came from. You may ask yourself, "What is the relevance of this legislation today?" The racist climate created by the adherence to that law created a separation of the races that is still felt and observed in many communities today, even though there is no law saying that someone of one race cannot live in the same area as someone of a different race or socialize with them.

While racism started and has continued due to the political or economic interests of others, we need to end racism to build a cohesive nation and body politic. By keeping us separate from Black america, those who would use racism for their own ends have helped to keep us from truly being one nation, indivisible.

Now let's look at how and why racism still exists today. In order to do this we need to examine why stereotypes exist and how stereotypes about race have continued to spread and thrive in American society.

Stereotypes

Why in the world do we have stereotypes if they are so destructive and enable such negative mentalities as racism? Let us begin by thinking of a harmless stereotype that is ingrained in our minds. People don't touch the burners on an electric stove because it has been reinforced in their minds that it would be painful to do so, regardless of whether the stove is off. The person with this stereotype need not be burned by the stove, only to have exposure to the Western culture that would tell them that touching the burner is dangerous.

The example given for this methodologies and theories can answer why and how racial stereotypes can be created. Some racial stereotypes that you have probably heard are "All black men are good at basketball" and "All bald, young white men are skinheads", "All latinas can salsa meringue", "All Asians get straight A's".These stereotypes have negative implications and show how stereotyping is pervasive in our society. The things said here are bold, hurtful, and untrue and moreover, are spread on a daily basis by people who should know better.

After examining how stereotypes are communicated through process and practices you see how history has played a major role in how stereotypes are reinforced today. Would you agree that both religion and politics have had a significant impact on our perception of all things, including identity, over the decades?

To examine how this is reinforced today, let us begin by looking at the media and how it continues our racial prejudices.

Racism and the Media

You might ask yourselves how black people are victimized by the Media. Well, in his documentary "HipHop: Between Beats and Rhymes", Byron Hurt talks about how hip hop/rap music contributes to violence, homophobia, misogyny, and racial self-segregation in the black community. He discusses how hip hop/rap music went from "Fight the Power", a popular hip hop song of the time which helped to empower the black community, to "Bitch Better Have My Money" a popular rap song of it's time that contributed to the objectification of women in the black community.

Solutions

What are the benefits and solutions to a society free of harmful stereotypes and prejudices? Can there truly be a harmonious place that is reason free from conceptualizing the notion of race? These are questions that we can ponder as we watch our children grow up.

Can man today ever truly be free of racism? This question is something that only time will tell. We can only that we can stray away from the status quo, because it is not working.

Summary

Now, imagine if Trayvon Martin was your brother, son, nephew or friend? How much would it impact your thoughts and lives? Would you be able to face the heartbreak? Now, imagine what if Trayvon Martin was Asian, Caucasian, or Latino? Would this change the way the media viewed this tragedy?

We talked about the history of racism and self-segregation. Then, we examined, through process and practices, how racial stereotypes are reinforced in our society. Finally, we went deeper and examined how racism is perpetuated through the media.

In closing, I leave you with a poem by Nellie Wong's Plain English that celebrates multiculturalism. I am leaving you with this poem in celebration of all cultures.

Plain English

by Nellie Wong

Plain English is not the flatlands.

Not doughnuts with holes in tact. When we speak plainly in poetry,

it is not to say we deflower the English language. Its richness. Its golden light.

When an Asian-American speaks.

When an African-American speaks.

When a Native-American speaks.

When a Latin-American speaks.

He sings. She sings the language of cultures.

Of songs and festivals and bells and rhythms and dialects

of ancestors long buried, but alie.

Why a poem? Why not an essay?

Ah, but you see, we write poems in our essays

and essays in our poems. We do not confuse the form from the content

We fuse them. See threads of cord and silk intertwine.

We make love in the heart of sense, in the abdomen of pain and struggle.

In the eyes that see clarity. In the roar and dancing of lions.

If you say, I am being ethnic

If you say I am being a reducationist.

If you say I am being limited.

I say no. I do not consent to your reducing me

My language, my learning, my life.

I say no. I resist what white America has taught me to obey its standards of beauty.

Because beauty, is the mountain in our eyes.

Because beauty, is the glow of our yellow, black, and brown skins. And if we dance like you've

never seen. We say, 'we are, we are".

If we see other colors other than red, white, and blue,

Do not accuse us of being unpatriotic. Do not say that we do not belong,

for our generations prove you wrong. For our history in slavery, incarceration, exclusion.

We sing in Plain English not to blend in a melting pot, but to see the dignity and elegance

of our people who seek to rise and not be silenced by a gun.

By censorship. By ignorance.

Physical death is no monster. Cultural genocide snakes around our necks.

And until we loosen free. Until you hear as we've heard you.

Until you see our backs break, we will sing in Plain English flowering from our tongues.

Bibliography

Alaniz, Y., & Wong, N. (Eds.). (1999). *Voices of Color*. N.p.: Red Letter Press.

Goldstein, B. (2012, March 28). Trayvon Martin: A dead boy becomes a brand. In *Washington Post*.

Hurt, B. (Director). (2006). *Hip Hop: Between Beats and Rhymes* [Motion picture]. God Bless The Child Productions.

Plessy v. Ferguson, 163 U.S. 537

Foundation **1**

PART 1
FOUNDATION

introduction
The Value of Public Speaking Skills

C hances are you will soon have the opportunity to give a public speech, perhaps in the context of a public speaking class, or because you need to give a presentation at work or in another public venue. Whatever the context, this *is* an opportunity and this *is* a good thing.

For some, the statement "You will soon have the opportunity to give a public speech" may sound a bit ominous. Most people approach the idea of speaking in public with some apprehension. Your feelings might range from mild apprehension to severe panic. But there is one thing worse than being called on to give a public speech when you *don't* want to—that is not being *able* to give a public speech when you *do* want to.

Do any of the following scenarios sound familiar?

▶ You listen to your acquaintances telling stories of funny things that have happened to them, and you would like to share your own experiences, but you are too shy to speak up.

▶ You sit in class, knowing the answer to the instructor's question, but you lack the confidence to raise your hand.

▶ You begin a presentation on a topic you know well, but you soon forget your key ideas and hastily end the speech.

▶ You attend a business meeting to discuss a problem. You think you have some insights that could be part of the solution, but you can't formulate your thoughts clearly enough to present them.

▶ You would like to take on a leadership role in a work or social group, but you struggle to persuade your peers to follow your lead.

▶ You are being interviewed for a job you really want and think you are qualified for, but your ideas come out jumbled and lack clarity, confidence, and depth.

▶ You attend a public meeting on an issue crucial to your family and you disagree with the ideas being discussed. You believe you have a valid concern that is being overlooked, but lack the confidence to express your reservations.

Social and Societal Benefits of Public Speaking

A democratic society requires the free exchange of ideas so people can listen to each other's views, understand the implications of policies, and select the best courses of collective action. In the words of historian Daniel J. Boorstin, "Disagreement is the life blood of democracy."[1] Likewise, U.S. Senator J. William Fulbright noted, "The citizen who criticizes his country is paying it an implied tribute."[2] All citizens must be willing to contribute positively to their democracy and be able to speak up to protect their own rights and the rights of others.

Not only are communication skills important to our democracy, but they are also important to business. Organizations of all kinds depend on people's willingness to pool their expertise through communication. Perhaps most of all, our families and communities need people who are sensitive to and skilled in communication, because it is through storytelling and personal sharing that we are able to form healthy family and community bonds.

Personal and Professional Benefits of Public Speaking

Experience with analyzing information and expressing your opinions through public speaking will not only increase your confidence in day-to-day activities, but it will also help you get more out of your classes. Participating constructively in class discussions and applying the skills of preparation, organization, development, and presentation will enhance your learning experience.

Regarding professional benefits, a quick glance at job descriptions at websites such as indeed.com, careerbuilder.com, and monster.com reveals regular and frequent use of phrases like "strong communication skills," "excellent verbal and written skills," and "ability to motivate others." Clearly, the skills you develop as a public speaker not only will help you land a job, but will also help you succeed and advance in your profession. In an interview, the candidate who gives concise and direct answers, who expresses ideas in memorable ways, and who remains calm under pressure will make a stronger impression. Once you get the job, you can use these communication skills to improve your work place and product, influence those around you, and gain personal satisfaction while being an effective and valued professional resource.

Improving Your Public Speaking Skills

For the most part, the factors that inhibit people from speaking in public can be addressed through education and coaching. Effective speaking is a skill almost everyone can learn. Why else would so many colleges and universities require courses in public speaking? Why else would thousands of people voluntarily join groups like Toastmasters International? Why else would corporations and public agencies spend millions of dollars on presentation training? Each of us can improve our speaking skills, regardless of our prior experience.

As with any other skill (such as basketball, dancing, martial arts, or brain surgery), there are principles to be mastered with public speaking, there is a need for concentration and practice, and there are benefits to working with a skilled teacher and supportive co-learners. As classroom faculty and speech coaches, we have seen reticent speakers gain confidence and poise. We have observed people develop the ability to effectively analyze and create mutual understanding with their audience. We have watched as people, who initially detested speech outlines, admit the improved clarity and structure afforded by outlining and the resulting improvement of their messages. Believe it or not, some of the most reluctant speakers have discovered that making a presentation can even be fun. They find it exhilarating to make compelling points that clearly interest, and even persuade, their audience. More importantly, lives are improved and opportunities are expanded by the willingness and ability to speak.

We all like to receive compliments and applause when our ideas resonate with others. We enjoy a sense of effectiveness when our ideas are taken seriously and can contribute to improving understanding, or advancing the public dialogue. In short, there is power and personal satisfaction in finding our voices in the public sphere.

Critical Thinking Questions

▶ What dollar value would you put on the ability to speak publicly with confidence?

▶ What will it take to improve your public speaking skills?

▶ Are you willing to work at improving your public speaking skills?

chapter 1
Understanding Speaking

Understand that public speaking is the act of creating meaning with your listeners, and that by consciously combining communicative resources you already possess, you can speak successfully.

I n the course of preparing a public speech, we make dozens of decisions. When we deliver a speech, the complexity increases as we coordinate mind, body, and voice from moment to moment. Giving a speech can never be made simple, but thinking about it can be greatly *simplified* if we understand the basics of communicating and speaking. Understanding some fundamental communication principles and the theoretical framework of public speaking can reduce complexity, bring clarity, and guide the choices we make in planning and presenting a speech.

Understand What It Means to Be a Public Speaker

When most people hear the words *public speaking*, they imagine a podium, a stage, and an auditorium with a large audience—the components of a classic "capital S" Speech. This handbook presents a broader picture of public speaking. This picture includes the capital S Speech—and the authors hope users of this book will become more skilled at that—but it includes more. We are speakers not only when we stand behind the podium at an awards banquet or when we approach the microphone at a planning commission meeting, but also when we sit at a table with a few members of our work group and present a problem. We are speakers in class, at work, and among friends and family. In each of these situations we are the same speakers working with the same set of communication skills, but we will apply those skills differently in each situation.

But let's not broaden the context too much. Not all oral communication in a group setting is public speaking. **Public speaking** is an event in which a group of people agree that one person, the speaker, will direct the event. Because the speaker directs the event,

FIGURE 1.1
Communication is similar to the give and take between dancers

AP Photo/Chris Pizzello

it would be easy to assume that speakers and listeners are vastly different in the public speaking situation. However, there are probably more similarities than differences between these roles. In essence, speakers create meaning that is transmitted to listeners. Communication theorists stress that meaning is socially constructed in a mutual transaction between speakers and listeners. The speaker and listener are therefore involved in a sort of dance, a give-and-take that develops over time into a meaningful exchange (Figure 1.1). Continuing with this metaphor, the more experience two dance partners have together, the more effectively each is able to anticipate the moves (intended meaning) of the other and respond appropriately. This mutuality of concern is central to the effective communication of any message.

This view of speaking as a mutual transaction does not relieve the speaker of certain basic responsibilities, nor does it mean every speaking situation is an improvisation. To uphold their end of the agreement, speakers are obliged to lead their audience partners and create an effective, efficient, perhaps even enjoyable event. To achieve this sort of event, speakers must follow certain guidelines, but like good dancers, they must also be creative and bring something that is uniquely theirs to the interaction. Just as we want our dance partner to know the basics but not follow the same pattern for every dance, each new speech situation calls for certain basic elements but allows for those elements to be arranged into countless combinations.

Recognize the Theoretical Foundations of Effective Public Speaking

Although this handbook emphasizes practical advice for speakers, its recommendations are distilled from a number of communication theories and traditions. Table 1.1 summarizes the many insights of four prominent theoretical foundations of public speaking: oral cultures, classical rhetoric, communication studies, and dialogic perspectives.

TABLE 1.1
Insights from theoretical foundations of public speaking

THEORETICAL FOUNDATION	INSIGHTS AND WHERE THIS BOOK DISCUSSES THEM
Our ancient oral traditions	• Public speaking existed in preliterate societies. It is a form of communal experience that bonds people together. • Public speaking, despite the visual, textual, and electronic aids that enhance it today, still finds its essence in the sounds made by the human voice. • Speech is a medium characterized by immediacy and concreteness. Rhythm, repetition, participation, conflict, and vivid details make it powerful and memorable. • Human beings are innately storytellers. The narrative form is the most natural way to engage an audience. *You will encounter some of these principles in* Chapters **1, 18, 26, 27, 33.**
Our rhetorical heritage	• Public speakers are, above all, decision makers. They choose among many possible ways to speak their truth, seeking the one that is most effective for the situation. • Speech influences people by appealing to their rationality, but effective speakers view rationality as more than logic. They integrate appeals of motivation and credibility into their speeches. • Speech is complex and it is helpful to analyze its various components and the demands of various speech situations. • Because speech is used to influence others and shape common decisions, it always has an ethical dimension. *You will encounter some of these principles in* Chapters **1, 3, 6, 7, 16, 19, 20, 22, 34.**
Information transmission theories	• Speech is a process and can be studied scientifically. • Public speakers are information managers. They need to control the flow of information to keep it from flooding the listeners, and they need to minimize and compensate for the noise present in every encounter. • Communication is impossible without a shared code. Using words and language to convey meaning is crucial, but so is an understanding of the nonverbal, social, and cultural codes that shape the interpretation of meaning. • Receivers are not passive recipients of speech; they bring their own filters to the decoding process. • Communication is never complete until feedback has been received and interpreted. *You will encounter some of these principles in* Chapters **15, 17, 21, 27, 31.**

Dialogic perspectives on communication	Though what we say is important, the ways we speak can change society for better or worse.
	• Speakers are not always trying to change other people; they may use communication to advance mutual understanding.
	• Even when someone seems to be presenting a monologue, it can be done with a dialogic perspective of humility, openness, and respect.
	• Empathy and consensus are built over time and start with finding common ground, which then expands to authentic speaking and listening.
	• It is possible to stand your ground about important principles and be receptive to other perspectives at the same time.
	You will encounter some of these principles in Chapters 1, 2, 3, 29.

Oral Cultures

Just as children speak before they write, humans developed systems of communal speech long before they created the first systems of writing. Scholars of preliterate societies remind us that speech is the most fundamental tool of social organization. Oral cultures relied on the spoken word to draw them together, affirm their connectedness, and preserve their traditions.

Walter Ong is one of the scholars who have identified a special feature of oral cultures: When the spoken word was the only form of preserving culture, speech had to be memorable.[3] Memorable speech took the form of dramatic stories of intense conflicts between powerful villains and heroes. These early stories were concrete and close to the "lifeworld" of the community. To aid memory and be sure the stories were passed on, the storytellers used repetition and rhyme to create songlike inflections.

After centuries of literacy based on books and printing presses, Marshall McLuhan[4] and other media scholars observed that the electronic media, especially television, had transformed communication into a sort of global village. They coined the term secondary orality to describe the rekindling of a preference for intense, visceral, immediate kinds of communication. The Internet, email, and presentation software have brought the written word back into the speech act in ways that differ radically from the textualized orations found in anthologies of great speeches. It is difficult to imagine what exciting combinations of speaking, writing, images, videos, and sound will evolve in the future. But recognizing the features of orality that characterized speech in the earliest human societies will always help us understand what makes public speaking so powerful.

Classical Rhetoric

The genesis of formal theorizing about speech is usually placed in the thousand years that straddled the beginning of the Common Era. The most influential texts were produced in Greece between the fifth and fourth centuries BCE and in Rome during the two hundred years following that period. In truth these texts share commonalities with teachings associated with the Egyptian philosopher Ptahhotep years earlier.

Classical rhetorical theories emerged in the context of expanding political participation. In the early forms of democracy, citizens of the Greek city-states were allowed to speak in the public assembly and were required to defend themselves in courtroom struggles over property. Traveling teachers known as *sophists* served as speaking coaches and speechwriters. *Sophist* translates generally as "wise one" or "one who makes a business out of wisdom." Undoubtedly, the useful tips of these well-paid teachers empowered a people who might have lacked political voice. But the sophists were severely criticized by philosophers such as Plato, who claimed that the sophists' emphasis on **rhetoric** encouraged people to employ tricks of persuasion instead of searching for the truth.

Aristotle, a student of Plato's and a scholar in many disciplines, tried to resolve this controversy in *The Rhetoric*, a comprehensive treatment of public speaking that was the basis of communication theory for centuries. Aristotle's definition of rhetoric as "the ability to find in any situation the available means of persuasion" differed sharply from the sophists' definition in that it made the speaker a decision maker, not just a technician. Aristotle's discussion of rhetoric also differed from Plato's philosophical notion of seeking one absolute, all-encompassing truth; Aristotle emphasized that what counts as truth varies with each situation. In other words, although speakers should not tell lies in order to persuade an audience, they are wise to recognize the many truths about each topic and to select the one that is most appropriate to the specific audience and situation.

Thus, much of Aristotle's *Rhetoric* deals with how a speaker analyzes situations, audiences, and issues in order to make wise choices. For example, Aristotle differentiates between three genres of speaking:

▶ *Forensic* speaking, as in a courtroom, where a speaker needs to convince a judge or jury that a certain claim is true or untrue;

▶ *Deliberative* speaking, as in a legislature or any decision-making setting, where a speaker is persuading others to make a certain decision or take a course of action; and

▶ *Epideictic* or *ceremonial* speaking, where the speaker is praising, blaming, or otherwise appealing to common values.

Each kind of speech requires different skills from the speaker. Audiences have different expectations and demands in these situations.

Most notably, Aristotle identifies three categories of persuasive appeals. The most fundamental of these, *logos*, refers not just to logic as its name might hint, but to all the intellectual substance of a speech—its arguments, reasons, evidence. In addition to logos, speakers can draw on *pathos*, or motivational appeals to the values, needs, passions, and emotions of listeners. Finally, Aristotle recognized a third kind of persuasive appeal—one that goes beyond the content of the message and the feelings it evokes, and springs from the *ethos* of the speaker. *Ethos* refers to the personal power or credibility that comes from a speaker's force of personality or depth of character.

Effective speaking is too complex to understand as a single skill. Instead, it is made up of five areas of study, sometimes called *canons* of rhetoric, each requiring instruction and practice.

▶ *Invention:* The process of creating something that did not exist before.

▶ *Organization:* The grouping of ideas with supporting evidence and arranging the parts of the speech in a way that makes sense and affects the audience in a particular way.

▶ *Style:* The selection of words to make the points clear and engaging.

▶ *Delivery:* The use of body and voice, unobtrusively but gracefully, to project a compelling message.

▶ *Memory:* The ways of focusing one's mind during a speech so that all of the speech's elements are coordinated with ease.

Communication Studies

In more recent times, attention has shifted from persuasive speaking to informative speaking. In the mid-twentieth century, some new perspectives emerged that treated communication more as science than as art, even examining features of machine systems to see what they might share with human communication. The model of human communication developed by Shannon and Weaver[5] in this period was a mechanistic view that emphasized one-way transmission from a sender to a receiver. From this line of thinking came the interactional and transactional perspectives. These two-way perspectives are represented in models of human communication such as the one in Figure 1.2.

Messages originate inside senders, or *sources*, who formulate their mental images into words or other symbols in a process of *encoding*. The sender then *transmits* the message through a *channel*, where it may encounter resistance or static known as *noise*. If the message gets past the noise, it is received at its *destination*. The signal must then be turned back into meaningful symbols through a process of *decoding*. If the resulting

FIGURE 1.2
A two-way communication model

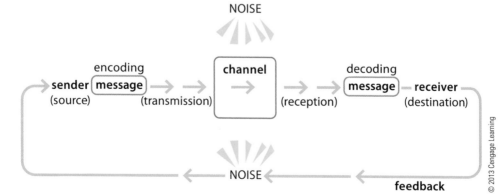

© 2013 Cengage Learning

mental image generally corresponds to the mental image of the sender, there is *fidelity* of communication. If the two images are significantly different, there has been a *communication breakdown*. The comparison of the intended message with the received message is accomplished through the process of *feedback*.

Feedback entails reversing the role of sender and receiver. Feedback can be formal, as in a critique, but more often it is less formal, taking the form of instantaneous nonverbal communication as a listener makes eye contact, smiles, frowns, or perhaps nods off with boredom. The speaker notices, reacts, and adapts to these micromessages. The shifts back and forth between sender and receiver are nearly simultaneous, with each participant sending–receiving–encoding–decoding constantly. Practically, the distinction between sender and receiver almost disappears as their interaction becomes more fluid.

Go to your *CourseMate for* The Speaker's Handbook *and click on* **WebLink 1.1** *to visit a site that discusses the sender's and receiver's different realities, perceptions, and experiences as communicators.*

These information-based approaches showed that even the simplest exchange is packed with dozens of opportunities for communication to break down. Applied to public speaking, the information transmission models reminded speakers that it is never sufficient just to say what they mean and assume communication will follow. Speakers must learn to pay close attention to the way they phrase messages to be sure there is a shared code, just as good dancers respond to music and to their partners while dancing. By including feedback in the communication model, scholars realized that in a situation where interference (visual and psychological as well as acoustic) was likely, communicators could clarify their messages through repetition and redundancy. And, perhaps most importantly, they learned that no communication is complete without feedback to confirm what has been received.

Dialogic Perspectives

A fourth important way to look at communication is through the lens of dialogic theories. Dialogue, associated with give-and-take, may at first seem incompatible with our definition of public speaking. But dialogic theories are less about the *format* of a communicative event—whether one person is leading the event, for instance—than they are about the *attitude* of the speaker. In a dialogue, the speaker is not setting out to change the listeners according to some blueprint, but engages in a much more open and collaborative event. Participants accept that points of view other than their own have validity and are open to changing their views; they avoid inflammatory language and statements of dogmatic certainty. In interacting with their audience, dialogic speakers show respect for different opinions and seek out areas of common understanding.

Some of the central ideas of dialogic theories can be traced to mid-twentieth century philosophers such as Martin Buber. He envisioned a kind of communication in which the primary goal is mutual understanding. Speakers recognize their differences and hold to their beliefs, but they seek out the "between" as the place where communication must start. Dialogue is possible to the extent that participants speak and listen with authenticity, and that they establish what Buber called I–Thou relationships, in which people recognize one another's unique humanness, rather than I–It relationships, in which people treat one another as means to an end. Perhaps you have experienced this sort of communication where you live or work, from effective leaders as they moved organizational members through a difficult change.

Consistent with the nonexploitative approach of dialogic theory is a contemporary notion called *invitational rhetoric*. Foss and Griffin[6] urge speakers to pay less attention to trying to change their audiences and instead to invite listeners to explore ideas together and discover common interests. This orientation is particularly relevant for discussions of controversial issues where people's positions reflect deeply held values. At the most practical level, the invitational approach is often the only way to begin discussion among people who strongly disagree. People are more likely to hear a speaker out if they know the speech will be followed by a genuine give-and-take of ideas. A group of communication scholars known as the Public Dialogue Consortium is committed to applying these principles to speech in the public sphere. Their goal is to promote ways of speaking that will lead to an inclusive society that handles conflict constructively and respectfully. In such a world, they say, people would speak so others are able to listen and listen so others are able to speak.

Go to your CourseMate for The Speaker's Handbook *and click on* **WebLink 1.2** *to visit the Public Dialogue Consortium's website and view some of their projects.*

Approach Public Speaking as Meaning-Centered

As different as the theoretical foundations of communication scholarship are, it is evident there are some common strands. People make meaning together, not alone, and what is effective varies from situation to situation. In recent decades, ideas like these have converged into a perspective that focuses on the *social construction of meaning*. This perspective provides the primary framework for the rest of this book.

Communication Is More than Information Transmission and Reception

As we've discussed, for decades after the dawn of the Information Age, *communication* was defined in terms of the clear transmission of information from a sender to a receiver. For some kinds of speaking and some aspects of speech preparation, this notion is useful. (See Chapter **21**.) But comparing speaking with delivering a package has severe limitations. This metaphor tends to convey the image of discrete, sender-controlled steps. "Giving a speech" becomes a matter of selecting ideas, packaging them, shipping them, and verifying their receipt. Of course, this simplistic approach is inadequate. A more collaborative and complex model of communication is needed.

Communication Is a Collaborative Creation of Meaning

The metaphor of collaborative creation evokes a different set of images. Think about a group of friends hanging out after work or a software design team. At any given time, one individual may put forth ideas while the others listen and react. The product is a composite that emerges from the interaction; it did not exist in any one person's mind at the outset. The shift in emphasis from messages (speaker controlled) to meanings (jointly created) has important implications.

An example of this joint creation is the difference between early web content and newer web resources that incorporate interactivity. Notice how much more dynamic web pages have become recently, allowing users to post content to others' pages (MySpace and Facebook), to change content on public pages (Wikipedia), and to influence the types of content they receive. It's useful to be able to upload a page of content that can be accessed by others on the Web, but it is much more useful to be able to collaboratively create web content, change it, and be changed by it for mutual benefit.

Meaning Is Social

No individual, sender or receiver, can control the "true meaning" of a statement. A speaker who has violated a social norm cannot get off the hook by saying, "I did not intend that statement to be offensive, so it wasn't." But neither can a single receiver unilaterally control what a statement or an action really means to others. A thin-skinned listener is not justified in overreacting to a rather innocent comment by declaring, "I felt offended, so that statement was offensive." Similarly, saying you didn't mean something the way it was taken doesn't take it back.

Meaning Is Contextual

Words or messages alone cannot tell us the "true meaning" of the communication. Words take their meanings not just from a dictionary but from all that surrounds them as they are uttered. The *context*, that which surrounds a text (con-text), must be considered to understand its meaning. This approach to meaning considers when and where a statement was made, who was present, what happened previously, and what tone of voice and expression accompanied the utterance. Perhaps the importance of context is demonstrated by the incident involving Shirley Sherrod in 2010. Her videotaped comments were edited out of context and posted to the Web by commentator Andrew Breitbart.[7] In this case, Ms. Sherrod, a U.S. Department of Agriculture employee, was forced to resign her job before the full context of her comments was brought to light and allowing her to defend her comments as appropriate within the context of their original form.

Meaning Is Negotiated

When the "true meaning" of a message is contested, appeals to the words themselves, to the speaker's intentions, or to the listeners' response have all been shown to be inadequate. Instead, groups work out meanings over time. For example, one court case does not settle what counts as sexual harassment in the workplace. The meaning of sexual harassment has been worked out in speeches, op-ed columns, letters to the editor, and countless personal conversations. Groups whose definition of sexual harassment included even friendly comments found their definition rejected. So did those whose definition excluded everything except physical assault. Gradually, a range of meanings of the term within contemporary US culture came into general understanding. However, because these meanings are social, contextual, and contingent, they will continue to change.

Draw on Three Familiar Communicative Resources

Public speakers should seek to create meaning with their audiences. Think of all the times you have successfully created meaning with different groups of people, in different contexts, and on different topics. When you enter the agreement that designates you as a speaker, you are not required to master a new skill. Rather, your challenge is to adapt several communication skills you already have in your repertoire: conversation, writing, and performance, as Figure 1.3 shows.

FIGURE 1.3
Three communication resources

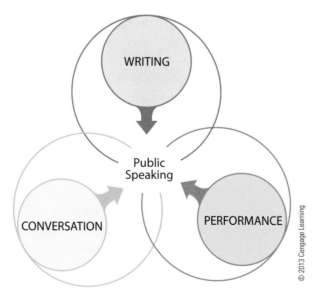

© 2013 Cengage Learning

Conversation Skills

In everyday conversations, you do certain things to be effective. You probably are relaxed, spontaneous, and responsive to the situation, and you express your changing feelings naturally. Your attention is centered on the person or people to whom you are speaking and on the ideas you want to convey. You don't worry about your exact words because the event is interactive, with meaning clarified in the give-and-take.

Conversation is a form of risk taking in that you are not sure of the outcome at any point. This uncertainty does not usually prevent you from conversing, even if you know disagreements may occur. A lot of apprehension about public speaking can be dissipated if you carry this aspect of conversation into the speaking event. One of the highest compliments a speaker can receive is to be called "conversational." The conversation skills that are useful to a public speaker include speaking in a comfortable and confident manner, listening to and considering the perspectives of others, and adapting constantly to feedback.

Composition Skills

Composing a written or oral work enables you to distance yourself from your ideas and to freeze them on paper. This distancing allows you to craft and tinker—to experiment with alternative forms and play them out in your imagination. This tinkering takes much longer than a conversational exploration of ideas, in which the vague "you know what I mean" to a friend can substitute for a few paragraphs of content.

When composing, you pay close attention to word choices and organization. Vocabulary in a speech is more precise than in conversation. By taking the time to enjoy wordplay, explore nuance, and find elegant phrasing you can make a message memorable. Composing can create the distance you need to view your ideas objectively, test them logically, and see how well they fit together. When composing, you can also incorporate additional authoritative sources with your own. Good composition requires time to polish your words to achieve the most economical and forceful way of conveying your message. When composing, then, a speaker draws on the attention to language, the order of ideas, and the internal unity of the speech.

Performance Skills

We are all performers, even if we have never appeared on *Dancing with the Stars*, acted in a Broadway show, or sung karaoke. In one sense, performance occurs whenever we do something rather than merely think about it. When you tell a story to your family, you are performing. Even telling a joke requires performance skills in order to know how long to pause before delivering the punch line. When this handbook talks about performance skills, it means your use of physical qualities—tone of voice, gestures, and movement—to create a focal point in a group.

To many, performance also connotes drama and talent: the flash of a track star, or the passion of an actor in a dramatic scene. In context and in appropriate forms, drama and talent are good things for a speaker to manifest. Communication can be more complete if your delivery is energetic and your movement intentional.

So strong has been the emphasis on conversation that the concept of performance has become taboo among speech teachers. This is because performance has for some time been seen as an end in itself rather than as an essential human activity. But to downplay the performance-related aspects of public speech is to deny the essential power that makes a speech more than conversation, a PowerPoint presentation, or a transcript. *Performance* refers not to display or phoniness, but to the enactment of an event between speaker and listeners that transcends the exchange of information, that makes people say, "You had to be there."

Performance skills that are useful to speakers include the ability to pay attention to the entire effect, the knowledge of how to use setting and timing, and the capacity to turn a collection of individuals into a cohesive group. Performers tie together visual effects, lighting, sound, music, humor, and drama. Performance skills that are useful to speakers include a sense of timing and an understanding of how to direct emotional buildup and choose the right moment for the climax.

Combine and Balance These Communicative Resources

To be successful, public speaking requires the ability to balance all three qualities of conversation, composition, and performance. A speaker needs to command the flexibility of conversation, the organization of composition, and the engagement of performance to earn the undivided attention of an audience. This is not to say that each resource merits equal emphasis in all situations for all speakers. Instead, effective speakers understand that any speaking situation requires a delicate dance in order to maximize impact and audience response. Similarly, giving too much priority to one element over the others can be dangerous. A speaker who spends too much time composing and too little time practicing may develop a great speech but falter during delivery; one who counts on stellar performance skills at the expense of organizing ideas could also face disaster. The "Balancing Communicative Resources" checklist describes some of the perils of leaning too much or too little on any one resource.

How you combine these resources depends on your level of consciousness of your competence (discussed later in this chapter) and on the kinds of feedback you receive in your practice sessions (see Chapters **2** and **25**). Next, let's look at some things to consider as you decide how to combine your communicative resources to create an effective speech.

Consider the Situation and Expectations of the Audience

Most of us understand that how we act on Friday night with friends is much different from how we behave Monday morning at work. We consider the situation and respond

CHECKLIST ~ Balancing Communicative Resources

Conversation

☐ Underreliance leads to stiffness, excessive formality, distance, and lack of spontaneity and immediacy.

☐ Overreliance leads to rambling, disorganization, overuse of vocal pauses, loss of focus, and failure to control distracting delivery habits.

Composition

☐ Underreliance leads to imprecise word choice, repetition, and scattered organization.

☐ Overreliance leads to unnatural use of language and a "canned" sound, inability to adapt to an audience, emphasis on message transmission, and a reliance on reading the text.

Performance

☐ Underreliance leads to monotony, low emotional impact, and reduced energy level.

☐ Overreliance leads to an overly stagy speaking event, distraction from the message, unnatural or melodramatic persona that distances the speaker from the audience, audience passivity, questions of sincerity and credibility, and the possibility of stage fright.

accordingly. As speakers we must do the same. The type of speech and the situation determine how you blend the skills of communication in various speeches. A formal occasion and a large audience often require a speaker to give a writer's attention to word choice and overall unity. Moderating a discussion with a smaller audience entails tapping the listening skills involved in conversation. A festive occasion in front of a larger audience may require a larger-than-life performance.

Chapter **7** gives some suggestions on how to learn more about the people to whom you will speak. Chapters **17** and **28** present guidelines about occasions and situations.

Consider Your Personality and Distinctive Speaking Style

Speakers differ even when speaking on the same occasion and topic. Each of us approaches every situation with a slightly different perspective and style. If you are a great storyteller or have a dramatic flair, you should use that resource to the appropriate extent. If you know you have trouble being spontaneous, let alone dramatic, in front of a group, you should focus on developing the content of your speech so your words and message bond you to your listeners. The choices you make depend on your strengths and weaknesses as a speaker, as well as on the context and situation of the speech event. Again, each dance and dancer is unique.

© geopaul / iStockphoto 3620311

Speaker's Workshop 1.1

Assess the resources you already have as a public speaker by thinking about your strengths and weaknesses as a conversationalist, a writer, and a performer. Which of these resources

▶ Will be the most transferable to your public speaking?

▶ Will be difficult for you to transfer to public speaking?

▶ Might you tend to draw too much from as a speaker?

▶ Offers you the most room for improvement?

Understand the Role of Consciousness in Skill Learning

We learn complex skills differently than we learn simple facts. A complex skill like public speaking involves combining a number of intellectual and physical operations. You know how to breathe, how to raise and lower your voice, how to move your hands, how to define a new term, and how to group ideas into categories. What you may not know is how to put all of these skills together to make an effective public speech.

The learning of skills is said to progress through four stages: unconscious incompetence, conscious incompetence, conscious competence, and unconscious competence (Figure 1.4).

▶ *Stage 1: Unconscious incompetence.* In this stage, people are not aware that they are making errors, and they may even be unaware that some particular skill needs to be learned.

▶ *Stage 2: Conscious incompetence.* People in this stage have come to the realization that they are doing something ineptly and need to improve. In many cases, this awareness creates anxiety, which then magnifies incompetence.

▶ *Stage 3: Conscious competence.* In this stage, people have worked to improve in an area in which they felt incompetent but must now consciously try to perform competently. If they do not make a conscious effort, they are likely to regress to more comfortable but less competent patterns. However, if they persevere, the awkwardness of the new behavior and the need for self-monitoring diminish.

FIGURE 1.4
The four stages of learning skills

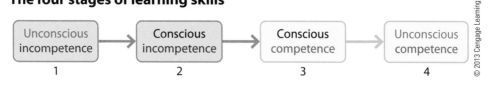

© 2013 Cengage Learning

Unconscious incompetence	→	Conscious incompetence	→	Conscious competence	→	Unconscious competence
1		2		3		4

▸ *Stage 4: Unconscious competence.* People in this stage have integrated the learned skills to the extent that competence comes naturally—there is no longer a need for conscious attention. Performing the skill becomes relatively effortless and may even be fun. Speakers at this level can do more than merely talk; they are free to pay attention to audience response and to make spontaneous adjustments that enhance the quality of the communication.

A great deal of communication behavior is unconscious. You don't think about how you move your lips to make sounds or why you speak one way with your friends and another with your boss. These are areas of unconscious competence. At the same time, you may not be aware you say "you know," mispronounce "library" and "February," twirl your hair when you are nervous, or often commit the fallacy of hasty generalization. These are examples of unconscious incompetence.

When do your communication behaviors receive your conscious attention? Usually when you are learning new skills or when you run into difficulties in communicating. As soon as a skill is mastered or a communication problem is solved, your behavior becomes unconscious again. This is an efficient system. You are constantly freeing yourself to direct your conscious attention to something more challenging.

As a developing speaker, you can set priorities for learning and decide where to focus your attention. Several of the misconceptions listed in the next section can be understood in terms of this approach to skill development. The person who thinks speaking should be effortless (Misconception 2) usually wants to jump straight to Stage 4, unconscious competence, without going through the process of discovering weaknesses and practicing new ways of communicating. The person who thinks speaking is impossibly hard (Misconception 3) does not trust that Stage 3, conscious competence, will eventually lead to unconscious competence (Stage 4). As we attempt to become conscious of what is usually an unconscious act, things may even seem to get worse before they get better. But if increased competence is the goal, the process is necessary, and it does pay off. Before you know it, the new, formerly awkward, behaviors are as habitual as the old ones—but they work better.

The person relying too heavily on the performance model is overly conscious of the physical and vocal delivery of ideas at the expense of the ideas themselves. Speakers holding this view who also see themselves as consciously incompetent can become paralyzed by self-consciousness and anxiety. At the other extreme are speakers who are overly conscious of what they see as competence in delivering a speech. They are so enamored with their own gestures and voice that the result is an affected and showy style. Their attention is on the presentation of self rather than on the presentation of ideas. For the audience this can translate into a speaker so distracting that their message is entirely lost.

Speakers who rely too much on composition skills misdirect awareness in the opposite direction. They may think too much about what they are saying and too little

© geopaul / iStockphoto 3620311

Speaker's Workshop 1.2

1. Compare the speeches by Elizabeth Lopez, Brian Sharkey, Nathanael Dunlavy, and Kayla Strickland that are available through your CourseMate for *The Speaker's Handbook.* Can you find specific examples of how each speaker uses the three resources of conversation, composition, and performance? Next, contrast the speakers in their use of these resources. Which resource did each rely on the most? Which did each use most effectively? Do you attribute the differences to individual style or to the nature of the occasion on which they spoke?

2. What are some of your areas of conscious competence as a public speaker? Conscious incompetence? Unconscious competence? Can you speculate about some areas of unconscious incompetence or remember examples from the past?

about how they are saying it. Or they may go on talking to the formulas on the board while the audience snoozes, or become incoherent when someone asks a question that derails them from their intricately constructed train of thought.

Speakers who think little of composition and performance skills while concentrating on conversation can end up being personable in a speaking event but delivering little substance. If a speaker, however, has been able to use composition and performing skills to develop the speech, the person's conversation strengths will further enhance the well-planned and well-practiced speech.

Recognizing that a speech really is an extension of interpersonal communication should keep you from being overly conscious of either your manner of speaking or the exact language of your message. In day-to-day interactions, you are usually conscious of a few basic things: your reason for speaking, the message you want to get across, your relationship with the other communicator, and the response you are receiving. These are the same things you should be aware of when you speak in public.

Beware of Common Public Speaking Misconceptions

There are many approaches to teaching public speaking and much folk wisdom about how speakers become effective. Mastery of speaking will come more quickly if you can avoid being affected by the four common misconceptions: (1) good speakers are born, not made; (2) good speaking should be easy right away; (3) speaking will always be as difficult as it is when you are first learning it; and (4) there are simple formulas for effective speaking.

Misconception 1: Good Speakers Are Born, Not Made

While it may seem that some people are born better speakers, in fact they are people who have already learned a number of speech skills or who happen to learn speech-related skills quickly. No one is born an effective speaker any more than one is born a good dancer, an accomplished skateboarder, or an expert guitar player. Although pre-dispositions and early learning mean some people learn faster and skate better, anyone who is moderately coordinated, is adequately motivated, and receives sound instruction can learn to dance, perform an ollie, or play a simple tune on the guitar. Similarly, virtually anyone can learn to give a clear, effective public speech.

Misconception 2: Good Speaking Should Be Easy Right Away

When we watch world-class figure skaters, we are fascinated by the apparent ease with which they perform what we know are extremely difficult moves. We appreciate the years of training, dedication, and discipline that have gone into making their movements seem so effortless. Not everyone figure skates—but everyone communicates. Skillful communicators can make public speaking look easy, but it takes work—and lots of it. While many of us have communicated for years, there's a difference between just communicating and communicating effectively. Effective communication takes regular practice and constant review.

Misconception 3: Speaking Will Always Be as Difficult as It Is When You Are First Learning It

Preparing an oral message on a substantial topic for a live audience is demanding. When, at least initially, you must spend hours preparing for a short presentation, there

YOUR
NEW
CAREER

FOR YOUR BENEFIT: **No Simple Do's and Don'ts for Every Situation**

We often joke with students that the answer to each question on our exams is the same: "It depends." This applies outside of school too. The key to become an effective speaker is to understand what it depends on. Although the chapters of this handbook are written as prescriptions, there are no do's and don'ts to apply automatically to every situation. The fundamentals of speaking are stated simply, but the application and combination of these principles depend on your good judgment according to the speaking situation.

Rtimages / www.BigStockPhoto.com

Speaker's Workshop 1.3

Which misconceptions about public speaking do you personally hold? Which do you think are most widespread? Are there other misconceptions that have not been mentioned here?

is a real temptation to say, "Forget this. I can't invest this much time and effort every time I give a speech." Remind yourself that learning a skill requires effort and attention, but it becomes easier once mastered. Recall the concentration required when you learned to drive a car. Now that you have mastered the skill, you simply think of the goal you want to achieve; the actions necessary to reach the goal happen on their own. When you get discouraged with a speech outline that just won't come together or with phrasing that just won't flow, remember: It *will* get easier.

Misconception 4: There Are Simple Formulas for Effective Speaking

Communicating with an audience is an incredibly complex and sophisticated act. Every public speaking event is unique. Each speaker has a distinctive style and personality, the audience has idiosyncratic needs and preferences, and the situation differs from case to case. How these three factors interact creates the meaning in any speaking event. No one can give an all-purpose formula for preparing or delivering a speech. Be wary of programs that promise instant speaking success. When you want to learn a skill well enough for it to become habitual, you need time to develop good habits. The advice in this handbook is based not on what is easiest or fastest but on what has proved to be effective based on years of application. It takes longer to develop a full-sentence outline than to jot down points in the order they occur to you. It is harder to sound conversational and look poised standing and speaking from notes than it is to read while leaning on a table. But once you master these proven techniques, you will be flexible and effective and ready for any speaking situation.

Follow Five Steps of Public Speaking

Preparing and delivering a speech is complex and can be a daunting process. However, the essentials of preparing any speech, even the most basic one, can be distilled into five steps: plan, investigate, compose, practice, and present. This list will help you get started. Later, you will add variations to these steps, master specialized formats, and incorporate specific strategies. Table 1.2 summarizes these steps.

TABLE 1.2
The five steps of public speaking (with chapter references)

STEP	PRIMARY TASKS	CHAPTER WHERE YOU'LL FIND HELP
Plan	Initial decisions and analysis	Prepare plan **5**
		Select and narrow topic **6**
		Consider occasion **7**
		Clarify purpose **6**
		Determine mode of delivery **23**
		Frame thesis statement **6**
		Analyze topic **6**
		Analyze audience **7**
		Counter anxiety **4**
Investigate	Research for resources and materials	Locate credible resources **8**
		Investigate articles, books, and websites **8**
		Conduct interviews **8**
		Keep research notes **8**
Compose	Development of speech materials	Develop rough working outline **9, 10**
		Develop full-sentence outline **11**
		Add supporting materials **15, 16**
		Add attention factors **18**
		Prepare transitions **12**
		Prepare introduction and conclusion **13, 14**
		Prepare presentation aids **27**
		Prepare speech notes **17, 24**
Practice	Preparation for oral performance	Give the speech aloud **17, 24, 25, 26**
		Practice with presentation aids **27**
		Work on vocal delivery **25**
		Work on physical delivery **26**
		Get feedback **24**
Present	The culmination of all your work—relax, enjoy, connect with your audience, and debrief to learn something for next time	Adapting to the speech situation **28**
		Answering questions **29**

© 2013 Cengage Learning

For simplicity, the five steps are presented in a linear fashion, but in practice a speaker may move through the steps in a different order. For a major speech, you might return to topic analysis in order to refine it after you have done some research. Or, when composing the speech, you may discover you need to return for further research. For any speech, it's critical to think through each step!

Review, Reconsider, & Act

Summary

In this chapter we defined public speaking and discussed insights we've gained from prominent communication theories and traditions: our oral culture and rhetorical heritage, information transmission theories, and dialogic perspectives on communication. We explored public speaking from a perspective that focuses on the social construction of meaning. We discussed three communicative resources we can draw on as we prepare public speeches: conversational skills, composition skills, and performance skills. We considered the role of consciousness in the four stages of learning skills. We identified a number of misconceptions about public speaking. And, finally, we outlined the five steps of public speaking: plan, investigate, compose, practice, and present. You will implement these steps throughout this class as you build your skills and learn how to become an effective speaker.

Critical Thinking Questions

▶ How does a meaning-centered perspective differ from a message-centered perspective?

▶ What impact does a meaning-centered perspective of communication have on your ability to speak publicly?

▶ What are your communicative resources, and how can you maximize their impact?

▶ What are the four stages of skill learning, and how might they help you improve your speaking skills?

▶ Which of the five steps of the public speaking process do you find most challenging and why?

Putting It into Practice

Go to your CourseMate for *The Speaker's Handbook* and click once again on **WebLink 1.2** to visit the Public Dialogue Consortium's website. There, review the seven principles for developing public dialogue in communities.

1. What are the community benefits of public dialogue?
2. How might your community benefit by addressing an issue publicly?
3. What issue would you have your community address?
4. What topic would motivate you to speak publicly?

chapter 2

Listening

Develop your skills as a listener to enhance
your own critical thinking and speaking and to
meet your obligations as an audience member.

L istening and speaking are closely tied. An effective speaker must learn to listen
to his or her audience prior to and during each presentation. To be able to speak
effectively a person must listen to understand the needs and wants of the audience. While we spend more hours of our day listening than speaking that doesn't make
listening easy or guarantee we are good at it. Doing something a lot is not the same as
doing it well. Understanding how we listen can help a speaker prepare a speech that will
be heard, understood, and remembered by his or her audience.

Recognize the Relationship between Effective Speaking and Listening

Throughout this handbook, listeners are cast as coauthors of every speech. A message
does not really exist until it is received and shaped by a listener. The act of listening is
defined as a complex and active process of receiving, processing, and evaluating an oral
message. It includes the reception of stimuli, their organization into usable chunks of
sound, the identification of comprehensible words or phrases, and the interpretation of
meanings. From this, it follows that listening is not passive but an active process involving specific skills that requires explicit attention and practice.

Effective speaking and listening go hand in hand. If you master the techniques
in this handbook, it's inevitable you will be more appreciative of good speaking when
you hear it, recognizing the art and craft that come into play to create a satisfying and
successful speaking event. You will also be a more critical listener of the speeches and
reasoning you hear.

Go to your CourseMate for The Speaker's Handbook *and click on* **WebLink 2.1** *to visit the International Listening Association website, which provides some short articles on the value of listening, a compendium of irritating listening habits, and some inspiring and entertaining quotations about listening.*

Prepare to Listen

It may seem silly to talk about "preparing to listen," but it is necessary if we are to become effective listeners. Athletic teams spend considerable time and effort preparing for competitive events. In the same way, it makes sense to prepare to listen, as it can quickly improve our ability.

Remove Distractions

In our multitasking society, we listen to the radio while driving, watch television while texting or talking on a cellphone, or make shopping lists while listening to a professor's lecture. When listening demands your full attention, you shouldn't be doing anything else. In a classroom, this means sitting up straight, looking at the speaker, and clearing away all materials except those needed for note taking.

Stop Talking

As obvious as this advice sounds, many people enter situations in which they need to gain information from others, such as interviews, and then proceed to do most of the talking. Even when they stop talking, many listeners continue to be distracted from genuine listening as they plan what to say next. Stop talking, look at the person who is talking, and listen.

Decide on Your Purpose as a Listener

Are you listening to learn? To understand a new point of view? To solve a problem? To evaluate a controversial argument? Or to enjoy a narrative by a talented storyteller? These are just four of many possible listening objectives—and to achieve any one of them requires different subsets of listening skills and approaches. Your empathy, your curiosity, your critical analysis, your concentration—all come into play in different ways in different situations. As listeners, if we understand the purpose for our listening we are more likely to match the situation with the appropriate listening intensity to meet our listening goals.

Be Curious and Critical

When participating as an audience member, it's unfair to the speaker if you are so resistant to a message that you close yourself off to new ideas or different opinions. You also do yourself a disservice if you accept the ideas and information you encounter without a critical eye. Effective listeners navigate between these two extremes. You'll want to balance a charitable and open receptiveness to what the speaker is saying with a critical assessment based on your life experiences and common sense.

Show Respect

Even if you disagree with a viewpoint or find a topic dull, recognize that speaking in public takes courage and effort. Give the speaker your full attention, and adhere to the courtesies of a public situation. This is important whether you are an audience member or the next speaker. Listeners show courtesy by looking at the speaker, asking questions if that is appropriate, and avoiding any verbal or nonverbal behavior that would distract either the speaker or other listeners. This includes reviewing your own note cards, checking for text messages, and any other activity that might diminish even the appearance of paying attention.

Be Open to the Speaker's Point of View

It is not really possible to suspend judgment until a speaker has finished. People cannot help evaluating everything they hear as they hear it. But instead of criticizing, be curious. While listening, ask yourself, "What, exactly, is this person saying? What led this person to that position? What assumptions underlie the speaker's position?"

The discussion of reasoning (see Chapter **16**) suggests that people can start with the same data but end up with different interpretations. Get inside the speaker's world with this analytic approach, and one of two things will happen: You will be able to put your finger on the exact points you want to ask questions about or refute, or you will find your opinion changing to accommodate part of the speaker's view.

Follow the Structure of the Speech

Try to identify the speech's thesis, main points, supporting materials, and crucial links, whether these are explicitly stated or not. Discerning the structure helps you retain content and evaluate its validity.

FOR YOUR BENEFIT: Failing to Monitor Your Nonverbal Behaviors as a Listener

YOUR NEW CAREER

Even when you disagree or are confused by a speaker, don't grimace or roll your eyes. Learn to monitor your facial expression. As a matter of courtesy and respect, assume a supportive and responsive listening demeanor. At times it may prove to be politically savvy to mask your initial reaction, whether you are listening to a classmate in speech class or to a colleague in a business meeting.

Rtimages / www.BigStockPhoto.com

CHECKLIST ~ Questions for Assessing a Speaker's Claims

- ☐ Do the main points, taken together, justify the thesis? (See Chapter **9**.)
- ☐ Is each claim stated clearly as a proposition that can be validated or rejected? (See Chapter **22**.)
- ☐ Is this claim a proposition of fact, value, or policy? (See Chapter **22**.)
- ☐ Is the support offered for each claim relevant to the point? (See Chapter **15**.)
- ☐ Does each piece of evidence pass the appropriate tests for examples, testimony, or statistics? (See Chapter **15**.)
- ☐ Are the links between the points logically drawn? (See Chapter **16**.)
- ☐ What premises are taken for granted without being stated? Are these assumptions valid? (See Chapter **16**.)
- ☐ Are any fallacies present? (See Chapter **16**.)
- ☐ Does the speaker misuse emotional appeals or substitute them for intellectual argument? (See Chapter **20**.)

Unfortunately, not every speaker will be skilled at highlighting important points and providing clear transitions to signal relationships. To get the most out of a speech, you may need to create a mental outline to structure the points you hear. Listen for the speaker's thesis. Can you discern the main point of the speech?

Critically Assess the Speaker's Claims

As you listen to any speaker who makes a controversial claim, engage your critical thinking skills to test the validity of the argument. Does the speaker rely on rational or emotional appeals? Use the "Questions for Assessing a Speaker's Claims" Checklist to ask yourself the necessary questions.

Ask Questions at the Designated Time

Jot down any points you want to return to during the question-and-answer period. Be sure you ask genuine questions: Do not turn your opportunity to ask a question into your own speech or an argument with the speaker, and avoid attempts to trap the speaker. Again, the spirit of curiosity should help you frame questions whose answers will lead yourself and others to an understanding of what the speaker is trying to communicate.

Provide Constructive Feedback

In one special situation, when you act as a critic or consultant, you agree to listen as more than an audience member and to provide feedback on the decisions a speaker has made and the effectiveness of the presentation. This may occur during a practice session of a speech that is still in preparation, or it may take place after a speech has been given, with the goal of helping the speaker improve future presentations. (See Chapter **24**.) In either case, the role of critic–consultant requires a special blend of honesty and tact. The supportive critic bears in mind the fragility of partially formed ideas and the close connection between a person's speaking personality and that person's self-image. The following guidelines are for listeners who have been asked to give feedback.

Start with the Positive

Acknowledge what the speaker has tried to do and how it has succeeded. By beginning with the positive, you help reduce defensiveness and maintain openness for the constructive feedback to follow.

Make Important Comments First

Begin your feedback with the most significant issues. Think first about whether the message makes sense and whether the overall strategy is effective. Resolve issues regarding main points before addressing lesser concerns.

Be Descriptive

It is more helpful to say, "You were discussing causes of the problem in Point 1 and then again in Point 3, which confused me" than "This speech was disorganized." With positive comments as well, it's better to describe what was effective by saying, "Comparing the greenhouse effect to the atmosphere inside a closed car really helped me understand," rather than "The speech is great."

Offer Suggestions, Not Orders

Acknowledge in your comments that your reactions are those of just one listener and others may differ. Also, recognize that some wonderful ideas can and should be rejected by a speaker because they simply don't fit that person's style. Bearing these things in mind, you might suggest something along the lines of "I have never cared for a heavily dramatic delivery, though I know it works for some people. Have you thought about . . . ?"

Restrict Speaker Feedback

Always consider the speaker's feelings when deciding what to say and how to phrase it. There is no need to comment on aspects of a person's speech style that are tied to cultural identity. Also, some delivery problems are so obvious that encouraging the speaker to view videotape is a less embarrassing way to confront them. Others are so complex that it would be better for a speech professional to address them.

Be aware of the time constraints a speaker faces. If you are giving feedback early in the development of the speech, you can make some larger suggestions for revision.

However, if the speech is in final rehearsal, it's probably too late to suggest going back to the drawing board. Try to offer a few suggestions that can improve the speech, rather than make the speaker wish for time to prepare a different one.

Use the 90/10 Principle

This principle, developed by one of the authors in teaching interpersonal communication, states that people's weaknesses are rarely the *opposite* of their strengths. More often, they are the *excesses*. This awareness suggests a way of phrasing feedback: "The first 90 percent of (quality A) is a positive addition to your speech, but the last

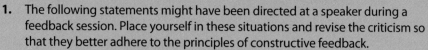

CHECKLIST ~ Constructive Feedback

- [ ] Start with the positive.
- [ ] Make important comments first.
- [ ] Be specific.
- [ ] Offer suggestions, not orders.
- [ ] Be realistic.
- [ ] Use the 90/10 principle.

Speaker's Workshop 2.1

1. The following statements might have been directed at a speaker during a feedback session. Place yourself in these situations and revise the criticism so that they better adhere to the principles of constructive feedback.
   ▶ Your manner is too abrasive.
   ▶ Talk more loudly.
   ▶ Your speech was very interesting.
   ▶ Take your hand out of your pocket; use more humor; your points don't prove your thesis.

2. Go to your CourseMate for *The Speaker's Handbook* and select one student speech from the book's interactive videos. As you watch it, prepare constructive comments and feedback you would give this speaker to help improve the speech.

3. Or go to Speech Studio and watch one of your classmate's first speeches. Prepare constructive comments and feedback you would give this speaker to help improve the speech.

10 percent of (quality A) begins to work in the opposite way." You are not suggesting that speakers eliminate a characteristic behavior, but that they hold it in check. Actual feedback phrased this way might sound like this: "Generally, the use of evidence made this speech especially compelling. Sometimes, though, the statistics were so dense I found them hard to comprehend, and I was hoping you would insert an example or a brief illustration."

Listen to Optimize Your Learning

Chapter **8** covers seeking information from other people as you research your speech. Effective listening in these situations will enable you to reach a deeper understanding of your topic and use your time more efficiently. In formal interviews of experts or in more informal conversations on your topic, use the following listening techniques.

Paraphrase

Check your understanding of the points being made by paraphrasing and clarifying. This involves restating what you think you heard so the speaker can confirm or correct your interpretations: "In other words, what you are saying is . . . " or "Would [give example] be an example of what you are talking about?" or "Are you using the term *discrimination* with the connotation of *conscious intent*?"

Ask Follow-up Questions

In Chapter **8**'s discussion about interviewing people, it is suggested that you devise a list of specific, open-ended questions, which keep the interview focused on the person's expertise but also allow the person to go in a fruitful direction you might not have anticipated. Careful listening will enable you to capitalize on this, as well as to focus on following up. As the expert answers the open-ended questions, follow up with more specific questions in response to those answers: "You said a minute ago that the global impact of biofuels may be more harmful than the environmental impact of burning fossil fuels. Why do you say that?"

Take Notes

Be sure to take notes as you listen to a speaker. At first, having to write as well as listen may seem to get in the way of actually hearing what is being said. However, because taking notes forces you to think about what is said, it will actually help you listen better. As you take notes, realize that it isn't necessary to capture the speaker's words verbatim. Instead, make notes of the key ideas offered by the speaker in order to help you comprehend and critically consider what the speaker is saying.

FOR YOUR BENEFIT: **Listening to Non-Native English Speakers**

YOUR
NEW
CAREER

American businesses and classrooms have grown increasingly culturally diverse. Developing a sensitivity for various accents will serve you well in our increasingly multicultural society. Practice listening to non-native speakers and consider studying a second language yourself. Remember that to communicate with you, the speaker has learned American English vocabulary, grammar, and syntax, and then has risked speaking publicly in that new language. With a small amount of effort, most listeners can adjust to nonnative speakers' inflection, unusual pronunciation or pauses, and understand quite well. When possible check your understanding with the speaker by paraphrasing your understanding.

Listen Holistically When Conducting Audience Analysis

Listening to understand the whole person—in context, in the moment—is called holistic listening. It requires the open and receptive attitudes that characterize caring friends and helping professionals when establishing empathy is a major goal of communicating. We listen holistically as audience members whether in a business meeting or classroom. A speaker might listen holistically when conducting audience analysis (see Chapter 7) to get a general sense of how audience members see the world.

Listen at Multiple Levels

All utterances have a surface message, but there are other deeper meanings that reveal how a person feels. The full richness of meaning can be discovered by being alert to word choices, metaphors, and tone of voice.

Listen between the Lines

Another implication of holistic listening is that the full meaning of an utterance is embedded in the nonverbal cues that surround the words. We listen not just with our ears but with our eyes and hearts. You can observe when a person's vocal tones or body language are emphasizing or contradicting some of the words. Practice noticing variations in emotional intensity, which can be revealing. It is in these nonverbal messages that television shows like *Lie to Me* and *The Mentalist* have focused.

Listen to the Silences

Sometimes, it's not the utterance that communicates. Form the habit of noticing what a speaker does *not* say. What topics are omitted or rushed through? When do long pauses occur? If a job applicant has a two-year gap in a résumé or a salesperson talks about every feature of a product except price, these omissions may be important.

Avoid Common Listening Pitfalls

Daydreaming, Doodling, and Disengaging

It's easy for your mind to wander during a speech, in part because it takes a speaker longer to state an idea than for a listener to think the same thing. Listening experts recommend using that time differential constructively. As you listen, use your extra processing time to think of questions to ask later, consider the implications of what is being suggested, or consider how your own speech might benefit from some of the strategies used by the speaker. Stay mentally active in ways that connect to the speech topic.

Becoming Distracted by Superficial Qualities of the Speaker

You may notice that a speaker mispronounces a word, makes a grammatical error, sways back and forth, or makes every statement sound like a question. Or you may notice another speaker has a charming accent, sounds like a radio announcer, or looks wonderful in that shade of blue. In either case, letting yourself become distracted with these traits hinders your ability to listen to the speech. As a listener, your job is to overcome superficial distractions and focus on the message.

Uncritically Accepting a Message

Don't automatically assume that if a speaker makes a statement it must be true. Listeners share an ethical responsibility for the meanings that come out of speeches. Passivity in listening abdicates this responsibility. Give a speaker's ideas the scrutiny they require.

Prematurely or Totally Rejecting a Message

Hear the speaker out. For instance, you may totally oppose capital punishment, but don't be quick to assume this speaker is the same as all other proponents. Listen attentively, and you may hear a new argument or find an intriguing point you hadn't considered.

Planning Your Response or Rebuttal to a Speech Instead of Listening to It

You can certainly be critical and analytical, but unless you are in a debate that requires on-the-spot refutation, don't divert your attention to the extent of composing your own messages.

Speaker's Workshop 2.2

 Go to your CourseMate for *The Speaker's Handbook* and access the book's video activities. First read the transcript of and then watch the video of Hans Erian's speech "No More Sugar."

▶ Are you distracted from listening by any aspects of the speaker's appearance or vocal or physical delivery?

▶ What steps do you take to help focus your attention to the message? What more could you do?

Failing to Monitor Your Nonverbal Behaviors as a Listener

Even when you disagree or are confused, don't grimace or roll your eyes. For that matter, don't look bored or allow your eyes to glaze over. Out of courtesy and respect, assume a supportive and responsive listening demeanor.

Review, Reconsider, & Act

Summary

In this chapter we have considered the importance of listening skills, both as an audience member and speaker. We have come to understand the important relationship between speaking and listening. We know that listening takes preparation, that we must be both curious and critical in our approach to listening, and that to truly listen well sometimes means being able to offer constructive feedback. The chapter also reviewed strategies allowing us to optimize our listening: paraphrasing, questioning, and taking notes. We explored holistic listening, or listening to understand the whole person, as a way of improving our listening effectiveness. Last, the chapter concludes with six common listening pitfalls to avoid.

Critical Thinking Questions

▶   How does listening relate to the process of effective speech making?

▶   What can you do to improve your listening behavior?

▶   What advice would you offer a friend required to give feedback to coworkers?

▶   Which listening pitfall do you find most challenging, and what could you do to overcome this difficulty?

Putting It into Practice

Go to your CourseMate for *The Speaker's Handbook* and click on **WebLink 2.2**. There, read Tanya Glaser's summary of the article "Dialogic Listening: Sculpting Mutual Meanings."

1. What listening techniques are suggested in the summary?

2. Pick two of the listening techniques suggested and use them as you listen to others at home, work, or school.

3. What differences do you notice in how others respond to you when you practice dialogic listening?

4. How could these listening strategies be useful to you?

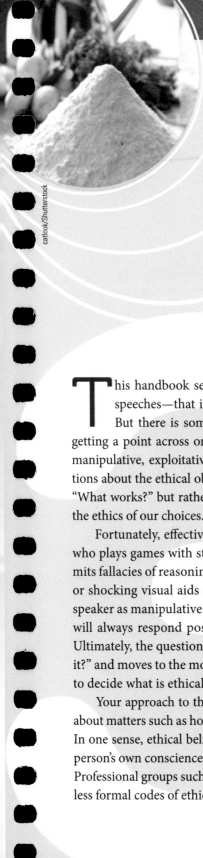

chapter 3
Speaking Ethics

Commit yourself to a set of ethical principles
that will guide you as a public speaker.

This handbook serves primarily to help you plan and present effective public speeches—that is, speeches that allow you to achieve your goals in speaking. But there is something more to consider. Sometimes, a speaker succeeds in getting a point across or in persuading an audience but does so in a manner that is manipulative, exploitative, dishonest, or otherwise offensive. These cases raise questions about the ethical obligations of all speakers. Ethical questions do not merely ask, "What works?" but rather ask, "What is appropriate?" As a speaker we must consider the ethics of our choices.

Fortunately, effective speaking and ethical speaking work together. The speaker who plays games with statistics or quotes authorities out of context frequently commits fallacies of reasoning in the process, and heavy-handed use of emotional appeals or shocking visual aids often backfires. Credibility suffers when listeners perceive a speaker as manipulative or insincere. There are no guarantees, though, that audiences will always respond positively to those speakers who take the moral high ground. Ultimately, the question transcends the simple yes/no choice of "Can I get away with it?" and moves to the more complex realm of personal values, where each speaker has to decide what is ethically justifiable.

Your approach to the ethical choices in public speaking grows out of your beliefs about matters such as how people should treat one another and what counts as honesty. In one sense, ethical beliefs are so individual they seem almost to be a matter of each person's own conscience. Yet other people influence our beliefs about right and wrong. Professional groups such as doctors and lawyers have formalized codes of ethics. Other less formal codes of ethical conduct come to us through family, religion, and culture.

Go to your CourseMate for The Speaker's Handbook *and click on* **WebLink 3.1** *to visit the National Communication Association's website. There, read the association's Credo for Ethical Communication. Your organization or educational institution may also have a code of ethics— learn it. Also check out* **WebLink 3.2** *to visit the Ethics Updates website. This site provides instructors and students with resources and updates on current literature that relates to ethics.*

Be Aware of Ethical Choices

We make choices based on values and ethics every day. Sometimes these choices are clear cut and easy but often they are less clear or perhaps a choice between the lesser of two evils. Our choices as speakers have significant ethical dimensions, are rarely clear cut, and the best choice may depend on the contextual issues relating to the context of our circumstance, or audience.

Recognize That Every Action Has an Ethical Dimension

No decision a speaker makes is morally neutral. We speak because we believe that what we say will make a difference. And it does. The results of a speech can be as serious as persuading others to follow a dangerous course of action or as apparently harmless as wasting their time with an unprepared and unfocused message. Every time you speak, you exercise power and assume responsibility for the consequences of what you do or don't say.

Recognize That Ethical Decisions Are Rarely Clear-Cut

Often, the answer to questions about what works in public speaking is, "It depends." Questions about what is the right or ethical course of action are just as complex. Ethics grow from our values, and values sometimes conflict. Classic communication dilemmas in everyday life deal with choices about whether to be honest and hurt someone's feelings or to be tactful and less than fully truthful. Rarely are there black-and-white choices. The best we can do most of the time is to select among various shades of gray. As communicators, we are obligated to consider each case and to make a judgment based on experience and reflection. As time goes by, we will likely be more discerning about the nuances of situations and more skilled in using language and nonverbal communication in sensitive and responsible ways.

Recognize That Ethical Decisions Vary with Context

In a speech tournament, a debater might argue for medical marijuana at 9:00 and argue against it at 10:30. In this context, it is understood that the rules of the game are to defend the assigned side of a topic as vigorously and skillfully as possible. This is considered no more unethical than the case of the football team that defends the north goal in the first and third quarters and just as vigorously defends the south goal in the second and fourth. However, if a political candidate gets caught taking one position when speaking to voters in Oregon and the opposite position in Kansas, we judge that to be unethical because we view such public speeches not as part of a game but as sincere statements of the speaker's true beliefs.

What you can pass off as your own words varies as well. We would expect the governor of our state to employ a speechwriter because the demands on public servants make it impossible to personally prepare each speech he or she gives. However, in an academic environment, it is understood that students must create and deliver their own speeches. So, for the student it would be unethical to buy a speech online or use a speech written by a friend, just as it would be unethical for one employee to take credit for another employee's work.

Respect the Integrity of Your Core Values

As a public speaker, you are not simply a transmitter of messages; you also put yourself in contact with an audience. Although you may adapt, adjust, and accommodate to meet your goals, you have an ethical obligation to be true to yourself. When you've finished a speech, regardless of how anyone else responds, you should always feel good about what you said and how you said it. Never be reluctant to speak from your heart, to express your passion and conviction on a topic. Yet, as the speaker, you must respect your audience.

Respect the Integrity of Your Audience

Public speakers have a special kind of power. When audience members entrust you with their time and attention, you take on an obligation to treat them fairly. In a democracy that means we must recognize that each human being in our audience as a unique individual with free will and autonomy. Within this value system, those who have power over others do not have the right to use people as a means to their selfish ends. We must treat our audience members responsibly.

You have every right to pursue your own reasons for speaking, but not at the expense of your listeners' welfare. As an ethical speaker, do not underestimate audience members' intelligence or try to trick them into making decisions that endanger their health, safety, financial security, or other interests. And at the end of each speech, you should feel confident that your listeners are better off than they were before the speech. Whether or not they agree with your points, you have given them a chance to consider ideas without coercion or manipulation so they can make informed decisions.

Respect the Integrity of Ideas

Because the "victim" of unethical behavior is not immediately obvious, speakers find the responsibility to honor the integrity of ideas to be the most difficult to understand and, thus, the easiest to overlook. To live and work together, people have to trust that, overall, communication proceeds honestly and reliably. Imagine the impact of one piece of misinformation in a speech presented to twenty people, who each share that information with three other people later in the day. The speaker has now misinformed eighty people.

Don't Plagiarize

In addition to yourself and your audience, there are others, not present, to whom you have some ethical obligations. These are the people whose ideas and words you draw into the speech situation. The ethics of public speaking generally prohibit the use of another's major ideas or exact words—even paraphrasing them—without giving credit to the source. Anything short of that is equal to theft. See Table 3.1 for a comparison of appropriate paraphrasing and bad paraphrasing that would be considered plagiarism.

Most institutions are clear about having a specific policy for addressing issues of plagiarism and academic dishonesty—it is not adequate to claim you did not know that plagiarism was unacceptable. It is incumbent upon you as a speaker to give credit to the sources that inform you. Careers have been ruined when students, journalists,

TABLE 3.1
Avoiding plagiarism through bad paraphrasing

PASSAGE FROM ORIGINAL SOURCE	BAD PARAPHRASE RESULTING IN PLAGIARISM	GOOD PARAPHRASE RESULTING IN AN APPROPRIATE CITATION
"Of the four phases of the creative process, most speech training emphasizes the logical, rule-bound processes of preparation and refinement. The middle two phases of incubation and illumination are rarely mentioned because they do not lend themselves to systematization. These middle steps touch the emotions.	"Most speech training emphasizes the preparation and refinement phases, of the creative process. This is because they are systematic, logical processes. The middle two phases, incubation and illumination, aren't mentioned because they are less systematic and more emotional."	"The two middle phases of the creative process don't get the attention in speech training that the other two do. According to Sprague, Stuart, and Bodary, incubation and illumination get less attention because they deal with less logical aspects of creativity than preparation and refinement, which are more logically ordered."
Sprague, Stuart, and Bodary, *The Speaker's Handbook*	Condensing, changing the order of some words, and substituting synonyms do not make this an honest paraphrase.	Attributing the ideas discussed to the original authors makes this an honest paraphrase.

and public figures have been exposed as plagiarists. To avoid even the appearance of unethical use of speech content, form the habit of taking careful notes of the sources of all your ideas, statistics, and evidence. It is your obligation to explain the source of your information as you use it in your speech. And when you hear a wonderful anecdote, story, or turn of phrase you might like to quote someday, make a note right then so you will remember to give credit to the source. (See Chapter **8.**)

A useful tool for gathering, organizing, and tracking your sources online is Zotero. Go to your CourseMate for The Speaker's Handbook *and click on* **WebLink 3.3** *to learn more about this free resource. In addition, click on* **WebLinks 3.4** *and* **3.5** *to access several resources available through Northwestern University and Purdue University that will guide you in avoiding even the appearance of plagiarism.*

Don't Lie

Nothing written here will stop the pathological liar or the ill-intentioned person. For the majority of us, the issues surrounding honesty are much subtler. Our courts require an oath to tell "the truth, the whole truth, and nothing but the truth," although rarely do we live up to that standard in everyday interactions. For example, out of kindness, someone compliments a friend's new outfit although it is not attractive. Acting on the best information available, a presidential candidate promises there will be "no new taxes." A nurse tells a child that the shot "will only sting a little bit." You exaggerate a funny story to better entertain your listeners. The phrase "it depends" always crops up in conversations about what counts as a lie, a white lie, a fib, a prevarication, or tactful phrasing.

In public speaking, most people would consider that at least the following categories of behavior cross the line between honest and dishonest speech.

Making Statements That Are Completely Counterfactual

"I have no financial interest in this fitness center. I just care about your health." [when you receive a commission for every new member you enroll]

Playing Word Games to Create a False Impression

Sometimes a speaker can use words with great precision of definition, being technically correct but totally misleading: "In response to allegations of illegal drug use, let me say that I have never broken the laws of this country." [when the drug use was in another country]

Leaving Out Some Part of "The Whole Truth" That, if Known, Would Completely Reverse the Impact of the Statement

"None of the studies in the dozens I reviewed show that smoking causes lung cancer." [But many show a strong link.]

Don't Oversimplify

Another dimension of the integrity of ideas has to do with faithfulness to the facts and realities of your subject matter. Although there is rarely one "real truth" on any complex issue, some accounts are so shallow or oversimplified as to provide a false picture. Before you speak in public, thus contributing to and shaping the public discourse on a topic, you have an ethical obligation to do your homework, to look beneath the surface, to weigh evidence carefully, and to explore a variety of viewpoints.

Weigh the Complex Factors and Competing Goals in Ethical Decisions

As a speaker, you perform a delicate balancing act in many of the decisions you make. Be especially aware of the ethical impact of choices you make about language, facts, emotional appeals, and persuasive strategies. Use the "Finding a Balance in Ethical Decisions" checklist to ask yourself the necessary questions.

Avoid Offensive Language

When occupying a public platform, speakers can cause pain by using words that some find demeaning, racist, sexist, or obscene. This is not to say that a speaker must rely on bland or wishy-washy phrasing. The wonderful richness of vocabulary, metaphor, and style provides many ways to be colorful, precise, and sensitive.

Avoid Sharing Opinions as Facts

Newspapers have editorial sections that clearly distinguish the opinions of the newspaper staff from articles about issues of news. Advertisements in magazines and newspapers are expected to be clearly marked. Similarly, public speakers have a responsibility to support their claims with evidence and should avoid presenting opinions or hearsay as fact.

Avoid an Overreliance on Emotional Appeals

When your argument is logically sound and well documented, appeals to your listeners' feelings are legitimate ways to support and emphasize your points. And it's perfectly acceptable when a speaker becomes a bit carried away when presenting a deeply held belief. However, an overreliance on appeals to needs, emotions, or values is distrustful when:

▶ A need is created that listeners had not perceived before causes considerable pain or discomfort, and the action required in response to this need directly benefits the speaker.

▶ Extreme emotional appeals are made to listeners at a time of great emotional susceptibility or are related to an area of their lives in which they are particularly vulnerable.

▶ Emotional appeals are part of a sustained, systematic effort to make listeners feel more confused, dependent, insecure, fearful, or helpless.

▶ The basic logical argument would not be validated by dispassionate and informed observers without the underlying the emotional appeal.

CHECKLIST ~ Finding a Balance in Ethical Decisions

☐ Have you used lively language that doesn't cause pain and offense?

☐ Have you appealed to your audience on an emotional level without abusing emotional appeals?

☐ Have you clarified the source of your information and avoided introducing opinions as facts?

☐ Have you used compelling persuasive appeals but avoided simplistic persuasive techniques?

Avoid Simplistic Persuasive Techniques

By definition, persuasion is not neutral. If you have decided to persuade, you have decided that a point of view is worth advocating. (See the persuasive strategies outlined in Chapter **22**.) But in your zeal to get across your point of view, remember that a good speaker never shortchanges the role of logical arguments supported by sound evidence. The classic list of propaganda devices identified by a group of journalists some decades ago sets forth the techniques unethical speakers can use to short-circuit an audience's rational processes.[1]

▶ *Name-calling.* By attaching a negative label to an idea or a person, a speaker can provoke fear or hatred in an audience. For instance, charged words such as *traitor, sexist, terrorist*, or *anti-American* can be used to short-circuit a listener's critical thinking. Such speakers hope this tide of emotion will gloss over the lack of substance in their positions. (See Chapter **16**.)

▶ *Glittering generalities.* At the other extreme is the speaker who generates a positive response to a statement by using words or phrases that represent some vague virtue. This technique attempts to convert listeners not on the merits of a position but because adoption of the position would be, for example, the patriotic thing to do.

▶ *Testimonials.* Another way to generate positive emotions is to link a popular figure with some cause or product. Here, the speaker replaces sound argument with inappropriate extension of the person's credibility. Thus, an actor may be admired in his role as a doctor, but when he endorses a headache remedy, he is way beyond his qualifications. In this case, the testimonial is based on a misleading impression.

▶ *"Just plain folks."* It is fine to build identification with an audience so that members are receptive to the ideas presented. This process goes too far, though, when the speaker implies, "You should believe me, not because of the inherent validity of what I say, but because I'm just like you." Examples of the "we are all just plain folks here" technique include politicians who roll up their flannel shirt sleeves on the campaign trail in, for example, Indiana.

▶ *Card stacking.* In this method, a speaker carefully uses only facts or examples that bolster his or her position, and the biased selection is passed off as representative. An opponent of hiring more police officers might stress accounts of police sexual misconduct and reports of pilferage of confiscated drugs and ask, "Do we want to spend money to put more of that kind of person in positions of authority?"

▶ *The bandwagon.* This technique is useful to a speaker who wishes to discourage independent thinking. The "everyone is doing it" approach appeals to the need for security and plays on fears of being different or left out. Speakers frequently cite public opinion polls to support their positions. However, the fact that many people are in favor of some proposal does not necessarily make it right. A proposition should be sold on its merits, not on its popularity.

▶ *Transference.* To make some unfamiliar thing more (or less) acceptable to an audience, many speakers will ascribe to it characteristics of something familiar. Often, there is no true relationship between the two. For example, characterizing video games as a "cancer spreading through our society" would inappropriately equate video games with losing someone you love to cancer.

This list is far from comprehensive. Effective modern persuaders also use such techniques as snob appeal (the opposite of "just plain folks") and stand-out-from-the-crowd

Speaker's Workshop 3.1

1. These clichés about right and wrong have come up repeatedly over the centuries. Relate each of these to problems a public speaker might face in trying to be ethical and fair.
   A. What would the world be like if everyone did that?
   B. Above all else, do no harm.
   C. The ends don't justify the means.
   D. Would you want your mother [favorite teacher/clergy member/most admired friend] to know you did this?

2. What can a listener reasonably expect from a public speaker? Write an "Audience Bill of Rights" you would like to see adopted.

3. Evaluate these uses of emotional appeals according to the principles suggested in this chapter.
   A. I saw a vision and knew that if I didn't raise $1 million by April 1, that I would surely die. Please send in your contributions.
   B. I know how shocked you are by the death of your two classmates last week. They would certainly want you to write your senator today, demanding stricter penalties for drug pushers. You can show your love for them and save others from going through the pain you are experiencing.
   C. You can make $50,000 a year in your spare time by becoming a distributor for our organization. But you must do exactly as I say. Put yourself in my hands, and I will make you rich.
   D. If you can pinch an inch of flesh at your midriff, you are disgustingly fat and should buy a membership in my health club.

(the opposite of the bandwagon). Such persuasive appeals are questionable whenever they serve to:

▶ Distract listeners from important issues.

▶ Cloud important distinctions.

▶ Introduce irrelevant factors in the decision-making process.

▶ Use emotional appeals inappropriately or excessively.

Review, Reconsider, & Act

Summary

Ethics are involved in every aspect of developing a speech. As ethical speakers, we must be aware of the ethical implications of our choices throughout the speech-making process, and we must reflect upon and respect the integrity of our own core values as well as the integrity of our audience and the very ideas we espouse. Ethical speakers don't plagiarize and don't lie; they avoid oversimplification; and they strive for fair balances in their use of language, emotional appeals, and persuasive strategy.

Critical Thinking Questions

▶ Make a list of the ethical issues speakers face.

▶ Explain what balance has to do with managing any ethical speaking situation.

▶ What makes plagiarism so heinous? How should a person who commits plagiarism be treated?

▶ Which of the propaganda devices listed in this chapter have you used? Was it ethical to do so?

Putting It into Practice

Make a list of three to five well-known people who have made errors in ethical judgment. Creating the list is easy: think of examples such as golfer Tiger Woods; Hewlett-Packard CEO Mark Hurd; former governor of New York Elliot Spitzer; former attorney general of Ohio Marc Dann; or James Frey, the author who fabricated stories in a book that Oprah Winfrey promoted on her talk show.

1. What factors contributed to their errors?

2. Were specific ethical or legal codes violated?

3. What effect did the errors have on the individuals' professional and personal lives?

4. How might these ethical errors have been avoided?

chapter 4
Overcoming Fear of Speaking

Understand, analyze, and accept your fear of speaking. Combine thorough preparation with relaxation and visualization techniques to increase your confidence.

Stage fright, communication apprehension, speech anxiety, reticence, shyness—these are among the most researched and analyzed variables in the literature on communication, precisely because so many people believe they fear public speaking. While there are no simple ways to eliminate the fear altogether, experts do offer some techniques that can help you become more comfortable and confident when you speak in public. Techniques you can use to work toward this goal include putting fear into perspective, building confidence through preparation and practice, managing the physical effects of fear, and using positive self-suggestion to combat anxiety.

Put Your Fear of Speaking into Perspective

We often give fear more power than it warrants. The more we anticipate our fears rather than face them, the more power they hold over us. Fortunately, there are several techniques you can use to help you put your fear into perspective and even make it work for you.

Accept Some Fear as Normal

Many speakers believe they must be completely calm in every speech situation. This is unrealistic; all speakers feel some nervousness. One out of five people experiences rather serious fear, enough to adversely affect performance. One out of twenty suffers such serious fear that he or she is essentially unable to get through a public speech. For most of us, though, the fear can be managed and sometimes even turned to positive effect, just as athletes benefit from the rush of adrenaline generated from competition to energize their performance.

The more speeches you give, the more confident you will become. You will recognize that fear is usually worst just prior to the speech and during the introduction.

Once your speech is under way and the audience responds to you, negative emotions are often replaced by exhilaration.

One way to test your level of communication apprehension is to take the PRCA-24, a self-report inventory, available through your CourseMate for The Speaker's Handbook. Click on **WebLink 4.1**.

Analyze Your Fear as Specifically as Possible

Although one survey found that people rank the fear of public speaking ahead of the fear of death, few people really believe the experience to be fatal. But just what are we afraid of? An amorphous, ill-defined fear cannot be dealt with. Dealing logically with this fear requires examining its components so you can isolate issues, understand them, and prepare accordingly.

List Your Fears

It may be helpful to write your fears down on paper. Be as specific as possible, using this format for your list, and try to identify the actual outcome you find troubling:

I am afraid [specific event] will occur and then [specific result] will follow.

Not: *I'm afraid I'll make a fool of myself.*

But: *I'm afraid I'll forget my points, and the audience will think I don't know what I'm talking about.*

Not: *I'm afraid I'll freeze up.*

But: *I'm afraid my heart will start pounding, and my mouth will get dry, and I'll feel terrible the whole time I'm speaking.*

Not: *I'm afraid they won't like me.*

But: *I'm afraid my listeners will see through my facade of confidence and feel contempt for me.*

Classify Your Fears

The mere act of writing the fears down makes them manageable and often points immediately to a solution. The additional step of classifying your fears into categories will show you common themes, as shown below.

▶ *Seeming incompetent.* For items like "I'm afraid my visual aids won't be clear," the solution is simple. Check out the clarity of your visual aids with a few people, and if there is any problem, redesign them. Many fears have roots in inadequate preparation.

▶ *Uncomfortable physical responses.* "I'm afraid my hands will shake and my voice will crack." If many of your concerns fall into this category, pay special attention to the tension release and relaxation suggestions offered later in this chapter.

▶ *Not measuring up to your ideal.* Perfectionists find this issue particularly troubling. Recognize the fear of failing to meet your own high standards as a positive motivation to do the best you can. But also realize that the power of self-fulfilling prophesies and understand that focusing on failure can create failure. Use some of the visualization and verbalization techniques recommended in this chapter to create positive self-expectations.

▶ *Negative evaluation.* Some speakers find themselves frozen by the fear of negative evaluation from their audience. Perhaps as a group, they seem threatening and critical. Remind yourself that an audience is merely a group of individuals and a speech is merely an enlarged conversation. If it would not be frightening to speak to any three or four of them, then it should not be frightening to speak to all of them together. Remember, audience members would much rather listen to you speak than speak themselves. They want you to succeed. This final, and probably most pervasive, category taps into widely held assumptions about speakers' vulnerability before an audience, the topic of the next section.

Reconceptualize the Role of the Audience

If one technique in particular has helped people cope with their fears, it is reconceptualizing the role of the audience.

▶ *Change the audience from "critic" to "recipient."* Remind yourself that you are there not to *perform* but to *share.* Think about how you might benefit your audience—even enrich their lives.

▶ *Realize that the listeners want you to succeed.* Most listeners are caring and supportive. They want to hear a good speech given by a confident speaker. Recall a time when you listened to a nervous speaker: Your discomfort and embarrassment were probably almost as great as the speaker's. This is testimony to the empathy of most audiences and quite possibly a biological response of mirror neurons in listeners.[1]

▶ *"Talk with" your listeners; don't perform for them.* All of this advice comes back to the importance of the conversational resource at the time of speaking. (See Chapter **1.**) It comes down to this: If you can think of yourself as "talking with" the listeners rather than "performing for" them, you will feel much more comfortable.

CHECKLIST ~ **Steps for Eliminating Your Fear**

☐ **Step 1.** List your fears, i.e., *"I am afraid people will laugh at me if I make a mistake."*

☐ **Step 2.** Consider the origin of that fear. What events in your life influenced your beliefs? *My grade school classmates laughed at me when I made a mistake in my speech in the fifth grade.*

☐ **Step 3.** Create a list of alternative interpretations for your experience. *My audience will not be insensitive like my fifth grade classmates. My classmates were nervous too and at ten years old their only coping mechanism was laughter. It really was kind of funny now that I think of it.*

☐ **Step 4.** Recognize that past beliefs, while reasonable then, may not be the only plausible interpretations in your present situation.

☐ **Step 5.** Decide not to be controlled by past experience.

Build Your Confidence through Thorough Preparation and Practice

The fact that good speakers make speech-making look effortless does not mean that it is easy. Their seeming lack of effort is based on extensive preparation over time. The confidence they exude is also a result of preparation, not genes, fate, or dumb luck. Speakers who have prepared thoroughly can be as confident as skydivers who know they will reach the ground in one piece because they have exhaustively checked all their gear.

If you feel uneasy about getting your speech started, perhaps your introduction needs more work. If you are fearful of losing the continuity of the speech, you may need to practice it aloud several more times to internalize the flow of ideas. If you find yourself becoming generally anxious, use this as a stimulus to go over your preparation yet again. Drill yourself on the particulars of your supporting material. Go over your outline a number of times. Whatever else you do, remember that time spent fretting about the outcome could better be used taking positive action to ensure a positive outcome.

Manage the Physical Effects of Fear by Releasing Tension and Relaxing

When we are fearful or anxious, our bodies react by tensing muscles to brace for attack and by releasing extra adrenaline to prepare us to fight or flee. However, these fight-or-flight responses, which are helpful when confronting a savage beast in the wild and were adaptive for our prehistoric ancestors, are not appropriate when the threat is less physical and more psychological—and often even imaginary.

Tension Release

When fear of speaking triggers our primitive sense of danger, we experience symptoms such as rapid heart rate, dizziness, butterflies in the stomach, trembling, perspiration, and dryness of the mouth. Muscular tension in the throat can cause a voice to quaver and sound strained and can even produce the unpredictable squawks of adolescence. These physical symptoms will probably diminish with time as your successful speaking experiences make disaster appear less probable. But some degree of physical discomfort is likely to persist. Fortunately, you can master techniques to help you feel more comfortable.

When too much adrenaline makes you jumpy, physical activity usually helps. Of course, heavy exercise before a speech is impractical. But a brisk walk around the block or a little pacing in the hall can be enough to bring your body back to normal. If you have a few moments of privacy, light exercise will feel good—just a few knee bends, arm swings, and neck rolls. If you remain in sight of your audience before the speech, clench and unclench your hands or toes unobtrusively. Once the speech begins, take advantage of the extra energy that the adrenaline provides to make your delivery more vigorous. Appropriate, dynamic gestures will help you release your nervousness.

Relaxation Techniques

You can also handle symptoms of nervousness by learning relaxation techniques. Relaxation, like any other skill, is achieved through practice. Using audio books or podcasts on stress, tension, and relaxation, you can learn first to isolate the areas of your body that are tense and then to relax them. Try meditation, biofeedback, or self-hypnosis. Explore such methods as tightening and then relaxing certain muscle groups, breathing deeply, visualizing serene settings, or imagining sensations such as warmth or heaviness in parts of your body. Experiment until you find a technique that is effective for you.

Chemical aids to relaxation—alcohol, drugs, and tranquilizers—are inadvisable for public speakers. Most have side effects that impair your mental and physical performance during a speech, not to mention fabricating a false sense of security.

Use Positive Self-Suggestion to Combat Your Anxiety

Self-fulfilling prophecies can hold you back or work for you. Through the power of the mind, we can increase or decrease our fear. Learning the power of positive thinking can help you diminished your fears.

Visualize Success

Psychologists have discovered the tremendous power of visualization in influencing performance. When we experience fear, we are visualizing the most negative outcome for our speech. Unfortunately if we avoid something out of fear we are never able to replace the imagined danger with a real lived experience. It is possible, however, to turn these fearful visions around. Tennis players, field goal kickers, and speed skaters have found it helpful to visualize what they are striving for in order to become more accomplished.

When you detect negative thoughts, try to replace them with a more positive scenario. For instance, "I will approach the lectern calmly, smile at the audience, and begin. My voice will sound strong and confident." Do not set unrealistic standards of perfection. Build some contingencies into your fantasy: "If I forget a point, I will use my notes to remember and focus on communicating each main idea." Run through these positive visualizations a few times a day before you speak. As you practice, picture the audience responding favorably to the speech. And just before you get up to speak, remind yourself of the general tone and image you wish to project: "When I get up there, I am going to communicate my sincerity and concern in a warm, natural, confident manner."

Replace Negative Internal Statements with Positive Ones

One technique for reducing fears is cognitive restructuring. In essence, it is used to probe mental commentaries, identify the unrealistic or irrational statements that cause fear, and replace them with more positive, realistic beliefs. We all have constant narrations running through our minds. These commentaries are so familiar we are barely conscious of them. With some introspection, we can bring them to the mental forefront and examine the effect they have on our behavior. Remember these are not statements of fact but statements of belief we have created that can be replaced if necessary. Become aware of your public speaking beliefs and replace the unproductive beliefs with positive ones. Table 4.1 gives some examples.

Your mental commentaries are habitual and will not change easily. At first, you will have to repeat the replacement sentences mechanically, as you might in memorizing

© geopaul / iStockphoto 3620311

Speaker's Workshop 4.1

What beliefs do you hold about public speaking? Is it possible that those beliefs were true in the past but not today? Research suggests that affirming your beliefs while considering alternative interpretations can help individuals to reduce their public speaking fears.[2] Make your own version of Table 4.1, and create positive replacement statements to counter these beliefs.

TABLE 4.1
Replacement belief statements

INITIAL BELIEF	REPLACEMENT BELIEF
My speech will be a failure unless everyone in the audience likes it.	I will be successful if most people respond favorably.
A good speaker never says "uh" or "er."	A few nonfluencies aren't even noticed unless attention is called to them.
My mind always goes blank.	I've practiced several times, and I know the basic structure of this speech. I can use brief notes to help me remember.
I will make a mistake and ruin everything.	My speech doesn't have to be perfect to be worthwhile.
No one will be able to understand me because of my accent.	My listeners will want to hear what I have to say, not how I say it.
Someone will ask me a question that exposes my ignorance.	I've researched this topic, and I'm prepared for any reasonable question. I am not ignorant.

Speaker's Workshop 4.2

Many articles containing practical tips for overcoming public speaking anxiety can be found by accessing InfoTrac® College Edition or another periodicals database and searching for *communication apprehension or stage fright.* You can access InfoTrac College Edition through your CourseMate for *The Speaker's Handbook.* Read one of the articles you find and share the suggestions provided for controlling nervousness with your class or colleagues.

a phone number. The reassuring nature of repeating the words may help you become physically calmer, and this more comfortable sensation acts to reinforce the new beliefs.

Practice Systematic Desensitization

A common strategy used to help people overcome all manner of fears involves systematic exposure of the subject to the stressor over time. For instance, a person who is arachnophobic (afraid of spiders) might systematically be exposed to pictures of spiders and then perhaps to spiders inside closed containers or at a safe distance. In addition, the person would be educated about spiders and trained in relaxation and visualization techniques. Over time, this systematic exposure can lead to a reduced apprehension of spiders. The same idea holds true for public speaking. By accepting minor speaking opportunities such as introducing yourself to a stranger or answering a question in front of classmates, a person can systematically reduce the apprehensions associated with speaking in public.

Many colleges and universities offer special sections of speech classes for fearful students. Others offer ungraded workshops to supplement regular classes. These programs use systematic desensitization, cognitive restructuring, skills training, or a combination of these and other methods. Psychologists and speech consultants also offer programs to help reduce fear of speaking. Such programs may be publicized under the names of *stage fright, communication apprehension, speech anxiety, reticence,* or *shyness.*

Seek Assistance Beyond This Book

Some deeply rooted public speaking fears cannot be remedied by the methods suggested here. If your fear of speaking is almost paralyzing, you may need additional help. Research shows that even severe fear of speaking can be reduced to a manageable level when treated by a qualified professional. In some cases, medications have been found to successfully reduce unproductive fear responses in individuals, allowing even the most fearful person to speak in front of others.

Review, Reconsider, & Act

Summary

Doing something for the first time—whether dancing, golfing, or giving a speech—can be scary and difficult. The more we practice the behavior, the less our nervousness impairs our ability to succeed. This chapter has focused on several strategies for overcoming the fear associated with speaking. First, we learned the importance of putting our fears into perspective. Second, we learned to build confidence through preparation and practice. Third, we learned several techniques for releasing tension and relaxing muscles. Fourth, we learned how to replace negative internal beliefs with positive ones. Finally, we considered the benefits of systematic desensitization.

Critical Thinking Questions

▶ What are your greatest fears about speaking in public?

▶ How might you restructure your beliefs to break free of old fears?

▶ Which of the relaxation and tension reduction techniques do you find most useful?

▶ How will you prepare your next speech to better manage your apprehension?

Putting It into Practice

 Go to your CourseMate for *The Speaker's Handbook* and click on **WebLink 4.2** to read Stephen Eggleston's story about overcoming his fear of public speaking.

1. What past experiences have you had that frame your feelings about public speaking?

2. How did Stephen Eggleston reframe his negative experience to overcome his apprehensions?

3. What false beliefs about public speaking do you need to replace?

4. Create positive replacement statements to counter your false beliefs.

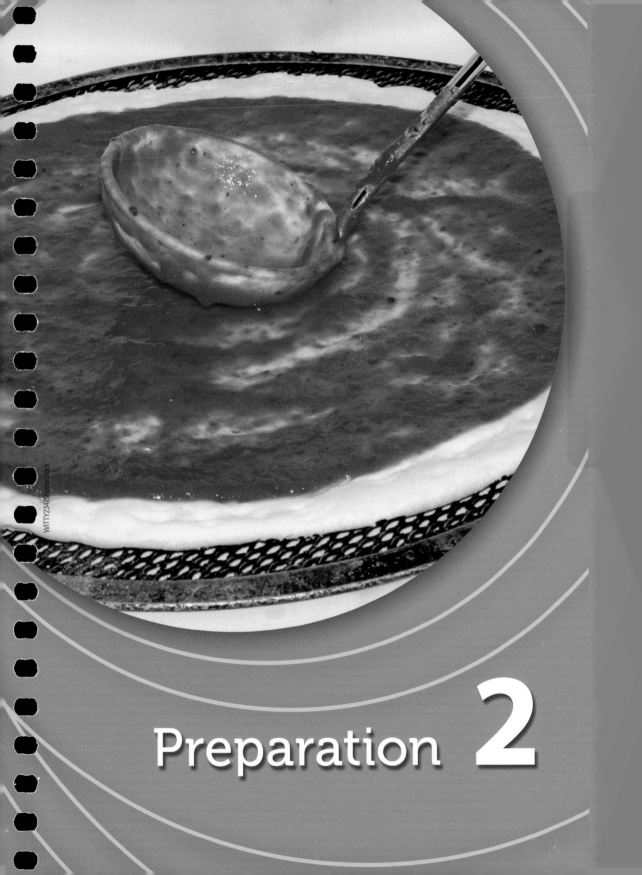

Preparation **2**

PART 2
PREPARATION

The First Stage of the Public Speaking Process

The ability to float doesn't make a person a proficient swimmer. Likewise, knowing how to speak doesn't make a person an effective public speaker. Floating and speaking are easy enough if we are relaxed, but tension or anxiety, which sometimes results from poor preparation, causes many of us to sink. When we are preparing to speak, tension can also arise if we focus on the final *product* of the speech, rather than on the creative *process*, and we experience a sense of urgency to produce something. That urgency can lead to poor choices, such as accepting the first topic that enters our minds. Experienced speakers save time and avoid wasted effort by organizing their preparation. They understand that the creative process progresses unevenly and that if they persist through all its steps, a respectable product will result. Part 2 of this handbook will help you develop a positive routine for preparing your speech, incorporating planning, topic selection, audience analysis, and research.

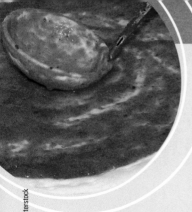

chapter 5
Planning

Make a schedule for the preparation of your speech so you will have time to progress through the four phases of creativity.

Preparing a substantial public speech is not a mechanical act like assembling a toy. It is a creative act in which you bring into being something that has never existed before, and that no one but you would have designed in exactly this form. Speech preparation is more like painting a picture, creating a dance, or inventing a product. Once you recognize the importance of creativity, you can strategically manage your preparation to allow time for each phase of the creative process.

Allow Time for Four Phases of Creativity

The creative process has four phases: preparation, incubation, illumination, and refinement.[1] For speakers, the preparation phase includes gathering the materials, analyzing the topic and audience, and making the first attempts at putting the parts together. Incubation is a phase marked by frustration, even despair, when the problems seem insoluble and the speech is often set aside. During this phase, the unconscious mind and peripheral awareness work on the problems. Suddenly, in a moment of illumination, the pieces fit together or there is a dawning awareness that grows in intensity. Illumination may occur while working on the project, but it is just as likely to occur when driving on the freeway, taking a shower, or just before waking. Exhilaration and relief accompany this phase. After the creative burst, there follows a comparatively long period of refinement that includes checking details, fine-tuning, and polishing. Like the preparation phase, this phase is largely cognitive and requires concentration and discipline.

It is essential that adequate time is allocated to *each* phase of the creative process. Too often first-rate ideas fail to be brought to fruition because they were never refined. Figure 5.1 summarizes the phases. The rest of this chapter supplies guidance for optimizing your planning so none of the creative phases is slighted.

FIGURE 5.1
The four phases of creativity

1. Preparation	2. Incubation	3. Illumination	4. Refinement
• Gather materials • Analyze topic and audience • Start putting pieces together	• Set the speech aside • Let your unconscious mind work on its problems	• You see how the pieces fit together • You see solutions to the problems	• Check the details • Fine-tune and polish your speech

© 2013 Cengage Learning

Make a Realistic Timetable

At one university, a group of public speaking instructors survey their students informally at the end of each term, asking what advice they would pass on to the next group of students. Consistently the students' response is "start early." They all regret underestimating the time necessary to prepare a good-quality speech.

When professionals plan a major project—whether it is organizing an event, designing a public relations campaign, or tooling up to manufacture a new product—they use a number of structured time management techniques. A few valuable project management tools, the Program Evaluation and Review Technique (PERT) and Gantt charts, are provided in this section.

The Speech Timeline *feature of Speech Builder Express can help you create a schedule for preparing your speech based on how much time you have available. It can also help you manage your time as your work progresses.*

List Tasks, Estimate Time

Speech-making involves many time-consuming intellectual tasks, such as analyzing your topic, and physical tasks, like going to the library or making visual aids. Effective planning involves identifying the most and least optimistic estimates of the time needed to complete each task. Certain parts of the creative process should not be rushed, and it's wise to allow extra time for emergencies. Speech research and rehearsal can go on when you have a headache or are in an emotional funk, but the creative aspects of speech organization require physical and psychological alertness. Establishing an honest estimate of the time needed for each task is a good first step in the speech-making process. Figure 5.2 clarifies the many tasks associated with the four stages of speech planning and practice.

FIGURE 5.2
Speech planning and practice

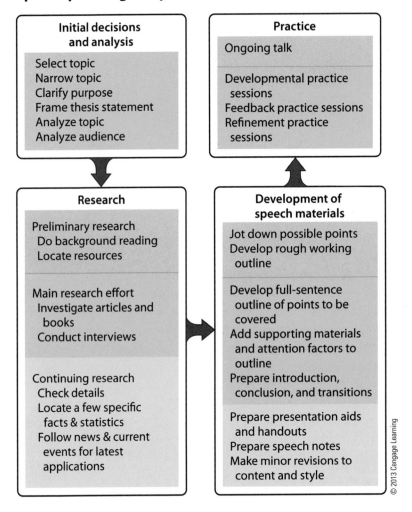

Initial decisions and analysis

Select topic
Narrow topic
Clarify purpose
Frame thesis statement
Analyze topic
Analyze audience

Practice

Ongoing talk

Developmental practice
  sessions
Feedback practice sessions
Refinement practice
  sessions

Research

Preliminary research
  Do background reading
  Locate resources

Main research effort
  Investigate articles and
    books
  Conduct interviews

Continuing research
  Check details
  Locate a few specific
    facts & statistics
  Follow news & current
    events for latest
    applications

Development of speech materials

Jot down possible points
Develop rough working
  outline

Develop full-sentence
  outline of points to be
  covered
Add supporting materials
  and attention factors to
  outline
Prepare introduction,
  conclusion, and transitions

Prepare presentation aids
  and handouts
Prepare speech notes
Make minor revisions to
  content and style

© 2013 Cengage Learning

Determine the Order for Completing Tasks

Professional project managers call this step *determining the critical path.* It is not enough to schedule three hours for speech practice and call that *planning.* Those three hours must occur after the speech outline is completed. The outline cannot be completed until you have articulated your speech's purpose and thought about the audience for the speech. When you lay out the entire project in this linear fashion and add up the time estimates for each task, you will determine the critical path.

Suppose your speech is due in three weeks, and the critical path adds up to five weeks. It is better to discover now that the plans are unrealistic rather than two days before the speech is due. In rare cases, a speech can be rescheduled for a later time, but more frequently, plans can be scaled back. Perhaps this means conducting two or three interviews by phone instead of five in person. Perhaps it requires minimizing development of PowerPoint slides. Ultimately, what's most important is that you decide on and keep to your schedule, or else you will end up skipping the crucial later steps of practice and refinement.

Set Intermediate Deadlines for Major Stages

The process of speech planning and practice are divided into four stages: initial decisions and analysis, research, development of speech materials, and practice. (See Figure 5.2.) The chart will help you to see how the central tasks of one stage cannot really be started until the central tasks of the previous stage are completed. At some point, you must make preliminary decisions regarding a narrowed and focused topic, purpose, and thesis, and then get into your serious research.

Eventually, you must stop gathering material and start putting the speech together, because you must leave yourself adequate time to develop your speech and practice it. There is no point in scheduling your feedback practice sessions so late that adjustments cannot be made based on the feedback.

Occasionally, you might retrace your steps. Maybe important new evidence presents itself, or a feedback session suggests more visual aids are needed. Such backward steps should be minimal; under almost no circumstances should you be returning to significant tasks, such as changing your topic. Nor should you make any substantive changes to the speech at the last minute. During the final practice sessions, you should have complete mastery of the organization and basic content so you can concentrate on refining your phrasing, delivery, and timing, and on attaining the desired audience response.

Make Your Speech Preparation an Oral and Collaborative Process

Because a speech is delivered orally, it must be composed orally. And because the meaning of a speech depends on the interaction between speaker and listeners, it should be created collaboratively. Keep the speech conversational, even during those parts of preparation that require you to draw on your skills as a writer or performer.

YOUR NEW CAREER

FOR YOUR BENEFIT: Estimating Preparation Time

Novice speakers and professionals alike often underestimate the time needed to research, compose, practice, and deliver a speech. A general rule of thumb is to plan to spend approximately one hour of preparation time for each minute of a speech. While this may seem extreme, it is better to overestimate and have extra time than to underestimate and be inadequately prepared.

Although you cannot practice the speech until your basic outline exists, one form of oral preparation begins with your first idea. This is the ongoing talk suggested by the large orange section in the Practice column of Figure 5.2. Talk to yourself about your topic. Talk to other people. Try out your ideas and words to see if they make sense. Work your ideas into conversations over lunch and chats with colleagues and friends. After talking to a number of people, you will find you have begun to work out the wording of the speech. Continue to incorporate feedback throughout your preparation and practice phases as suggested in Chapter **24**.

Focus on Different Resources during Preparation and Presentation Phases

As speakers, most of you already have substantial resources at your disposal. You are conversationalists, writers, and presenters. These resources should be present throughout the planning and practice stages of a speech, but they may be utilized in different amounts at different times to achieve a successful final presentation. Figure 5.3 illustrates these changing priorities.

Generally, during the preparation stage, writing skills come to the fore. *This does not mean that you write out your speech!* Rather, it means that you consciously begin selecting points, arranging them, choosing your support, and thinking of appropriate illustrations. Focus your attention on transitions between ideas and refine the language of the speech.

Once the speech exists in some form, you move into a practice phase, in which the importance of performance-related elements increases. Through oral practice, you can experiment with vocal and physical dynamics to emphasize certain points and create certain effects. Here, you also introduce visual aids, props, and movements to begin to see how the entire presentation will engage your audience.

If these resources are fully explored during preparation and practice, the writer and performer sides of you will recede during the actual speech, and the conversationalist will come forth. By using enhanced conversation, the speaking style effective for almost all speech situations, and emphasizing a relaxed, informal delivery despite following a well-planned, carefully organized outline, you will seem conversational

FIGURE 5.3
Key communicative resources for different phases

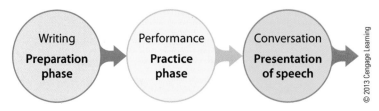

© 2013 Cengage Learning

and natural, and your conscious attention will be centered on the give-and-take with the audience. When proper time is devoted to the planning stages, speakers are able to develop a natural conversational style. That is because the writing and performance elements emphasized during the preparation and practice phases are revealed as areas of unconscious competence during the presentation phase. The nature of these changes is detailed in various chapters of the handbook. (See Chapters **17, 23, 25,** and **26**.)

Avoid Common Planning Pitfalls

The errors speakers make in their planning are fairly predictable, reflecting common human tendencies such as procrastination. Knowing the pitfalls listed here will help you prevent the accidental sabotage of your efforts.

▶ *Failing to allow time for idea incubation.* The creative process cannot be forced, so be sure to give yourself time for reflection before settling down to the job of composing your speech. The best ideas come when we live with our topic for a while and let our unconscious and conscious minds interact.

▶ *Failing to allow an adequate margin for error.* If you overrate your efficiency, you may cut your preparation time so close that even minor interruptions endanger the success of your presentation. And if a major catastrophe occurs, you may not be able to fulfill your commitments at all. Put together a schedule that gives you some breathing room.

▶ *Stalling progress because of writer's block.* Although speech preparation differs from writing, this pitfall is much like the paralysis many writers face. You may find yourself doing more research, more thinking, or even more time on Facebook than is really needed just to avoid the awful moment of confronting a blank sheet of paper. For your speech to succeed, you must stop getting ready to create and start creating—well before the final deadline.

▶ *Not practicing orally.* Begin working orally early in the process. You will need to practice a speech aloud many times to showcase its strengths. Make sure the first time you give the speech aloud is not in front of the audience.

Review, Reconsider, & Act

Summary

This section of the handbook emphasizes the planning stage of the preparation process. Above all, we learned that effective planning takes time to allow for creativity to develop through preparation, incubation, illumination, and refinement. Allow yourself adequate time for this process to emerge. Create a schedule that identifies the time you'll need for each task, prioritizes the order of tasks, and sets deadlines throughout the process. The preparation process is an oral and collaborative process, and relies on different communicative resources during each phase: writing during the preparation phase, performance during the practice phase, and conversation during the presentation phase. The process can be accomplished successfully if you plan effectively and avoid common planning pitfalls.

Critical Thinking Questions

▶ Why is it important to allow time for creativity in the speech development process?

▶ Why is oral preparation preferable to practice "in your head"?

▶ How will you overcome your personal planning pitfalls?

Putting It into Practice

Go to your CourseMate for *The Speaker's Handbook* to access **WebLink 5.1**. Read the article there about why it is sometimes best to cancel a speech, even when you've been asked to give it: "Cancel That Speech! Lucubrations of a Fusty Rhetorician" by Ed Vilade.

1. Why does the author suggest that canceling a speech is sometimes the best thing to do?

2. What is the author's view on public speaking?

3. How would preparation be different for an audience that disagreed with you rather than one that agreed with your major points?

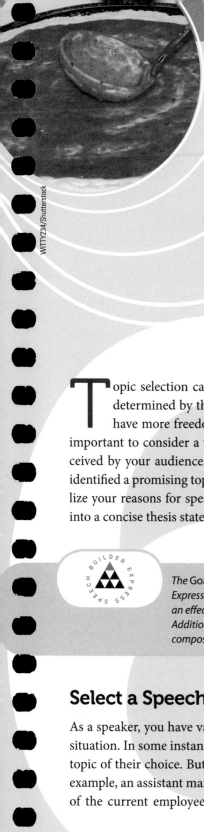

chapter 6
Topic Selection and Analysis

Select a topic that is interesting, manageable, and likely to evoke the desired response. When you have chosen a promising topic, create a thesis statement to help you stay focused as you develop your speech.

Topic selection can be a difficult process. However, many speakers' topics are determined by their roles and responsibilities. Students in a speech class may have more freedom in choosing a topic than most speakers after college. It is important to consider a variety of different topics, as well as how they might be perceived by your audience, early in the planning process. When you believe you have identified a promising topic, clarify your speaking goal, narrow your topic, and crystallize your reasons for speaking to your specific audience about that particular subject into a concise thesis statement.

The Goal/Purpose *and* Thesis Statement *sections of Speech Builder Express can help you choose an appropriate topic and formulate an effective thesis statement for many different types of speeches. Additionally, the* Title *section of Speech Builder Express can help you compose a title if your speech needs one.*

Select a Speech Topic

As a speaker, you have varying degrees of freedom in topic choice, depending on the situation. In some instances, respected speakers will be given free rein to speak on the topic of their choice. But it's more common to be given a specific subject matter. For example, an assistant manager might be told to give an oral report on the effectiveness of the current employee scheduling system or a student is told, "Two weeks from

Friday, you will speak third and give a persuasive speech on the dangers of social networking sites."

Most speaking situations fall between these extremes. You may be asked to welcome delegates to a conference or to speak to the Rotary Club about a service project. In these cases, you still have to select a theme for your talk. Even when the general topic is set, you need to zero in on an approach that will fit you, the audience, and the situation.

Draw from Your Experience, Expertise, and Interests

You bring a body of knowledge to the speech situation. Perhaps you have been asked to speak about your experiences in the Marines or with Habitat for Humanity. Your background will be the springboard for narrowing in on a topic, which can be developed into a compelling and substantial speech.

Brainstorming is a great way to generate possible topic ideas based on your experiences. This can be done alone or with others. The principle behind brainstorming is that even an unworkable idea may trigger one or more good ideas, or a group of mediocre ideas may combine to make a great one. Therefore, don't judge any one idea until you have generated many. Later, you will select your best topic for the audience and occasion. Consider the following questions to help you to identify a meaningful and manageable topic.

What Unusual Experiences Have You Had?

Consider places you have traveled, jobs you have held, and events you have experienced. Perhaps you have met a celebrity or traveled to a foreign country. Do not overlook aspects of your life that you take for granted but that might be interesting to others. If you are adopted, have always been self-employed, or grew up speaking one language at home and another at school, you can introduce your audience to unfamiliar life experiences.

What Special Knowledge or Expertise Do You Have?

Each of us has developed mastery in certain areas. How do you make your living? If your work in real estate has provided you with a good income, you can be certain there will be people eager to hear about your techniques. Yet a job need not be high paying or prestigious to generate speech topics. People like to know how things work. They are often quite interested in hearing about procedures, even ones the people performing them consider mundane. For instance, you might share how a person's credit score is determined or what goes on backstage at a concert.

Your course of study in school or your hobbies may have given you knowledge about topics that are obscure to your potential audience. Could you build a speech on the risks and benefits of tanning salons, playing a musical instrument as relaxation therapy, or the health benefits of proper posture? Or you may have researched a topic simply because it interests you: Quentin Tarantino movies, radio ID technology, the wines of Argentina, Sudanese culture, stem cell research, and so on.

What Strong Opinions and Beliefs Do You Hold?

Have you ever overheard someone arguing fervently about the importance of free speech? What topics stir your passions in this way? Issues that touch on your core values (see Chapter **20**) frequently make good speech topics. You will be less self-conscious if you are speaking from a sense of deep conviction. And the audience will be more generous in spirit, even when they are in opposition, if they see you are passionate and sincere about your topic. You may also be motivated to investigate your topic more thoroughly than one assigned to you arbitrarily.

Besides issues that can provoke you into heated debate, others may fascinate you intellectually. Do you have a pet theory about why the number of marriages has declined, what makes a good teacher, or whether fossil fuels can be effectively replaced? Explaining and exploring the basis of your beliefs can make an excellent speech.

What Would You Like to Know More About?

Perhaps, you are curious about the workings of the Federal Reserve System. Or after reading about shifting alliances in the Middle East, you have become interested in the history of the U.S. role there. Perhaps after filling your gasoline tank you decide to investigate what influences the price of a gallon of fuel. Use the occasion of giving a speech as an opportunity to research a topic that has piqued your curiosity.

How Are You Uniquely Prepared to Assist Your Audience?

Perhaps your role at work or in an organization affords you unique knowledge or insights that others need. Organizations often require people to share knowledge, perspectives, and priorities with co-workers. Perhaps your topic could come from your work role expertise.

Select a Topic Appropriate to the Audience and Occasion

By brainstorming, you have created a possible subject list of great variety. To choose the one topic you will speak about, think about the audience and the occasion. (See also Chapter **7**.) There are two more questions you can ask yourself at this point:

▶ What does the audience expect? (audience)

▶ What might the audience expect on the day you speak? (occasion)

Knowing who your audience is and why its members are gathered together can help you rule out a number of topics. A speech on the fluctuating gold market could be interesting, but not to a class of seventh-graders at an assembly just before summer vacation.

When you have removed the inappropriate subjects from your list, find the *most* appropriate of the remainder. Place yourself in the audience's shoes. What topic do you think the audience would find worth hearing? Don't be the speaker that wastes an audience's time with a speech that doesn't meet their needs and interests or is beyond their comprehension.

Select a Topic That Is Timely and Timeless

After considering your audience and the occasion, you may still have more than one possible topic on your list. Other things being equal, the best topics are those that are both timely and timeless. Certain issues have always been and always will be part of human discourse. People have been discussing the rights of the individual versus the rights of the state and the need for security versus the need for adventure for centuries and will continue to do so far into the future. When you tie a contemporary event to one of these enduring human dialogues, you link the timely and the timeless.

Neither one of these conditions by itself is an indication the topic will be a good one. Consider the criterion of timeliness. If an event has been front page news for two weeks, a speech on that topic may be timely. But unless you can tell your audience what it all means in more universal terms, you will probably give them little they do not know already. The reverse is true as well: your audience can miss or fail to be interested in the depth of your topic if you do not tie it into the fabric of their current existence. A profound, timeless topic needs a timely application.

Table 6.1 shows how topics that are too narrowly contemporary or too broadly universal may be altered to meet these criteria. Notice the different kinds of speeches to which the timely–timeless standard can apply.

© geopaul / iStockphoto 3620311

Speaker's Workshop 6.1

Suppose each of the following topics is of great interest to you and you are qualified to speak about all of them:

1. Martial arts
2. Mediation before litigation
3. Problems of our health care system
4. The way television commercials are made
5. Western misconceptions about Islam

Which of these topics would be best for each of the following audiences? Select more than one if you wish, but justify your answers.

A. A speech class in which the assignment is to support a thesis with factual and statistical evidence from several different sources
B. A community service club luncheon
C. A neighborhood youth group
D. A current-events study group
E. A keynote address at a business conference

TABLE 6.1
Timely and timeless topics

TIMELY (BUT POTENTIALLY TRIVIAL)	TIMELESS (BUT POTENTIALLY DIFFUSE)	TIMELY AND TIMELESS
There was a major confrontation last week when the Ku Klux Klan held a rally downtown.	Freedom of assembly must be protected for everyone.	Last week's confrontation over the Ku Klux Klan rally raised important questions about what restrictions, if any, should be placed on freedom of assembly.
I took a trip to Quebec.	Travel helps people understand diversity of human cultures.	My trip to Quebec helped me understand my own culture by contrasting it with another.
Our company has adopted a new profit-sharing plan.	The best management philosophy is one that treats employees like partners.	Our new profit-sharing plan will benefit the employees directly and reflects an enlightened philosophy of management.

Select a Topic That Is Meaningful and Manageable

Perhaps the most difficult aspect of topic selection is finding a topic that is both meaningful, in the sense that it is timely and timeless, *and* manageable. A manageable topic is one that can be discussed in the time allotted for your speech. For example, if you have only ten minutes in which to explain your main points, can you cover *all* the aspects of Sudanese culture? Focusing on just one or two key aspects of the culture will make your topic more manageable.

Narrow Your Topic

To get into a topic, to get under the surface, you have to limit yourself to the number of points that can be adequately developed in the time available. You can expedite your research and preparation by narrowing your topic from the beginning. Thus, instead of looking up all the books and articles about the impact of the Internet on society, you can focus on those related to the influence of social network sites in higher education.

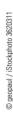

Speaker's Workshop 6.2

Explain how each of the topics in Speaker's Workshop 6.1 (page 68) could be developed to reflect both timely and timeless concerns.

Determine the Number of Ideas Time Will Allow

The average speaker utters 100–150 words per minute. If you speak very rapidly or very slowly, you may fall outside this range. Chances are, though, your rate of speaking is somewhere near 125 words per minute. If you want to check your rate, see Chapter **25**.

A typical journalistic paragraph of simple sentences runs about 125 words. Thus, a general rule of thumb is that an average speaker speaks about one short paragraph per minute. If your material is technical or interspersed with statistics, dialogue, and dramatic pauses, or if you speak slowly, you had better allot two minutes per paragraph. This system, though rough, might help you to realistically adjust your topic to the time allotted.

For instance, if you plan on speaking informatively for eight to ten minutes on the U.S. electoral college system, you need to set aside at least one to two minutes for the introduction and one minute for the conclusion. This leaves six to seven minutes for the body of your speech. If you plan to talk about the history of the electoral college system, the cause for its inception, the way electoral college votes are determined, and the influences of an electoral college process on the 2008 and 2012 elections, you can spend about one to one and a half minutes on each subject. That would hardly be adequate. By narrowing the topic to one of these areas, you can develop two subpoints for three minutes each or three subpoints for two minutes each—a more realistic plan. The same principle can be applied to longer speeches, business presentations, and lectures. A twenty-minute speech can be thought of as twenty short, simple paragraphs or ten longer, more developed paragraphs.

Table 6.2 shows how the speech about the electoral college might be broken down.

TABLE 6.2
Time allotment of speech elements

SPEECH PART	MINUTES
Introduction	
Welcome audience	1
Share startling statistic about 2008 U.S. election	1
State topic and preview main points	1
First main point	
Explain and define	1
Subpoint	2
Subpoint	2
Second main point (including subpoints)	5
Third main point (including subpoints)	5
Conclusion	2
TOTAL	20

Select a Few Main Ideas to Cover

Knowing that the electoral college system speech in the preceding section should be cut to one or two main points does not tell you *which* one or two to select. To develop your ability to narrow a topic effectively, consider the following questions.

▶ *Which aspects of your topic are best covered in the public, oral mode?* Is it wise to spend five minutes reading a list of numbers? Might this data be included in a handout for further study and the *meaning* of the key numbers discussed instead? Ask yourself: Is this an important topic to discuss in a public speech? A speech should not be used to transmit routine information, to discuss specialized problems of a small portion of the audience, or to indulge the speaker's ego.

▶ *Which aspects of your topic are best suited to this audience and occasion?* Let audience analysis direct the emphasis of your speech. Select those points that relate most directly to the needs, attitudes, knowledge, and expectations of your listeners. Will it give the audience "more for their money"? (See Chapter **7**.)

▶ *Which aspects of your topic can you present most effectively?* Select those points on which you have the most knowledge and in which you have the most interest. Do you excel at explaining complex material? At making abstract ideas personal? Are you better with human interest stories than statistics or vice versa? Select those points that best fit your speaking style.

Go to your CourseMate for The Speaker's Handbook *and click on* **WebLink 6.1** *to read a good article about how to narrow your speech topics. Also check out* **WebLinks 6.2** *and* **6.3** *for good advice about how to choose good topics for informative and persuasive speeches.*

```
Speaker's Workshop 6.3
```

1. A speech has 2,900 words. Roughly how long would it take for the average person to deliver it?

2. Go to your CourseMate for *The Speaker's Handbook* and select a transcript from the sample speeches available in the interactive video activities. Suppose you were allotted one third of the time needed to give that speech. How would you limit the topic?

3. Look at the outline on comic books in Chapter **10**. If you were to present that speech to avid comics collectors, how would you limit the topic? Look at the outline on women in the labor force in Chapter **11**. How would you limit that topic if you were given fifteen minutes to speak to a high school social studies class?

Clarify the Purpose of Your Speech

Each speech has a general purpose, a specific purpose, and a set of desired outcomes.

Identify the General Purpose

What is your intention? Are you trying to change people's minds, to teach them something, to entertain them, or to explore attitudes on a topic?

For instance, if you decide on "rock and roll" as your topic and then narrow that topic further to "lead guitarists of classic rock," there are several possible speeches you might give. Do you want to explain the feedback-manipulating guitar work of Jimi Hendrix to your audience? Or do you want to convince them that Mark Knopfler has not been given the attention he is due? Or perhaps you want to inspire your audience by telling of the comeback of Joe Walsh. The general purpose of a speech can be classified in one of four ways:

▶ *Inform:* A speech designed to explain, instruct, define, clarify, demonstrate, or teach.

▶ *Invite:* A speech designed to explore a topic with an audience or invite the audience to respond.

▶ *Persuade:* A speech designed to influence, convince, motivate, sell, preach, or stimulate action.

▶ *Evoke:* A speech designed to entertain, inspire, celebrate, commemorate, or bond, or to help listeners relive a significant event.

The speech to evoke is often called the "speech to entertain," but this is too narrow a definition. An evocative speech elicits a certain feeling or emotional response. The emotion or feeling can be one of fun, escape, and diversion—entertainment, if you will—but it can also be solemn and serious, as in a eulogy, in which a sense of community and an appreciation of individual worth may be evoked.

You will quickly discover that no speech has only one purpose. Most have a combination, but with one purpose usually dominant. For instance, a classroom lecture is used primarily to teach, but at the same time, it can be used to shape attitudes. The purpose of a campaign speech is to drum up support for the candidate, but the speech can also entertain. An excellent sermon might do all four: inform, invite, persuade, and evoke.

Determine the Specific Purpose

Knowing which of the four purposes—to inform, invite, persuade, or evoke—is predominant in your speech will help you in the next step: deciding what you really want to accomplish with your topic. In phrasing this purpose, isolate your central reason for speaking. You will have many incidental goals, but you cannot select and organize your materials without a clear set of priorities. Be both specific and realistic about the purpose you set for yourself. Do you want to teach your listeners all about chess in a

Speaker's Workshop 6.4

Describe how each of the following topics could be made into

A. A speech to inform

B. A speech to invite

C. A speech to persuade

D. A speech to evoke

Topics

International travel

Natural childbirth

Investing in gold

Football

Water conservation

ten-minute speech? Or do you simply want to give them the basic principles of the game? Do you want the audience members to buy your company's telecommunications system? Or do you want them to learn about it so that you can gain their insights about how to best train new users? Do not go any further until you can complete this sentence: If there is one goal I want to achieve in this speech, it is to….

At this point, your topic should have a clear focus:

Not: *My specific purpose is to inform the audience about politics.*

But: *My specific purpose is to inform the audience about the role of the two-party system in American politics.*

Not: *My specific purpose is to invite the audience to discuss traffic safety.*

But: *My specific purpose is to invite the audience to understand red-light-camera laws and share their perspectives about the use of the laws in our community.*

Not: *My specific purpose is to persuade the audience against illegal immigration.*

But: *My specific purpose is to persuade the audience of the need for stronger enforcement of existing illegal immigration laws.*

Specify the Desired Outcomes

Once your goal is phrased in the terms of what you want to do, turn it around and phrase it in terms of what you want your *audience* to do: If there is one action I want my listeners to take after my speech, it is to….

In other words, if your speech is a success, what will your audience do? This is called the **primary audience outcome.**

Not: *My desired outcome is to sell this product.*

But: *My desired outcome is to <u>have you buy</u> this product.*

Not: *My desired outcome is to explain photosynthesis.*

But: *My desired outcome is to <u>have you understand</u> the workings of photosynthesis.*

After you have identified the single most important audience outcome you are looking for, you can clarify your speech goals even further. Implicit in every general goal statement are many contributing subgoals that may also be phrased in terms of concrete audience behaviors. If your overall goal is to persuade members to take up the guitar, you want them first to *decide* that this is a good idea, second to *purchase* a guitar, third to *sign up* for lessons, and last to *continue* to practice. Notice the significance of the verbs in each case. The emphasis is on the behavior you want the audience to adopt.

The same procedures will help you plan your speech. Break the primary audience outcome into components, paying particular attention to using phrasing with verbs that describe overt actions rather than general states of mind. "I want my audience to *appreciate* art" is fine for a primary audience outcome, but you must go further and ask yourself how you will know if you have succeeded. What, exactly, are people doing when they are appreciating art? If you think about the specific behaviors or operations that contribute to appreciating art, you will come up with a list like this:

▶ *Go* to galleries.

▶ *Read* books on art.

▶ *Create* pieces of art themselves.

Observe how speech purposes and outcomes can be crystallized for each type of speech: informative, invitational, persuasive, and evocative.

Informative Speech

General purpose: To inform.

Specific purpose: To inform the audience of the uses for radio frequency identification (RFID).

Primary audience outcome: I want my audience to know how RFID can be used.

Contributing audience outcomes: I want my audience to

▶ *differentiate* RFID from other forms of identification systems

▶ *understand* what RFID is

▶ *recognize* some current uses of radio ID

▶ *contemplate* some future uses of RFID

Invitational Speech

General purpose: To invite.

Specific purpose: To invite my audience to explore the impact of a statewide smoking ban in all restaurants and bars.

Primary audience outcome: I want my audience to become familiar with the actual impact of the smoking ban.

Contributing audience outcomes: I want my audience to

▶ *consider* the negative impacts of the smoking ban on bars and other businesses

▶ *recognize* the benefits of the smoking ban on patrons' health

▶ *discuss* additional impacts of the smoking ban on restaurant and bar employees

Persuasive Speech

General purpose: To persuade.

Specific purpose: To convince the audience to change their eating habits.

Primary audience outcome: I want my audience members to start eating locally grown, organic foods.

Contributing audience outcomes: I want my audience to

▶ *minimize* consumption of fast food

▶ *shop* at local farm markets when in season

▶ *buy* organic food when possible

▶ *eat* organically grown foods when possible

Evocative Speech

General purpose: To evoke.

Specific purpose: To celebrate the successful conclusion of a complex community project and honor the individuals responsible for the success.

Primary audience outcome: I want my audience to experience a sense of community with all those who participated in the Habitat for Humanity Blitz Build.

Contributing audience outcomes: I want my audience to

▶ *recognize* the contribution and achievement of each group: builders, fundraisers, donors, and support staff

▶ *feel* pride in their individual contribution

▶ *relive* some of the accomplishments

▶ *identify* with each other by telling a story common to those involved with the project

▶ *share in* the warmth felt for Diane, the "spark plug" of the organization

Develop a Clear Thesis Statement

Many organizations devise a short mission statement to focus the energy of its staff, to guide their choices. In a similar vein, your topic analysis needs a thesis statement that gives you something concrete against which to test ideas. In contrast to your "purpose" and "outcomes," your thesis sentence states your topic as a proposition to be proved or a theme to be developed. This sentence, sometimes referred to as the **central idea**, gives

Speaker's Workshop 6.5

▶ Go to your CourseMate for *The Speaker's Handbook* and watch the speech videos by Harriet Kamakil and Brian Sharkey that are available among in the interactive video activities. Identify these speeches by their type—informative, invitational, persuasive, or evocative. State the one-sentence specific purpose you think each speaker had.

▶ List at least four contributing audience outcomes that might be developed for each of the following primary outcomes. Use specific, concrete verbs to describe the behaviors.
   A.   I want my audience to learn about genetic engineering.
   B.   I want my audience to experience the thrills of visiting the Galápagos Islands.
   C.   I want my audience to drive more safely.

your speech focus. It helps you make the transition from thinking about where you want to end up (your goal) to how you will get there.

Formulate a Single Declarative Sentence

A thesis statement should not merely announce your topic. It should encapsulate what you plan to say about the topic. By writing your thesis as a complete sentence you ensure the clarity of thought that comes from delineating both what you are talking about (the subject of the sentence) and what you are saying about it (the predicate of the sentence). A thesis statement whose single declarative sentence is "Today I will talk about cell phone plans" makes *you* the subject and makes the fact that you *are talking* the predicate—hardly the essence of your speech's content. However, "Cell phone plans are confusing and need to be simplified" makes the topic (cell phone plans) serve as subject and the point being made about it (they are confusing and need to be simplified) the predicate. See Chapter **11** for further discussion of the role of propositional phrasing in testing the relevance and completeness of ideas.

Be sure your thesis statement includes enough information to differentiate your approach from other possibilities.

Informative Speech

Not: *My speech is on gangs.*

Or even: *Young people find gangs attractive.*

But: *There are a number of sociological and developmental reasons why young people find gangs attractive.*

Invitational Speech

Not:　　*Exploring credit promises and pitfalls.*

Or even:　*There are many credit promises and pitfalls.*

But:　　*Today, we will explore the promises and pitfalls associated with credit card use.*

Persuasive Speech

Not:　　*Something must be done about human papillomavirus.*

Or even:　*HPV is on the increase and should be combatted.*

But:　　*The threat of human papillomavirus requires a program of education and treatment.*

Evocative Speech

Not:　　*We are here to dedicate the new hospital wing.*

Or even:　*The opening of this wing is a great day for O'Connor Hospital and the community.*

But:　　*This new surgical wing reflects the efforts of many dedicated fund-raisers and increases the quality and quantity of medical care available in our community.*

Break Your Thesis Statement into a List of Questions

When chemists analyze a substance, they identify its components. As a speaker, you analyze the topic to find all the subtopics within it. All types of speeches require this type of analysis, and in persuasive speeches, this takes the form of a structured issue analysis. (See Chapter **22**.) To perform this analysis, consider the set of questions your

Speaker's Workshop 6.6

1. Read one or more of the speech transcripts available among the book's on-line resources, and formulate a single declarative sentence that best sums up the content. You may find the actual sentence in the speech itself or you may, in the case of an implicit thesis, have to draft a sentence of your own.

2. Evaluate the following as thesis statements for a speech. If they are not effective, rewrite them.
   A. What shall we do about the problem of racism?
   B. Cambodia—its history, its people, its problems—will be the topic I will cover today.
   C. To explore the need for mandatory drug testing of athletes!
   D. Taxpayers should not have to subsidize art that is pornographic or unpatriotic.
   E. How to make a Caesar salad.
   F. There are three causes of congressional gridlock.

thesis statement brings to mind. These questions are the ones your listeners will expect to be answered before they accept your thesis. Thus, they are the ones you should identify before proceeding with your research. The analysis will help anticipate your audience's reaction to your speech, direct your research, help you develop your main points and subpoints, and prevent you from committing any glaring oversights. You'll find the answers to these questions as you research your topic.

Consider this thesis for a persuasive speech:

> Today I will demonstrate the problem of homelessness in our community, share a solution being offered by St. Vincent Hotel and Booth House, and help you to recognize the benefits of supporting this local organization.

Embedded in this thesis are three questions your audience will be asking as they listen:

▶   Is homelessness a problem that needs to be addressed?

▶   Does the St. Vincent Hotel and Booth House effectively address this problem?

▶   Do the benefits outweigh the costs necessary to move listeners to action?

For a speech about comic books, you might develop the following thesis sentence:

> With their scope, history, and influence, comic books are an interesting component of American popular culture.

For this informative speech, four questions present themselves:

▶   What is the scope of comic book themes?

▶   What is the history of the comic book?

▶   What influence have comic books had?

▶   Are comic books an interesting component of American popular culture?

Even in an invitational speech to a classroom audience, you might encapsulate your message into this thesis sentence:

> We will explore the advantages and disadvantages of a motorcycle helmet law in our state and I will invite you to share your perspective.

This thesis brings to mind several questions you ought to investigate:

▶   What would a new motorcycle helmet law entail?

▶   What are the possible advantages of a motorcycle helmet law in the state?

▶   What possible disadvantages of a helmet law could be identified and for whom?

▶   How might the audience members' perspective be invited?

To answer these questions, you can investigate the impact of helmet laws in other states, perhaps interview some motorcycle owners you know to learn their perspective, speak to a police officer or your insurance provider about the possible impact of a law, and plan to invite your audience's perspective as part of your speech's main points.

Speaker's Workshop 6.7

1. Look at each of the thesis statements you have identified or written for Speaker's Workshop 6.6. Identify the questions implicit in each. Do the speakers address each issue?

2. Identify the questions embedded in each of these thesis statements:
   A. The conceal carry law has been in effect for one year with both positive and negative effects.
   B. Together we will explore the promise and pitfalls of credit card use.
   C. Because the property tax is essentially regressive, it is an uncertain and inequitable source of revenue for the city and therefore must be changed.

Select a Speech Title If Necessary

Although every speech needs a thesis and a purpose, not every speech needs a title. A title is necessary when there is to be advance publicity, when there is a printed program, and, usually, when the speaker is going to be formally introduced. Unless there is a definite deadline to announce your title, you can defer selecting one until after the speech is composed.

A title can take any grammatical form. It can be a declarative sentence, question, phrase, or fragment:

▶ "Freedom of Speech Is in Jeopardy"

▶ "Is Free Speech Really Free?"

▶ "Threats to Free Speech"

▶ "Free Speech: An Endangered Species"

An effective title should stimulate interest in your subject and make the audience eager to listen. Sometimes, a metaphor, quotation, or allusion that is central to the speech can be part of the title:

▶ "Who Will Be David to This Modern Goliath?"

▶ "The Quiet Revolution"[1]

▶ "Women's Progress Is Human Progress"[2]

▶ "Are We Ready for Tomorrow, Today?"[3]

▶ "Educated Citizens in a Changing World"[4]

▶ "From Tentative Twig to Mighty Branch"[5]

In an effort to be clever or profound, do not devise a title that will mystify your audience, like "Whoot, Whoot!" or "The Heraclitus of Sycamore High." Nor should you select a title that promises more than you can deliver. That is false advertising. Do not announce "How to Double Your Income While Working Two Days a Week" and then give a speech on how to make one's first investment in income property. This may sell tabloids at the supermarket, but it is not considered good speaking technique.

Speaker's Workshop 6.8

© geopaul / iStockphoto 3620311

1. Go to your CourseMate for *The Speaker's Handbook* and evaluate the titles of the speeches by Hans Erian, Harriet Kamakil, and Brian Sharkey in the interactive video activities. Are they effective?

2. Select titles for the comic book speech outlined in Chapter **10** and the speech on women in the labor force outlined in Chapter **11**.

3. Match each of the numbered categories to a lettered example.

Categories

1. General topic
2. Narrowed topic
3. General purpose
4. Specific purpose
5. Primary audience outcome
6. Contributing audience outcome
7. Thesis statement
8. Analysis question
9. Title

Examples

A. Have more lives been saved when a CPR-trained person has been present?

B. To convince the audience that the greater the number of people who know CPR, the better the chance of more lives being saved every day.

C. Encourage friends to take a class in CPR.

D. Cardiopulmonary resuscitation (CPR).

E. I want my audience to actively work toward increasing the number of people who know CPR.

F. Learn CPR and make the world a safer place.

G. As many people as possible should learn CPR to increase the probability that a person trained in this life-saving technique will be available in the event of a heart attack or similar medical emergency.

H. To persuade.

I. The value of learning CPR.

Review, Reconsider, & Act

Summary

Selecting a speech topic is our first step in developing an effective speech. We can draw from our experiences, expertise, interests, opinions, and beliefs when considering possible topics. Also consider topics you'd like to know more about. Brainstorming is a good way to generate multiple ideas. Select a topic that is appropriate to the audience and occasion, that is timely and timeless, and that is meaningful and manageable. Narrow your topic by determining the number of main points that time will allow. When you've identified a topic, identify your general and specific purposes, specify the desired outcomes, and develop a clear thesis statement that encapsulates the main ideas of your speech. Finally, consider giving your speech a catchy title.

Critical Thinking Questions

▮ Explain the process and benefit of selecting a topic appropriate to the audience and occasion.

▮ How might one's audience influence topic selection?

▮ Brainstorm a list of possible speech topics, choose the topic you're most interested in speaking about, and create a general purpose, specific purpose, primary audience outcome, and contributing audience outcome for this speech.

Putting It into Practice

Brainstorm and then choose a topic that would be appropriate to deliver where you work. Identify a general purpose and specific purpose for this speech.

1. What topics would be appropriate for your workplace? What would be inappropriate?

2. Who would attend your speech? Why would they attend?

3. Would the speech be informative, invitational, persuasive, or evocative?

4. What audience outcomes would you desire? What outcomes would your direct supervisor desire?

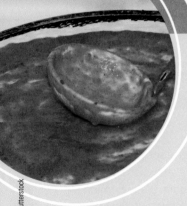

chapter 7
Audience Analysis

Base your speech preparation on thorough audience analysis.

Speakers do not give speeches *to* audiences; they jointly create meaning *with* audiences. The ultimate outcome of any speech situation is a product of what the speaker actually says and how the listeners process and interpret what is said. Therefore, audience analysis is much more than a step in planning a speech. It involves the constant awareness of those who are the "coauthors" of your speech—your listeners.

You speak to a particular group of people because you want a certain response from them. If you do not know the composition of that group, you cannot make intelligent decisions about what to include, what to emphasize, and how best to arrange and present your ideas. Research your audience thoroughly. Their age, sex, beliefs, attitudes, and expectations are all relevant to your planning.

The composition of audiences varies. The members of one audience may have many similarities; the members of another, little in common. Within a given audience, the degree of homogeneity or heterogeneity can differ for each of the characteristics discussed in this chapter. For instance, an audience can be fairly homogeneous (similar) in terms of sex—predominantly female, say—and heterogeneous (diverse) in its composition of people who agree or disagree with your position.

We approach each of these characteristics as a discrete factor and describe the techniques to be used with various kinds of homogeneous audiences. You have to mix and match these techniques as you uncover the actual composition of your potential audience even if that audience includes your classmates.

Later in the process of preparing your speech, you can use the information to tailor your speech to your audience and situation.

Seek Information through Many Channels

When you ask an audience to listen to your ideas, you are asking them to come partway into your experience. It is your obligation, in turn, to go partway into theirs. Every person is also a member of multiple discourse communities that are tied to specific cultural heritages, geographical locations, occupational groups, and so on. Each of these communities has its own code of conduct and specialized vocabulary. By observing and reflecting on your audience from different perspectives, you can discover what communication links are already present between you and them—and what gaps need to be bridged.

The following are valuable ways to gain information about your audience. But it's important not to limit yourself to any one of them; these techniques work regardless of whether your audience includes attendees at a business luncheon or classmates in your public speaking class.

Use Direct Observation

You know what will interest an audience with whom you share much in common. However, observing a less familiar audience will help you generate interest with them too. Notice the group's demographics such as age, gender, and ethnicity. Consider what examples or evidence might resonate with them. In addition, try to determine their attitudes, beliefs, and values. Observing a group, be it at a meeting or during class, can help you a great deal.

Do Systematic Data Collection

One excellent way to become informed about your audience is to ask them directly. Politicians and advertisers spend millions on public opinion and market surveys. Such research reveals who their audiences are and how they think. Do not discount even a simple form of data gathering, such as distributing a three- or four-item questionnaire before your speaking opportunity. You might arouse interest and curiosity while gaining valuable information.

Conduct Selected Interviews or Focus Groups

When you cannot get information on the whole audience, arrange to talk to one or two members of the group. If that is not possible, talk to someone who shares characteristics with your potential listeners. For a speech to a group of teenagers, talking to one teenager—even if she or he will not be a member of that audience—can provide you with useful information. The same applies to interviewing someone who manages a bank if bank managers will be in your audience. Similarly, you will benefit from conversing with a friend who is active in the local chapter of the American Red Cross, at whose regional conference you will speak.

In these interviews, try to find out not just *what* people think but also *how* they think. Ask open-ended questions and encourage respondents to expand on their answers by probing with follow-up questions. Listen to the language they use. You can gain insight into what is most meaningful to people by tuning in to the words and metaphors they use. (See Chapter **17**.)

Talk with the Contact Person

The person who asked you to speak has certain expectations about the interaction between you and the audience; otherwise, you would not have been invited. Ask this contact person to elaborate on his or her perceptions of the audience. Ask about previous speakers, both best and worst, to better understand what to do and what to avoid.

Use Intelligent Inference and Empathy

When you have no specific information about an audience, draw on your general knowledge of human behavior and groups. What are reasonable assumptions about a college audience at 9:00 a.m. on your campus, or at a Rotary Club monthly luncheon meeting? It probably isn't too much of a leap to realize that a 9:00 a.m. speech will require some extra attention to awaken the audience and the luncheon meeting may have some predictable distractions.

Let empathy lead your understanding. Get outside yourself and adopt your listeners' frames of reference. Recall a similar situation in your life: Ask yourself, "When have I felt as they likely feel?" and "What would be my main concerns?" Plan to address the resulting feelings and concerns through your speech. Use that empathy to plan appropriate responses to your audience's concerns.

Analyze Audience Demographics

There is no such thing as an average audience. Obtaining each audience's vital statistics enables you to make general predictions about their responses. The "Pertinent Demographic Questions" checklist provides questions you can use to analyze the demographics of your audience.

Obviously, all demographic characteristics are not equally important for any given speech. For example, knowledge of the religious configuration of your audience will be important in preparing a speech on issues such as euthanasia or whether prayer speeds healing. But religion might have no bearing whatsoever on another topic. Despite differences in relative importance to a particular topic, each demographic characteristic should be noted, if only to give you a general picture.

In spite of the limitations of demographic analysis, you will benefit from identifying various characteristics that may affect your audience's response—including age, gender, and race. Holding an image of your audience in mind as you prepare and practice your speech will affect dozens of minor decisions affecting your speech success. On the basis of your general cultural awareness, you will tailor your language, humor, and style of delivery to match your audience and situation. In addition, Chapters **22** and **23** will help you plan more specific adaptations.

Generational Culture

It is likely that your classroom or workplace has at least three different generational groups, including: Traditionalists, Boomers, Gen Xers and Millennials.[1] These groups have been influenced by very different environmental, political and sociological circumstances leading to quite different perspectives.[2] Of course, not every person in a particular generation will espouse the values of that generation but some tendencies are worth consideration.

▶ Traditionalists have been shaped directly or indirectly by the Great Depression and World War II. They tend to value privacy, hard work, trustworthiness, formal communication authority, and social order. They tend to be fiscally conservative.

▶ Boomers have been shaped by a post–World War II economic boom. They tend to value competition, change, hard work, and inclusion, and take a more collaborative approach to work.

▶ Generation X has been shaped by greater independence at a younger age than previous generations and raised with instant access (latchkey kids). They tend to be highly independent, creative, entrepreneurial, and comfortable with change. They tend to value feedback, balance, fun, informality, information, and access to that information instantaneously.

▶ Millenials have been shaped by technology and instant access to information. They tend to value positive reinforcement, autonomy, flexibility, diversity, technology, multitasking, and constant access to information available through their extensive social network.

CHECKLIST ~ **Pertinent Demographic Questions**

☐ What is the average age of the audience members?

☐ What is the age range?

☐ Which generational group would audience members most closely associate?

☐ What is the proportion of males and females in the audience?

☐ What relational arrangements are represented (married, single, divorced, in a civil union or domestic partnership)?

☐ What cultural groups are represented, in about what proportions?

☐ What is the socioeconomic composition of the group?

☐ What occupations are represented?

☐ What religious groups are represented?

☐ What is the political orientation of the group?

☐ How homogeneous or heterogeneous are the audience members for each of the above characteristics?

Sex and Gender

Sex is the demographic category that relates to biological maleness or femaleness. *Gender* refers to the socialized roles we have learned as appropriate for our sex. There may be a few experiences that are directly linked to sex; a speech on breast-feeding or circumcision might take the actual male–female composition of an audience into account. Far more commonly, however, gender issues enter into audience analysis. The issue is not how many males and females are present, but how audience members of either sex think about masculinity and femininity. These gender expectations are culture bound and have changed dramatically in recent years. The failure to recognize this change could seriously harm a speaker's credibility.

As a speaker, you are well advised to avoid statements that may offend a sizable portion of your audience. Women, especially as they become aware of past oppression, are naturally sensitive to slights to their dignity and their roles as autonomous adults. Avoid referring to women as "girls," "gals," or "ladies,"—all of which tend to trivialize their status. Many women believe that references to their clothes and appearance, however complimentary and well-meant, focus on them as sex objects or decorative accessories. To be on the safe side with any audience, avoid such comments as

▶ "I was chatting at dinner with your lovely vice president, Professor Ruhly."

▶ "To Mr. Davis's left, the charming young lady in the pretty blue dress is our sales manager, Lydia."

▶ "If you had a son about to take over your business, you would probably tell him . . . "[Why not a daughter?]

▶ "I saw a father babysitting his daughter at the mall the other day." [Should we think fathers as "babysitters" when we think of mothers as parents or caregivers?]

Race and Ethnicity

Ethnicity refers to a person's "identity with or membership in a particular racial, national, or cultural group and observance of that group's customs, beliefs, and language."[3] The term "race" is more problematic. Although it has historically been used to group people along lines of physical appearance, particularly skin color, most biologists think of race as an arbitrary social construction that does not align with genetic and biological boundaries. Regardless of the biological reality, people do self-identify as members of a particular "race," and that identification and the perception of racial differences has great sociological and political force.

Because a single community or organization may be composed of dozens of cultures, it is not a reasonable goal to become an expert on the cultural values and symbols of each group. But you can familiarize yourself with their experiences. For example, the common experience of nonwhite racial groups and most other ethnic minorities in the United States has included discrimination and oppression. Members of these groups,

FOR YOUR BENEFIT: Limitations of Demographic Generalizations

YOUR NEW CAREER

Few generalizations can be made on the basis of demographic factors. The studies from which generalizations are drawn are often flawed. Also, social change occurs so rapidly that by the time research is reported, the situation may have changed. Social science research, even when carefully controlled and well designed, tells us how one group on average differs from another group on average. With respect to almost any trait, the differences among all women or among all men are far greater than the differences between the average man and the average woman.

Still, demographic data let us make some probability statements. That is, we can say many people in an audience are likely to respond in a certain way even though we cannot say any individual in that audience definitely will respond in a given way. Knowing that an audience is all female or all over sixty-five or all Asian American is more helpful than having no information about the audience at all, but by no means does this data tell us everything we need to know.

similar to women, are justifiably sensitive to any communication that reduces their status or reflects old stereotypes. Use an individual's proper title and don't address one group any more or less favorably than another.

Beyond showing sensitivity to the relationships between members of dominant and nondominant cultural groups, a speaker can also demonstrate an appreciation of cultural diversity. People of any ethnic group can tend to look at things from the standpoint of the group's own history and culture. Taking the time to investigate other cultural views can open up a number of refreshingly different avenues to good communication. Making the effort to pronounce unfamiliar names and phrases correctly, and avoiding the most stereotypical cultural generalizations, show your goodwill and openness.

This kind of investigation is worthwhile only if it is put to appropriate use. The superficial approach, equivalent to the politician who is filmed eating her way through every ethnic restaurant in her constituency, results in a speech that rings false. The focus should be on the factors that influence communication: What constitutes a credible image? What level of eye contact is appropriate? How much controversy or intensity becomes discomforting? What is an appropriate greeting or social distance?

Go to your CourseMate for The Speaker's Handbook *and click on* **WebLinks 7.1** *and* **7.2** *to visit helpful websites at University of Hawai'i Maui Community College and Texas A&M University. These sites provide information about how to gather and analyze data about your audience before you give a speech.*

Rtimages / www.BigStockPhoto.com

YOUR
NEW
CAREER

FOR YOUR BENEFIT: **Multiple Identities of Audience Members**

Audiences are not only culturally diverse, but they are also composed of individuals who themselves are multicultural. This is most evident in the case of President Barack Obama, whose father is from Kenya, whose mother is from Kansas, and who lived in Hawaii and Indonesia as a young person.[4] It is increasingly rare to find someone whose heritage is monocultural in any real sense. One person may have one European parent and one South American parent and have lived on four continents. Another individual may be part of an ethnic group that has largely been oppressed but may personally have had a privileged upper-middle-class lifestyle and education. A third-generation Korean American will share most of the cultural experiences of other native-born US citizens but may have had different experiences or treatment based on having a Korean name or "Asian" features. Because people's experiences, not their traits, shape them as listeners, there are no simple prescriptions for analyzing an audience's cultural background.

Try to Understand What Is Meaningful to Your Audience

Because speakers are not transmitting information, but rather are jointly constructing meanings with listeners, no part of audience analysis is as important as learning *how a particular group of people makes meaning.* The demographic data you collect can be useful, but only if treated within the context of this complex process. Age, race, and sex all contribute to a person's interpretation of the world. But so, too, do religion, social class, educational level, economic status, sexual orientation, health, physical

TABLE 7.1
Relating to an audience

LEVEL OF UNDERSTANDING	ANALYSIS
Being oblivious to the audience (poor understanding).	Here is how I see this issue. You should see it the same way.
Adapting to the audience's traits (better understanding; although be cautious to avoid hasty generalizations).	Because you are male, you are probably competitive and would respond to statements about being a winner. Because you are older, you may be conservative and would be skeptical about sudden change.
Understanding and respecting how the audience interprets the topic (best understanding).	Because of your experiences (which may or may not be linked to your demographic traits), you have this set of values and this way of defining yourself. I can see how your worldview makes sense to you, and here is how my position overlaps and resonates with what is most meaningful to you.

ability, and many other factors. As the incredible diversity and constantly changing profile of US society have made clear, no formula can tell a speaker how each of these variables relates to a particular topic, let alone how they all interact. In a sense, as a speaker, you have been freed from the unrealistic goal of making predictions based on static traits of your listeners. Instead, your task is to consider thoughtfully how they engage in a constant process of constructing, and reconstructing, the world. Table 7.1 lists ways to relate to an audience.

This third and most useful way of understanding audiences requires both empathy and intellect. From this perspective, you can begin to grasp how different people can observe the same events but interpret them "logically" to come to opposite conclusions. (See Chapter **16**.) In this sort of audience analysis, you are trying to glimpse what some describe as *core values* (or *worldviews, personal construct systems, frames of reference, informal theories,* or *master narratives*). (See Chapter **20**.) What do your listeners draw on to organize their experience and make sense of it?

There are two sources of such information. You can learn about cultural and group differences by reading, traveling, and exposing yourself to literature and art forms that shake up your own worldviews. You can also learn by listening openly to and participating in dialogues with the people you want to understand. Many times, people can tell you explicitly about their beliefs and attitudes, but often, the processes by which they make meaning are taken for granted and are difficult for them to articulate. You may not get the insights you want through questionnaires or traditional interviews, so you need to rely on extended observation and careful attention to the ways their talk reveals their values, priorities, and conflicts. (See Chapter **17**.)

Determine the Audience's Attitudes toward Your Topic

Theoretically, you could spread every possible reaction a person might have to the thesis of your speech across a continuum that ranges from extreme disagreement to extreme agreement. Much social science research is based on asking people to clarify their attitudes on scales like this one:

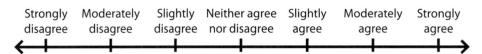

| Strongly disagree | Moderately disagree | Slightly disagree | Neither agree nor disagree | Slightly agree | Moderately agree | Strongly agree |

If your goal is to bring about some specific act, your listeners' responses will range across these categories:

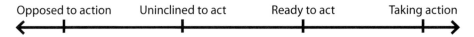

| Opposed to action | Uninclined to act | Ready to act | Taking action |

If the majority of your audience falls to the left on either continuum, that audience should be considered *unfavorable*, and if it falls to the right, it is *favorable*. If it is in the middle, it is *neutral*.

Most speakers agree that knowing the audience's predisposition toward the topic is the single most important bit of information in planning their speech strategy. If your speech deals with a controversial topic, it is crucial that you interview people who differ from you in terms of attitude and experience. Listen carefully and respectfully to their accounts of the world. At the information-gathering stage, your goal is not to plan a strategy for changing them, but rather to see how their views and yours might be connected. Once you determine whether your audience is favorable, neutral, or unfavorable, you can follow the specific suggestions offered in Chapter **22**. Although attitudes toward your topic are most obviously relevant to persuasive speaking, they can influence the speech to inform, invite, or evoke as well.

Speaker's Workshop 7.1

Suppose you are the contact person for a speaker who will talk about state funding cuts in education. Prepare an audience profile of at least two paragraphs summarizing the most relevant demographic and attitudinal data. If you are enrolled in a speech class, use the class as the audience you will describe. Otherwise, describe a group you know well, such as your department at work or an organization to which you belong.

Gather Details about the Specific Speech Situation

We have stressed the importance of knowing your purpose in speaking, but what is your audience's purpose in listening? Why are they sitting there giving you their valuable time? Knowing the predominant audience expectation is vital to the preparation of your speech. An excellent speech can fail miserably if the audience expected something different from the speech you gave.

Think about the situation of your audience. Did your listeners just arrive from home, or have they been sitting in session since 8:00 this morning? What length of speech do they expect? Have they just come from a big meal? The overly relaxed audience can be a challenge to a speaker, but so can the antsy or hungry one. Is your speech the key note, or are they anticipating the election of officers, a well known performer, or another speaker to follow? This is not to say you must be bound by the audience's expectations. You can lead them to a new mind-set, but to do that, you need to discover what they know and expect. Start with the questions in the "Audience Expectations" checklist.

You obviously cannot control all the conditions surrounding your speech, but this makes it all the more important to find out as much as possible about audience expectations beforehand. Then you can direct your time to preparing a speech ideally suited to the occasion.

© geopaul / iStockphoto 3620311

Speaker's Workshop 7.2

Go to your CourseMate for *The Speaker's Handbook* and watch the videos of Megan Soileau's and Kayla Strickland's speeches. Both speeches were prepared for college-aged audiences. After watching the speeches, what assumptions do you think they made about that audience? Imagine a situation where either of these student speakers had the opportunity to address an older "public audience" on the same topic. Identify the characteristics of the audience and suggest several specific adaptations that could be made in these speeches.

CHECKLIST ~ **Audience Expectations**

☐ *What do they know about your topic?* Avoid making blanket assumptions about the sophistication of your audience; rather, use the techniques of audience analysis to determine accurately audience attitudes. No one likes to be talked down to or to waste time listening to what she or he already knows. In both cases, listeners become irritated and tune out the speaker. People listen and learn best when exposed to information that is just beyond their current level of comprehension.

☐ *What do they think about you?* Learn what your audience has heard, read, or assumed about you. If they believe you are an unquestioned expert, a misguided fanatic, or the funniest speaker their program chair has ever met, it will surely influence how they listen to you. Knowing what your credibility is prior to the speech helps you decide how much you need to bolster it during the speech. (See Chapter **19**.)

☐ *What is the history of your audience as a group?* Audiences come in many different forms, with varied levels of group cohesion. Most audiences have some common history, but that may range from a long association at work to a few weeks together in a classroom. Learn all you can about this collective history. What projects have they undertaken? What have they shared or accomplished? What other speakers have they heard? You may find possible connections to your speech topic.

☐ *What is the program surrounding your speech?* To understand an audience's expectations of you, it is essential to learn your speech's place in the context of their immediate situation. Whether you are part of a three-day professional conference or a high school assembly, familiarize yourself with the agenda and where you fit into it.

Review, Reconsider, & Act

Summary

In this chapter we addressed audience analysis, stressing the importance of learning your audience's background and perspectives in order to tailor your speech to their needs and expectations. Learning about an audience's demographic makeup, their attitudes toward your topic, and details about the speech situation can improve your ability to meaningfully tailor your speech to their interests and needs.

Critical Thinking Questions

▶ What demographic information would you request in the event you couldn't gather the information through direct observation?

▶ How might you best determine your audience's attitude and expectations toward you and your topic?

▶ What does audience analysis affect in the process of speech development and delivery?

Putting It into Practice

Prepare a speech for a club or organization that you belong to or can easily access, perhaps a service organization such as Lions Club, Rotary Club, or Sertoma.

1. What do you know about the organization's membership?
2. What do the members expect of speakers presenting at their meeting?
3. What situational elements might make speaking to this group a challenge?
4. What topics that you have knowledge about would be welcome?

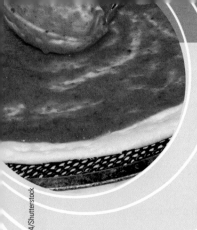

chapter 8
Research

Research your topic. Plan to gather information from a broad range of sources.

I magine you have been invited to listen to a speaker give a talk on your state's concealed carry gun laws. Which of the following speakers would you prefer? Speaker 1 will speak from personal experience about your state's concealed carry legislation, sharing personal anecdotes and her impression of the impact the law has had. Speaker 2 will offer an organized discussion of the impact of the concealed carry legislation, including informed opinions from her reading of a number of articles on the subject, statistics located through research, and some stories from a local police officer. Assuming both speakers are similar in delivery skills, which speech will afford you the more accurate view of the topic? Which is more likely to inform you? Which would you rather hear? A well-researched topic provides a number of benefits to both speaker and audience members, including its opportunity to effectively inform and persuade.

Have a Research Strategy

A well-researched topic doesn't happen accidentally. A well-planned research strategy optimizes your effort for the time allotted. A research strategy requires you to reflect upon your topic and the situation before dashing off to research it. How much time do you have? What facts must you look up based on the nature of your topic and the knowledge you already have about it? What aspects of your topic require investigation? Other questions center on where you will get your information. What can best be found in text sources? Which research can be done online? Whom can you interview to inform your topic?

Fit Your Research to the Time Allotted

Your approach to research can vary widely according to the time you have to prepare and the nature of your topic. Chapter **5** advises having a realistic timetable for preparation. With one day's notice, you cannot make an exhaustive study of the literature, but you can draw from general references like encyclopedias, whether at the library or online. With more time, a broader effort is possible, starting with the information gleaned from general resources and perhaps a few specific sources, including interviews with local experts.

The Speech Timeline *in Speech Builder Express can help you plan your research based in the amount of time you have.*

Work from General to Specific

Start with an investigation of the "big picture." As you move further into your research, you can become more focused. Knowing from a broad standpoint what you can afford to ignore and what areas are essential will allow you to conduct your research strategically.

As the planning chart in Chapter **5** indicates, a round of preliminary or exploratory research precedes your main research effort. Many people turn to broad research tools like encyclopedias and even some might use Wikipedia for initial information, but research can't stop there. There are two basic sources to tap for research: published information and people. By starting first with published information, you will be better able to consider what questions to ask of a peer or an expert later.

FOR YOUR BENEFIT: Information Everywhere

Finding information is easy these days. Unfortunately, finding accurate, timely, relevant information is not always easy. Learning to utilize your information resources will be one of the smartest and most efficient things you can do in this age of information. If possible, ask for a tour of your library. Learn the name of the librarians at your institution. Approach your information search strategically, keeping in mind what information you need and how you wish to use it. The skills you develop researching your speech will prove equally valuable as you research a possible employer, treatment alternatives for a medical condition, or the history of your family name.

Rtimages / www.BigStockPhoto.com

One of the most useful talents in the early stages of research is the ability to skim. Even if you have unlimited time to prepare, it makes little sense to grab all the available books and articles on a topic and read them cover to cover. Before checking out any text resources from the library (or buying them, for that matter), look through a number of them quickly. Because you will not have time to read everything, try to get a feel for the most important approaches and theories. Use the table of contents or quickly skim key paragraphs of an article or the first and last chapters of the book. Jot down the names of the frequently cited scholars and public figures, as well as recurring concepts and studies. Do not feel obligated to read every single sentence.

Develop a similar technique as you search online. Especially on the Web, it is easy to be seduced by a long set of links that are fun and interesting but may lead to useless information. One way to sidestep this problem is to start with subject directories such as About, the Open Directory Project (**dmoz.org/**) or the Librarian's Internet Index (**ipl.org/div/subject/**) rather than search engines such as Google. If you do use search engines, you should be able to develop, after a time, a sense for the ranking algorithm used by each engine, and can skip some highly ranked hits that really don't match your criteria. Be aware that, often, the top few links returned by a search engine have paid for prominent placement and may be less relevant to your search than those further down the list.

As you begin, look for summary or state-of-the-art articles and books and sites that synthesize current thinking on your subject. Pieces that trace the history of your topic are also useful. Often, these sources are readily identifiable by their titles:

▶ "What Is a Working Woman?" [H. H. Stipp, *American Demographics*]

▶ "The Lasting Changes Brought by Women Workers" [*BusinessWeek*]

▶ *Women in the American Economy* [Juanita M. Kreps, Prentice-Hall]

Skimming several sources and reading a few general ones will give you a good overview of your topic. You can then further narrow your topic and focus the remainder of your research.

Develop a List of Key Terms

Beginning to study a new topic is almost like learning a new language. As you start exploring your topic, make a list of key terms that come up. In researching women in the labor force, for example, you will find you need to understand the distinctions made between *equal opportunity, affirmative action,* and *comparable worth.* You will notice certain phrases, such as *glass ceiling, queen bee syndrome,* and *pink-collar workers,* that have been coined by earlier writers and that are widely used in the discourse on this topic. Familiarity with the language of your topic is essential as you continue your research because you need to identify key words as you search through the literature. This is particularly useful in searches for electronic information—using precise language is one way to obtain a manageable number of hits with your Internet search.

Use Your Audience Analysis Questions

When you've made one pass through for background research, but before you launch your main research effort, go back and analyze your topic. Consider whether you want to narrow your topic, adjust your speech objectives, or fine-tune the wording of your thesis statement. Carefully follow the suggestions in Chapter **6** to list the questions about your topic your audience will want answers to. These questions become the basis of your research objectives.

Suppose this is your thesis:

Since the beginning of the Industrial Revolution, women in the United States have been exploited as a cheap and expendable source of labor.

Your audience may want to hear the answers to questions like these: Are women a cheap source of labor? Are women an expendable source of labor? Can the labor practices appropriately be labeled as exploitation? Has the treatment of women been consistent since the Industrial Revolution? Clearly, then, your list of research objectives will include goals like these: Find out how women's salaries compare with those of men who do the same job. Find specific examples of women having been treated as an expendable source of labor. Find an expert definition of *exploitation*. Find out how women's work changed at the time of the Industrial Revolution, and so on.

Like a shopping list you take to the store, this set of questions can provide focus and direction. Armed with this list of research objectives, you are ready to make the best use of your research time and to ask for the help you need.

Use the Library

Most every college or public library has a connection to a larger system through which it can order what you need. If your library gives tours of the facility, be sure you go on one so you will know what the library offers. Even with the advent of the Internet, the library is still the place to find the widest variety of research tools (including access to the Internet) and, most importantly, the place to find professional researchers who can quickly help you locate valuable resources.

Talk to a Librarian

Librarians are service-oriented information specialists and, contrary to the image presented in popular culture, are not there merely to shush people who forget to whisper. They are there to help you find the materials you need. Do not hesitate to ask your librarian questions. He or she will welcome the challenge of trying to understand your requirements and directing you to the answers you seek—whether you have questions about key terms, general resources for a particular topic, the best databases, Internet search strategies, and any other part of your research.

Locate Books and Articles on Your Topic

In addition to the librarian, important library resources include the online book catalog, periodical indexes and databases, and specialized dictionaries and encyclopedias.

The Book Catalog

In most libraries, the book catalog is an online resource. These database systems let you search for entries in a number of ways. For instance, you may choose to search by some combination of subject, author, and title. Or you can focus on topics as they are grouped in the Dewey decimal system or the Library of Congress classifications. Or you can search by keywords or *descriptors*—words or short phrases that the database uses to identify entries on related topics. (In our example of women in the labor force, some keywords might be *labor market, women, wages and salaries,* and *sex discrimination.*) Or, in some cases, you may make a *free text search,* in which the computer does not limit itself to defined descriptors, but rather looks for words and combinations of words you have chosen within the titles and content summaries of the books in the database. If you encounter difficulty, do not hesitate to ask for assistance from a library staff member.

Periodical Indexes and Databases

You can locate magazine, journal, and newspaper articles on your topic by using the periodical indexes and databases available at the library. This may entail searching a computer database or perusing bound volumes. Some of the indexes and databases are general in their coverage; others are about a specific field. Whether your topic is art, criminal justice, religion, engineering, business, music, tax law, or any one of a multitude of topics, there is a good chance a specialized index or database exists for it. Once again, do not hesitate to approach the librarian for guidance in finding these sources.

Your library probably provides access to one or more electronic databases. InfoTrac College Edition, LexisNexis, Gale (AccessMyLibrary), Dialog, EBSCOHost Research Databases, BRS (Bibliographic Retrieval Service), and Wilson OmniFile are some of the services that provide information retrieval. A service can have hundreds of databases to choose from, each of which can cover hundreds of thousands of articles and papers. Many times the information available through these services would not be accessible through the public Internet resources available through search tools like Google, Bing, or About. Many public libraries subscribe to at least one service. College and university libraries are likely to have a search service, usually available only to students, staff, and faculty. Many companies have access to at least one of the major systems. Figure 8.1 shows a search conducted on InfoTrac

FIGURE 8.1
A search using InfoTrac college edition

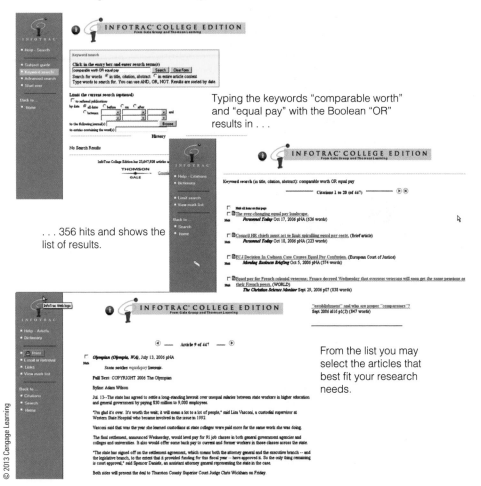

Typing the keywords "comparable worth" and "equal pay" with the Boolean "OR" results in . . .

. . . 356 hits and shows the list of results.

From the list you may select the articles that best fit your research needs.

College Edition, using the keywords *comparable worth* and *equal pay*. (InfoTrac College Edition is one of the resources available to you through your CourseMate for *The Speaker's Handbook*.)

Specialized Dictionaries, Encyclopedias, and Other Resources

Special dictionaries and encyclopedias are useful tools, especially for clarifying terms and concepts in fields in which you may have little knowledge. Many such reference works cover world history, finance, law, medicine, science, philosophy, music, literature, and other subjects of significance.

Depending on its size, the library may have many other sources of information available, including atlases, photographs, art collections, video recordings, compact discs, and all nature of digital media.

Use the Internet

Electronic information accessible by personal computer ranges from web pages, to online editions of encyclopedias and news magazines, to stock market reports, to government statistics, to sports and entertainment news and weblogs (blogs). Apps for iPod Touch, iPad, and iPhone as well as other "smart phones" have become widely available, creating easy access to reliable information from anywhere.

Search engines and metasearch engines are like indexes for the World Wide Web. You type in a keyword or a URL and the engine looks for links. Metasearch engines combine the results from several search engines. Here are some examples of both:

▶ Google
google.com

▶ Yahoo!
search.yahoo.com

▶ Bing
bing.com

▶ Yippy (metasearch engine that clusters results by topic, source, or URL)
yippy.com

▶ Dogpile (metasearch engine)
dogpile.com

If a search engine is like the index of a book, a subject directory is like the library's book catalog. You find the general subject and then browse around in it to see what may be useful. Subject directories consist of links organized by topic. The topics on the first page of a directory are general, but each of them leads to lists of more specific subtopics. Two of the major search engines—Google (**google.com/dirhp**) and Yahoo! (**dir.yahoo. com**)—also have subject directories. In addition, subject experts and librarians have created several smaller, but more select, subject guides. Here is a sampling:

▶ About (summaries and links from experts in 500 subjects)
about.com

▶ Internet Public Library (subject directory and online reference books)
ipl.org

▶ Infomine (searchable virtual library with 100,000 scholarly links)
infomine.ucr.edu

▶ The Scout Report Archives (searchable virtual library of more than 20,000 selected websites)
scout.wisc.edu/Archives/

In addition, a few search engines look for information on the *invisible* Web, or databases (such as Census Bureau statistics and reports from government agencies) that are not accessible via standard search engines.

▶ FirstGov (search or browse U.S. government websites)
usa.gov

▷ Federal Digital System (search information databases produced by the U.S. government)
gpo.gov/fdsys/

▷ THOMAS (search engine for legislative information from the Library of Congress including: U.S. Congress bills, treaties, votes, and more)
thomas.loc.gov/

Also invisible to standard search engines are the messages and articles on Listserv email discussion groups, Usenet newsgroups, and blogs. If you know your subject well and want a special piece of information, these may be worth checking out. Some search engines do special searches of groups and blogs. Here are a few:

▷ CataList (browseable catalog of public Listserv lists)
lsoft.com/catalist.html

▷ Google Groups
groups.google.com/

▷ Yahoo! Groups
groups.yahoo.com/

▷ Google Blogsearch
blogsearch.google.com/

▷ Technorati (blog search engine)
technorati.com/

If you want to learn more about blogs, go to your CourseMate for The Speaker's Handbook *and click on* **WebLink 8.1** *to visit the Internet Public Library's Blog List, which lists blogs by category, or* **WebLink 8.2** *to visit DeepBlog.com, which provides an extensive list of high-quality blogs and a guide to newcomers to the blogosphere.*

Search Efficiently

Some search engines and subject directories let you focus your search with *Boolean operators* ("this AND that," "this OR that," "this NOT that"). For example, if you search for "Finland" in hopes of finding some information on Finnish exports in 2010, you may have to wade through websites extolling Grandmother Kovanen's cookie recipes, Bob and Diane's trip to Helsinki, and so on, before finding anything useful. With Boolean operators, you can specify "Finland AND exports" or "Finland NOT recipes." Many engines permit users to specify that one word in the search should be near another and offer other tools (such as wildcards and required terms) to be as precise as possible; check the Help feature of your favorite engines to learn their searching shortcuts. Most search engines also have an advanced features option with additional tools. For example, you can limit your search to a specific domain (such as .edu, or educational sites) or to pages that were updated recently. Figure 8.2 shows Google's Advanced Search page.

The Web Search Guide is an excellent place to find information on various search engines and subject directories and strategies for using them. Visit this site by going to your CourseMate for The Speaker's Handbook and clicking on **WebLink 8.3.** See especially its tutorials for web searches and its comparisons of search engines. Another extremely valuable site is the UC Berkeley Library's "Finding Information on the Internet: A Tutorial," which you can find at **WebLink 8.4.**

FIGURE 8.2
Google's advanced search page

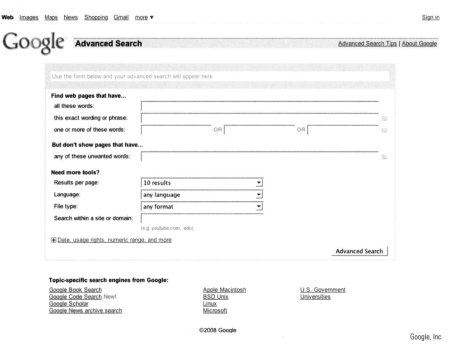

Google, Inc.

For the most efficient use of any electronic resource, create a research strategy by narrowing your topic after considering different avenues of approach. Then you can decide on the most likely categories and keywords related to your topic. Being prepared for your search will help you avoid going down too many blind alleys.

If you need to fill in the holes in your background knowledge about a topic, you can go to online versions of basic reference books, such as encyclopedias, dictionaries, and almanacs. Table 8.1 lists some useful references that could be the starting point for your Internet research. You can also use them to double-check facts.

TABLE 8.1
Useful references on the Web

Dictionaries and pronunciation guides	
Merriam-Webster Online Dictionary and Thesaurus—includes audio pronunciations	**merriam-webster.com/**
VOA Pronunciation Guide—audio guide for names in the news	**names.voa.gov**
Glossarist—searchable directory of glossaries and topical dictionaries	**glossarist.com/**
Encyclopedias and other reference works	
Encyclopedia Britannica—free condensed articles; full articles available to subscribers	**britannica.com/**
Bartleby—reference collection with *Columbia Encyclopedia, Encyclopedia of World History, Columbia Gazetteer,* and *World Factbook* (Note that many of the references posted on this site are in the public domain, so they were published at least 75 years ago. Nonetheless, this is still a useful resource.)	**bartleby.com/reference/**
LibrarySpot—multipurpose resource center	**libraryspot.com**
Quotations	
Quotations at Bartleby—search *Bartlett's Familiar Quotations, Grocott's Familiar Quotations,* and *Respectfully Quoted*	**bartleby.com/quotations/**
Statistics	
FedStats—links to statistics collected by the US government	**fedstats.gov**
NationMaster—creates graphs for comparisons among countries	**nationmaster.com/**
StateMaster—creates graphs from comparisons among US states	**statemaster.com/**
Population Reference Bureau—worldwide data about population trends, health, and the environment	**prb.org/**
Media links	
OnlineNewspapers—links to newspapers around the world	**onlinenewspapers.com/**
Center for Communication—exposes readers to the issues, the ethics, the people, and the creative products that define the media business.	**cencom.org**
US history and government	
Library of Congress—US history resources	**loc.gov**
THOMAS—searchable database of federal legislation	**thomas.loc.gov/**
US National Archives and Records Administration—historically important US government documents and records	**archives.gov**
Science	
Eric Weisstein's World of Science—links about math, chemistry, physics, and astronomy	**scienceworld.wolfram.com**
BrightSurf—science news stories	**brightsurf.com/**
How Stuff Works—brief articles and weblinks about how all sorts of things work	**howstuffworks.com/**

CHECKLIST ~ **Questions for Evaluating Internet Sources**

☐ *Who created it?* Is it a personal page? If so, what are the person's credentials and how compelling are they? If it is an organization's page, does it provide enough background information (e.g., an "About Us" page) for you to make a judgment about its credibility?

☐ *What's its bias?* Why was this site created? Was it to provide information, advocate a position, or just rant? If it's providing information, how is that information influenced by the underlying assumptions of the site's creator or funding by its sponsors?

☐ *Is it up to date?* Does the site have regular maintenance that keeps it on top of developments?

☐ *What company does it keep?* That is, who does it link to? Are those sites credible and competent?

☐ *How does it compare to reliable print sources?* Does the information square with what you know about the topic and with information from traditional sources? Especially if something on a web page seems questionable, be sure to check it against a reliable print source. For specific techniques on evaluating websites, see the UC Berkeley Library's tutorial (**WebLink 8.4**) and the guidelines from Johns Hopkins University's Sheridan Library, "Practical Steps in Evaluating Internet Resources" (**WebLink 8.5**). You can find these links at your CourseMate for *The Speaker's Handbook.*

Carefully Evaluate Internet Sources

Scrutinize web-based materials with special care. Although *any* information you gather in the course of research should be subjected to tests of credibility and reliability as described in Chapters **15** and **19**, the wide-open nature of the World Wide Web requires a particularly critical eye. In contrast to the various review processes applied to getting ideas into print or onto film, all it takes to mount a website is the software and a server. Many websites are the equivalent of an opinion forcefully stated at a party: The authority resides in the volume, not the merit. With this in mind, consider the "Questions for Evaluating Internet Sources" Checklist as you review a site.

Talk to People

Research is more than delving into piles of web pages, books, and papers. You are surrounded by potential sources of information in the form of other people. These sources can supplement and complement your library and electronic research.

Locate People with Information

Human resources are all around you—at home, at school and work, and in the community. As you consider your topic and the information needed to support your thesis, ask yourself who you could talk to to help bring insight to your effort.

Acquaintances, Family, and Coworkers

Share your developing speech ideas with the people you come in contact with every day. You may encounter surprising sources of expertise. Your neighbor who's always walking her dog the same time you are may turn out to know quite a bit about long-haul trucking, or your dentist may have gone to China last summer. On many topics, what these people can offer you is not so much expertise as a lay perspective you will not find in any book. What are your closest friends' most amazing computer foul-ups? What do they think is the most urgent economic problem the country faces? (You might turn this into an informal survey, or even go a step further and develop a brief questionnaire.)

Note, though, this is only the beginning. Do not stop your research at this point, but use these contacts as a springboard to other, more specialized resources.

Experts

In every community there are people with specialized expertise in your topic. They can make a significant contribution to your research, perhaps by telling you of unpublished

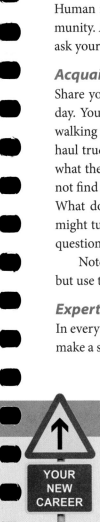

FOR YOUR BENEFIT: Beware of Spreading Urban Legends

YOUR NEW CAREER

Rtimages / www.BigStockPhoto.com

Because electronic information travels so fast, rumors and hoaxes can quickly turn into "facts." If a friend tells you about a barely believable story that happened to "a friend of a friend," check it out before you pass it along. Here are two searchable websites where you can find out if a story is true or just an urban legend.

▶ *About.com's page on current hoaxes, email rumors, and urban legends (**WebLink 8.6**)*

▶ *Snopes.com, a popular site for verifying online rumors and hoaxes (**WebLink 8.7**)*

 You can find these links at your CourseMate for The Speaker's Handbook.

data, local applications, or local examples of your subject, or by directing you to obscure sources. The information provided by local experts will likely be seen as more interesting and more credible than information obtained through less credible online resources. Isn't it far more interesting to say, "According to Officer Jeff Burian of the local police department" than to say, "According to the data I read in a book about violent crimes"?

Educators   At whatever level—high school, trade school, college, or university—educators are usually approachable experts. Dissemination of information is their business. If you do not already have a specific person in mind after your research to this point, call the appropriate department or school or check with your local librarian for a referral. They will direct you to someone knowledgeable.

Public officials and agencies   People elected to public office consider it one of their duties to make information available to their constituents. Most have staffs whose job it is to locate and send out government documents, copies of bills pending, and so on. In addition, scores of public agencies are staffed by experts who are ready to help you. If you do not know where to start, call the main switchboard of the local or regional government and outline the direction of your research. The operator can tell you the department with which to begin.

Independent agencies and special interest groups   Groups such as the American Cancer Society, Planned Parenthood, and the local Lions Club can be excellent sources of information. Be aware, however, that such groups often represent a limited perspective. Talk to a spokesperson from, say, the National Rifle Association or the Sierra Club, but consider your source's biases. (See Chapter **15**.) When possible, interview experts who have differing orientations toward your subject, especially if the subject is controversial.

    A useful resource for making contact with such groups is the Encyclopedia of Associations, available at the library or through Dialog (**WebLink 8.8**). This encyclopedia contains descriptions of the groups and information on how to get in touch with them. Many of the groups listed have a toll-free telephone number you can call.

 You can find this link at your CourseMate for The Speaker's Handbook.

Potpourri   Judges, athletes, businesspeople, police officers, doctors, merchants, and accountants can all be experts. If you do not know a person in the particular field, see if you have a one-step link to one through a colleague or friend. Failing that, be alert to people mentioned in the newspapers. Chances are, if they were interviewed once, they will be willing to answer other questions. If you have no contacts in a large organization, start with the public relations officer. However, when you know who you want to talk to, there is no harm in calling that person's office and explaining your request. Maybe you will not get an appointment with the mayor, the chief of police, or the head football coach, but you may be able to meet with a top aide or assistant.

Look also for experts who may have credentials of a less formal sort. A homeless person, for instance, is an expert on certain dimensions of homelessness. In short, do not skip a potential source of useful information and possibly a fresh viewpoint by limiting your definition of "expert."

Experts are also accessible by computer. Newsgroups and web conferences available online can introduce you to knowledgeable people around the country and even around the world. Thousands of forums exist, covering just about every topic—from Celtic music, to calculus, to corporate law, and from bicycling, to boycotts, to Barbie dolls. In these groups and on message boards, people carry on extended dialogue on many issues. Questions are asked and answered, challenged and rebutted. Join in by asking your own questions and engage in the multifaceted discussion that can result.

Before asking a specific question, check to see if it is one that has come up many times before. Questions of this sort, along with their answers, are usually posted in a Frequently Asked Questions (FAQ) file. If there is such a posting in your area of interest, read it first—you may find many answers immediately, and you may also find answers to questions you had not yet thought to ask.

 Links to Usenet FAQs of all kinds can be found at the Internet FAQ Archives, which you can access by going to your CourseMate for The Speaker's Handbook and clicking on **WebLink 8.9**.

Conduct Interviews

As with all aspects of public speaking, in interviewing, preparation is just as important as the process itself.

Preparing for the Interview

Prior to any interview, think about who the person is, and ask yourself in what ways she or he can best contribute to your research. If the person has written an article or a book on the subject, read it. You should devise a list of questions specific enough that you will not be wasting this person's time by asking for information you could have found elsewhere. Prepare open-ended questions rather than yes/no questions or simple factual queries, but at the same time, don't be so vague that you give the person no starting place. For instance, suppose you are studying the history and current condition of women in the labor force, and you are directing your questions to the chair of the County Commission on the Status of Women:

Not: *How many women are there in the workforce in this county? [You could have looked up the figure before].*

Not: *What are the problems working women encounter? [This is too vague].*

But: *I've read that in this county the average woman's salary is 32 percent less than the average man's. To what do you attribute this?*

Conducting the Interview

Spend the first few minutes establishing rapport and setting a context for the interview. Explain who you are, why you need the information, and how far you have gotten. Also, confirm your understanding of the time available, even if you did this when setting up the meeting. If you wish to record the interview on tape or with a digital voice recorder, ask permission at this point, but technology can fail so plan to take a few notes as well. Notes can help you keep track of potential questions and needed clarifications as you go along. They also provide a written key to assist you in finding important points when you later go over the recording.

When you begin to ask questions, be sure to let the expert do most of the talking. (See the suggestions on listening in Chapter 2.) Do not interrupt, disagree, or offer your own opinions. Be supportive verbally and nonverbally: nod, smile, and use your posture and facial expressions to express interest and concern. Encourage the person with short, noninterruptive comments such as "mm-hmmm," "I see," "That's interesting," and "Then what happened?"

Also, use questions to summarize and direct the interview: "So far you've talked about four problems working women face—unequal pay, lack of training, sexual harassment, and inadequate child care. Are there others?" You can also use what's known as a **clearinghouse question,** such as, "Is there anything else you can share that might be useful to me?"

Allow for a closing phase for the interview. Respect the interviewee's time limit, and if you are approaching it, stop—even if you have gone through only half of your questions. Summarize your perspective of the interview. Ask if they might be contacted in the future and, of course, convey your thanks.

Keep a Complete Record of Your Sources and Know How to Cite Them

Form the habit of identifying the source for every piece of information you use and of recording complete bibliographic information for each source. Think about the battering your credibility will take if you are questioned about a bit of evidence and your only reply is, "I found this on the Internet, but I don't remember exactly where." With electronic catalogs your task often will be easier—you may be able to print out the bibliographic information for each of your potential sources or perhaps email it or save it to your flash drive. When you print pages from the Internet, make sure your print command will include the headers and footers from your browser, which contain the page title and the page's uniform resource locator (URL). Some people use an online tool called Zotero (see **WebLink 3.3**) to collect, manage, and cite research sources. In other situations, you will need to record them yourself. Writing down volume numbers of journals, or the cities of publication of books, or the telephone numbers of interviewees—details you will never mention in your speech—may seem unnecessary, but routinely recording all such information will help you retrieve sources if you need to check them again. And if you later develop your speech into a written report or article, your research notes will be priceless.

The Works Cited *section of Speech Builder Express can help you develop* *a record of your sources and create your list of references.*

Citing Sources for a List of References

Because you are recording all the details about your sources anyway, we recommend you master one of the standard formats for citing references. Then, if you need to append a reference list to an outline or decide to produce a handout for your audience, the sources of your research will be appropriately laid out. Three of the most popular formats for the humanities and social sciences are found in *The Chicago Manual of Style* (CMS), 16th edition (2010), usually referred to simply as Chicago style; the Modern Language Association's *MLA Handbook for Writers of Research Papers,* 7th edition (2009), referred to as MLA style; and the *Publication Manual of the American Psychological Association,* 6th edition (2009), or APA style. For the sciences, two other popular formats are found in the 2007 *IEEE Standards Style Manual* (Institute of Electrical and Electronics Engineers) and *The CSE Manual for Authors, Editors, and Publishers,* 7th edition (2006), a publication of the Council of Science Editors.

MLA and APA styles are the ones most likely to be used in the context of a speech class. Individual variations notwithstanding, all five styles require an alphabetical listing of research sources that includes author, title, date, and publication details. An easy way to remember these categories is to include the who, what, when, and where information for every source possible. In addition to the conventions for citing books, articles, chapters, and abstracts, there are established ways to cite nearly every known type of source, including interviews, TV shows, websites, and email. Table 8.2 shows the APA and MLA styles for thirteen types of reference citations. Note the different

TABLE 8.2
Selected reference list entries in APA and MLA styles

	PUBLICATION MANUAL OF THE APA	MLA HANDBOOK
Book, two authors	Lastname, A. A., & Lastname, B. B. (date). *Title of work*. City: Publisher.	Lastname, Firstname, and Firstname Lastname. *Title of Work*. City: Publisher, date.
	Crossan, J. D., & Reed, J. L. (2001). *Excavating Jesus: Beneath the stones, behind the texts*. San Francisco: HarperSanFrancisco.	Crossan, John Dominic, and Jonathan L. Reed. *Excavating Jesus: Beneath the Stones, Behind the Texts*. San Francisco: HarperSanFrancisco, 2001.
Periodical, journal	Lastname, A. A. (date). Title of article. *Periodical,* volume, pages.	Lastname, Firstname. "Title of Article." *Periodical* volume (date): pages.
	Hughes, M. (2002). Moving from information transfer to knowledge creation: A new value proposition for technical communicators. *Technical Communication,* 49, 257–285.	Hughes, Michael. "Moving from Information Transfer to Knowledge Creation: A New Value Proposition for Communicators." *Technical Communication* 49 (2002): 257–285.
Periodical, magazine	Lastname, A. A. (date). Title of article. *Periodical,* volume, pages.	Lastname, Firstname. "Title of Article." *Periodical*, date: pages.
	Schoenfeld, S. (1997, May/June). An experience in culture. *Timeline,* 33, 3–4.	Schoenfeld, Samantha. "An Experience in Culture." *Timeline*, May–June 1997: 3–4.
Newspaper	Lastname, A. A. (date). Title of article. *Newspaper* [add city in brackets if necessary], pages.	Lastname, Firstname. "Title of Article." *Newspaper* date [edition, if named]: pages.
	Guido, M. (2003, September 11). Lawmakers seek to plug loophole: Chipmakers got refunds but paid no tax to state. *San Jose Mercury News*, C1–2.	Guido, Michelle. "Lawmakers Seek to Plug Loophole: Chipmakers Got Refunds but Paid No Tax to State." *San Jose Mercury News* 11 Sep. 2003, [Peninsula/SF ed.]: C1–2.
Internet document (nonperiodical, no author)	Organization publishing website. (date). *Document title*. Retrieved date from address	"Document Title." Site. Date. Organization publishing site. Date of retrieval <address>
	League of American Bicyclists. (2003). *How to commute by bicycle*. Retrieved August 4, 2008, from http://www.bikeleague.org/resources/better/commuters.php	"How to Commute by Bicycle." League of American Bicyclists. 2008. League of American Bicyclists. 08 Aug. 2008 <http://www.bikeleague.org/resources/better/commuters.php>

	PUBLICATION MANUAL OF THE APA	MLA HANDBOOK
Email	[Personal communication not included in reference list.]	Lastname, Firstname. "Subject Line/Description." Email to Firstname Lastname. Date.
		Thor, Leifur. "Info on the Design Science Initiative Project." Email to Doug Stuart. 2 May 2003.
Interview conducted by the speaker	[Personal communication not included in reference list.]	Lastname, Firstname. Personal/Telephone/Email interview. Date.
		Thor, Leifur. Telephone interview. 5 May 2003.

sequence of information required by each, and also the differences in capitalization, punctuation, order of names, and so on. Again, keep in mind this list is just a sampling of the types of publications and communications that can end up in a reference list.

Citing Sources in Your Speech

In the discussion on supporting materials in Chapter **15**, we talk about weaving them smoothly into the speech while citing the source. The form this citation takes is, like many choices in speaking, dependent on the context. In some cases there is a rigid and stylized form, in others there is a lot more flexibility available to the speaker. The college debate or speech contest may have a strict form, developed by tradition. Otherwise, you can choose the *density* level of your citation—how much information you need to include about the source as you speak—according to how much you think your audience has to hear to accept the source as legitimate (although they don't have to agree with it).

One context is your listeners' attitude toward you and your topic: Chapter **22** discusses the adjustments you may have to make, depending on whether your audience is *favorable, neutral,* or *unfavorable.* As you might imagine, the more unfavorably your listeners regard your position, the more useful it may be to include denser citations as you introduce your supporting material (and to have a complete reference list printed up and ready to hand out). Another determinant in the density of your citations is your judgment on projecting credibility. (See Chapter **19**.) You may find in some cases that citing your sources more fully would be to your advantage, especially if a goal is to impress upon your listeners your competence and trustworthiness.

Here are three examples along the continuum of citation density. The first introduces the information with no citation at all. This is inappropriate as it lacks credibility and smacks of plagiarism. The second presents the name of the source, which indicates you are not picking numbers out of the air. The third example is fairly dense, giving your listeners enough information that they can jot down and use to check your source if they so wish.

No Citation

Only 17 percent of all bicycle accidents are car–bike collisions, and in only 10 percent of those collisions was the car overtaking the bike from the rear.

Light Citation

According to transportation engineer John Forester, only 17 percent of all bicycle accidents are car–bike collisions, and in only 10 percent of those collisions was the car overtaking the bike from the rear.

Dense Citation

In his 1993 book Effective Cycling, published by MIT Press, transportation engineer John Forester notes that only 17 percent of all bicycle accidents are car–bike collisions, and in only 10 percent of those collisions was the car overtaking the bike from the rear.

If you must be dense in your citing, make it as conversational as possible, as in the last example above. Avoid the "big parenthetical speed bump" that interrupts the flow of a sentence, as in "Transportation engineer John Forester notes (*Effective Cycling*, MIT Press, 1993) that only…" It may take a few more words to come up with a smooth version, but the result will be more natural to the ears.

Check out Speech Studio to see how other students cited sources in their speeches. Or record a speech you're working on, upload it to Speech Studio, and ask your peers for their feedback. What feedback could you use to fine tune your source citations before you give your speech in class?

Capture Information and Ideas in Discrete Units

In the process of doing your research, gather and record your information and ideas in a way that makes it as easy as possible to find things later on and to work with them creatively. The ability to download pages and pages of text from the Web does not make it any easier to review the information you have. Smaller, more manageable units will promote creative flexibility as you arrange and rearrange, and structure and restructure your thoughts and data.

We talk about index cards in this section, but the important thing is not the media or the cardstock but the activity—and if you use an outlining tool or idea development software on a computer, these suggestions are just as pertinent. That said, traditional 4-by-6-inch index cards are easy to manipulate and don't require a power source nearby.

Index Cards from Print and Electronic Sources

As you read the book or article, jot down each discrete idea or bit of information onto a separate card, being sure you add the identifying code (discussed shortly) and page number. Use only one side of each card. There are three kinds of data you might record: direct quotations or citations (Figure 8.3), paraphrased ideas (Figure 8.4), and references for later use (Figure 8.5). Do not neglect to do this for materials obtained online.

FIGURE 8.3
Direct quotations or citations

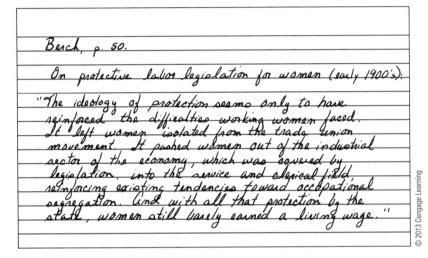

Berch, p. 50.

On protective labor legislation for women (early 1900's):
"The ideology of protection seems only to have reinforced the difficulties working women faced. It left women isolated from the trade union movement. It pushed women out of the industrial sector of the economy, which was covered by legislation, into the service and clerical field, reinforcing existing tendencies toward occupational segregation. And with all that protection by the state, women still barely earned a living wage."

© 2013 Cengage Learning

FIGURE 8.4
Paraphrased ideas

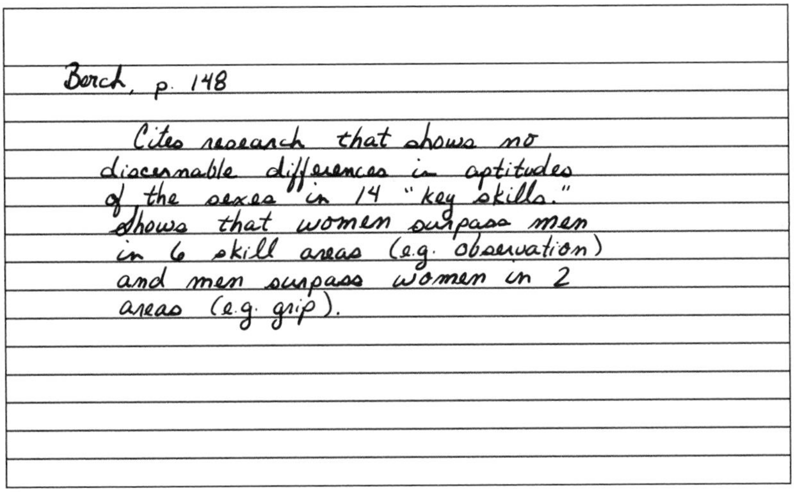

Berch, p. 148

Cites research that shows no discernable differences in aptitudes of the sexes in 14 "key skills." Shows that women surpass men in 6 skill areas (e.g. observation) and men surpass women in 2 areas (e.g. grip).

© 2013 Cengage Learning

FIGURE 8.5
References for later use

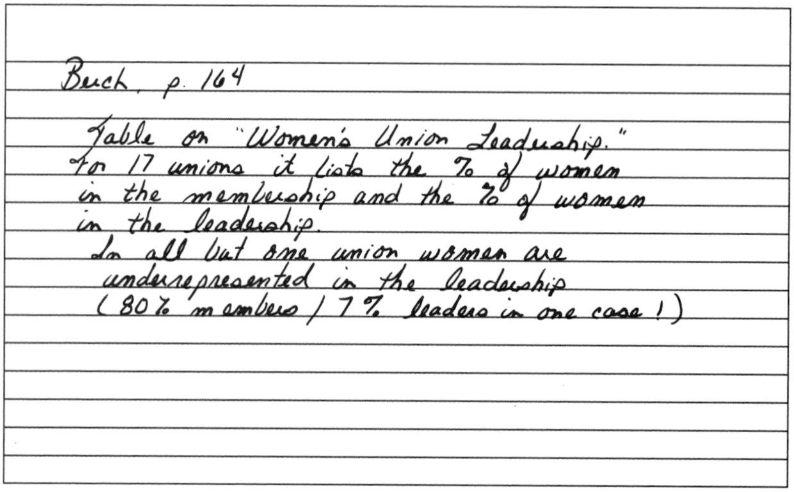

Berch, p. 164

Table on "Women's Union Leadership."
For 17 unions it lists the % of women
in the membership and the % of women
in the leadership.
In all but one union women are
underrepresented in the leadership
(80% members / 7% leaders in one case!)

© 2013 Cengage Learning

Even if you have a printout, it is valuable to go through the process of paraphrasing or quoting so you isolate and internalize the key points that drew you to the source in the first place.

If you decide now or later that the table mentioned in Figure 8.5 is valuable, you may want to photocopy it rather than tediously transcribe it by hand. If you photocopy lists, diagrams, tables, and other technical material, immediately head the sheet as you would an index card. Be certain to keep track of the bibliographic information for each and every source you utilize.

For each source, select a one- or two-word identification code that refers to that source and no other. Usually, the author's last name is sufficient: "Berch." If there is another book by Berch among your references, you may need to use "Berch, 2001" and "Berch, 2009." Or, if there are two sources from that author and year, you could use "Berch, *Endless Day*" and "Berch, *Work and Worth*." Or, of course, if you have different authors with the same last name, then "Berch, B." and "Berch, F."

If you copy entire articles or chapters, be sure to make a bibliography card for each. Many people find it helpful to photocopy the title page and copyright page of the book or periodical to make sure they have the title and year accurately recorded.

Index Cards from Interviews and Surveys

Make a bibliography card or some other notation for each interview, citing the person interviewed, his or her qualifications, the date of the interview, and the person's telephone number or address. As you listen to the voice recording or review your notes, consider transcribing the information onto cards.

Grouping Your Ideas

When you have gathered your information or index cards, you may want to organize them under categories such as "History," "Causes," and "Solutions." As you will see in Part **3** on organization, this grouping of ideas and naming of categories usually occurs later in the process of preparing your speech.

The Thesis Statement *section of Speech Builder Express can help you develop the categories you use to group your ideas.*

Review, Reconsider, & Act

Summary

We focused on how to build speech content through careful research. This stage starts with a clear and efficient research strategy that will allow for both a broad scope of the topic and a thorough understanding of the material within the time allotted. Regardless of where the information comes from, content must be credible, captured in a way that will allow for the creative process to flow, and recorded clearly so that we can cite your sources accurately in your speech.

Critical Thinking Questions

▶ What are the advantages and disadvantages of using a source like Wikipedia in the early stages of research?

▶ What are the advantages and disadvantages of local interviews as a source of information on a topic?

▶ Why is it important to carefully track your sources in the preparation stage of speech development?

Putting It into Practice

Think of a topic for a speech that you could give.

1. What are the most effective sources of content for your topic and audience situation?

2. Would experts, educators, public officials, or special interest groups be well received by your audience?

3. What level of citation within your speech is customary for this audience?

4. What would be the advantages of increasing the specificity of your source citations for this group?

Organization 3

PART 3
ORGANIZATION

introduction

Bringing Order to Your Ideas

Of the four phases of the creative process (described in Chapter **5**), most speech training emphasizes the logical, rule-bound processes of preparation and refinement. The middle two phases of incubation and illumination are rarely mentioned because they do not lend themselves to systematization. These middle steps touch the emotions. The process of creating a rap song, story, painting, melody, or speech can produce intense feelings of discouragement and excitement. This process is rarely straightforward and systematic. Even with adequate preparation, you can find yourself pacing the floor, staring into space, and filling your wastebasket with false starts. Rest assured you are not alone if this has happened to you.

In writing this book, we did not sit down at the computer, type the title *The Speaker's Handbook*, and then proceed unerringly through to the last page. The naming and arranging of categories took hours: Should practice be dealt with as an aspect of preparation? Can style be separated from content? Does the motivated sequence fit under patterns of organization or under motivational appeals? Even when we had settled on a general outline, we altered the details of that outline again and again as the actual writing progressed. At times, the topics seemed so interconnected that we felt we were trying to untangle a skein of yarn rescued from a marauding cat. Would it ever come out in one straight line?

This frustration is an inherent part of the creative process. When you have read only one article on a topic, it is easy to write a summary of it. But when you have researched and analyzed a topic fully, you begin to suffer from information overload. First, you are overwhelmed by the amount of information; second, you see so many connections among the facets of the topic that you have trouble dividing it. This frustration is a sign you have gone beyond the "book report" stage and are imposing your own creative structure on the topic. Keep in mind that by experiencing this frustration and struggling until you have developed conceptual clarity, you are saving your audience from the agony of information overload.

The analysis and synthesis of information have appropriately been called *invention*. *Analysis* is the taking apart of a topic, a process that follows specified rules. *Synthesis* is the remolding of the parts into a new whole—truly creating or inventing an interpretation that did not exist before. There are no set rules for synthesis. Although many people can collect the same information and divide a topic into certain logical parts, no two people will prepare the same speech. The synthesis you create reflects your own personality, values, and perspective.

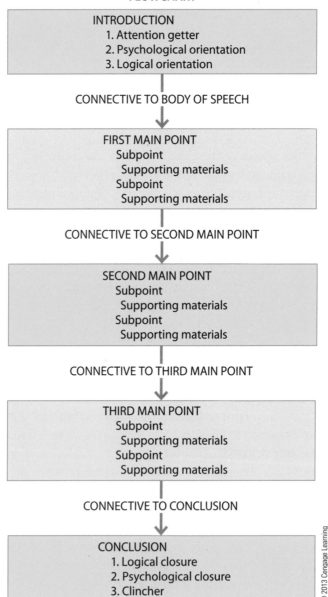

**SPEECH STRUCTURE
FLOWCHART**

INTRODUCTION
1. Attention getter
2. Psychological orientation
3. Logical orientation

CONNECTIVE TO BODY OF SPEECH

FIRST MAIN POINT
Subpoint
Supporting materials
Subpoint
Supporting materials

CONNECTIVE TO SECOND MAIN POINT

SECOND MAIN POINT
Subpoint
Supporting materials
Subpoint
Supporting materials

CONNECTIVE TO THIRD MAIN POINT

THIRD MAIN POINT
Subpoint
Supporting materials
Subpoint
Supporting materials

CONNECTIVE TO CONCLUSION

CONCLUSION
1. Logical closure
2. Psychological closure
3. Clincher

Once you've done all this work, you can put the pieces together in an organization that connects the information and presents it in a coherent and compelling flow. (See the Speech Structure Flowchart.)

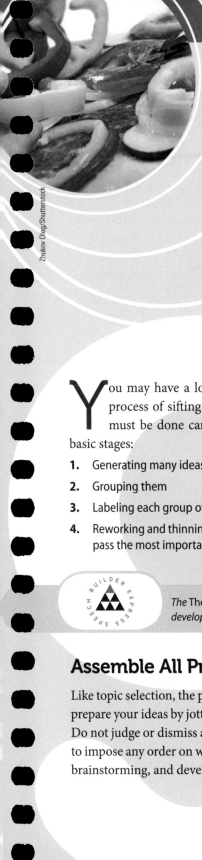

chapter 9

Transforming Ideas into Speech Points

Look for logical groupings of ideas that could be developed as main points and subpoints of your speech.

You may have a lot of good ideas, but prioritizing them can be difficult. The process of sifting through all the ideas and establishing a satisfactory pattern must be done carefully and thoughtfully. The process of organizing has four basic stages:

1. Generating many ideas
2. Grouping them
3. Labeling each group of ideas
4. Reworking and thinning out the ideas until you have two to five major groups that encompass the most important ideas and that can be developed in your allotted time

The Thesis Statement *section of Speech Builder Express can help you develop, limit, and organize the main ideas related to your thesis.*

Assemble All Promising Ideas and Information

Like topic selection, the process of assembling ideas begins with brainstorming. Start to prepare your ideas by jotting down every item you might possibly cover in your speech. Do not judge or dismiss any idea, but instead write them all down. There is no need yet to impose any order on what you are writing. Work quickly, following the techniques of brainstorming, and develop quantity rather than quality at this point.

Use a Variety of Tools to Identify Potential Points

Review the brainstorming list you made and consider how you might cluster the entries. Are there any that stand out as possible main points? Are there any that seem to fit together? Are there any that are naturally subordinate to others?

There is no one correct way to group these ideas. Some ideas will be omitted altogether, and others will have to be forced to fit into a category. You may notice that the points in one group are not of equal importance. Sometimes, one or more of the ideas from your brainstorming list can serve as a category around which to group lesser points. Other times, you will group several minor ideas and then try to figure out the category.

You can use a number of different techniques to begin your organization. You can use only one, or you can use a combination that suits how you work best, either textually or visually.

Create a Working Outline

Perhaps the most traditional technique of speech organization is to arrange ideas in the hierarchical, indented outline format. At this early stage of development, however, you do not want to be constrained by the requirements of the formal *full-sentence outline.* (See Chapter 11.) The full-sentence outline will be important later in helping you elaborate points and subpoints, but a less rigid form, the topic outline, is more useful now. A **topic outline** uses words or phrases to identify the essential points a speech will cover. Complete examples of both types of outlines are shown in Chapter 11; however, an excerpt from that topic outline is shown here to provide an immediate example.

Topic Outline

Topic: The History of Working Women in the United States

I. Preindustrial

   A. Colonial women

      1. Soap

      2. Clothing

   B. Frontier women

      1. Indian attacks

      2. Farmwork

II. Increased industrialization to Civil War

   A. Women in factories

      1. Smaller hands suited to weaving

      2. One dollar per week, less lodging

B. First union attempts

    1. 1824

    2. Lady Shoe Binders, Lynn, Massachusetts

Because you are likely to experiment with several different groupings of ideas, don't spend time on phrasing or format. Just try to fit ideas under one another, nesting them in various ways until you discover the pattern that seems to make the most sense.

If the topic outline is a comfortable method for you, you will have a head start on developing the full-sentence outline. However, even this loose form of outlining may be premature if it blocks your thought processes. Next, we describe other, more spatially oriented ways you can collect your thoughts.

Use Concept Mapping

Concept mapping is a visual method of showing how your ideas relate to each other. In its most basic form, you quickly draw a simple diagram made of labeled circles and squares, connecting them with lines.

Starting with your central idea—your topic—write it in a box or circle in the center of a sheet of paper. Based on your brainstorm, jot some major ideas around the topic, leaving enough room to add more subpoints. As you write down each new idea, draw a line to connect it to its related point. This doesn't have to be done hierarchically, however. Subpoints might come to you before a broader point does. You can redraw as relationships become clear.

A variety of styles exists for doing this, under the names of *clustering, mindmapping, branching,* and *ballooning.* Figure 9.1 shows a simple concept map. (This led to the comic book outline you'll find in Chapter **10**.)

Manipulate Movable Notes

You can manipulate notes spatially or linearly. For example, you can jot down your ideas on sticky notes and stick them to a wall or desktop. Cluster the ideas according to themes, moving items from group to group until you are happy with the organization. (You can also group your research note cards under subject cover cards, which was suggested in Chapter **8**). You can write ideas, connectives, and syntheses on additional sticky notes or cards and plug them in where you think they fit. These two paper-based approaches can also be duplicated on a computer, using the simple outlining function of word processing software or specialized idea development software. You can find one example of idea development software at MindMeister.com.

By beginning with a brainstorm, you will have a set of potential points for your speech. The next step is to choose the points that work best for your audience and purpose.

FIGURE 9.1
Simple concept map

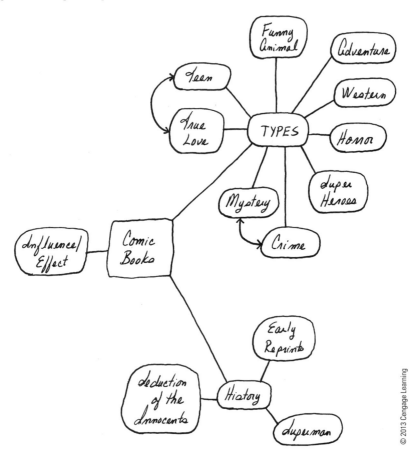

© 2013 Cengage Learning

Choose Main Points That Correspond to Your Thesis

Main points are primary ideas, those that are central and indispensable to the development of the thesis. To decide which main points to include in your speech, first look at your general purpose, specific purpose, and thesis statement. Follow the steps discussed in Chapter **6** to identify the essential questions you must answer for your thesis. For persuasive speeches that develop propositions of fact, value, or policy, consult Chapter **22** for information on how to identify the essential questions with more precision. Once you know what a complete development of your topic requires, use the thesis statement as a standard against which to test your main points. Ask yourself these two questions:

1. Is there any part of my thesis that is not developed in the speech?
2. Is there any main idea of the speech that is not reflected in my thesis?

To see how this works, look at the following thesis and main points:

Thesis statement: The jojoba plant is an effective energy source capable of eliminating US dependence on foreign oil.

A. The jojoba plant is a virtually untapped source of energy.
B. Energy can be produced from the jojoba plant efficiently and safely.
C. Given an adequate educational program, the public would come to accept jojoba plant energy.

Obviously, something is missing. Either the thesis should be changed by deleting "capable of eliminating US dependence on foreign oil," or another main point should be added to establish that jojoba plant energy has that ability.

The following set of main points corresponds exactly to the thesis statement; nothing essential is missing, and nothing superfluous is included:

Thesis statement: The jojoba plant is an effective energy source capable of eliminating US dependence on foreign oil.

A. The jojoba plant is a virtually untapped source of energy.
B. The jojoba plant is a safe, efficient, and marketable source of energy.
C. The jojoba plant could create sufficient energy to eliminate US dependence on foreign oil.

Sometimes, you may need to adjust your thesis to reflect the refinement of your ideas that resulted from the organizing process. Such changes are acceptable so long as your resulting thesis still fulfills the purpose and other requirements established for the situation.

© geopaul / iStockphoto 3620311

Speaker's Workshop 9.1

Do the main points correspond to their thesis statements in the following two examples? If not, rewrite the main points or the thesis so that they correspond.

Thesis statement: A four-day workweek would be beneficial to our company, our employees, and our community.

I.   The company will benefit from increased productivity.

II.   Employees will enjoy longer weekends.

III. The community will benefit from reduced carbon emissions and rush-hour traffic.

Thesis statement: Skateboarders are discriminated against wherever they ride.

I.   Public facilities have "No Skateboarding" signs.

II.   Skateboarders are needlessly harassed by private property owners.

III. Skateboarding is a difficult sport that encourages agility and physical fitness.

Select Main Points That Are Mutually Exclusive

Sometimes, when you are grouping ideas under potential main points, you will find that many fit into two or more categories. When this overlapping occurs, you know you have not yet found an effective system for classifying your ideas. For maximum clarity, the ideas in your main points should be mutually exclusive. Settling on a single organizational pattern is essential. If you do not know where an idea fits, your audience certainly will not. If you were unsure of your pattern, the result might be an outline like this:

Topic: Great Films

I. Action

    A. *Saving Private Ryan* (1998)

    B. *The Lord of the Rings: The Return of the King* (2003)

    C. *Avatar* (2009)

II. Science fiction

    A. *The Matrix* (1999)

    B. *Iron Man* (2008)

    C. *Inception* (2010)

III. Black-and-white

    A. *Stagecoach* (1939)

    B. *Citizen Kane* (1941)

    C. *Raging Bull* (1980)

A quick look shows that this speaker began to lay out the structure of the speech before thinking through the topic completely. Apparently, the speaker was unable to decide whether the discussion on film should be by dramatic category or by color or the lack of it. Whether a movie was shot on color or black-and-white stock has no intrinsic relationship to genre. These three main points—action, science fiction, and black-and-white—are not parallel categories.

Ideally, if you have mutually exclusive main points, you will know how to classify any film and list it under one point only. If we put the sample outline to the test, however, we encounter uncertainty. *Lord of the Rings* could fit not only under "Action" but also under "Science fiction." So, although each main point by itself seems a plausible way to classify movies, the three main points taken together do not constitute a sensible way to look at the topic.

Here is another example of an outline on the same topic:

Topic: Great Films

I. Black-and-white

    A. Drama

        1. *Stagecoach* (1939)

        2. *Citizen Kane* (1941)

        3. *The Manchurian Candidate* (1962)

        4. *Raging Bull* (1980)

    B. Comedy

        1. *The General* (1927)

        2. *Bringing Up Baby* (1938)

        3. *Some Like It Hot* (1959)

        4. *A Hard Day's Night* (1964)

II. Color

    A. Drama

        1. *The Adventures of Robin Hood* (1938)

        2. *Rear Window* (1954)

        3. *The Shawshank Redemption* (1994)

        4. *Fight Club* (1999)

    B. Comedy

        1. *Singin' in the Rain* (1952)

        2. *Monty Python and the Holy Grail* (1975)

        3. *The Princess Bride* (1987)

        4. *Toy Story 3* (2010)

Here, the topic is divided into main points along a single dimension: color or lack of it. These two main points are each divided into the same two subpoints.

FOR YOUR BENEFIT: **Tailor Main Points for Your Audience and Situation**

When you are faced with decisions about which point(s) to cover in a speech, the decision must come back to questions of audience. Exclude points that have limited interest to your audience. Focus on main points that are essential issues for the people you will be addressing. That means you may need to make adjustments when giving a speech to different audiences. For instance, if your job requires you to inform plant employees about upcoming health care changes, the issues of importance to members of the day shift might be very different from the issues of the night shift members. Your choice of main points should be adjusted accordingly. Items not covered in your speech might be introduced in a question-and-answer period.

Rtimages / www.BigStockPhoto.com

This same topic could be organized in many other ways. For example, the main points might be organized chronologically, topically, or spatially. (Additional organization patterns are discussed in Chapter **10**.) For instance, a speech about award-winning movies could be organized by when they were made, who directed them, or where they were filmed.

Include Two to Five Main Points

Although this rule sounds arbitrary, it is not as unreasonable as you might think. As a speaker, you should be able to cluster your ideas around a few main themes. Your audience is unlikely to remember more than few main points. So gather a few of the most relevant points (main points) and support them with examples, statistics, or testimony and avoid the perception of an unorganized barrage of information.

Express Points to Reflect Relationships

Ideas of equal importance are called coordinate points. Points of lesser significance that support, explain, or contribute steps of logical development to other ideas are called subordinate points. Points of greater significance are called superordinate points. The relative importance of the various points must be very clear in your mind. Every point in the speech is subordinate, coordinate, or superordinate to every other.

If you were to classify methods of transporting goods, you might come up with a list like this one:

Transportation of Goods

Trains

Trucks

Airplanes

Ships

In this example, the modes of transportation (trains, trucks, airplanes, ships) have a coordinate relationship to each other, and they all have a subordinate relationship to the larger, or superordinate, category of "Transportation of Goods."

Each mode of transportation, in turn, may have more specific divisions:

Types of Trucks

Tractors

Vans

Dump trucks

Tankers

Flatbeds

Here, each type of truck bears a subordinate relationship to the larger category of "Types of Trucks" and a coordinate relationship to each other.

Logical relationships can also be shown through subordination and coordination, as in this example:

> **Trucks are an efficient means of transporting goods.**
>
> [*because*] They have a wide network of destinations.
>
> [*because*] They have great versatility of design.
>
> [*and because*] They are relatively cheap to operate.

It is evident that the reasons are subordinate to the points they establish.

Subordinate Points Should Fit within a Larger Idea

Sometimes, ideas that are too big for the points they are intended to support can slip in. Consider the following example from a speech on the role of aircraft carriers in World War II, and think about the fit of these points.

I. Aircraft carriers were instrumental in winning the war in the Pacific.

　A. The successful use of aircraft carriers at the battles of the Coral Sea and Midway blunted the Japanese drive across the Pacific.

　B. Planes launched from aircraft carriers were able to inflict damage on enemy bases out of the range of land-based aircraft.

　C. Antisubmarine warfare was instrumental to winning the war in the Atlantic.

In this case, subpoint C is not related to the major idea, nor is it subordinate in importance. The use of antisubmarine warfare in the Atlantic does not belong under the use of aircraft carriers in the Pacific. The two ideas bear a coordinate relationship, and the statement in subpoint C should probably be main point II.

Coordinate Points Should Be of Equal Importance

Occasionally, an idea is too small to fit with the others at its level. In the following outline, the subpoints are not coordinate:

I. Aircraft carriers were instrumental in winning the war in the Pacific.

　A. The successful use of aircraft carriers at the battles of the Coral Sea and Midway blunted the Japanese drive across the Pacific.

　B. A number of new aircraft carriers were named after carriers sunk earlier in the war.

　C. Planes launched from aircraft carriers were able to inflict damage on enemy bases out of the range of land-based aircraft.

Notice how subpoint B stands out when compared to the other two subpoints. There may have been some initial benefit from the confusion that such naming caused among the intelligence services of the Japanese, but it was hardly "instrumental."

If you have one main idea that seems much less important than the other(s), omit it altogether, or create another main point so that this less important idea can become a subpoint, or mention the idea only as part of the introduction or conclusion. You might also occasionally consider a catchall main point, such as "There are several other factors . . . ."

Each Subpoint Should Directly Relate to the Point It Supports

Do not group unrelated subpoints, as was done here:

   I. Aircraft carriers were instrumental in winning the war in the Pacific.

      A. The successful use of aircraft carriers at the battles of the Coral Sea and Midway blunted the Japanese drive across the Pacific.

      B. The F4F fighter was redesigned to have folding wings so that aircraft carriers could carry more planes.

      C. Planes launched from aircraft carriers were able to inflict damage on enemy bases out of the range of land-based aircraft.

Subpoint B is interesting and may be appropriate as a subpoint somewhere in this speech, perhaps supporting a superordinate point about steps taken to make the carrier force more efficient. Clearly, though, subpoint B has no *direct* relationship to the point about the war in the Pacific.

Check out Speech Studio to see how other students handled their main points. Do their main points correspond to their thesis statements? Are they mutually exclusive? How many points did they include? Do their points reflect relationships? Or record a speech you're working on, upload it to Speech Studio, and ask your peers for their feedback. What feedback could you use to fine tune your main points before you give your speech in class?

Review, Reconsider, & Act

Summary

In this chapter we have discussed brainstorming and concept mapping as two tools useful in the development of ideas for the content of a speech. Movable notes and topic outlines, created with brief words or phrases, can be a flexible, helpful way of testing out various organizational strategies during the speech. When selecting main points, you should take care to ensure that they match your thesis and that they are mutually exclusive, limited in number, and worded to reveal coordinate, subordinate or superordinate relationships.

Critical Thinking Questions

▶ What would you do if you found your main points didn't fit your thesis?

▶ How does understanding the effort required to transform ideas into main points change the way you will prepare your next speech?

▶ How might mind-mapping software or the sticky-note technique simplify the process of preparing your speech?

Putting It into Practice

Write the thesis for an informative speech to be given where you work or volunteer.

1. Brainstorm the main points for the speech thesis you have written.

2. Check to ensure that your main points correspond to your thesis and adjust if necessary.

3. Review your main points. Are they clear? Are the coordinate points of equal importance?

4. Consider how you could order your main points for your particular audience and situation?

chapter 10
Organizing Points

When you organize your points, consider the traditional patterns of speech organization and select the one that is best suited to your topic and purpose.

O nce the main ideas of a speech are selected, you need to arrange them in the order that will maximize effectiveness. In some cases, the decision is virtually made for you. For an argument to seem logical to an audience, the premises must unfold in a certain order, as is explained in Chapter **16**. Debate speeches or closing arguments to juries, for example, have such strict requirements that they almost always unfold according to stock issues, as shown in Chapter **22**. Many ceremonial or special occasion speeches are so stylized that they follow a formula. (See Chapter **33**.) We can expect a commencement speaker to begin by congratulating the graduates and their parents, and then to posit a challenge for the future. We can anticipate that at a retirement dinner, the speaker will begin by summarizing the honoree's achievements and then speculate humorously about the honoree's coming leisure time. But for the usual informative, invitational, or persuasive speech, there is no given pattern. You, as a speaker, must select the best arrangement of ideas.

The Organization *section of Speech Builder Express can help you choose an arrangement pattern that presents your main ideas effectively, is appropriate for your speech's goal and purpose, and supports your thesis.*

Arrange Your Main Points

There are several traditional patterns of speech organization: chronological, spatial, cause–effect, problem–solution, and topical.

Using Chronological Patterns

Probably the most ancient form of extended discourse is the narrative unfolding of a story. Many contemporary speeches still follow this time-ordered format. *Historical* development is the most common **chronological pattern**. If you were giving a speech on the influences of early rock music, you might arrange it this way:

I. Rhythm and blues (1940s–1950s)

II. Rockabilly (mid-1950s)

III. British Invasion (1960s)

For another example, look at the outline on women workers in Chapter **11**.

Another chronological pattern divides a topic into *past–present–future*. In a speech on automobile propulsion, you might arrange your ideas in this manner:

I. In the days of cheap oil, auto engines did not need to be energy efficient.

II. Today, fossil fuel costs have risen, creating a demand for more efficient hybrid vehicles.

III. Future projects suggest that alternative power sources may soon replace fossil fuel-burning engines altogether.

A third way to look at a subject chronologically is to analyze a process *step by step*. The topic "How to repair a hole in drywall" could generate this outline:

I. Gather materials, including a tin can lid, string, a small stick or pencil, patching compound, and tools.

II. Punch holes in the lid and place string through the holes.

III. Holding the string, place the tin can lid inside the wall and position it behind the hole, tie the string to a pencil or a small stick, and twist until solidly in place.

IV. Fill the hole with plaster, let dry, add a finish coat, let dry, and sand until smooth.

Using Spatial Patterns

The **spatial pattern** of speech organization arranges points according to the relationships among physical locations, and is often based on geography. This can be global geography or the geography of the two blocks around your house:

Topic: Afghanistan occupation zones

I. Northern zone

II. Central zone

III. South central zone

IV. Southern zone

Other geographically organized speeches might look at troop deployment in Europe, Asia, Africa, and Latin America.

Geography is not only areas on a map but also other spatial divisions of society:

Topic: Schools

I.   Rural schools

II. Urban schools

III. Suburban schools

Spatial organization can also be applied to smaller areas, such as the floor plan of a house or the arrangement of a library. The following example of a spatial pattern describes a very small area indeed:

Topic: An Aircraft Instrument Panel

I.   Instruments needed to maintain controlled flight are on the left side of the panel.

   A. Compass

   B. Altimeter

   C. Artificial horizon

   D. Turn and bank indicator

   E. Air speed indicator

II. Instruments providing information on the operating condition of the aircraft are on the right side.

   A. Tachometer

   B. Manifold pressure gauge

   C. Oil temperature gauge

   D. Oil pressure gauge

   E. Fuel gauge

Using Cause–Effect Patterns

This pattern is used to show that events that occur in sequence are, in fact, causally related. A **cause–effect** pattern is well suited to a speech in which the goal is to achieve understanding or agreement rather than overt action, as here:

I.   The recent economic recession has decreased housing values in many communities.

II. [*This is the result.*] Real estate prices have dropped to record lows in many areas, making it a good time to buy some properties.

Occasionally, the pattern may be reversed to an effect–cause sequence:

I.   Mortgage rates and housing prices are at record lows

II. [*This is the cause.*] There has been a sharp drop in home values.

Of course, when using the cause–effect pattern, you must be sure the causal relationship you propose is a valid one. (See Chapter **16**.)

Using Problem–Solution Patterns

The problem–solution pattern begins with a topic of concern, and then explains how that concern can best be addressed. It is often used in persuasive speeches that advocate a new policy or a specific course of action, as in the following:

I. The current system of financing health care in the United States is inadequate.

II. [*This is the solution to that problem.*] A system of national health insurance would provide medical care to all citizens.

On rare occasions, speakers choose a solution–problem pattern:

I. A system of national health insurance would provide adequate medical care to all citizens.

II. [*That is the way to solve the following problem.*] The current system of financing health care in the United States is inadequate.

This pattern tends to be weak both stylistically and psychologically because most audiences will resist accepting a proposed change before hearing why the change is needed.

Using Topical Patterns

This is the most frequently used speech pattern. It is also the most difficult in that you must understand the range and limitations of the subject in order to select an effective topical pattern. This pattern consists of simply developing each topical area in turn, with no implication that these points have a specific logical relationship or a relationship in time or space. Some topics obviously fit a time or space sequence; many subjects, however, do not lend themselves readily to any of the arrangements discussed so far. In these cases, you need to generate an original system for structuring the speech. Because a pattern intrinsic to one subject will not work with another, the application of any topical pattern you select will be unique to that one speech.

Often, the best structure for a speech is a list of the components of a whole or a list of reasons that add up to the thesis. The following is an example of a topical pattern that lists reasons for a conclusion:

Thesis statement: Capital punishment should be abolished.

I. Capital punishment does not deter crime.

II. Capital punishment is ultimately more costly than life imprisonment.

III. The risk of executing an innocent person is morally unacceptable.

Sometimes, topical patterns combine aspects of other organizational patterns. For instance, a *cause* leads to an *effect*, which is seen as a *problem* that requires a *solution*. Here's an example:

I. Children watch a great deal of television.

II. [*Therefore*] Children are not developing skills in reading and creative play.

III. [*And this is a problem; so, to remedy it*] Parents should limit children's viewing time.

Other topics easily suggest their own arrangements, such as grouping the pros and cons on a controversial issue or answering questions that have been laid out checklist style by some expert on your subject.

Check out Speech Studio to see how other students organized their speeches. Or record a speech you're working on, upload it to Speech Studio, and ask your peers for their feedback. What feedback could you use to fine tune your speech's organization before you give your speech in class?

For more ideas about how to organize speeches, go to your CourseMate for The Speaker's Handbook *and access* **WebLink 10.1**. *In addition to organizing speeches according to the patterns described in this book, you can organize by an acronym, by opinions, by storylines, and more.*

When you are building a speech that supports a controversial thesis, as in most persuasive speeches, arranging your main points is more complex than merely choosing a pattern. Your speech will consist of an *argument* for your thesis, and the main points may be parts of that argument or may be a series of smaller arguments that add up to your overall conclusion. You have important decisions to make about how best to lead your audience through your reasoning pattern. For an unfavorable audience (see Chapter 7), this requires spelling out every step of the process. Besides these logical considerations, you also may need to think about the psychological impact you are attempting to create. See Chapters **15** and **22** for discussions of these advanced organizational patterns.

Speaker's Workshop 10.1

1. By generating separate sets of main points, show how each of these topics could be presented in three different organizational patterns:
   ▸ Smoke-free laws
   ▸ National parks
   ▸ Racial discrimination in the United States
   ▸ Fundamentalism in Christianity and Islam
   ▸ Cajun cooking

2. Which patterns are used in the speeches "No More Sugar!" by Hans Erian, "The 54th Massachusetts" by Nathanael Dunlavy, and "The Four Ways Sound Affects Us" by Julian Treasure? You can find these speeches in Part 7 and in your CourseMate for *The Speaker's Handbook*.

Group Subpoints According to a Pattern

After your main ideas are set, look at the subpoints under each. These, too, need to be arranged in an effective order. You do not have to repeat the pattern you used for the main points; you can choose the format that makes the most sense for each set of subpoints. Notice the different arrangements of subpoints in the following detailed outline, whose main points are organized topically.

Thesis statement: With their scope, history, and influence, comic books are an interesting component of American popular culture.

I. Comic books are not merely "comic," but rather explore a range of subject matter.

Topical

  A. Funny-animal comics and kid comics are parables and parodies of the human condition.

    1. Elmer Fudd and Bugs: Tradition versus the pioneering spirit.

    2. Barks's ducks: Epic adventure and human foibles.

    3. Harvey's rich kids: Capitalism with a human face.

  B. Western and adventure comics concentrate on the triumph of good over evil.

    1. Western cattle barons learn that saviors slinging six-guns arise naturally from oppressed common folk.

    2. Adventure stories pit virtuous types against the blind malice of uncaring Nature.

  C. Horror and mystery comics investigate ethics and morality while titillating and scaring readers.

    1. Eternal punishment for an unethical choice is a recurring theme of horror comics.

    2. The tempting hedonism of wrongdoers is graphically displayed in mystery comics—until the ironic twist of fate on the last page.

  D. Superhero comics manifest the unspoken and sometimes frightening fantasies and aspirations of the American people.

    1. Superman is the supremely powerful spokesperson and law enforcer for the American definition of the "right way."

    2. The jackbooted hero Blackhawk was created in World War II to fight totalitarian fire with fire.

    3. Mar-Vell personifies the desire for total knowledge and the wisdom needed to use it.

    4. Spider-Man is the embodiment of the perennial underdog triumphant.

II. Comic books started as anthologies of another medium but soon grew into a separate art form developing along a path of its own.

Chronological

  A. Early comic books were mostly reprints of Sunday newspaper comic strip sections.

    1. "Foxy Granpa" was reprinted in a number of comic books just after the turn of the century.

    2. The following decades saw strips like "Mutt and Jeff," "Little Orphan Annie," and "Moon Mullins" reprinted.

Chronological

3. Reprint books in the 1930s included titles such as "Tarzan" in *Tip Top Comics* and "Terry and the Pirates" in *Popular Comics*.

B. By 1938, the majority of comic books contained original work, and, with the appearance of Superman, the golden age of comics began.

1. *Detective Comics* was the first single-theme, all-original comic.

2. Superman, the first costumed superhero, was featured in *Action* no. 1.

3. More than 150 titles were in print by the end of 1941.

C. By the late 1950s, comic books had started to overcome their tarnished image.

1. In creating the Comics Code Authority, publishers hoped to reassure worried parents and legislators.

2. The silver age of comics began with the reintroduction of long-dormant golden-age characters.

D. In the early 1990s the trend toward darker storylines grew, the effects of which were eventually felt in the other comic genres.

1. Darkness and nihilism was manifested in DC's production of "A Death in the Family," in which Batman's sidekick Robin is murdered by the Joker.

2. Comic books and graphic novels became accepted by a wider, more literate adult audience.

3. Concern with ethical and even political questions became more evident in cartoons and graphic novels.

III. Comic books have an effect beyond their entertainment value.

Cause–Effect

A. Comic books are a unique and vigorous art form.

1. Comic books have developed exciting and innovative methods for transcending the static nature of the panel format (series of distinct pictures across and down the page) to produce a sense of motion and drama.

2. The art of comics is not confined to the work within a single panel, but also touches the arrangement of panels on a page.

B. [*As a result*] Comic books have influenced other media.

1. Many filmmakers' use of split screens and quick cuts demonstrates a stylistic adaptation of the comic panel format.

2. The 2010 Universal Studios movie Scott Pilgrim vs. the World is based on the graphic novel series Scott Pilgrim by Canadian cartoonist Bryan Lee O'Malley.

C. [*Also as a result*] Comic books are in demand with collectors.

1. Some issues of rare comics can bring prices in the thousands of dollars.

2. Every year there are many large conventions around the United States where comics can be bought, sold, and traded.

Speaker's Workshop 10.2

Identify which organizational pattern Megan Soileau uses in her speech, available through your CourseMate for *The Speaker's Handbook*. Would you call this a well-organized speech? Why or why not?

YOUR
NEW
CAREER

FOR YOUR BENEFIT: Organizational Patterns Are Handy Devices

Organizational patterns are useful far beyond giving a speech. These same organizational schemes can be used to clarify events, policy papers, and all nature of public and private writing. Even short impromptu speeches require structure and an organizational pattern provides the necessary structure allowing listeners to more easily comprehend and remember your ideas. The topical pattern is highly flexible while the problem-solution is selling an idea.

Review, Reconsider, & Act

Summary

A speech's main points can be organized in a variety of organizational patterns, including the topical, chronological, spatial, cause–effect, and problem–solution patterns. The appropriate organizational pattern depends on what will best help the speaker inform, invite, persuade, or inspire the audience regarding a particular topic.

Critical Thinking Questions

▶ How would you arrange a speech addressing the equipment used in the game of lacrosse?

▶ What type of speech is a problem–solution format best suited for? Why?

▶ Why is topical organization the most frequently used organizational pattern?

▶ What makes the topical pattern both easy and difficult to use effectively?

Putting It into Practice

Read or watch Barack Obama's "Remarks on a Historic Revolution of Egypt," delivered on February 11, 2011. For easy access to this speech, go to your CourseMate for *The Speaker's Handbook* and click on **WebLink 10.2.**

1. How does Obama organize this speech?
2. Could it be organized another way?
3. What impact does Obama's speaking situation have on his choices of main points and the organization of those points?
4. How does Obama tailor the speech for this audience and situation?

Development **4**

PART 4
DEVELOPMENT

INTRODUCTION: SHAPING YOUR SPEECH

introduction
Shaping Your Speech

Rudyard Kipling, author of many popular story books, is quoted as saying that, "Words are, of course, the most powerful drug used by mankind." The next eight chapters deal with words and our ability to use them effectively with an ethical impact on our audience. Of all the choices you make as a speaker, by far the most important is how you will craft your message.

Too often, people think of a speaking assignment as a block of time to be filled instead of a chance to affect the people we care about positively. It is a powerful opportunity to make an impact on the lives of our audience. A seven-minute speech may not seem like a big deal until you consider that with an audience of twenty-five people you have been granted nearly three hours of human time. This view of the speaking situation dramatizes your opportunity and your responsibility.

Being entrusted with these precious hours of human time should motivate you to prepare extensively. You do not want to waste your listeners' time by underestimating their intelligence, stating the obvious, boring them, or taking twice as long as necessary to make a point. Remember, you are not doing all this work for a seven-minute result; you are getting set for three hours of potential influence.

Effective speakers invest considerable time not only in gathering compelling material, but also in designing an overall speech strategy. The word *strategy* may bring to mind the movement of armies by generals or secret game plans by football coaches, but in speech it carries none of the combative or manipulative connotations of these images. A speech strategy is only this: a master plan for combining your content with other elements of speaking to meet a certain goal.

Particularly when the goal is to inform or persuade, we believe that speakers, to show good faith, have an ethical obligation to respect the audience's interests as well as their own. Of course, speakers always have a purpose in speaking, but they should not abuse the power of the platform. Emotional appeals, loaded language, and personal charisma may mesmerize listeners, but their misuse would be unethical.

A good speech can be emotional, but it should never substitute emotion for reason. Supporting materials including definitions, examples, statistics, and expert testimony can be combined with emotional appeals, stories, and personal testimony for an effective balance of logic and emotion. When you presume to command people's time and attention, you owe it to them to know what you are talking about. Your message should be logical, factual, and coherent. Only after developing a sound, rational base should you move on to making the message personal and palatable.

chapter 15
Supporting Materials

Clarify and justify each of your points with
supporting materials through the use of
definitions, examples, statistics, and testimony.
Be sure these materials are varied, provide
sound evidence, and are smoothly integrated
into the speech.

After you have set up the basic structure of your speech, your next step is
selecting the materials—whether from your research or from your thinking—
that will make up its real substance. This process is similar to fleshing out a
sketch of a figure or adding the siding to the frame of a building. These supporting materials are crucial to the success of your speech. They are the "stuff" it is made of. They
may well determine whether your listeners characterize your statements as believable
or unbelievable, interesting or boring.

You can select the forms of support only after your basic structure is in place. It
is impossible to judge the appropriateness of supporting materials unless you are very
clear about what you are supporting. It is extremely important, as Chapters **6** (on topic
selection and analysis) and **9** (on transforming ideas) stress, that you measure every
component of your speech against a logical outline. If your point is that crime is on
the increase, then the story of a single crime, however graphic and compelling, is not
enough. To *support* your point, you need comparative data—examples collected from
at least two periods of time to establish a trend.

Supporting materials may take the form of clarification or of proof and can
include definitions, examples, statistics, or testimony. Often, especially in speeches to
inform or evoke, supporting materials clarify or expand on ideas. Supporting materials can also be used as evidence to support the claims you make in your speech.
Although it may be impossible ever to *prove* a point completely, we speak of supporting
materials as proof because they can serve to justify an idea, adding to the probability
of its acceptance. Frequently, a single piece of support, such as a statistic, functions

as both clarification and proof of a point. Some kinds of support, though, like hypothetical examples or definitions, can be used only as amplification; they never serve to prove anything. For a fuller discussion of methods for clarifying ideas, refer to Chapter **21** ("Informative Strategies"). For further advice on proving controversial claims, see Chapter **22** ("Persuasive Strategies").

Select the support for your ideas first on the basis of relevance, then on soundness, and then on interest value. By using a variety of supporting strategies, a speaker can avoid falling into the rut of relying exclusively on examples, testimony, or explanation.

Define Unfamiliar Words and Concepts

Does "regressive taxes" mean poor people pay more, or less? Does "left-brain function" refer to the logical or the creative side? And what does it mean to "deglaze the pan"? Speakers must be careful not to confuse audience members with the words they choose. One way to clarify the various terms you use in your speech is by using definitions, but there are different types of definitions you can use. Depending on your situation and the needs of your speech, consider using one or more of these types to clarify the terms you use.

Note that within Speech Builder Express, at the top of each screen, you'll find a search field with a link to an online dictionary (and a thesaurus), so you do not have to switch to another window or program to check definitions quickly while preparing a speech.

Logical Definition

Logical definition, also known as *dictionary definition*, has two steps. It first places the concept to be defined into a category; then it explains the characteristics that distinguish the concept from all other members of the category. For example:

ANTHROPOLOGY IS A . . .

| **Step 1: Category** | *. . . formal field of academic study that studies the human species . . .* | *[not a religion or a political system or a health food]* |
| **Step 2: Distinguishing characteristics** | *. . . as a whole to develop a comprehensive understanding of human nature and history.* | *[which differentiates it from physics, sociology, biology, psychology]* |

Etymological and Historical Definitions

One way you can explain a word's meaning to your audience is to explain how the word was derived, either as linked to some historical event (historical definition) or as drawn from root words in an older culture (etymological definition):

Historical

In 1880, Charles G. Boycott, an English land agent in Ireland, refused to reduce rents. In response, his tenants refused to pay them. The word *boycott* has entered the language to mean the act of refusing to engage in social or economic interaction with some entity, either to coerce or to express disapproval.

Etymological

Anthropology is drawn from the Greek *anthropos*, meaning "human being," and *ology*, meaning "the study of."

Operational Definition

One way to explain a term is to tell how the object or concept referred to works or operates, providing an operational definition. Such definitions may simply indicate the steps that make up a process:

▶ The *arithmetic mean* is what you get when you add up all the scores and divide by the number of scores.

▶ *Blogging* consists of writing an online journal or web-based log.

Social scientists use operational definitions to explain how conceptual terms are measured:

Returning to the anthropology example, you might define the field by telling what an anthropologist does:

▶ An *anthropologist* makes systematic observations about past or present human behavior and then synthesizes these observations into generalizations about human nature and history.

Definition by Negation or Opposition

Socrates said, "Nobody knows what justice is, but everyone knows what injustice is." In many cases, the best way to clarify a term is to explain what it is not, a practice known as definition by negation or opposition. Abstract notions such as fairness, clarity, and power can sometimes be better defined by describing actions that are unfair, relationships that are unclear, or people who are powerless. Reference to opposites can be used to explain concrete terms too:

▶ Hypoglycemia is something like the opposite of diabetes.

▶ Forensic anthropologists do not amass specialized data on a whim. They don't go digging for bones because they need the exercise.

This sort of definition can be powerful and intriguing. For a well-rounded picture, however, negation is best combined with other forms of definition.

© geopaul / iStockphoto 3620311

Speaker's Workshop 15.1

1. Use two different methods to define each of these terms:
   A. Eco-friendly
   B. Marriage
   C. Inflation
   D. Tachometer
   E. Sibling rivalry

2. Read or watch Harriet Kamakil speech on the Maasai people of Africa, available in Part 7 and through your CourseMate for *The Speaker's Handbook*. Identify at least four definitions she presents. How would you classify each definition? Are they effective?

Definition by Authority

This method of defining is useful for controversial or vague terms for which a choice must be made among plausible alternatives. When you use **definition by authority**, the arbiter of meaning becomes the person with the most credibility or the most power:

▶ I don't know what *you* mean by "a little late," but the boss says anything more than fifteen minutes goes on your record.

▶ Free speech cannot be suppressed unless a "clear and present danger" exists. The Supreme Court has defined it thus: "No danger flowing from speech can be deemed clear and present, unless the incidence of the evil apprehended is so imminent that it may befall before there is opportunity for full discussion.... Only an emergency can justify repression."

Definition by Example

Using a **definition by example** is a common and effective way to explain something by pointing at it, verbally or literally:

▶ When I talk about a charismatic leader, I mean someone like Raymond A. Kroc (founder of McDonald's), or Martin Luther King, Jr., Herb Kelleher (CEO of Southwest Airlines), Oprah Winfrey, or Estée Lauder.

▶ There are two basic ways to cause the strings of the guitar to vibrate: strumming, which sounds like this [strums], and picking, which sounds like this [picks].

Make Frequent Use of Examples

Few sentences perk up an audience better than "Now let me give you an example." Beyond the universal appeal of a good story, examples provide audience members with a chance to check their perceptions of a speaker's message. When concepts are linked to actual cases, the listeners can see if their images coincide with those of the speaker. As a speaker, you need to decide whether to use real examples or hypothetical ones and how long these examples should be.

Use Factual Examples

Factual examples rely upon facts. A *fact* is an assertion that is universally accepted. Sometimes, it is directly verifiable, as in "Elena Kagan is a justice of the Supreme Court." Even if you were not at the swearing-in, you could find plenty of sources to help you verify that this is a factual statement. "The earth is 93 million miles from the sun" is another assertion accepted as a fact although it is not *directly* verifiable through any of the five senses. But we accept it, because we know scientists have studied it and through calculations have arrived at the same answer. When you use such examples for explanation, it is essential that they be clear, relevant, and varied. When you use examples to prove a point, though, specific logical tests must be met. These tests are the essence of *inductive reasoning* as discussed in Chapter **16**.

Are Sufficient Examples Given?

To establish the point that high schools in your county are failing to teach basic literacy skills, it would not suffice to tell about one or two functionally illiterate graduates you know personally. The more examples you give, the less likely your listeners are to dismiss the phenomenon as the product of chance.

Are the Examples Representative?

Even if you gave a dozen examples of local graduates who are functionally illiterate, the conclusion would be suspect if all the cases were from one remedial class in one school. To be credible, examples should represent a cross section of students in the county from a variety of schools.

Are Negative Instances Accounted For?

When you reason by example, you must look into and account for dramatic negative examples. If your friend points out that her cousin was a National Merit Scholar or that test scores at Arbor Estates High School were above the national average, you might reconsider your conclusion about the failure of the schools. Perhaps the niece has an IQ of 175. Maybe Arbor Estates High School has a cadre of charismatic English teachers. Your obligation, if you wish to carry your point, is to show how these examples are atypical and why they should be excluded from a consideration of the general status of most students in most schools in the county.

Use Hypothetical Examples

Sometimes, when no factual example quite suits your purpose, or when you are speculating about the future, you might give a brief or extended hypothetical example. Here are two illustrations of *extended hypothetical examples.*

▶ Why should you get out of debt? Well, let's imagine that you have $1,000 worth of debt. If you pay only the minimum amount on a credit card with 18 percent interest, it would take you twelve years and $1,115 in interest fees to pay off the $1,000 debt.

▶ Picture a young woman—let's call her Katie—heading toward her car after working overtime. Because she's so tired, she doesn't hear the footsteps behind her until she's some distance from the building. Katie quickens her pace. . . .

Obviously, hypothetical examples cannot *prove* anything. They are useful for clarification because they can be tailored to fit the subject exactly. As such, hypothetical examples can be used to explain or supplement real examples, particularly if a real example is complex, a bit confusing, or doesn't quite illustrate the point you're trying to make.

Hypothetical examples do not have to be long. Here is a speech segment that uses three *brief* hypothetical examples in quick succession:

▶ What would happen if this tax law were to pass? Well, Miguel over there couldn't deduct his business lunches. Audrey wouldn't be able to depreciate her buildings. You, Tom, with kids about to start college . . .

As the previous example demonstrates, hypothetical examples allow you to bring the members of your audience into your speech. You'll find tips for designing your examples in Chapter **18**.

CHECKLIST ~ Tests of Factual Examples

☐ Are sufficient examples given?
☐ Are the examples representative?
☐ Are negative instances accounted for?

© laurent Renault / iStockphoto 14363693

FOR YOUR BENEFIT: Standpoint and Bias

YOUR NEW CAREER

Our standpoint can bias how we interpret the world around us. Because each of us sees the world from a different standpoint or perspective, sometimes that view biases what we see. If I attend my local football team's game and sit with the home team in the box seats, my view of the game will be far different than if I stand on the visitors side by the bench, or from the end zone with the band. Be sensitive to possible bias formed by your standpoint. If your examples imply that you see the world in terms of inaccurate stereotypes, some audience members will rightfully be offended. We live in a pluralistic and rapidly changing society, so examples including names, sexes, races, and roles should fully reflect that diversity.

Rtimages / www.BigStockPhoto.com

Speaker's Workshop 15.2

1. Read or watch the speech by Megan Soileau, available in Part 7 and through your CourseMate for *The Speaker's Handbook*. How many examples are used in this speech? Label each as brief or extended, and as factual or hypothetical.

2. Select one of these topics:
   Teenage suicide
   Media impact on elections
   Organ transplants

   Now develop an example in each of the following categories, and briefly explain in what sort of speech situation it would be most appropriate:
   A. Brief factual
   B. Extended factual
   C. Brief hypothetical
   D. Extended hypothetical

Use Appropriate Detail

When you use examples, you must decide how long or short to make each one. Examples in a speech can be kept brief when you can safely assume the audience already accepts them. To clarify an idea you might say, "The employee benefits manager handles all of the forms of reward that are not wages—including medical insurance, dental insurance, bonuses, profit-sharing plans, and company scholarships, for example." To prove a proposition, you could also point to familiar and accepted cases: "The 2012 presidential election will hinge on a few swing states, including Ohio, Michigan, and Pennsylvania, much like the elections of 2000, 2004, and 2008." But, obviously, these *brief factual examples* will not be effective with listeners who have never heard of profit sharing or who know nothing of prior presidential elections. In such cases, more detail will be needed.

When a succession of quick references will not illuminate a point for your listeners, develop the example into an illustration. Though these scenarios take time to develop, they create vivid images that might make the point with more emphasis than would shorter examples.

Use Statistical Evidence

When examples are systematically collected and classified, they are reported as statistics, the source of statistical evidence.

In the case of the literacy topic discussed earlier, it would not be feasible to discuss, by name, all the students who illustrate your point. It would simply take too much time to give

There are many excellent source of statistical information online. For example, you can find government statistics classified by topic, state, and agency at the website FedStats.gov. The website for the US Census provides all sorts of information about the US population, including statistics about ethnicity, employment, and geography. And the US Bureau of Justice website provides statistical information about crime, the courts, law enforcement, and more. You can go to your CourseMate for The Speaker's Handbook *to access these sites with* **WebLink 15.1** *(FedStats. gov),* **WebLink 15.2** *(census), and* **WebLink 15.3** *(crime statistics).*

enough examples to show the seriousness of the problem. This is when you turn to statistical evidence. By examining labor statistics, reviewing available data from state offices, or interviewing teachers, you could clarify and support your speech with material like this:

▶ Full-time workers age 25 and over without a high school diploma had median weekly earnings of $465, compared with $630 for high school graduates (no college) and $1,140 for those holding at least a bachelor's degree (Bureau of Labor Statistics).[1]

▶ Eighty percent of Ohio inmates are high school drop outs. Approximately 30 percent of the males and 20 percent of the females are considered functionally illiterate, reading at less than a sixth grade level (Ohio Department of Corrections).[2]

▶ Per year, 23,000 young adults drop out or complete school needing basic skills (Ohio Literacy Network).[3]

Test Accuracy of Statistical Evidence

Before you use a statistic, use the tests of who, why, when, and how.

Who Collected the Data?

Investigate the qualifications and competence of the researchers. Was the work done by a professional pollster or the host of a call-in radio show? A noted scholar or a graduate student? A government task force or an advertising agency?

Why Were the Data Collected?

Most people have more confidence in studies rooted in a desire to advance knowledge. Although not totally free of bias, independent pollsters, investigative journalists, scientists, and academics tend to be more objective than people committed to selling a product or promoting a cause. For example, statistics from research done by a political candidate's staff, purporting to show massive support for the candidate, may better reflect a need to demoralize the opposition than a need to show a true picture to the public.

When Were the Data Collected?

Be sure your evidence is up to date. Attitudes change as swiftly as prices, and some data are obsolete by the time they are published. If you are dealing with a continuously

CHECKLIST ~ Tests of Statistical Evidence

☐ Who collected the data?
☐ Why were the data collected?
☐ When were the data collected?
☐ How were the data collected?

active subject, like oil prices, it won't hurt to consult a credible resource for the most recent data.

How Were the Data Collected?

Find out as much as you can about the design of the research and the details of its execution. If a certain statistical finding supports an essential point of your speech, do not settle for a one-paragraph reference from Wikipedia. Track it back to the original source and learn more about the study.

First, compare definitions. You may find the title of the study promising, but a closer reading could show that the investigator defines important terms in ways that do not apply to your speech.

Next, check how the cases were chosen. Subjects and examples should have been selected randomly or through some other logical and unbiased system.

Finally, evaluate the method of data collection—observation, experiment, or survey conducted by phone, mail, or personal interview. If possible, look at the actual questionnaire used. Are there leading questions or unrealistic forced choices in the interviews and questionnaires? Even if you are not an expert, you can spot bias introduced into the research method—for example, through the phrasing of directions or the way the findings are analyzed and presented.

Avoid Misleading Statistics

We know language is ambiguous, but we tend to believe that numbers make straightforward statements; there is no mystery in $2 + 2 = 4$. However, numbers *can* be just as ambiguous, with statistical pitfalls to trap the unwary.

The Fallacy of the Average

A critic once said, with tongue in cheek, that a person could stand with one foot on a block of ice and one foot in a fire and be *statistically* comfortable. Although the average can be a useful tool for analysis, it sometimes gives a picture absurdly at odds with reality.

The *median* (the number or score that falls at the midpoint of the range of numbers or scores) or the *mode* (the most frequently occurring score or number) can be more

FIGURE 15.1
Sample graph showing median, mode, and mean

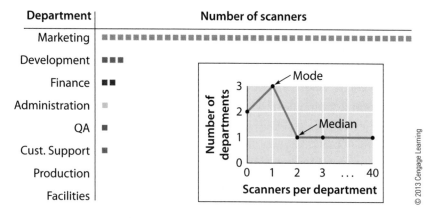

meaningful averages to use in some cases, although they, too, can be abused. See Figure 15.1 for a graphic representation of the scanner distribution in a fictitious company. In this case, although the *mean* is 6, the *median* is 2 (scores of 0 and 1 below it, scores of 3 and 40 above it), and the *mode* is 1 (the largest number of departments, three, have this score).

The Fallacy of the Unknown Base

When speakers use percentages and proportions, they can imply that a large population has been sampled. In fact, data are sometimes reported in this manner to give credence to unscientific or skimpy evidence: "Two out of three dentists recommend this whitening toothpaste." Most listeners would see this as shorthand for "We polled 300 dentists around the country, and 200 of them recommended this toothpaste." How valid would this recommendation seem if it came to light that in reality only *three* were polled?

Similarly, "Of all the crimes in this county, 80 percent were committed by teenagers" seems to point to a serious problem. It certainly has more impact than "We had five burglaries this year, and four were committed by teenagers." But four instances do not make a crime wave, and 80 percent is not necessarily an epidemic.

The Fallacy of the Atypical or Arbitrary Time Frame

An executive of a computer circuit board company told the authors of this book that sales in February were double those of the previous month. These data could be misleading unless you know that January is always the worst month in the yearly cycle of the computer industry. If the executive had compared February to November, the month in the cycle in which the pre-Christmas home computer and video game buying frenzy reaches its peak, then the picture would have been quite different. A more valid example to demonstrate company growth would have compared February with February of the previous year.

By choosing longer or shorter time frames, this executive could give varying spins on the company's health. If he chose November–December–January, with its downward trend, he might convince employees that this is no time to talk about raises. Or he might reassure stockholders by reporting a gradual but steady upward trend revealed by the figures from the last five Novembers.

Make Statistics Clear and Meaningful

The stereotypical dry, plodding speech is one that is overloaded with statistics. After a short while, the audience becomes overloaded too, and listeners start to build a mental dike against the numbers flowing over them. When you do use statistics, round them off. Say "about fifteen hundred" instead of "one thousand four hundred eighty-nine point six."

Use comparisons to make the numbers more understandable:

▶ For the amount of money they propose to spend on this weapons system, we could provide educational grants in aid to all the needy students in the eleven western states, or triple the government funding for cancer research, or upgrade the highway system in this state and its three neighbors.

Avoid overused comparisons. Too many dollar bills have been laid end to end and too many large objects have been improbably dumped onto football fields or placed next to the Empire State Building. Furthermore, audiences are no longer shocked to consider the "five people in this room" who will suffer some fate, or the dire toll of outside events that will be racked up "by the end of this speech" or "by the time I finish this sentence."

Speaker's Workshop 15.3

1. What additional information would you need to have before accepting the following statistical evidence?
   A. Studies show that over two thirds of the total meaning a person communicates is conveyed nonverbally.
   B. Of people who chew gum, four out of five surveyed prefer sugarless gum.
   C. Researchers have found that the average social drinker has eight serious hangovers a year.
   D. Dozens of cases of police harassment have been brought to my attention during my opponent's term of office.

2. Identify the use of statistical evidence as support in the speeches by Dianna Cohen, Hans Erian, and Kayla Strickland, available in Part 7 or through your CourseMate for *The Speaker's Handbook*. Which are used to clarify and which are used to prove controversial claims?
   Evaluate the statistical support according to the tests discussed in this section. Find examples of how the speakers made the statistics clear and meaningful.

For more on how to use statistics effectively, go to your CourseMate for The Speaker's Handbook *to access* **WebLink 15.4**. *The web page "Statistics Every Writer Should Know" explains the basic concepts of statistics in a way that's useful to writers and public speakers.*

Draw on Testimony from Authorities

Often, we call on statements from other people to get our point across. These statements, known as **testimony**, can be viewed as an outward extension of the speaker's own fact-finding. When we do not have the opportunity to verify something through our own senses, we rely on the observations of others. For instance, even if you have never had an accident due to distracted driving or never been a public safety officer, you can give a credible speech on the dangers of distracted driving by making thoughtful use of testimony.

It might be effective to share the words of a friend or colleague involved in a distracted driving incident. You can draw on eyewitnesses or on the authority of experts.

▶ Remembering his accident, Joe Jones said, "One second everything was fine and then next my bumper was buried in the back of the truck ahead of me. It all happened so fast. Until then I thought I could easily text and drive but now I won't do it. Messages will have to wait."

You can cite testimony directly or you can paraphrase it:

▶ **Direct quotation** David Strayer, Ph.D., director of the University of Utah's Applied Cognition Lab, said, "We directly compared drunk drivers and cell phone drivers and found that cell phones were every bit as bad, if not worse, as drunk driving."[4]

▶ **Paraphrase** Based on his study of distracted driving conditions, noted researcher David Strayer concluded that drivers are four times more likely to crash if they're talking on the phone while driving.[5]

Evaluate Credibility of Authorities

You do not have to research a controversial topic for very long before you find that there are seemingly authoritative quotations to support every side of an issue. It is easy to find citations that say almost anything; it is much more difficult to select those that provide legitimate support for your points. Test the credibility of the authorities you're considering quoting by asking whether the apparent authority has access to the necessary information, is qualified, is an expert on this subject, and is free of bias.

Does the Authority Have Access to the Necessary Information?

A person does not have to be famous to be an authority. The eyewitness to an accident can tell you authoritatively what happened in the intersection. Your neighbor does not have to be a Chinese diplomat to report on her trip to Beijing. The farther removed someone is from the source, however, the less trustworthy that person's information.

A quotation from the accident eyewitness is preferable to a quotation from an acquaintance recounting what the eyewitness said, but even eyewitness accounts can differ.

Ambiguous descriptions can be misleading. "My brother works for the government, and he says there's a massive conspiracy to cover up the cost overruns in the Defense Department" or "It is the opinion of a noted psychologist that the murderer is definitely insane" is testimony that loses its effect when we learn that the brother is a postal clerk and the psychologist has only read the newspaper accounts of the trial. When you use an authority, be sure that the person had firsthand experience, direct observation, or personal access to relevant facts and files.

Is the Authority Qualified to Interpret Data?

Anyone can credibly describe what she or he saw. It is when a person starts making interpretations, forming opinions and conclusions, and proposing recommendations that the standards of credibility become stricter. People earn the right to be considered experts either by holding specific credentials—such as a law degree, Ph.D., or Realtor's license—or by establishing a record of success and experience.

Is the Person Acknowledged as an Expert on This Subject?

Actor William Petersen (*CSI*) was featured in a public service announcement on behalf of Court Appointed Special Advocates (CASA) for children. Though his character, Gil Grissom, certainly is portrayed as having concern for children, does that make Petersen a qualified expert? There are other cases in which experts' opinions have subtly stretched beyond the range of their expertise. A tax attorney may be presented as an expert on constitutional law, a social psychologist may express an opinion on the causes of schizophrenia, or a well-known chemist may receive national attention for her or his views on the efficacy of vitamin C. The opinions they express may or may not be valid, but their expertise in a related field makes them, at best, only slightly more credible than an informed layperson.

Is the Authority Figure Free of Bias and Self-Interest?

It is not very surprising when the chair of the Democratic National Committee characterizes the party platform as a blueprint for justice and prosperity, or when a network spokesperson describes a new television season as "the most exciting line-up ever." Nor is it very persuasive. We give much more credence to the opinion of a political analyst or a television critic who appears to have no personal stake—ideological or financial—in the response to the opinion. What would be surprising, and highly persuasive as well, is reluctant testimony. If you can find testimony from a person speaking *against* his or her interests, presumably because of honesty or as a duty to a larger concept, then it certainly will be an effective addition to your presentation: "Even the National Committee chair admitted that the platform is fuzzy on foreign policy."

CHECKLIST ~ Tests of Testimony

- ☐ Does the authority have access to the necessary information?
- ☐ Is the authority qualified to interpret data?
- ☐ Is the person acknowledged as an expert on this subject?
- ☐ Is the authority figure free of bias and self-interest?

Don't Distort Quotations

Shortening quotations to highlight the basic thrust of the message is perfectly acceptable. What is unacceptable is editing a person's statements to such a degree that they appear to support positions other than or even opposite those espoused in the actual quotations.

Political candidates frequently criticize their opponents by citing portions of their statements on various issues. What results is an incomplete summary of a candidate's position on an issue. For instance, if a person were to say: "About the job-retraining program, the mayor has said that it 'is a disappointment.' The president of the Chamber of Commerce stated that it 'has not fulfilled our expectations.' The chair of the Council of Unions labeled it 'a failure.'" In this instance, although the people cited may be authorities on the subject, their reservations may arise from issues unrelated to the speaker's point. For instance, each may be criticizing the funding adequacy rather than the concept of the program. The program shortcomings may be impossible to discern from cryptic quotations. It is also possible that these experts could be wrong. Listeners need to hear the *why* of the experts' conclusions along with *what* they concluded.

Cite Sources Smoothly

When you have chosen appropriate definitions, facts, examples, statistics, and testimony, you still have to marshal these supporting materials and integrate them effectively. You want to emphasize the quality of your materials, make them clear and understandable, and incorporate them appropriately in relation to the points they support.

Speaker's Workshop 15.4

 Evaluate the credibility of the authorities cited in the persuasive speech by Hans Erian, available in Part 7 or through your CourseMate for *The Speaker's Handbook*. To what extent does it meet the tests discussed in this section?

Speech Builder Express provides a framework and prompts specifically designed to help you effectively incorporate supporting materials into your speech and to cite your sources within the Supporting Material and Works Cited sections of the program.

Cite Sources of Supporting Materials

By giving credit for, or *citing* the sources of, your supporting materials, you build your own credibility by showing the range of your research. You are also providing information your listeners are almost certain to want. Very few audiences will settle for "studies show . . . " or "one researcher found . . . " or "a friend once told. . . ." To evaluate these statements, listeners need to know more about where the information came from.

This does not mean you are required to present regulation footnotes in oral form, citing volume and page numbers. Nor do you need to recite an authority's complete biography or necessarily explain a study's design intricacies. Although you should know the *who, why, when,* and *how* of every bit of data you use, you will probably mention only a couple of these in introducing the evidence.

How do you decide which to include? You can follow two basic approaches. First, consider the questions your audience will have. Place yourself in the listeners' place and adopt a skeptical outlook: What would you question about the data? A hostile audience might want to know whether your expert was objective; a group of social scientists might question whether the opinion poll you cite was scientifically conducted. Second, stress what is most compelling and impressive. If you have a thirty-year-old quotation from a Supreme Court justice but think the sentiment expressed is timeless, stress the

---

Speaker's Workshop 15.5

1. Compare the ways Nathanael Dunlavy and Kayla Strickland introduce supporting materials in their speeches, available in Part 7 or through your CourseMate for *The Speaker's Handbook*. Does either speaker "over-introduce" or "under-introduce" the citations? Identify some examples of citation that you find most effective.

2. Review the supporting materials used in the sample speeches by Julian Treasure, Harriet Kamakil, and Kayla Strickland, available in Part 7 or through your CourseMate for *The Speaker's Handbook*. Note the presence of explanation, definition, examples, statistics, and testimony in each.
   ▶ Does each speech use a variety of methods?
   ▶ What are the two favored forms of supporting material in each speech?

© geopaul / iStockphoto 3620311

who and not the *when*. What is the best feature of the evidence—its recency, the large size of the sample, the prestige of the journal in which it appeared, or the authority of the speaker? Look at Chapter **8** for more discussion of citing sources in your speech.

Use a Variety of Lead-Ins

Do not get into the habit of introducing all your illustrations, statistics, and so on with the same phrase: "Some figures about this are . . . some figures about that are . . . ." Be prepared enough that you can employ a number of lead-ins for each kind of supporting material. There are many possibilities:

▶ To support this idea . . .

▶ This point is verified by . . .

▶ _____ put it well, I think, when she said . . .

▶ In the words of _____ , . . .

▶ What causes this situation? One answer to that question was offered by _____ when he wrote last year . . .

▶ Let me tell you about a survey taken in the early eighties by a Brandeis psychologist . . .

▶ There are several examples of this. Let me share just two . . .

▶ I was immediately struck by the similarity to an experience I/he/ _____ once had . . .

However you decide to introduce a quotation, do not say "quote, unquote" or wiggle pairs of fingers in the air to approximate quotation marks. A subtle change in your voice or posture is enough to indicate to your listeners the boundaries of a direct quotation.

Check out Speech Studio to see how other students cite sources in their speeches. Or record a speech you're working on, upload it to Speech Studio, and ask your peers for their feedback. What feedback could you use to fine tune your oral citations before you give your speech in class?

Review, Reconsider, & Act

Summary

Effective incorporation of supporting material requires thoughtful consideration of what the audience will need in order to understand and be affected by your speech. Define unfamiliar words and concepts, use examples to clarify difficult concepts, offer statistical support for the claims made, and draw on testimony from recognized authorities. Most importantly, boost your credibility by citing sources of support clearly, sharing the most relevant aspects of who, why, when, and how.

Critical Thinking Questions

▶ Why is it better to use a variety of supporting materials such as quotes, examples, statistics, and stories from a variety of sources?

▶ When are specific examples preferable to broad generalizations in a speech?

▶ What are the tests of credibility for testimony cited in a speech?

▶ Which statistical fallacy is most common? What can you do to avoid it?

Putting It into Practice

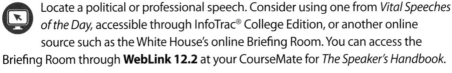 Locate a political or professional speech. Consider using one from *Vital Speeches of the Day,* accessible through InfoTrac® College Edition, or another online source such as the White House's online Briefing Room. You can access the Briefing Room through **WebLink 12.2** at your CourseMate for *The Speaker's Handbook.*

1. What types of definitions are offered in the speech?
2. What examples does the speaker offer?
3. How effectively does the speaker incorporate statistics?
4. What expert testimony does the speaker use?
5. How does the speaker smoothly integrate the supporting statements?

chapter 16
Reasoning

Use sound reasoning to develop your speech.
Avoid logical fallacies.

P eople reason every time they make links between ideas. When people disagree about an argument, it is often because they disagree about the facts and evidence offered rather than over the rules of logic used. Whereas Chapter **15** is devoted to ensuring the validity of our supporting material, this chapter addresses how to make sure your reasoning, or interpretation of the evidence, is valid *and is understood as valid by your audience.*

To develop a logical line of thought and test its validity, we need to understand a little more about the basic building blocks of reasoning, to become familiar with standard patterns of reasoning and with a few of the common fallacies. Only then can we decide how best to use reasoning in our speech.

Building Blocks of Reasoning: Claims, Data, and Warrants

Reasoning is made up of claims, data and warrants. **Claims** are any statements that you need to substantiate because they are not taken for granted by your listeners. Your thesis sentence might be thought of as a "super" claim, your main points are claims that support that "super" claim, and even some of your subordinate points have to be reasoned through before they become acceptable.

Some of our claims may not be disputed (e.g., "murder is wrong") or may be obvious (e.g., "most people would prefer not to pay higher taxes"). But many other points will need to be supported. The supporting material used to bolster your point is known as **data,** or evidence. Sometimes however, the connection between the claim and data is not understood clearly. This link between a claim and the data to support it is known as the **warrant**. Warrants allow an audience to bridge the connection between data and a claim, to understand the speaker's reasoning.[1]

Evidence Can Lead to More Than One Claim

Suppose you have a claim that you want your listeners to accept, and you have some evidence or data that you believe support that claim. Clearly, everyone who confronts the same facts and figures does not automatically come to the same conclusion that you do. Reasoning links the data to the claim and warrants the acceptance of the claim. For example, suppose two different people are confronted with the fact that more people go to the doctor in countries with national health care programs than in countries with privately funded health care. Person A concludes that this is an argument in support of adopting national health care in the United States. Person B concludes that it is an argument against national health care.

The reasoning offered in a speech provides a bridge to span the distance between the evidence and the claim. Through reasoning a person's interpretation of the evidence becomes clear and the logic of the argument is revealed. Like a bridge the reasoning might be complex or it might be simple. Of course the more complex the reasoning the less likely listeners will follow the speaker's thinking and come to the same conclusions.

As Figure 16.1 shows, there is no connection between evidence and claim except through the reasoning link that you provide.

People Look for Familiar Patterns

In the health care example, Person A is drawing on a pattern observed in the past—namely, that people who cannot afford a service they need will seek out that service when it becomes affordable. This is perfectly reasonable and logical; we all can think of plenty of commonsense examples.

FIGURE 16.1
Reasoning links evidence and claim

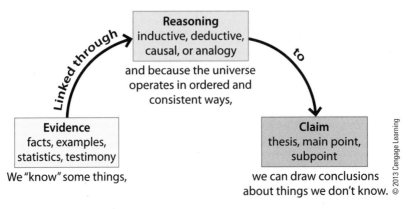

© 2013 Cengage Learning

Person B is also being logical and reasonable in linking the evidence of increased medical visits to the claim that national health care would be undesirable. This person is drawing on another observed pattern of human behavior—that people who see a resource as free and unlimited may use it inappropriately and wastefully. There is also plenty of support for this view.

The issue here is not what the facts *are*, but what the facts *mean*. For our purposes, the significance of these opposing views is to show that there are many sensible ways to interpret the same piece of evidence. A speaker who uses evidence to support a claim cannot simply present the evidence and hope it speaks for itself. The speaker must explain the relevance of the evidence and justify the link to a particular claim.

Speaker's Workshop 16.1

1. For each of these claims, list at least three pieces of evidence you could use to support it.
   A. Smoking should be banned in all indoor public places.
   B. Bicycles are a good choice for reducing fossil fuel consumption.
   C. Drivers over the age of seventy should have to take a road test every year to renew their driver's licenses.

   After you have listed the evidence, explain how each piece of evidence supports the point.

2. Explain how the evidence in these examples can be linked to the two different claims. What logical pattern is drawn upon in each case?

   Example A

   Evidence: The form of government in the United States has existed for over two hundred years.

   Therefore

   Claim 1: We should maintain our present form of government because *[link or reasoning]*

   or

   Claim 2: We should change our present form of government because *[link or reasoning]*

   Example B

   Evidence: Deaths from firearms have increased in the past few years.

   Therefore

   Claim 1: We need even stronger gun control laws than the ones we have because *[link or reasoning]*

   or

   Claim 2: We should get rid of gun control laws because *[link or reasoning]*

Recall that speakers do not merely transmit information to listeners. Rather, speakers and listeners create meaning together. Therefore, for any complex and controversial topic, you need to show your audience what your evidence means and build the argument with them. This is done by spelling out your interpretation of the data and showing how this interpretation fits one of the common patterns of reasoning familiar to your listeners, including inductive, deductive, causal, and analogic reasoning, as explained next.

Inductive Reasoning

The simplest and most common kind of reasoning is induction. Induction assumes an orderly universe: a universe where we believe that much of what has happened before will happen again. We step in front of oncoming traffic because we believe from previous experiences that the cars will obey the traffic signals. Dozens of times a day, we draw inferences based on past experiences and expectations derived from those experiences. Inductive reasoning involves making an educated guess about something that is based on a subset of known factors. Figure 16.2 depicts the process of inductive reasoning.

Base Inferences on Sufficient and Representative Cases

Inductive reasoning consists of collecting enough instances to establish a pattern. Remember the logical tests in Chapter **15**. A typical line of inductive thought can be portrayed as follows:

Orchid$_1$ has no fragrance.

Orchid$_2$ has no fragrance.

Orchid$_3$ has no fragrance.

Orchid$_n$ has no fragrance.

Therefore, it is probable that all orchids have no fragrance.

FIGURE 16.2
Inductive reasoning draws inferences from observations

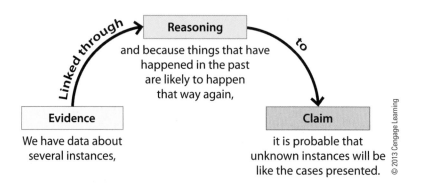

The extent to which you can generalize from such observations is linked to the extent of your sampling. If you smelled only the orchids in one corner of one hothouse, you would be less able to make a general conclusion than if you had smelled orchids in different hothouses throughout the country.

By far the greatest problem in this kind of reasoning is determining how many cases to consider before drawing a conclusion. Obviously, you want to test several cases before drawing a conclusion, but how many are enough? If you use five brand name USB flash drives and they all have problems, is that enough to say that all brand name flash drives are defective? If a researcher finds that 132 out of 150 students surveyed encountered no problems registering for classes, is that enough to justify a conclusion about that group? At best, you can say, "It is likely that many brand name USB flash drives are defective," and "Students will probably not encounter problems registering for classes." The conclusions drawn from induction are always *probable* rather than *absolute*. The only way you could say that *all* brand name USB flash drives are defective would be to test every one. This would be counting, not reasoning. Reasoning, as you will recall, is defined as drawing conclusions about the unknown.

Be cautious in drawing inferences from limited data. The following questions are helpful when you are considering the adequacy of your inductive reasoning. How many cases did you examine? Were they selected fairly? Are the contrary instances accounted for?

Recognize the Degree of Probability of Your Claim

An inductive conclusion can fall anywhere along this continuum:

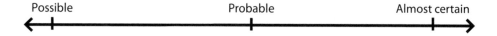

| Possible | Probable | Almost certain |

The degree of certainty depends on the methods used in making our observations and on the number of observations made. A conclusion like "The last two times I've gone to that restaurant the service has been lousy—I'll bet they've changed management" would fall far to the left. Two observations is a very small number, and there are many other viable explanations for the poor service. At the other end of the continuum is a statement like "The new drug therapy cures patients of malaria." This conclusion is based on a great many observations collected systematically. In fact, according to an April 2010 article in *The Lancet,* the new drug combination is 99.5 percent effective.

How strong must this probability be before you can consider the conclusion of an inductive argument to be valid? A 51 percent probability, or 75 percent, or 99 percent? Unlike deductive reasoning, for which there are agreed-upon tests of validity, the test of an induction varies in every case. There is no mathematical or logical answer to the question. The issue of how much is enough is more a psychological question of individual perception. Each of us would have a different threshold for how much we might be willing to bet on a coin flip. For many those odds are good enough for a dollar bet, but few would bet their life on it.

Demonstrate Your Cost–Reward Analysis

When induction is used in a public speech, the speaker's task is to convince the audience members that the conclusion arrived at is probable enough to warrant their acceptance. The so-called inductive "leap" occurs when you lead the listeners to a certain point with your data and then ask them to jump across an imaginary divide to your conclusion. Here, as in the preceding examples, the level of how much is enough is contingent on the risks and benefits perceived.

Suppose you know of a new drug rehabilitation program that has been found quite effective in pilot studies in three different communities. In urging its adoption in your city, your line of reasoning might go like this:

The program worked in Community A.

The program worked in Community B.

The program worked in Community C.

Therefore, it is probable that the program is effective and will work here.

Because these other cases were not studied systematically (e.g., with control groups, random sampling, and follow-up studies) and because there are only three cases in your sample, you cannot state your conclusion at a high level of probability. You must recognize that the drug rehabilitation program could fail in your community. Imagine that it were possible to assign concrete levels of probability and that both proponents and skeptics of the program agreed that there was about a 75 percent chance of its success. A member of your audience might well ask, "Why should we spend $650,000 for just a three-out-of-four chance we might help a bunch of junkies?" You cannot change the 75 percent odds, but you can influence your audience's assessment of the costs and rewards. Tell them how the program, if it works, will benefit the whole community: It will decrease crime, put former addicts back into the workforce, and lower the temptations for adolescent drug use. Also minimize the costs: "I know $650,000 sounds like a lot, but it's only 85 cents per citizen." When the listeners reassess the costs and rewards, and see them as you do, the 75 percent odds may look more attractive.

Consider another example, in which the conclusion's probability is very high:

Nuclear power plant A has had no accidents.

Nuclear power plant B has had no accidents.

Nuclear power plant C has had no accidents.

Nuclear power plant n has had no accidents.

Therefore, it is probable that nuclear power plants are safe.

© geopaul / iStockphoto 3620311

Speaker's Workshop 16.2

1. Think of the audience for your next speech. What costs or risks would you need to minimize and what benefits would you need to maximize to establish a high probability of acceptance for these conclusions?
    A. This new treatment for herpes should be marketed.
    B. Every school bus should be equipped with seat belts.
    C. We should hire only college graduates for our sales department.
    D. You should cut aspartame out of your diet.

2.  Read or watch Hans Erian's speech, available in Part 7 or through your CourseMate for *The Speaker's Handbook*. Analyze Hans's use of specific instances in the subpoint under his first main point regarding the reason people consume so much sugar. How does he attempt to establish the degree of probability of his claim that ignorance is a major factor?

Suppose the conclusion could be granted a 95 percent level of probability. Even so, you or someone else might not feel the evidence is sufficient to make the inductive leap that nuclear power plants really are safe. In explaining your concerns to the audience, you would minimize the rewards of nuclear plants—perhaps by pointing out that most of the energy we would get can be obtained through other sources—and maximize the risks by describing just how awful a nuclear accident would be. Your argument is: "I'm not willing to subject my family to even a 5-out-of-100 chance of this sort of destruction just to have cheap electricity."

We see from these examples that no inductive argument is innately logical or illogical. In the case of the drug program, a low probability met the test of how much is enough for the speaker. In the case of the nuclear power plant, even 95 percent was not enough. The difference lies in the perception of risk and reward. The validity is negotiated between you and your audience.

Deductive Reasoning

Unlike *induction*, in which the emphasis is on collecting observable data, **deduction** consists of making verbal statements, or premises, according to formal rules. Deduction, then, involves not bringing new data into play, but rather rearranging what you already know. A common example is the Sherlock Holmes type English murder mystery. In the obligatory denouement of the murder mystery, the detective

FIGURE 16.3
Deductive reasoning finds the patterns in what you already know

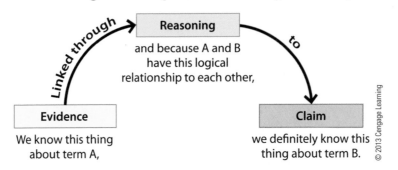

© 2013 Cengage Learning

patiently explains to a roomful of suspects the meaning of the details known but not assimilated by the reader:

> Everyone who had a motive appeared to have an alibi at the time of the murder. Because people cannot be in two places at once, I deduced that the time of the murder must have been earlier than we thought. Remember the maid who discovered the body in the bedroom, saying it was as cold as ice? But the bedroom was quite warm from the fire in the fireplace. A corpse is not as cold as ice unless it has been stored in a very cold place for hours and only later returned to the bedroom. And then there were the cobwebs almost imperceptible against the corpse's silver hair. What place in this manor is both cold and cobwebby? The wine cellar. Only Peters, the butler, had a key to the wine cellar!

Having the clues is not enough; it takes a supersleuth to recognize how the clues uniquely fit together. Figure 16.3 depicts the process of deductive reasoning.

In our everyday lives, we have that "Aha!" experience when we suddenly discover the pattern underlying disparate facts. Just as you are falling asleep, you might sit up abruptly and realize the connection between events that you had been struggling with all day. This kind of reasoning is quite different from induction, which involves gathering data. In deduction, facts that are already known are put together in a way that reveals their implications.

Deduction: Major Premise - Minor Premise - Conclusion

Because a deduction must adhere to certain rules in order to be valid, experts in deductive reasoning learn complex symbolic formulas by which they test arguments. For the purpose of this book, we need only touch on the basic concept of deduction: If we know certain things about how two terms (concepts, events, characteristics) are related, we can discover other relationships that are logically entailed or implicated:

Term A is related in a known way to Term B.

We know certain things about B.

Therefore, we can draw certain conclusions about Term A.

To use deductive reasoning in a speech, you need to transform this into a series of steps:

Step 1: Establish that a relationship exists between two terms.

Step 2: Establish the actual condition or status of one of the terms.

Step 3: Show how a conclusion about the other term necessarily follows.

Step 1 in deduction—establishing the **major premise** or broad statement of relationship—takes many forms. It always involves an absolute relationship between two terms. Here are examples of four common relationships.

One term may be an intrinsic characteristic of the other:

▶ All ducks have webbed feet.

▶ Conflict is inherent in the collective bargaining model.

One term may be a category that includes the other:

▶ All Volkswagens are motor vehicles.

▶ The food stamp program is part of the social welfare system.

One term may be inevitably linked to the other:

▶ If you heat water to 212 degrees at sea level, then it will boil.

▶ If corporate taxes are cut, then investment will increase.

The two terms may be the opposite of or exclude each other:

▶ Either that fabric is natural or it is synthetic.

▶ Unless we crack down on drunken drivers, fatalities will rise.

When you have established one of these basic major premises, you have set up a formula that will serve as the linking device at the top of your arc of reasoning. When you move to Step 2, you establish something about one of the two terms—in what logicians call the **minor premise**. A piece of evidence like "Daffy is a duck" might mean many things, or nothing, in some lines of argument. But in the context of the first major premise illustrated earlier, it is the minor premise, and the resulting, relevant implication is that Daffy has webbed feet.

Feed in the data you have, follow the rules of deductive logic, and certain **conclusions** are inevitably entailed:

▶ This blouse is made of a synthetic fiber, *so it is not made of a natural fiber.*

▶ We did not crack down on drunken drivers, *so traffic fatalities must have increased.*

The beauty of deduction lies in its certainty. If your listeners accept the premises, they *must* accept the conclusion.

This seems so attractive that you might wonder why a speaker would use any other method. Why waste energy on the probable conclusions of induction? Why not stick with deduction, in which the rules are clear and the conclusions have to be accepted? The problem with deduction is that for its conclusion to be absolute, its premises must be absolute. Unfortunately, most absolute statements of relationships are either untrue or trivial. Who really cares if ducks have webbed feet or really needs to reason about it? The things we do have to reason about, and tend to give speeches about, are complex issues of public policy, human behavior, and social values. In these domains, we rarely find acceptable statements that "*all X is Y*," or "if *X*, then *Y always* follows," or "either *X* or *Y* and *no other alternative*." The requirement of having an all-or-nothing beginning premise is so restrictive that true, formal deductive reasoning is rather rare. In speaking it is acceptable to use a slightly less rigorous form of deduction.

Probable Premises Lead to Probable Conclusions

In the if–then statement about tax cuts, does a reduction on corporate taxes absolutely *have* to result in increased investment? A more honest syllogism would be:

> It is highly probable that a cut in corporate taxes will increase investment.
>
> Congress is almost certain to cut taxes.
>
> Therefore, it is highly probable that investment will increase.

But now we have lost the tidy inevitability of deduction. The rules of logic no longer force our listeners to accept our conclusion. We are back to the same kinds of problems we face in induction—persuading the audience to weigh the probabilities as we do. Our appeal to them would be:

> If you grant this premise as probable,
>
> and
>
> if you grant this other premise as probable,
>
> then it is logical to grant this conclusion as probable.

When you look at deduction this way, you can take some liberties not available to the logician. You may build a deductively structured argument with premises that are not absolute, recognizing, of course, that the conclusions you derive will not be absolute, either. Each point needs to be supported sufficiently to persuade a member of the audience to say, "I'll grant that point; it's reasonable; it's probable." Thus, the degree of probability of any conclusion is a product of the degree of probability granted to each premise.

The form of a deductive argument is an elegant way to justify a conclusion, even when it has been qualified to be more realistic. It can provide an effective structure for part or all of a speech. When the conclusion you want your audience to reach can be arrived at through logical steps, seriously consider arranging your points in a deductive format.

Lay Out All Premises of a Deductive Argument

One of the real advantages of structuring ideas deductively is that you must state the relationships among the concepts with which you are dealing. When you clearly state the major premise on which your argument rests, you call to your listeners' minds certain values, assumptions or truisms. The audience can then apply these concepts when you move on to specific cases in developing your minor premise. In the following logical arguments, notice how the major premise serves in each case to direct the listeners' awareness to a statement that the speaker might otherwise have left implicit.

▶ It has always been the goal of our social welfare system to help recipients become self-sufficient.

▶ Certain current programs encourage dependency and discourage initiative.

▶ Therefore, these programs should be changed.

▶ A good friend is a person who helps you reach your potential.

Several people in this organization have helped me strive toward my potential. Therefore, as I say good-bye, I feel as if I am leaving a number of good friends.

© geopaul / iStockphoto 3620311

Speaker's Workshop 16.3

1. What unstated assumption or absolute statement of relationship underlies each of these arguments?
   A. She must be doing a good job. She hasn't been fired.
   B. You should buy a condominium. It's cheaper than a house.
   C. Well, it's not a win for labor, so I guess management wins.
   D. I thought he had some self-respect, but now I learn he's on welfare.

2. Watch "Let's Move! Launch Anniversary Speech to Parents" by First Lady Michelle Obama available online. A link has been provided on the CourseMate for *The Speaker's Handbook* under **WebLinks** for this chapter. Identify at least two different lines of deductive argument used in this exchange and lay them out as syllogisms. In some cases, you will need to make explicit a premise that was implicit in the statement.

3. Here are some conclusions that could have been reached either inductively or deductively. Briefly lay out an inductive and a deductive argument that leads to each.
   A. Natural childbirth is best for parents and infants.
   B. More states should institute regulations protecting computer users from workplace conditions that can cause carpal tunnel syndrome and other repetitive strain injuries.
   C. The Academy Awards are rarely given to the best films.

4. Identify the basic reasoning pattern in a sample speech or two, available in Part 7 or through your CourseMate for *The Speaker's Handbook*. Are they inductive or deductive? Can you lay out the underlying argument in three or four sentences?

Sometimes, speakers have so internalized a point of view that they leave out parts of their argument, which they consider obvious. When audiences and speaker share common values, these assumptions may be acceptable. On controversial topics with diverse audiences, neglecting to lay out all parts of the argument is dangerous. In excellent speeches, speakers take the time to articulate and justify their premises. Consider the previous examples. The first point of each argument might have been omitted or tossed in as an aside rather than developed. By the same token, in saying, "We couldn't possibly pass this bill; it endangers the free enterprise system," you are assuming that your audience accepts your assumption that "anything that endangers the free enterprise system is undesirable." If they do not accept those assumptions, your efforts to prove the bill's effects are wasted. If they do agree, you will not have lost much time by reiterating those points. Listeners will be more likely to remember your specifics if they have a logical framework for them.

Like the detective with the clues, your task is not merely to list the facts, but to demonstrate how they fit together and what they ultimately mean. Often, the conclusion of the speech is the place to weave together the threads of a deductive argument:

> So, I've shown that it is our goal to reach full employment and that the only available paths are through direct provision of public sector jobs or through indirect stimulation of private sector jobs. Because I went on to give you several reasons for rejecting the public sector alternative, there is only one conclusion left. To create full employment, the private sector must be stimulated.

Causal Reasoning

Causal reasoning is the backbone of all speeches that deal with policy and problem solving. In most cases, if a person says, "I don't favor your policy (or program, or solution)," what that person is really saying is, "I disagree with you that X causes Y." This means you must carefully scrutinize the relationship between two events to satisfy yourself that it is causal. Then you must provide your listeners with information indicating how thoroughly you tested this relationship. Figure 16.4 depicts the causal reasoning process.

FIGURE 16.4
Causal reasoning links cause and effect

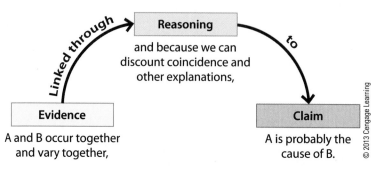

© 2013 Cengage Learning

Of course, in a problem-solving or policy speech, there is rarely one lone cause. To assert that there is would be a gross oversimplification, jeopardizing the acceptance of your conclusions. Still, it helps to understand the rigorous tests you have to apply to a statement if you are to assert a pure causal relationship in it—that is, "one cause leads inevitably to one effect."

Test the Validity of Causal Relationships

A causal relationship is stronger than mere correlation, coexistence, or coincidence. Two events may occur together or in sequence without one causing the other. For instance, morning sickness and weight gain often occur together, but neither causes the other; they are the result of a third condition, pregnancy. To be sure that the relationship is a causal one, apply these tests.

Do the Alleged Cause and Alleged Effect Occur Together?

To prove that a causal relationship exists, at least two formal comparisons must be made, as with a control group and an experimental group. It is not enough to show that the cause is present with the effect; you must also show that, in the absence of the alleged cause, the alleged effect does not appear:

> If a rash appears every time you eat tomatoes, and never appears when you haven't eaten tomatoes, this is strong evidence that tomatoes cause the rash.
>
> There are three groups of arthritis sufferers, matched in all-important characteristics such as age, sex, diet, and general health. Group A receives the drug Painaway, Group B receives a placebo, and Group C receives no treatment. Members of Group A experience dramatic relief, and there is no change in the condition of members of Group B and Group C. This supports the claim that Painaway causes a reduction in arthritis symptoms.

To prove a causal relationship, you must show both concurrent presence and concurrent absence. Technically, all that is needed to *disprove* a suggested causal relationship is to point to a case in which the alleged cause was present without the alleged effect, or vice versa. So, if you found that your rash occurred occasionally when you had not eaten tomatoes, or if you had once eaten tomatoes and not gotten the rash, a pure causal relationship does not exist. For example:

> For years, I believed the other teachers who said students would read the book only if they were given weekly quizzes. Then, one semester, I dropped the quizzes and found that students were as well prepared each week as before.

Do the Alleged Cause and the Alleged Effect Vary Together?

Another test of causation is to determine whether the magnitude of change in the cause matches that in the effect:

> If one bite of tomato gives you a small rash, and consuming many tomatoes gives you a big rash, this is one more bit of evidence to suggest that tomatoes cause your rash.

High school graduates, on average, earn more than high school dropouts. People with some college education earn more than high school grads, but less than college graduates. People with advanced degrees, taken as a group, have the highest incomes. Though you can think of individual exceptions, research on groups of people shows that each increment of formal education is accompanied by an equivalent increase in earning power.

Don't Oversimplify Causal Relationships

In the worlds of physics and chemistry, there are some clear, straightforward causal relationships:

An action results in an equal and opposite reaction.

Adding silver nitrate solution ($AgNO_3$) to sodium chloride (NaCl) will cause silver chloride (AgCl) to precipitate.

This type of relationship between cause (C) and effect (E) could be represented as

$$C \rightarrow E$$

However, in the areas of politics, psychology, medicine, economics, and the like, more complex patterns usually exist.

Some Effects Have Multiple Causes

If smoking were the single cause of lung cancer, then every smoker would have lung cancer, and every victim of lung cancer would be a smoker. Obviously, this is not the case. Yet research does show smoking to be one causal factor contributing to lung cancer. The simple cause-and-effect tests outlined earlier cannot be the sole criteria for providing cases of multiple causation. If you speak of issues like poverty, crime, divorce, and economic recession as though they had a single direct cause, you will justifiably lose credibility with your audience.

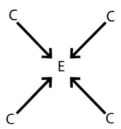

Some Causes Are Also Effects, and Some Effects Are Also Causes

When we designate a cause of a certain event, we can look at the immediate cause or a more distant factor. A doctor might say that the cause of a particular death was a cerebral hemorrhage. What, though, was the cause of that? Perhaps a fractured skull, which was caused by going through a windshield, which was caused by the impact of a car with a tree, which was caused by excessive drinking, which was caused by worry over being unemployed, and so on:

$$C \rightarrow (E/C) \rightarrow (E/C) \rightarrow (E/C) \rightarrow E$$

In a speech, you need to discuss enough of these links to give a realistic picture and to demonstrate to your listeners that you understand the complexity of the process— without going so far back in the chain as to be absurd.

It is sometimes important to point out the cyclical nature of certain causal chains. For example, ignorance about a particular group may lead to prejudice, which in turn results in lack of contact with that group, which perpetuates ignorance. This sort of analysis is far more interesting than positing a single cause of racial disharmony.

Some Effects Result from a One-Time Cause, and Some from Ongoing Causes

Effects that are labeled undesirable can be dealt with in two ways, either by treating the effect directly or by blocking the cause that produces the effect. To decide which strategy makes the most sense in a given context, you need to determine whether the cause is one-time or ongoing.

Picture a neighborhood with bare dirt for landscaping, busted windows, broken furniture in the yards, and residents in need of medical care. You are concerned about

Speaker's Workshop 16.4

1. Explain two ways you might disprove each of the following causal assertions, using principles discussed in this section:
   A. Supreme Court rulings on arrest procedures have allowed criminals to go free.
   B. Unfair laws have caused discrimination against women.
   C. Strokes are caused by stress.
   D. Lack of educational expenditure has produced an inferior generation of college students.

2. Explain how each of the causal statements in Exercise 1 might reflect one or more of the kinds of oversimplification referred to in this section.

3. Read or watch Mitt Romney's speech, available in Part 7 or through your CourseMate for *The Speaker's Handbook*. Can you identify his claims and support for those claims? How important is his ability to support his claims before this audience? Then watch Rauf Feisal Abdul's speech, "There Is Everything Right with Being an American Muslim," also available in Part 7. What support does he offer for his claims? How does the audience affect requirements for reasoning and support?

these symptoms and want to take some action. If you find that a tornado whipped through the area, you may push for emergency relief, intervention by the Army Corps of Engineers to clear wreckage, and loans to rebuild. However, if you learn that the area is depressed and that poverty is chronic, you may choose to advocate organizing retraining programs, launching campaigns to attract businesses to the community, and setting up health clinics. A mistake in evaluation, whereby the effect of an ongoing cause is treated as if it resulted from a one-time cause, will lead to the eventual reappearance of that effect.

Attempting to remedy problems through minor adjustments in laws and institutions when the real causes lie in basic attitudes and values is the worst kind of oversimplification. Nearly as bad is the tendency to advocate "education" as the answer to all social ills. It is better to lay out a two-phase solution, with short-range steps to deal with the symptoms complemented by a long-range attack on the underlying causes.

Explain Your Causal Claims Fully and Fairly

Pure, simple causal arguments like those scientific truths cited earlier deal with absolute relationships. In this sense, they are like deductive arguments. Like deductive major premises, however, valid but nontrivial examples of absolute relationships are rare. More common are lines of reasoning that lead to probable causal claims, like the following:

X was present in these cases, and Y occurred.

X was absent in these cases, and Y did not occur.

Changes in the amount of X have often led to corresponding changes in the amount of Y.

Therefore, it is probable that X causes Y.

Probable to what degree? To the degree that your examples are sufficient and representative, and that conflicting examples are minimized or explained. With this sort of causal argument, do not overstate your claim. Say, "This is a major cause," and not "This is *the* cause." Say, "There is strong evidence of a causal link between . . . " and so on.

The establishment of a probable causal claim requires the same sort of risk–benefit analysis that inductive reasoning requires. If it is highly likely that eating red meat causes cardiovascular disease, what are the risks of ignoring this link? What are the benefits of accepting it?

Also, whenever possible, explain the way the causal connection operates. Otherwise, even if you demonstrate perfect correlation between two factors, you may succeed in establishing only that one is a sign, signal, or symptom of the other. Causal reasoning tells more than *what* is connected; it tells *why* things are connected. Whenever applicable in your speech, include a brief explanation of how the cause leads to the effect. Cite expert testimony if possible or useful. The more explicit your analysis of causation, the less likely your audience is to dismiss your causal claim as mere coincidence.

Reasoning by Analogy

When we reason by analogy, we compare two things that can be placed in the same category. In the process, we assume that, because we know that A and B have a number of characteristics in common, we can conclude that those things we do not know about B are highly likely to resemble their counterparts that we do know about in A. Figure 16.5 depicts the process of **reasoning by analogy**.

Reasoning by analogy is a natural and powerful way to make links. People intuitively look to similar examples when they want to understand something. Suppose the president's foreign-policy advisors are trying to decide whether to intervene in a foreign country's internal struggles, or a judge is pondering whether to admit expert testimony on battered wife syndrome, or you are wondering whether to take the freeway or back streets to work. In all these cases, from the most cosmic policy issues to the most mundane everyday decisions, people ask themselves, "What is this like that I already know about?"

Like the other forms of reasoning we have explored, analogies can be used to support contradictory claims. Some of the president's advisors will argue that the foreign country is just like Somalia, and so intervention will be fruitless. Others will insist that it is more like Panama and that vital matters of principle are at stake. One lawyer will tell the judge that the case at hand is like one in which such evidence was admitted. Opposing counsel will insist that it is more like another one in which expert testimony of this sort was excluded. One member of your carpool will claim that today is like other Mondays, when traffic is light on the freeway. Another will point out that on other rainy days like today there are often accidents that slow things down on the freeway.

FIGURE 16.5
Analogy compares two things in the same category

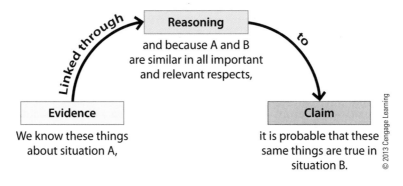

Although reasoning by analogy is so innate—or *because* it is—you need to approach it with a careful eye on the analogies you use. The following cautions are worth considering when reasoning by analogy.

Be Sure the Two Cases Are Similar

Here is the sort of unconscious analogy we all use every day. Does it pass the test?

> Requiring school uniforms for students helps maintain order for parochial schools. Therefore, requiring all students to wear school uniforms will help maintain order in the public schools as well.

There are certain similarities between parochial and public schools: Both are places of learning, both work with school-age children, and both benefit from a certain amount of order. It is also easy to point out differences: Parochial school students have a long history of uniform codes, and public school students have historically not been prescribed a uniform; parochial school students tend to be quite homogeneous, and public school students tend to be more heterogeneous. No cases are identical, and simply pointing out differences does not discredit an analogy automatically. Do they differ in relevant and important ways? In this instance, perhaps. Historically, differences exist between parochial and public school students and parents. Certainly all are interested in a decent education, but the freedoms they are willing to relinquish to achieve that may vary greatly. These stated differences may be important enough to lead a person to reject the conclusion that requiring all students to wear school uniforms will help maintain order in the public schools.

When comparing cases from different geopolitical areas, be especially aware of cultural differences. The identical institutional changes might be adopted in Scandinavia, Syria, or Sri Lanka with radically different effects. Even within a national culture, microcultural differences exist. A university faculty will not respond to management practices the same way a business organization does. The innocent belief that "people are people" must be modified by our increasing awareness of the role played by gender, social class, race, sexual orientation, and numerous other factors in influencing people and shaping their experiences, even when living under externally similar conditions.

Reasoning by analogy should also be tempered by an awareness of the impact of history. Comparisons between the Vietnam War and the Iraq War have often been made, yet the very experience of Vietnam irreversibly altered U.S. perceptions of foreign policy, military strategy, and media coverage. Any war following Vietnam will be different *because* of Vietnam.

Don't Confuse Literal and Figurative Analogies

Reasoning by analogy requires a comparison of two members of the same category. *Figurative analogy* compares the members of different categories:

© geopaul / iStockphoto 3620311

Speaker's Workshop 16.5

1. Identify at least three similarities and three differences between each of the following pairs of concepts. Now go back and think about how these enter into the way we reason by analogy. Write one argument for each topic in which the similarities are sufficiently relevant and important to justify the conclusion. List other lines of reasoning on each topic that would probably be discounted due to the differences you identified.
   A. A football game and a war
   B. A family and a group of employees
   C. "Ethnic cleansing" in Sudan and racial discrimination in the United States
   D. The national debt and one's personal checking account

2. Read or watch Julian Treasure's speech on the effects of sound, available in Part 7 or through your CourseMate for *The Speaker's Handbook*. Treasure compares using sound clips in advertising to a bowl of spaghetti. Analyze and evaluate his argument.

▶ Convincing my boss, Fred, to adopt a new procedure takes as much persistence, luck, and timing as starting my 1985 Mustang on a January morning.

▶ Fighting a war with Mexican drug lords would be like tap-dancing on quicksand.

These analogies may have stylistic impact, but they cannot support a conclusion.

The examples about school uniforms and the Vietnam War versus the Iraq War, however flawed in their logic, did make comparisons within the same categories—two school environments or two wars. The two examples just mentioned compare a human relationship with a human–machine relationship, and a war with an physical impossibility.

Avoid Common Reasoning Fallacies

Speakers commit fallacies when they use reasoning improperly, drawing unjustified conclusions. Some people do this knowingly, with dishonest intent. Others commit fallacies due to a lack of practice or skill in doing their own thinking. The good public speaker wants to avoid the appearance of either. Once you have built your speech around sound, logical arguments, go through it to detect any constructions that even hint of sloppy thinking. One glaring fallacy in your speech will make all your other conclusions suspect. It is not necessary to learn all the fallacies—more than one hundred have been categorized—but you should be familiar with the most common of them.

A bonus of learning about these fallacies is that you can improve your critical listening skills. Not only will you be able to construct a logically sound speech, but you also will be able to detect thoughtless, sloppy, or false lines of reasoning.

Ad Hominem Fallacy

The **ad hominem fallacy** attacks a person based on some attribute or circumstance rather than addressing their ideas. This strategy is widely used and can be recognized by attempts to redirect the discussion away from the issues toward some personal frailty of those involved. For instance,

> "Of course she would say that, what would we expect from an ignorant piece of trailer trash anyway?"
>
> Or "We would expect that from a tree hugging liberal such as yourself."
>
> Or "Sounds reasonable except that you stole the idea from your colleague. Why would we listen to a thief?"

Fallacy of the Absurd Extreme (Reductio Ad Absurdum)

The **fallacy of the absurd extreme** makes a potentially sound argument appear groundless by extending it to a point at which it can be ridiculed. Often, this extension goes beyond reasonable interpretation of the original point. In challenging current methods of criminal sentencing, a speaker might say:

> The average criminal is condemned to a bleak cell while top government wrongdoers lounge around in "country club" facilities. The logic is that the latter have already been punished considerably by loss of face, prestige, and professional standing. This seems to say that punishments should be harsher on those who have the least to lose. By this reasoning, the senator who commits murder might get off with a citation and public embarrassment, while an unemployed ghetto dweller who shoplifts should be put on bread and water, with regular sessions on the rack.

> This kind of fallacy relies on the humor of the cockeyed image it creates. Disarmed by a ludicrous example, listeners lose sight of the real issue.

Slippery Slope Fallacy

The **slippery slope fallacy** consists of making the false assumption that taking the first step in any direction will inevitably lead to going to dangerous lengths in that direction. The image is of someone sliding down a slope without being able to stop.

- If you ever take just one drink, you will become an alcoholic.
- If we let the government ban the sale and possession of assault rifles, banning all firearms is next.
- If we let the government abandon support of the arts, artistic freedom will die.

Circular Reasoning

Circular reasoning assumes as one of its premises the very conclusion it sets out to establish. Most of us know the hopeless feeling of trying to deal logically with such dead-end arguments as "you can't get a job in a field without experience in the field." Often, circular reasoning results from granting absolute authority to some source, and thus being blinded to the fact that others might not attribute similar authority to it, as in this example:

▶ I know that God exists. It says so repeatedly in the Bible. And everything in the Bible is true because it's the word of God.

   Other instances of circular reasoning come out of definitional word games:

▶ No sane person would consider suicide, because it's insane to want to take your own life.

Semantic Fallacy

The connotative nature of words can lead to faulty reasoning also known as a semantic fallacy. This misuse of the meanings of words can be funny, such as in "not a single burglar was arrested this month; they must all have been married." However, subtle and dangerous shifts in definition can occur in various critical parts of an argument, for instance:

> The free enterprise system, which we all cherish, could not exist without *competition*. This bill to protect small businesses threatens our whole economic structure. There can be no true *competition* when one group is given special protection.

In the underlying value premise, the word *competition* is used in the general sense of a market mechanism. In claiming that the bill endangers competition, the speaker uses the term in a much narrower sense, as in "a specific contest between individuals." The semantic fallacy is especially difficult to identify and frustrating to respond to because the form of the argument appears to be valid. The problem arises from the slight change in meaning when a term is used in different contexts.

False Dichotomy

A **false dichotomy** is reasoning based on an *either/or* statement when the two alternatives are not really mutually exclusive or when other alternatives exist. Many speeches set up artificial choices:

> Would you rather have a football program or a band and orchestra at our school?

> This can be a false dichotomy. Even in tough economic times, most schools would allocate resources so that both can be maintained if only minimally.

> Here's another example:

> Either we stand up to naked aggression, or we lose the confidence of our allies.

This basic premise so oversimplifies a complex issue that no conclusions can be drawn from it. Do not set up a deductive argument with a false dichotomy as its major premise.

Affirming the Consequent (Denying the Antecedent)

Another kind of deductive reasoning is based on an "if X, then Y" relationship. A common fallacy results from a faulty reversal of an if–then statement. This fallacy, known as **affirming the consequent** or **denying the antecedent**, occurs when a speaker assumes that, because *Y* necessarily follows *X*, the reverse is also true: that *X* necessarily follows *Y*. Political candidates so fear this kind of faulty reasoning by voters that they often publicly repudiate the endorsement of extreme groups and their supporters. They cannot count on the electorate to recognize the difference between a group endorsing a candidate and a candidate endorsing a group. Guilt by association is the most common manifestation of this fallacy.

For example:

> Barack Obama attended the church where Reverend Jeremiah Wright is pastor. Reverend Wright supported Barack Obama. Therefore, Obama supports what Reverend Wright says as pastor.

This is a fallacious conclusion because there is nothing in Reverend Wright's support of Barack Obama that requires Obama to fully agree with Reverend Wright. It is entirely possible that Obama has chosen to attend this church for reasons unrelated to Reverend Wright.

Hasty Generalization

A **hasty generalization** entails making a premature inductive "leap" based on insufficient evidence. Assumptions should be based on representative information. Making generalizations based on small samples can lead to this fallacy in reasoning. Consider the following:

> I saw a person smoking and talking on a cell phone run a red light this morning. Smokers are out to kill us.

Although time may not allow you, as a speaker, to include all the data supporting your conclusions, it is especially important to have the supporting data at your fingertips so you can respond should any accusations of hasty generalization be raised.

Post Hoc Fallacy

The Latin label for this fallacy—*post hoc, ergo propter hoc*—translates as "after the event, therefore because of the event." It is natural to try to understand the world around us by looking for cause–effect patterns wherever possible. So strong is this motivation that we are frequently guilty *confusing sequence with cause*, like Chanticleer the rooster, who firmly believed that it was his predawn crowing that caused the sun to rise each day.

A famous example of the **post hoc fallacy** is the "Tut Curse." Not long after he opened the burial chamber of the pharaoh Tutankhamen in 1923, Lord Carnarvon died in Cairo from complications following an insect bite. At the moment of his death, Cairo was said to have experienced a power blackout, and this was interpreted by many to be a manifestation of an ancient curse. Thereafter, if anyone remotely connected to

Speaker's Workshop 16.6

1. Identify the fallacy or fallacies in each statement:
   A. I'm surprised you health food nuts eat granola packaged in cellophane bags. Aren't you afraid the synthetic chemicals will poison the contents?
   B. Anyone who drives a foreign car doesn't care about this country anyway.
   C. It always rains on Easter. I remember it has for the last three years.
   D. Well, either you support your country, or you are critical of the government. Which is it?
   E. The jury system should be abolished. Last year a jury awarded $3 million to a woman who didn't like the nose job she got. The next month the doctor committed suicide.

2. In the marijuana outline at the end of the chapter, what kind of reasoning is being used in each of the four main points? Do you see any potential fallacies in the reasoning of the speech?

Egyptology died, it was attributed to the curse, regardless of what the true cause of death really was.

To avoid this fallacy, never assume that because something happened closely after another event that the first caused the second. Test every causal hypothesis against the criteria discussed earlier in the section on causal reasoning.

For more on effective arguments and how to avoid logical fallacies, go to your CourseMate for The Speaker's Handbook *and click on* **WebLink 16.1** *and* **WebLink 16.2.**

Link Evidence to Your Claim

It is not enough to have a speech that is well reasoned and free of fallacies. The reasoning process must be made clear to listeners. When speakers present only a cluster of evidence or a cluster of reasons for a claim, they are acting as if communication occurs through the simple transmission of messages. The perspective taken in this book is that communication consists of *making meaning together.* Therefore, as a speaker, you need to show listeners what makes your evidence meaningful to you.

The Organization *section and* Supporting Materials *under the* Outline *section of Speech Builder Express provide a framework and prompts to help you ensure that your speech clearly indicates the connections between your reasoning, evidence, and claim.*

Organize Points to Show Logical Relationships

Controversial claims can be found at all levels of a speech. How overall patterns of reasoning come into play is determined by how you lay out the speech. Sometimes, the thesis statement is supported by a line of reasoning, and each main point is part of the argument. For example:

> Thesis statement: Prayer should not be allowed in schools because it violates the doctrine of separation of church and state, which is a central tenet of U.S. society that must be preserved.
>
> I.   The doctrine of separation of church and state is a central tenet of U.S. society that must be preserved.
>   A. Why we have this doctrine
>   B. Why it must be preserved
> II. Prayer in the schools violates the doctrine of separation of church and state.
>   (Develop through testimony and examples.)
> Therefore: In conclusion, (restate thesis).

In other cases, the thesis statement might be an "umbrella claim" that is supported by several separate and somewhat independent claims:

> Thesis statement: Preschool programs such as Head Start are economically, socially, and morally justified.

The economic, social, and moral claims are separate main points where most of the reasoning of the speech will be found.

In still other cases, reasoning is necessary at specific subpoint levels in the speech to justify important claims.

There is no one way to display your lines of reasoning in a speech outline, but it is very important that you phrase points to show the connections. Do not simply group "reasons." Show reasoning.

> ***Wrong:***
>
> **I.** The United States cannot afford a middle-class tax cut.
>   **A.** Tax cut would lead to a bigger deficit.
>   (Support by testimony and statistics.)
>   **B.** The loss of revenue would hurt vital programs.
>   (Support by testimony and statistics.)
>
> ***Better:***
>
> **I.** The United States cannot afford a middle-class tax cut.
>   **A.** To adjust for a tax cut, we would have to either cut spending or go into debt.
>   (Briefly explain why these are the only alternatives.)

    B. It is not desirable to cut spending.

      (Support by testimony and statistics.)

    C. It is not desirable to go into debt.

      (Support by testimony and statistics.)

Wrong:

  I. Having a longer school day does not improve learning.

    A. They tried it at Riverdale High School, and test scores were unchanged.

    B. They tried it at Glenbrook High School, and test scores actually went down.

    C. At Creekside High School, test scores have gone up even though their school day has not been lengthened.

    D. Braeburn High School shortened their school day, and test scores did not change.

Better:

  I. Having a longer school day does not improve learning.

    A. In cases in which the school day was lengthened, test scores did not improve.

      1. Unchanged at Riverdale High

      2. Went down at Glenbrook

    B. In cases in which the school day was not lengthened, test scores were not lower.

      1. Improved at Creekside

      2. No change with shorter day at Braeburn

Summary transitional statement: If there were a causal relationship between the length of the school day and learning as measured by test scores, we would logically expect that scores would be higher where the school day is longer and lower where the school day is shorter. I have just demonstrated that this is not the case. Sometimes, the opposite is true. So you can see why I conclude that having a longer school day does not improve learning.

Remember the difference between points and support for the points. (See Chapter **11** and the introduction to Chapter **15**.) Do not use sources in place of reasoning. In the first example that follows, a speaker attempts to support a causal claim by saying that experts have agreed with the claim. But the listeners do not know why these people came to the conclusion they did. In the second example, the reasoning behind the causal claim is explained, with experts used to back up specific points.

Wrong:

  I. The use of sexist language perpetuates discrimination against women.

    A. Dr. Deborah Stone says sexist language causes problems.

    B. Professor Lydia Sorenson says sexist language is the root of many social problems.

    C. Linguist Chris Nupriya states that language affects behavior.

Better:

    I. The use of sexist language perpetuates discrimination against women.

        A. Language shapes social perception.

        (Cite experts and studies.)

        B. Speech that leaves women out can lead to people overlooking them.

        (Cite experts and studies.)

        C. If people subconsciously exclude women from certain roles, they discriminate against women.

        (Cite experts and studies.)

Select Language That Shows Logical Relationships

In addition to setting up a speech structure that highlights your reasoning, you should give thought to selecting language that illuminates the logical linkages between your ideas. Never merely jump from one point to the next. Practice adding phrases that are specific cues to the kind of reasoning you are using as suggested in Table 16.1.

As is stated in Chapter **12**, connective phrases are more important in speaking than in writing because listeners cannot look back at previous points. These cueing phrases play a crucial role in developing an oral argument. In an outline, claims are stated before their supporting reasons and evidence. This is an organizational artifact and should not obscure the fact that claims are reached only at the end of a line of reasoning. However, for purposes

TABLE 16.1
Language for different kinds of reasoning

STRATEGY	PHRASES AND EXAMPLES
For inductive reasoning	
Show the strength of your examples.	One case that supports my claim is . . .
	Another example that adds to this pattern is . . .
	These statistics illustrate a widespread . . .
	These instances are just a sample of . . .
	Across many levels of income, the same pattern holds true. For example, . . .
Acknowledge the probability of your data by using qualifiers.	Many . . .
	Most . . .
	Virtually every study in the literature . . .
	Evidence strongly indicates . . .
	I can say with near certainty . . .
	From these cases, I feel quite confident in concluding . . .

Demonstrate costs and rewards.	I'm willing to bet my tax dollars that this program will work . . .
	I think these are good/bad odds because . . .
	This is a gamble we can't afford to take . . .
	The risks, though they do exist, seem minimal compared to the rewards . . .
	Is it worth it to you to . . . ?
For deductive reasoning	
State your premises.	I base this on a core value of mine that . . .
	Underlying my position is . . .
	The argument for my claim rests on one basic assumption that I hope you will agree with. It is . . .
	Either . . . or . . .
	If . . . then . . .
	Only when . . . can . . .
	Anyone who . . .
	To the extent that . . . , then to that extent . . .
Spell out your reasoning.	Because I've shown you *X* and *Y*, . . .
	Therefore, . . .
	This entails . . .
	From this it follows that . . .
	What this means is that . . .
	We have no choice but to conclude that . . .
	Based on this, I reason that . . .
	It seems logical to conclude that . . .
For causal reasoning	
Show how the cause and effect are related in a predictable way.	In state after state where *X* happened, *Y* followed.
	This is no coincidence. When *X* occurs, then *Y* occurs.
	For every unit of increase in *X*, there is a proportional increase in *Y*.
Qualify your causal claims.	There may be many causes, but the one I have identified is a major causal factor.
	It is highly probable that . . .
	In the vast majority of cases, *X* causes *Y*.
	At least in middle-class white families, where most of the research has been conducted, there seems to be a strong causal link between . . .

(continued)

TABLE 16.1
(continued)

STRATEGY	PHRASES AND EXAMPLES
Explain the mechanism of the cause.	Except in small family-owned companies, employee morale is greatly enhanced by ...
	The reason all these experts have concluded that *X* causes *Y* is that ...
	I've shown you all these cases in which .... Let me explain how that happens.
For reasoning by analogy	
Stress the points of similarity.	In Ecuador, as in neighboring Colombia and Peru, ...
	In three similar cities, the same pattern recurred.
	For eight of the ten universities in our conference, adding women's sports to the athletic program has ...
	Likewise, ...
	Similarly, ...
	In a parallel case, ...
Explain points of difference that your listeners may be concerned about.	Although that case was tried in district court, the principle still applies here because ...
	Despite differences in size, our company can learn from this story because ...
	I realize that some of these instances happened a long time ago, but ...
Spell out the link.	If it worked in New Jersey and Idaho and Georgia, it will work in the rest of the country.
	The analogy holds true. We can apply these solutions to our problems.
	The groups who tried such proposals were disappointed. Let's learn from their mistakes.
	Let's not wait too long to plan for earthquake safety. We put off dealing with flood control, and the results have been tragic.

of signposting and keeping your audience informed about the direction you are taking, it is generally a good idea to first state the claim and then explain the reasons for it. Listeners may become lost as the steps of an argument unfold, though. By the time you reach the end of your reasoning, they may forget what claim you were trying to support. Therefore, it is also generally a good idea to restate the claim after you have presented the argument.

In the following example, the speaker's thesis is the claim that marijuana should not be legalized. Each main point is a separate claim supported by a different form of reasoning. Observe how at the end of each main point the speaker summarizes her reasoning to show

how it led to her claim, which she then restates. These brief statements can help audience members understand the logical relationship between evidence offered.

I. People are dangerous when they are under the influence of marijuana.
   (examples of accidents that were caused by people who were under the influence of marijuana)

   Summary of Main Point I: These five tragic stories about innocent people who were killed by someone who was under the influence of marijuana provide us with one reason marijuana should remain illegal: People are dangerous when they use marijuana.

II. Marijuana is a highly addictive drug like cigarettes and alcohol.
   (testimony from doctors and other experts)

   Summary of Main Point II: We all know how easy it is for some people to become addicted to nicotine and alcohol, and the problems that can result. Marijuana is very similar. It, too, can be addictive.

III. Smoking marijuana often causes people to use "harder" drugs.
   (statistics and testimony from drug users and doctors)

   Summary of Main Point III: Therefore, even though many marijuana users do not go on to use harder drugs, many do. These experts claim that contact with criminals and experiences with "getting high" serve as significant causal factors in predicting subsequent usage of harder drugs.

IV. Marijuana use reduces intelligence.
   A. Reduced number of brain cells lower intelligence.
   B. Marijuana kills brain cells.

   Summary of Main Point IV: Because anything that kills brain cells reduces intelligence, and because marijuana has been shown to kill brain cells, you can see that it follows logically that marijuana reduces intelligence.

Conclusion: (restatement of thesis, showing how the points are linked to it) I have shown that marijuana use puts innocent people in danger, is addictive, leads to use of hard drugs, and reduces intelligence. It seems logical that we should not legalize any practice that has these serious consequences.

Go to your CourseMate for The Speaker's Handbook and click on **WebLink 16.3** to access The Argument Clinic at the University of Northern Colorado. This site allows you to submit your arguments to see if they are valid and to see other people's submissions.

Check out Speech Studio to see how other students handled arguments in their speeches. Do any of their speeches include logical fallacies? Or, record a speech you're working on, upload it to Speech Studio, and ask your peers for their feedback. What feedback could you use to fine tune your arguments and avoid logical fallacies before you give your speech in class?

Review, Reconsider, & Act

Summary

Sound reasoning is essential to effective speech making. Reasoning is the process by which we come to understand something new by analyzing what we already know. The key to effective reasoning is offering evidence linked through reasons to support claims. Reasoning patterns include inductive, deductive, causal, and analogic. Many speeches use these reasoning patterns in combination. Common reasoning fallacies should be avoided because they lead to unjustified conclusions and can negatively affect your credibility. By learning to link evidence to a claim through reasoning, a speaker can help *make meaning together* with an audience.

Critical Thinking Questions

▶ What is needed for inductive reasoning to be considered valid?

▶ What makes "absolute" deductive reasoning difficult to use?

▶ How can deductive reasoning still be effectively used?

▶ Which reasoning fallacies described in this chapter have you committed?

Putting It into Practice

Locate a political or professional speech. Consider using a State of the Union speech, available through the American Presidency Project website. Click on **WebLink 16.4** to access this resource, available through your CourseMate for *The Speaker's Handbook*.

1. Highlight the claims made in the speech.
2. Label the claims supported with inductive reasoning.
3. Label the claims supported with deductive reasoning.
4. Label the claims supported with analogic reasoning.
5. What surprises you regarding the reasoning used in the speech you've chosen?

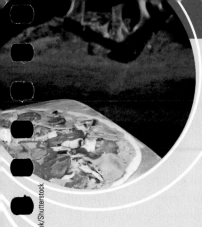

chapter 17
Language and Style

Choose language that makes your ideas
clear and memorable. Respect the power
of language.

Certain interpretations of classical rhetoric tended to treat language as an
adornment to ideas—a sort of gift wrapping put on the package to make it
appealing. Some modern communication models similarly suggest that an
idea is first fully thought out before it is encoded for transmission. Current under-
standings of language grant it a much more central role in communication: Language
is the essence of thought, not a mere vessel for it. People no longer believe that their
ways of thinking are "programmed in"; rather, they develop as individuals interact,
linguistically, with others. This means much more than learning to speak English
instead of Cantonese. It means that if you had been born in a different time and place,
you would not only use language differently, but you would also think differently. So,
language reflects culture and shapes our society.

Because of the pervasive and largely unconscious power of language, we are leery of
any treatments that relegate language to a single step late in the communicative process.
This handbook therefore stresses the importance of "talking ideas into being" throughout the entire process of speech preparation. Competent speakers are conscious of the
ways they develop their ideas through language to achieve an effective speaking style.

Style is a word of many meanings. A "stylish" person is one who conforms to the
latest fads and fashions. A "stylized" drawing is one with the least amount of detail
needed for comprehension. "Style" is the latest decorator colors, and it is tight jeans or
loose jeans, depending on the year. But in the context of speaking, style is simply your
choice of words and the way you string them together. "Good" style involves choosing
and combining those words so that your audience can easily understand and assimilate
your content. Although both demand clear, appropriate, vivid, and varied language,
good oral style differs from good writing style.

Understand How Oral and Written Styles Differ

Although oral style and written style use the same components, the styles are not interchangeable. Listeners expect to hear patterns that reflect the norms of conversation, if more refined. The natural-sounding speaker understands how oral style differs and talks *to* an audience rather than delivering a ten-page monologue. The ideal balance between the orality and literacy of a speech depends on the audience and occasion. (See Chapter **1**.) Sometimes, you will draw more heavily on the communicative resources of the writer. Other times, you can use the language and cadences of conversation.

There are some important ways in which oral style differs from written style. A written essay exists as a time machine: It allows a reader to return to a place where the eye had been a few seconds or many years before, or to jump ahead at will. Public speech is closely connected to time: Words are uttered, and immediately start to fade. Although technology allows us to record speeches, these rebroadcasts often lose their contextual meaning when replayed. Listeners have but one contact with each word, and memory is the only instant replay. Because a listener cannot look back or ahead, oral style uses more repetition, signposting, internal summaries, and internal previews to ensure comprehension and make the organization clear. (See Chapter **12**.) Shorter sentences and words of fewer syllables are characteristic of oral style as well. Sentence fragments are more acceptable in speaking, as are contractions. Even in a formal setting, a speech will still be more colloquial than an essay on the same topic. Table 17.1 lists some key differences between oral and written style.

TABLE 17.1
Differences between written and oral style

WRITTEN STYLE	ORAL STYLE
As mentioned above …	As I said a few minutes ago …
One cannot avoid individuals with this characteristic.	We can't avoid people like that.
Hypothetically, the government might …	Imagine this. Suppose Uncle Sam …
That is unlikely to result.	Well. Maybe.
Subjects were randomly assigned to either a control group or one of three experimental treatment groups. The four groups were pretested for initial attitudes toward the topic, and then post-tested after each experimental group had received a persuasive message containing one of three levels of fear appeals.	Here's how we did our research. First, we randomly assigned the subjects to four groups. Next, we gave all four groups a pretest to see what attitudes they held toward the topic. Then, three of the groups heard persuasive messages. One had a high level of fear appeals, one a medium level, and one a low level. Last, we post-tested the attitudes of all four groups, including the control group that received no message.

© 2013 Cengage Learning

Speaker's Workshop 17.1

Notice how the rhythms and word choices vary among the speakers featured in Part 7 or through your CourseMate for *The Speaker's Handbook*. For example, speakers like Hans Erian, Nathanael Dunlavy, and Kayla Strickland, who prepared from manuscripts, display more features of written style than Rauf Feisal Abdul, who uses more of a story style in his presentation.

Appreciate the spoken word and take advantage of its unique features. The rhythm and meter of speech aid memory. The physical immediacy creates a bond between speakers and listeners. Attune your ear to the music of the spoken word, and use it to your advantage as you phrase your ideas. Drawing on the resources of performance—part of every effective speech to some degree—involves a feel for the power of the spoken word.

Strive for Clear Language

We know that language does more than label objects, concepts, and actions. Words are acts. They do things, like promise or threaten; they can even serve to marry or excommunicate people. Because of this power, we sometimes make messages intentionally vague—perhaps to save face or build solidarity. For the most part, though, clear messages are paramount. "Bear come. We go. Now!" may not be subtle or poetic, but it certainly conveyed an important image from one early human to another. If you understand the priorities of communication, the first question you will ask yourself is, "Did my listeners get the picture?" When speaker and listeners end up with totally different mental images, something has gone awry. Perhaps the speaker has used words in nonstandard ways, or has chosen words so general that they evoke many different responses, or has buried the significant words in an avalanche of extraneous phrases.

To construct clear messages, you must do two things. First, know exactly, not approximately, what you want to communicate. Second, consider who the receivers of your message are and what the words are likely to mean to them.

Be Precise

To avoid fuzzy and ambiguous communication, you need to seek out the word that means precisely what you wish to convey and use it in a structure that illuminates, not obscures, its meaning.

Use the Proper Word

Many words can denote the same object or idea; however, each may have a slightly different focus. Do not say a person was "indicted" for robbery if in fact you mean

TABLE 17.2
The simpler oral style

PRETENTIOUS	BETTER
I was appalled at the feculence that oozed from the typewriter of this so-called greatest living American novelist.	I was appalled at the filth that oozed from the typewriter of this so-called greatest living American novelist.
Then I butted heads with the misoneists of the planning commission.	Then I butted heads with the planning commission, which seems to have a pathological hatred of change.
Hear my supplication!	Hear my plea!

© 2013 Cengage Learning

"arrested" (less serious) or "convicted" (more serious). Learn important distinctions and honor them.

Be careful around words that sound similar but have no similarity of meaning. *Allusion* means "a passing mention," and *illusion* means "a false perception." Some other troublesome near-homophones are *affect/effect, imminent/eminent, casual/causal,* and *aesthetic/ascetic.*

Remember that oral language is simpler than written language. Avoid using a precise word when it may seem pretentious. Table 17.2 offers some examples.

Don't Misuse Your Metaphors

In attempting to convey your picture vividly, do not throw discordant images together. For example, the wife of an official charged with taking a bribe accused the government of entrapment in this manner:

> The FBI has created the *illusion* of a crime. It's like raping Alice in Wonderland.

No doubt the speaker knew what she meant, but the rest of us were not so lucky. Wonderland is a crazy, illogical world where the powers-that-be are unpredictable—and that is a good image to accompany an accusation of entrapment. But used as it was, it only left her listeners deaf to the rest of her words while they struggled with the meaning of the image.

Use Specific and Concrete Language

The more specific and concrete your words, the less is left to your listeners' imaginations. When a speaker says, "NCAA academic standards for college athletes are ineffective," one listener may think, "Yes, they are racist"; another may think, "Yes, they are too low"; and still another may think, "Yes, they should be set by the faculty at each college." Yet all of these may be at odds with the intentions of the speaker, who perhaps feels that the standards are too high. Do not have your words name a broader category than they need to. Table 17.3 gives examples of specific, concrete language.

TABLE 17.3
Specific, concrete language

DO NOT SAY	IF YOU REALLY MEAN	OR EVEN
We need to attract people.	We need to attract customers.	We need to attract grocery shoppers.
This will cause problems.	This will be expensive.	This will cost us $2,500 we don't have.
Our committee has studied it.	Our committee researched and discussed it.	Our committee read documents, heard testimony, and deliberated for several hours.

© 2013 Cengage Learning

Minimize the use of abstract words such as *love, freedom, justice,* and *beauty*— words that have no tangible, physical referent. When you have no option but to use abstract words, supplement them with concrete examples:

> What is more important to me than peace? Freedom is more important to me than peace.
>
> If I weren't able to travel where I wish, if I weren't able to worship as I please, meet to discuss grievances, read and write what I want, then I would struggle to regain all these things.

Be Economical in Your Language

In the interest of clarity, express yourself with the fewest, most straightforward words that convey your meaning. Reasons why speakers use long words, extra words, and convoluted constructions are listed in Table 17.4.

Most often, though, wordiness results from lack of discipline. Editing is not simple, and many people shy away from it. These speakers prefer a machine-gun style of word choice, repeating the message in hopes that one version of it will hit its mark. The clear speaker is more like the sharpshooter who takes careful aim and makes every word count.

TABLE 17.4
Motives for bloated language

	UNECONOMICAL	ECONOMICAL
To hide meaning, as with doublespeak	We sustained losses through friendly fire.	We shelled our own troops.
To avoid responsibility, as with the passive voice	It has been determined that your services are no longer needed.	I have decided to fire you.
To soften unpleasant messages, as with euphemism	Jesse has gone on to his reward.	Jesse died.

© 2013 Cengage Learning

Wordy

Some individuals express their feeling that it is objectionable to eliminate and remove laws that serve to protect female members of the labor force. No one could really be in favor of doing away with protective laws for workers if the elimination of these laws would lead to the exploitation of the people no longer covered. The question I want to raise, however, is whether there is really any relevance to the sex of those workers who should be protected from exploitation, because wages and working conditions ought to be equitable for all employees.

Economical

There are objections to wiping out laws protecting women workers. No one would condone exploitation. But what does sex have to do with it? Working conditions and hours that are harmful to women are harmful to men; wages that are unfair for women are unfair for men.

—*Shirley Chisholm, Democratic congresswoman from New York*

Use Appropriate Language

There is no standard style to use in speaking. Different audiences and topics require different approaches. In the light of your audience analysis, you must make decisions about how formal to be, which part of your personality to project linguistically, and how deeply to descend into specialized language. Your age, status, and personality also determine what language is appropriate for you. Listeners have different expectations about the vocabulary and stylistic level of, say, a senior executive, a teenager, or a poet-in-residence.

Language is not fixed. New words and phrases are always coming into our language, and others fading out. Meanings change, as do standards of appropriateness.

Adapt Your Language to the Formality of the Occasion

Just as you dress differently for formal and casual events, so should you tailor vocabulary and usage to fit the situation. It would be a little startling if the organizer of a PTA bake sale finished an announcement in the following fashion:

This, then, is my plea to you: For the sake of our children, for the sake of our school, for the sake of our PTA, give of yourself for this culinary endeavor.

Equally inappropriate would be a CEO's annual address to stockholders that began:

Well, folks, things look kinda grim, but don't get bummed out, we'll be OK if we just hang in there.

In general, the more formal the occasion,

▶ the more serious the tone,

▶ the more subtle the humor,

▶   the more elaborate the sentences,

▶   the greater the number of figures of speech, and

▶   the greater the departure from everyday words.

More formal occasions include debates, presentations of policy statements, and ceremonial speeches. Less formal occasions include business conferences, roasts, rallies, and after-dinner speeches. In short, the more formal the occasion, the less you can rely on conversational language and the more you must incorporate language you'd use in writing or in a performance.

Use Jargon or Slang Carefully

Both jargon and slang can be used to create a bond with a specialized audience. At times, jargon—a special vocabulary used primarily within a particular group—can also allow you to get a point across more quickly. Slang—words and phrases that are nonstandard substitutions for more formal language—can enrich the texture of your language when used in appropriate situations. But there can be problems with using jargon and slang. You may confuse your audience with technical terms or sacrifice your credibility by using slang expressions that are offensive or out-of-date.

Notice how this excerpt from a talk on preventive maintenance is made understandable to a larger audience by substituting plain English in the second version:

Slang and Jargon Version

Let's look at how Jack could have benefited from a little PM. He burned a lot more number two than he needed to before he got around to running the rack on his Slambang. A maintenance schedule would have pointed out any problems long before the engine started smoking. Same thing with the front SQ drop-in. He wouldn't have cooked it if he had periodically checked and renewed the oil.

Plain-English Version

Let's look at how Jack could have benefited from a little preventive maintenance. He burned a lot more diesel fuel than he needed before he got around to adjusting the fuel injection system on his dump truck. A maintenance schedule would have pointed out any problems long before the engine started smoking. Same thing with the drive axle gears. They wouldn't have overheated and failed if he had periodically checked and renewed the oil.

Avoid Substandard Usage

Remember that a speaker perceived as competent by the audience will also most likely be considered credible. Although acceptable usage varies from place to place, many words and constructions are considered substandard. Speakers who consistently use *ain't* for *isn't* or who get sloppy with noun–verb agreement will find that many audience members will not seriously consider their points. Of course, you can sometimes break the rules for dramatic effect, like ending your opposition to a proposal with "Ain't *no* way!"

TABLE 17.5
Substandard and standard English

SUBSTANDARD	STANDARD
Ten items or less.	Ten items or fewer.
. . . said to my friend and I . . .	. . . said to my friend and me . . .
I could care less!	I couldn't care less!
A large amount of people attended the rally.	A large number of people attended the rally.
Where'd you put it at?	Where'd you put it?
He hits the ball good.	He hits the ball well.
They couldn't hardly see what happened.	They could hardly see what happened.
I would have went there myself.	I would have gone there myself.

© 2013 Cengage Learning

Where can you find a guide for what is standard? Expose yourself to models of literate and graceful usage by reading good magazines, blogs, and literature and by listening to respected public speakers and commentators. This exposure often leads to an intuitive recognition of correct usage. If you have never heard one of your language models say, "This here's the nexus of the problem," then you would be wise not to say "this here" yourself. Table 17.5 gives some more examples of standard versus substandard language. Part 8 addresses errors in pronunciation and usage.

Go to your CourseMate for The Speaker's Handbook *and click on* **WebLink 17.1** *to visit the Merriam-Webster's Dictionary website. This site's dictionary and thesaurus can help you use the right words, find more economical language, check your use of jargon and slang, and more.*

Use Language That Is Respectful and Inclusive

Referring to a group or individuals by the name they prefer is a sign of respect. When changes are made, those changes are often symbolic of a new status or image. For those used to the word *Negro*, the transition to *black* in the late 1960s caused some problems, yet now the term seems natural. In fact, many people use it in interchangeably with the term African American. Today, many adult females want to be called *women*, not *gals, girls*, or *ladies*. It is not possible to please everyone or to be on top of every trend. (Is it *Mexican American, Chicano, Hispanic,* or *Latino*? There are differences in the meanings of these terms and the preferences as to their use.) What you can do is make a reasonable effort to learn which reference people prefer. You can make a commitment to flexibility. Acknowledge that it is worth the temporary inconvenience of changing a language habit if that change is highly symbolic and important to the person or people involved.

A more complex stylistic issue involves the use of the generic *he–man–mankind*. Now that attention has been focused on these images, no speaker or writer can feign innocence of their impact. You may not mean to exclude females by such usage, but you should be aware that many listeners—male and female—now find "generic-he" terms jarring. If you want to avoid distracting, and possibly offending many listeners, use alternatives such as *he or she*, and replace *man or mankind* with *humanity, people,* or *humankind*. Sometimes, in a series of singular examples, you can provide gender balance by alternating pronouns, using *he* in one sentence and *she* in the next. If you are worried about distracting the dwindling segment of an audience offended by the current preferred usage, you can avoid the issue altogether by using plural and collective nouns instead of pronouns and by replacing words like *chairperson* with *presiding officer* and *mail person* with *letter carrier*.

Some guidelines for the use of inclusive language can be found on the websites of various universities and publishers. The guide by the University of Hawaii at Honolulu is a good example of inclusive language in general. And the University of Pennsylvania provides a good guide to gender inclusive language. Go to your CourseMate for The Speaker's Handbook *and click on* **WebLink 17.2** *(Hawaii) and* **WebLink 17.3** *(Pennsylvania).*

FOR YOUR BENEFIT: Not All Nonstandard Language Is Substandard

YOUR NEW CAREER

Sometimes, when people try to "standardize" the language others use, they are actually trying to change the content or to mold the identity of the speaker. While it is important to speak in a way that allows you to be understood by your audience, women should not have to talk like men and people from New Orleans should not have to talk like they are from Connecticut. You will not feel comfortable or seem authentic if you abandon your own language style. Strive to speak so that everyone in your audience will understand you while maintaining your cultural, ethnic, and individual identity.

Rtimages / www.BigStockPhoto.com

Use Vivid, Varied Language

You can keep your listeners attentive and interested by avoiding generic, bland and predictable language. Your audience is much more likely to remember your message if it is filled with vivid imagery, descriptive language, and memorable phrasing. Anyone can infuse energy into a speech by utilizing the following verbal devices.

Use Imagery

When you describe something, put the senses and the imaginative capacities of your listeners to work:

Not: *The life of the long-haul trucker is rough. Aside from being worn down by the effort of driving, the trucker can get discouraged by the tedium.*

But: *The long-haul trucker pulls to the side of the road. Throughout the day, the road has fought back through the springs and steering wheel. Even though the truck is stopped, his arms up to his elbows still throb to the rhythm of hitting four hundred miles of highway expansion joints. The harsh roar of the engine and the rattle of the cab rivets leave him with an infuriating ringing of the ears. After a boring, wholesome dinner, the trucker slips into the cramped womb of the sleeper cab, hoping to rest. In the morning, the pounding cycle of noise, sweat, and stress starts anew.*

Use Stylistic Devices

Enliven your language with figures of speech and memorable arrangements of words and phrases.

Simile and Metaphor

You can add vigor to your speaking by using language that connects objects or ideas to vivid images. A simile makes a comparison between two things ordinarily dissimilar: "When she came in from shoveling off the walk, her hands were like ice." No one would mistake a hand for a chunk of ice, but in this case they share the characteristic of extremely low temperature. A metaphor creates a figurative equation that implies two unlike things are the same: "Her hands were ice cubes" or "We stand in horror as our money disappears down the gluttonous maw of the federal government." Making the government a shark forms a more compelling image than "We stand in horror as the federal government operates with fiscal irresponsibility."

Personification

Objects or ideas can be brought to life by imbuing them with human qualities. We know that a room cannot really be "cheerful," that winds do not actually "whisper," and that the economy cannot possibly "limp." Nevertheless, all of these images are potent because they reflect human behavior. Here's another example:

> Today, we begin a new chapter in the history of Louisiana. I've said throughout the campaign that there are two entities that have the most to fear from us winning this election. One is corruption and the other is incompetence. If you happen to see either of them, let them know the party is over.
> —Bobby Jindal, Louisiana Governor-Elect victory speech delivered October 20, 2007[1]

Hyperbole

To emphasize a point, you may deliberately overstate it in a way that is clearly fanciful and not meant to be taken literally:

▶ This paperwork will be the death of me.

▶ I thought about nothing else for the next three days.

▶ The governor has repeated this same promise to you a million times.

Repetitive Language or Structure

By repeating keywords or phrases, you make your listeners feel that your points are snowballing to a certain conclusion. Use parallel structure to emphasize relationships.

Sometimes, a syntactic construction is repeated, such as the questions and brief answers in this paragraph:

> How serious is the morale crisis? We have lost several key employees. What has caused the problem? Lack of clear upward and downward communication. How can we change things? By hiring an interpersonal and organizational communication trainer for a series of workshops.

Notice that no phrases are repeated, but the question–answer format creates a sense of momentum.

The same phrase can begin consecutive paragraphs. For instance, a speaker can build a sense of urgency or dedication by repeating the phrase "We must act now to . . . " as each problem is presented.

Within a paragraph, you can achieve a similar effect by starting a series of sentences with the same words or by using a sentence as a connecting refrain.

> You see, I was born to a teenage mother, who was born to a teenage mother. I understand. I know abandonment, and people being mean to you, and saying you're nothing and nobody, and can never be anything. I understand. Jesse Jackson is my third name. I'm adopted. When I had no name, my grandmother gave me her name; my name was Jesse Burns 'til I was twelve. So I wouldn't have a blank space, she gave me a name. To hold me over. I understand when nobody knows your name. I understand when you have no name. I understand.
> —*Jesse Jackson, minister and civil rights activist*

Or you might end several sentences with the same words:

> What remains? Treaties have gone. The honor of nations has gone. Liberty has gone.
> —*David Lloyd George, former British statesman*

Additionally, for emphasis, you can repeat key words or phrases within a sentence:

> But, in a larger sense, we can not dedicate—we can not consecrate—we can not hallow this ground.
> —*Abraham Lincoln, sixteenth president of the United States*

Alliteration and Assonance

Use of these devices involves saying the same sound in a sustained sequence. Whether it is with consonants alliteration or vowels assonance, this repetition can make an idea more memorable, or at least charge it with a sense of poetry. Consider first alliteration as demonstrated here:

> Somewhere at this very moment a child is being born in America. Let it be our cause to give that child a happy home, a healthy family, and a hopeful future.
> —*Bill Clinton, 1992 Democratic National Convention Acceptance Address*[2]

Or assonance as in this example:

> Our flag is red, white, and blue—but our nation is rainbow. Red, yellow, brown, black, and white, we're all precious in God's sight.
> —*Jesse Jackson, 1984 Democratic National Convention Address*[3]

Antithesis

To contrast two ideas, you can use antithesis, which sometimes uses or implies word pairs like these:

▶ Not …, but …

▶ Not only …, but …

▶ Never …, unless …

Consider this example:

> We live in a society that emphasizes military expenditures over education. We spend millions teaching young people how to kill and be killed, but we won't spend money teaching them how to live and make a living.
> —*Harry Edwards, sociologist and civil rights activist*

In his acceptance of the 2001 Nobel Peace Prize, United Nations Secretary General Kofi Annan used antithesis, alliteration and assonance, and repetitive structure in one sentence:

> Today's real borders are not between nations, but between powerful and powerless, free and fettered, privileged and humiliated.

CHECKLIST ~ **Verbal Devices to Make Your Language Vivid**

- [ ] Images that appeal to the senses
- [ ] Similes and metaphors
- [ ] Personification
- [ ] Hyperbole
- [ ] Repetition of key words
- [ ] Parallel structure of key phrases
- [ ] Alliteration and assonance
- [ ] Antithesis
- [ ] Fresh language
- [ ] Varied sentence rhythms

Use Fresh Language

The power of figurative language lies in the images stimulated in the listener's mind. After too many repetitions, the original psychological impact is lost. The phrases, "At the end of the day" and "Easy as pie," while once pleasantly descriptive, are now tired and overused.

Certain fad words attract a following. *Cutting edge, iconic,* and *24/7* become overnight sensations and are used to the exclusion of many good (and fresher) synonyms. Rid your language of such phrasing. Take time to select original combinations of words and phrases that capture the image, mood, or thought you want to get across.

Vary the Rhythm of Your Sentences

Although oral style is characterized by simpler, shorter phrases with fewer different words, you are not trying to breed boredom. The "sing-songiness" associated with children's rhymes can creep into a speech if you fail to pay attention to how you are stringing your sentences and phrases together. Use parallelisms and repetition sparingly. Consider this plodding passage:

> The association's annual convention should be user supported. The convention is attended by a core of regulars. The average association member doesn't benefit from the convention. These average members shouldn't have to bear more than their fair share.

The choppiness of this tedious passage results from the sameness of sentence length and structure. Recasting the sentences will create a more fluid and graceful paragraph:

> The association's annual convention should be user supported. Who attends the convention? A core of regulars. The average association members, who don't benefit from the convention, shouldn't have to bear more than their fair share.

Speaker's Workshop 17.2

1. Rewrite these statements in a style more appropriate to oral communication.
   A. After having removed the air filter, one can begin to investigate the origins of the problem.
   B. All clerical and administrative personnel will undergo semiannual performance appraisals designed to evaluate their competence and clarify objectives for the next appraisal period.

2. Rewrite the following sentences so that they are more concrete, economical, correct, and inclusive.
   A. It's a very unique sort of thing how Karen just makes everybody feel sort of good. She's real notorious as the most respected girl on our whole staff of salesmen.
   B. At this time I'd like to say that one point to consider is the fact that we were totally surrounded by smokers who caused us considerable irritation and distress and aggravation.
   C. Plus, I personally feel that we also face a serious crisis of psychological morale. We need to get off our duffs and sit down and talk about this epidemic that has us running on only three cylinders.

3. Read aloud paragraph 16 of President Barack Obama's speech transcript that is available among this book's online resources and in Part 7, and take special note of the rhythm of the sentences (and the use of repetition). Find another paragraph in the same speech that illustrates at least two other stylistic principles from this chapter.

4. Use at least two different stylistic devices to enliven each of these phrases:
   A. A cold, rainy day
   B. An unworkable policy
   C. A delicate, intricate procedure
   D. A very stern leader
   E. A huge crowd

5. Think of fresh ways to replace these overused phrases:
   A. Like comparing apples and oranges
   B. Caught between a rock and a hard place
   C. Two steps forward and one step back
   D. Always darkest before the dawn

6. Read or watch the speech by Barack Obama, available in Part 7 or through your CourseMate for *The Speaker's Handbook*. Identify at least three different examples of imagery or stylistic devices Obama uses.

Use the Language Style of Your Listeners

Language is not solely the possession of speakers. Our words are shared with our listeners, drawn from a shared pool of possible statements. Speech consists not of messages sent, but of meanings jointly constructed within the context of a discourse community. Among the many possible ways to talk about a topic, the most effective way is the one that overlaps and resonates with your listeners. When you use phrases and metaphors that are comfortable for your audience, you're creating a bond that goes beyond the literal definitions of the words you use and lays the foundation for more communication. This sort of bonding is particularly important with an unfavorable audience.

In the process of bonding, be careful not to parrot phrases you do not understand, mock anyone's accent, or seem to talk down to your listeners. As a speaker, you must be yourself. But you have many facets, and without being artificial, you can choose to bring into your speech those aspects of your own language that best match your audience.

Synchronizing your language with your listeners' language involves close audience analysis. Listening to them and engaging in genuine dialogue will reveal the terms and categories that organize their reality. Every aspect of style can be subtly adjusted—level of formality, use of jargon or abbreviations, selection of figures of speech and metaphors. Matching words or phrases is important because paying attention to the

Speaker's Workshop 17.3

1. Suppose you are going to speak on the topic of why a two-day strategic planning retreat is a good investment for an organization. You visit three departments to which you will be making separate presentations. Based on the following observations, how would you characterize each audience, and how might you adapt your topic and your language to establish a tone that is in sync with theirs?

    ▶ Group A uses these terms: the real go-getters, on the fast track, it's a rat race every day, pressure cooker.

    ▶ Group B uses these terms: dotting the i's and crossing the t's, getting your ducks in a row, doing your homework.

    ▶ Group C uses these terms: our family here, the team, touching base, backing each other up.

2.   Find President Barack Obama's speech in Part 7 or through your CourseMate for *The Speaker's Handbook*. The speech opens with the premise that the people of Egypt have "spoken" that their "voices have been heard." Review the speech to locate additional references to voice and being heard.

audience's words gives you clues about how they see the world. If you respect your listeners, you will almost subconsciously scan for terms that reveal that respect. If you do not understand them, there is the potential to offend them. For example, the board member of an orchestra who talks to the musicians about Beethoven's Ninth Symphony as a good "product" may alienate them. Or the lack of understanding may not be as dramatic: It may be simply a feeling of not really connecting, though neither speaker nor listeners can explain why.

Check out Speech Studio to see how other students use language in their speeches. Or record a speech you're working on, upload it to Speech Studio, and ask your peers for their feedback. What feedback could you use to fine tune your language before you give your speech in class?

Review, Reconsider, & Act

Summary

Language reflects culture and shapes the perceptions of its users. How we use words determines our ability to connect with an audience and influences that audience's perception of us and our ideas. Because an oral style differs from written style, speakers must give careful consideration to linguistic choices. Language should be clear, appropriate, vivid, varied, and matched to the language style of the audience.

Critical Thinking Questions

▶ Why is a choice of words considered a choice of "worlds"?

▶ When might a speaker intentionally use abstract words over more concrete language?

▶ What effect does making a poor choice in language or style have on an audience?

▶ Offer an example of a speaker who failed to effectively match language choices to the situation.

Putting It into Practice

 Read or watch Barack Obama's "Address to the Nation on the End of Operation Iraqi Freedom," delivered on August 31, 2010. The text and video of this speech are available at the White House's Briefing Room website. You can also access them though **WebLink 17.4** at your CourseMate for *The Speaker's Handbook*.

1. As you review the speech, notice its style: oral or written.
2. Identify examples of both concrete and abstract language.
3. What instances of vivid and varied language can you identify?
4. What stylistic devices does Obama use? With what effect?
5. How does Obama adapt his language to the occasion and audience?

chapter 19
Credibility

Establish your credibility, both before and
during your speech, by projecting competence,
concern, trustworthiness, and dynamism.

W hat is it about some speakers that makes you want to accept what they say,
while others make you want to reject what may be an identical message?
Your content and delivery determine, to a great extent, whether your listeners believe what you say. However, an independent force is at work that can doom
even the best planned and practiced speeches. Beyond what you say and how you say
it, your audience is influenced by who you are or, more accurately, by the person they
think you are. Your credibility is that combination of perceived qualities that makes
listeners predisposed to believe you.

For centuries, scholars have been fascinated by credibility, from classical discussions of ethos to contemporary investigations of concepts like *image, personality*, and
charisma. Aristotle observed that audiences who view a speaker as having good sense,
goodwill, and good character are more likely to believe him or her. Modern social scientists have tried to isolate the characteristics that distinguish the most credible speakers
from others. Their lists include competence, dynamism, intention, personality, intelligence, authoritativeness, extroversion, trustworthiness, composure, and sociability.

You can enhance your credibility, and thus the chances of meeting your speech
objective, by projecting these qualities. You can build your image or reputation before
the speech, and you can take steps to improve your credibility as you are speaking. The
first step, though, is to assess your image.

Assess Your Speaking Image

The perfect speaker is seen as competent, concerned, trustworthy, and dynamic in
discussing all topics with all audiences, but most of us fall short of this ideal. One
speaker might seem warm, charming, and likable but somehow have trouble being

taken seriously on weighty issues. Another may have a demeanor that immediately inspires confidence but suffers from seeming dull or distant or not human enough.

Before you can work on improving your credibility, you need to see where you stand now. Is your overall credibility high or low? Which components of credibility are strongest for you? Which need to be developed? It may be very hard to gauge this alone. If possible, have some friends help you with this appraisal.

CHECKLIST ~ Assess Your Speaking Image

Are you perceived as competent?

- *Image prior to speech:* Do you have education, experience, or credentials to make you an expert on this topic? Does your audience know that?

- *Content of speech:* Have you researched broadly and deeply? Does your speech reflect this with well-documented, factual information?

- *Delivery:* Does your delivery connote competence? Do you seem to be on top of your information, well organized, and composed?

Are you perceived as concerned about your audience's welfare?

- *Image prior to speech:* If you have a history of generosity or selflessness on relevant issues, is it known? (For example, have you volunteered your time, informed yourself thoroughly, or made a sacrifice of some sort?)

- *Content of speech:* Do you stress the audience's needs and goals throughout the speech?

- *Delivery:* Is your delivery warm, unaffected, friendly, and responsive to the audience?

Are you perceived as trustworthy?

- *Image prior to speech:* Is your record one of honesty and integrity?

- *Content of speech:* Do you make an effort to be fair in presenting evidence, acknowledging the limitations of your data and opinions, and conceding those parts of opposing viewpoints that have validity?

- *Delivery:* Is your style of presentation sincere and honest, not slick or manipulative?

Are you perceived as dynamic?

- *Image prior to speech:* Is your image that of an active, assertive person, a leader rather than a follower, a doer rather than an observer?

- *Content of speech:* Does your speech have a sense of movement? Do the ideas build to a climax? Is your language lively and colorful?

- *Delivery:* Is your delivery animated, energetic, and enthusiastic?

Suggestions for improving your credibility in each of these areas are provided later in this chapter.

Speaker's Workshop 19.1

1. Use the "Assess Your Speaking Image" checklist to complete your image inventory. In a few sentences, describe your prior image as a speaker in your speech class or in a social or professional group you relate to regularly. Which is your strongest area: competence, concern, trustworthiness, or dynamism? Which is your weakest?

2. Consider how your credibility varies from topic to topic. Name three topics on which you already have high credibility and three on which you would have to work very hard to establish credibility.

3. Rate the last four U.S. presidents' credibility as high, medium, or low in each of the four areas of competence, concern, trustworthiness, and dynamism. Discuss your choices and reasons.

4. Is there a public figure you regard as competent, concerned, and trustworthy but whose image suffers due to a lack of dynamism? Can you think of a public figure for whom the opposite is true?

Build Your Credibility Before Your Speech

In a speech class, you know you have a certain image. Consider this image as your personal "brand." Based on daily classroom interactions, you can tell if you are considered serious, funny, prompt, lazy, cheerful, argumentative, intelligent, informed, and so on. Perceptions of your brand will affect the way your speeches are received.

YOUR
NEW
CAREER

FOR YOUR BENEFIT: Provide the Contact Person with Information about Your Qualifications

Even if you are not a professional speaker, you may have opportunities to speak outside the classroom. When you do, do not be overly modest when asked for information for advance publicity. Send a résumé that lists your background and achievements. Include clippings, testimonials about your speaking, a list of your books and articles, and a photograph if appropriate. In addition to providing written information, be available for consultation by phone or in person with the person introducing you. If there are aspects of your background you would like stressed for a particular speech, be sure to say so. It is acceptable to draft your own introduction.

A similar situation exists if you are to speak in front of the service group or profes-sional association to which you belong.

Speaking before an unfamiliar audience is different. Because these people have lit-tle basis on which to form an impression, their entire perception of you initially will be based on your nonverbal communication. Your brand will be based almost entirely on your appearance, friendliness, professionalism, confidence, and ability to make small talk prior to the speech will be very influential.

Build Your Credibility through Your Words

As you prepare your speech outline and select your supporting evidence and examples, think about ways to communicate your competence, concern, trustworthiness, and dynamism. The following suggestions are especially relevant in the opening minutes of the speech, when the audience is forming its first impressions. (See Chapter **13**.) But many credibility boosters can be woven throughout the entire speech as well.

The framework and prompts provided throughout Speech Builder Express can help you ensure your credibility as a public speaker. The following sections would be especially helpful: Goal/Purpose, Organization, Supporting Material, Introduction, *and* Works Cited.

Present Your Credentials

Most inexperienced speakers find it difficult to blow their own horns and do not do as much credibility building as they should. Do not be reluctant to provide information about your qualifications to speak. Do this even if you think your audience should remember you from the last speech you gave. For instance, you might say:

▶ In my five years as an Assistant Manager for Target, . . .

▶ The most common error I see in the twenty to thirty loan applications I look at each week is . . .

▶ I've had a special awareness of the barriers the physically handicapped face since 2009, when my brother Dave returned from the Iraq War.

Judgment and tact are important in deciding which qualifications to mention and how to work them into the speech. Our culture frowns on bragging and name-dropping; however, you can include many statements of your qualifications without seeming boastful if you play it straight and present them matter-of-factly. Include only relevant qualifications. Do not talk about well-known people you know unless it relates to the topic, and do not expound on your financial success unless the speech is specifi-cally about making money.

Demonstrate a Thorough Understanding of Your Topic

To communicate a sense of expertise, let listeners know you've done your homework. Mention the nature of your research when appropriate:

▶ The three judges I interviewed all agreed on one major weakness in our court system.

▶ I read the minutes of all the committee hearings on this bill, and not one expert mentioned…

▶ There is considerable disagreement on this point in the articles I read. Several scholars say…

Use concrete examples, statistics, and testimony. Be sure you have your details straight. One obvious error early in the speech can ruin your credibility:

> Just imagine what it would have been like for the Union soldier crouching in the trenches around Richmond, his jacket *zipped* up tight in a futile battle against the cold and the wet.

The people listening to this would probably think, "If this speaker doesn't know the zipper wasn't invented until long after the Civil War, I wonder what other information is all wrong?"

Be Sure Material Is Clearly Organized

Your audience's opinion of your competence depends on their sense that you are in command of your material and know where you are headed. Listeners will view you as uninformed rather than unorganized if you wander from topic to topic or must apologetically insert, "Oh, one thing I forgot to mention when I was discussing . . . ."

Present a Balanced, Objective Analysis

To demonstrate you are fair, trustworthy, and of good character, go out of your way to acknowledge the limitations of your evidence and argument, if appropriate:

▶ Now, I know there are some problems with relying on surveys, but this one was carefully conducted. It seems safe to conclude that many, if not most, working mothers are dissatisfied with the quality of child care available to them.

▶ I'm not saying television is the only cause of these problems. I realize that's an oversimplification. But I do think TV has had a pronounced effect on the imaginative thinking of the last two generations.

Also, be sure to acknowledge the existence of opposing evidence and opinions:

▶ Some studies indicate that an alcoholic can return to social drinking, however…

▶ I recognize the contributions the administration has made to social welfare programs, but it has failed in so many other areas that I still maintain it is time for a change.

Acknowledge self-interest when it exists to prevent the audience from thinking you are trying to hide something from them.

▶ It's true I'm a real estate agent and I stand to profit by having folks invest in real estate. But that's not my main reason for urging you to invest.

Speaker's Workshop 19.2

1. Go to your CourseMate for *The Speaker's Handbook* and watch Nathanael Dunlavy's speech about the 54th Regiment. How does he directly establish his credentials to speak? Which examples do you find especially effective?

2. Go to Part 7 or to your CourseMate for *The Speaker's Handbook* and find an example of how Brian Sharkey and Nathanael Dunlavy explicitly establish concern for the welfare of the audience. Also look at the speech by Feisal Abdul Rauf: What sections of this speech seem to present the speaker as a fair, objective, and honest person?

Express Your Concern for the Audience

Let audience members know your speech is offered to benefit them:

▶ I'd do anything to save your families the headaches and heartaches that go along with having a relative die without a will.

▶ Taking up cycling has added so much to my life that I'd love to see some of you share in that fun.

Increase Credibility with Your Delivery

Too many expert and well-prepared speakers lose effectiveness because they cannot *transmit* these qualities to their audience. Dropping cards, reading in a shaky voice, or fumbling with whatever is at hand all suggest lack of competence. An unexpressive face and voice might be interpreted as disdainfulness and detract from perceived goodwill. Hesitancy and uncertainty are sometimes mistakenly seen as shiftiness or dishonesty. Listless, monotonous, colorless speaking is the very opposite of dynamism and does little to enhance credibility; however, an overly emotional delivery can signal credibility problems, too. To be seen as a believable source of information and opinion, seek a balanced delivery that includes plenty of eye contact, natural gestures, and a dynamic tone. Additional delivery suggestions are offered in Chapters 25 and 26.

Go to your CourseMate for The Speaker's Handbook *and click on* **WebLink 19.1** *to visit a Colorado State University site that addresses how you can establish your competence and credibility. Also check out* **WebLink 19.2** *to visit Duke University's site on how to maintain credibility by correctly citing sources using a number of different style manuals.*

 *Check out Speech Studio to see how other students demonstrate their credibility during their speeches. Or record a speech you're working on, upload it to Speech Studio, and ask your peers for their feedback. What feedback could you use to fine tune how you demonstrate credibility before you give your speech in class?*

Review, Reconsider, & Act

Summary

Credibility is that combination of perceived qualities that makes listeners predisposed to believe you. It starts with a speaker's image (nonverbal communication) and is enhanced before and during the speech by adequate preparation and practice. Credible speakers must not be timid about presenting their credentials, demonstrating knowledge of their topic, presenting a balanced and objective analysis, and transmitting both personal confidence and concern for the audience.

Critical Thinking Questions

▶ How is stating your credibility similar to positive self-suggestion discussed in Chapter 4?

▶ What can a speaker do to develop credibility before speaking?

▶ What can a speaker do to enhance credibility while speaking?

▶ What mistakes have you seen destroy a speaker's credibility?

Putting It into Practice

Review the article "Preparing American Students to Succeed in a Global Era of Change" by David Abney.[1] Go to your CourseMate for *The Speaker's Handbook* to access this article through **WebLink 19.3** or through InfoTrac® College Edition.

1. How does the speaker connect with his audience to open the speech?
2. How effectively does the speaker present his own credentials?
3. Does the speaker demonstrate a thorough understanding of the topic? How so?
4. How does the speaker demonstrate concern for the audience?

chapter 20

Motivational Appeals

Motivate your listeners toward your speech's purpose through appeals to their emotions, needs, and values. But be sure these appeals do not replace sound logic and evidence.

This handbook stresses the role of clear analysis in support of ideas, but it also emphasizes making those ideas meaningful to an audience. A good speaker is constantly aware of the humanness of the audience. To be human is to be rational, but it is more than that. Love sometimes overrules logic, reverence often transcends reason, and emotion frequently contradicts evidence. Understanding the humanity of your audience means presenting your case so it touches the listeners' hearts as well as their heads.

Consider the Emotional Impact of Your Words

Keep in mind that everything you say has the potential to trigger some sort of emotional response in your audience. Generally, you can strengthen your speech by selecting main points, supporting material, and language that engages your listeners' feelings. Positive emotions—hope, joy, pride, love—are surefire motivators. Negative emotions like fear, envy, disgust, and contempt can also motivate, but the motivational effects of negative emotions are less predictable. Moderate levels of fear appeal can enhance persuasion, but higher levels may work against the desired effect. Some presentations feature gory films of traffic accidents, vivid visual aids showing cancerous lung tissue, or detailed descriptions of the plight of a family whose breadwinner had no insurance. These can either cause the audience to tune out the unpleasantness or seem too extreme to be statistically plausible fates for the listener to worry about. When adding emotion to your speech, remember the old adage, "Although some is good, more is not always better."

Devoid of Emotion

Malaria is a disease that causes a high fever and chills.[1]

Moderate Emotion

Most malaria infections cause symptoms like the flu, such as a high fever, chills, and muscle pain. Symptoms tend to come and go in cycles. One type of malaria may cause more serious problems, such as damage to the heart, lungs, kidneys, or brain. It can even be deadly.[2]

Excessive Emotion

You've been bitten and you know that while death is not immediate, you face fever, chills, and uncontrollable muscle pain that comes in waves, one more serious than the next. If you are lucky enough to live near a properly supplied hospital, you might live. That is, if you realize your symptoms are malaria and not some more benign infection. Without treatment, your brain, hearts, lungs and kidneys are all at risk and you will likely die. In addition, you may be the cause of many other deaths in your village.

These three levels of emotion are possible for any topic. It's important to discern early on where your listeners draw the dividing lines. Try to include the optimal amount of emotional appeal—not so little that you fail to move them and not so much that you turn them off.

Relate Your Speech to Listeners' Needs

The best-known way of classifying human needs is **Maslow's hierarchy of needs.**[3] Figure 20.1 shows the hierarchy.

In this hierarchy, the lower-level needs have to be met or satisfied before an individual can become concerned with the needs on the next-higher level. For instance, on the topic of physical fitness, you could appeal to your audience at any of the following levels:

▸ The effect of exercise in reducing risk of cardiovascular disease appeals to the survival need.

▸ Security might be drawn in by mentioning how physically fit people are more likely to be able to resist or evade attackers.

▸ The need for belonging can be linked to becoming trim and attractive, as well as to making friends through physical activity.

▸ Esteem needs can be tied into the current popularity of fitness and the social desirability of an active image.

▸ Fitness can be related to the need for self-actualization—the highs of exercise and the mental and physical challenge of reaching one's potential.

The significance of Maslow's hierarchy to the speaker is apparent. You must analyze your audience well enough to determine which need is most salient. Listeners whose jobs are in danger and who are struggling to feed their families do not want to hear you

FIGURE 20.1
Maslow's hierarchy of needs

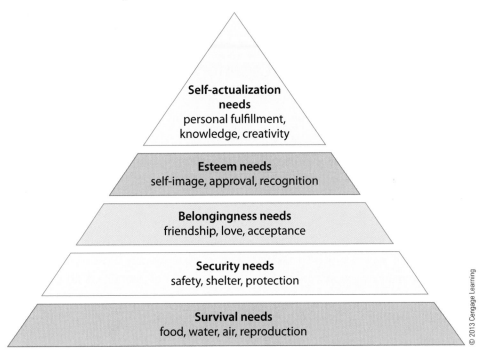

© 2013 Cengage Learning

contrast local economic programs in terms of the implications drawn from Keynesian theory. They want to know which one will create jobs. Being absorbed with their security needs, they are not likely to respond at the self-actualization level.

It is counterproductive to aim your emotional appeals too high, and unethical to aim them too low. Suppose a speaker wants to convince colleagues to adopt a different software system from the one currently in use in that department. If the company is doing well and the colleagues are satisfactory employees, then it would be inappropriate to use a fear appeal with visions of the organization going out of business and people being tossed into the street if the new system is not adopted. The more ethical approach would be to build a case related to the colleagues' needs for efficiency, productivity, success, and prestige (esteem and self-actualization levels).

To be fair, you should respond to existing needs and not foster an artificial sense of insecurity in your listeners. Speakers who abuse their influence in this way falsely assume that the most primitive needs are the strongest. Altruism is an extremely effective motivator. In fact, it might be possible to place another pyramid beside Maslow's, illustrating the belief that every person has a basic need to *protect* others' survival, to *give* security, to *spread* love, to *build* esteem, and to *nurture* self-actualization. Appeals to the idealistic, caring sides of human nature can be at least as powerful as self-oriented appeals.

Go to your CourseMate for The Speaker's Handbook *and click on* **WebLink 20.1** *for more on Maslow's hierarchy of needs, provided by the University of Hawaii at Honolulu.*

Relate Your Speech to Listeners' Values

Suppose, in a presentation, you use the argument, "and this procedure will speed up your assembly line," but you are actually unveiling only a part of the following syllogism:

> Anything that speeds up your assembly line is good.
> This procedure will speed up your assembly line.
> Therefore, this procedure is good.

You assume your listeners share increasing production speed as a value; as a result, you do not feel it is necessary to clutter your talk with the other parts of the syllogism. As it turns out, however, these particular listeners are currently satisfied with the speed of production but are more concerned with the accuracy of assembly. A little audience analysis could have alerted you to the fact, and you might have worked from the following syllogism:

> Anything that improves accuracy is good.
> This procedure improves accuracy.
> Therefore, this procedure is good.

Both arguments are logically sound, but the second is psychologically more effective because its underlying premise reflects the dominant value of the listeners.

We hold a certain value if we believe that a particular thing is either good or bad, in the broadest sense of those terms. Specifically, we *evaluate* concepts, people, objects, events, or ideas every day as we label them just or unjust, wise or foolish, beautiful or ugly, and so on. Whereas emotions and needs are considered innate (and therefore consistent across cultures, societies, and individuals), values are judgments or choices made by individuals. Looking at two people in isolation, we could predict that they both fear certain things, and both have a need for status, simply on the basis of their humanness. But we could not so easily predict whether one hates cats or the other is a passionate supporter of the free enterprise system.

Incorporate Appeals to General Values

Although values are individually chosen, the choice is rarely a totally conscious and rational one. Culture has a strong influence, shaping values through families, schools, media, and peers. Moreover, values are rarely formed in isolation; rather, they are organized and structured into related clusters. By knowing the culture of your listeners, the influences on them, and perhaps some of the other values they hold, you can make an educated guess as to how much particular values might shape their attitude toward your speech topic.

Sometimes, identifying values in your own culture can be extremely difficult; predominant values and trends often do not become clear until years later, much too late to do a speaker any good. However, paying attention to editorial writers and news commentators can help you get a clearer picture of the national mood. Many public opinion polls on specific issues like abortion, immigration, marriage rights, and energy policy contain questions specifically addressed to values.[4] You can also augment your audience analysis with an awareness of trends, mainstream values caused by economic and technical trends, counterculture movements, and liberation movements.

FOR YOUR BENEFIT: The Universality of Values

Research has found six universal value dimensions that together capture common values affecting human behavior.[5] Consider which value dimension best represents the majority of your audience members and how appeals to values that matter to them might improve your ability to motivate their behavior.

▶ ***Striver:*** *Values power, status, ambition, health and fitness, material security, courage, perseverance, public image, and wealth.*

▶ ***Fun-Seeker:*** *Values excitement, leisure, individuality, pleasure, enjoying life, having fun, adventure, and variety.*

▶ ***Creative:*** *Values open-mindedness, beauty, fulfilling work, self-esteem, creativity, self-reliance, freedom, curiousity, knowledge, wisdom, learning, internationalism, and music.*

▶ ***Devout:*** *Values spirituality, tradition, duty, obedience, respecting ancestors, traditional gender roles, faith, and modesty.*

▶ ***Intimate:*** *Values honesty, authenticity, protecting family, personal support, stable personal relationships, enduring love, romance, friendship, and sex.*

▶ ***Altruist:*** *Values being in tune with nature, preserving the environment, justice, social responsibility, helpfulness, equality, social tolerance, and social stability.*

Rtimages / www.BigStockPhoto.com

Identify and Relate to Listeners' Core Values

If the members of a culture share common values, why do we not see lockstep agreement on every issue? Obviously, not all members of a culture give equal importance to the common values, nor is there a standard ranking of them. Values are very general, and any particular issue can touch on many values, on both the pro side and the con. Examples of this value conflict can become common around election time. Suppose there is a proposed bond issue to build an expensive fine arts complex. Stella is drawn toward approving the bond because she holds the values of a world of beauty and a sense of accomplishment. But she may also have reservations about taking on a greater tax burden because of her belief in the values of a comfortable, prosperous life and family security. Stella's resolution of this conflict will depend on how she has prioritized these values.

Because nearly every topic stirs up such value conflicts, a list of audience values will not be useful unless it is supplemented by some estimate of the relative ranking. As Figure 20.2 shows, one way to illustrate this is to imagine a series of concentric circles, with the most strongly held values at the core, and the degree of importance of the other values determining their distance from the center. The innermost circle contains *core values*, the ones so central to a person that to change one of them would amount to a basic alteration of that person's self-concept. The next band out from the center contains the *authority values*, the values that are influenced by and shared with groups and individuals most significant to the person. *Peripheral values* form the outer band.[6] These are the more-or-less-incidental evaluations, easily made or changed.

FIGURE 20.2
Ranking of values

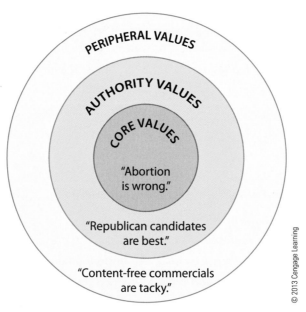

PERIPHERAL VALUES

AUTHORITY VALUES

CORE VALUES

"Abortion is wrong."

"Republican candidates are best."

"Content-free commercials are tacky."

© 2013 Cengage Learning

When speaking, try to make reasonable inferences about your listeners' core values and stress them in your speech or presentation. For example, suppose you have an educational innovation you want the local school system to adopt. In speaking to the school board, you might stress the values of practicality, efficiency, and local control of education. In speaking to the teachers, you might stress the more idealistic value of

Speaker's Workshop 20.1

1. Which of Maslow's needs found in Figure 20.1 are appealed to in each of these examples?
   A. Following the dress-for-success formula has helped countless people advance in their careers.
   B. Every home should have an electronic alarm system.
   C. Meditation will enhance your understanding of the universe.
   D. Some of the marijuana available on the street is laced with deadly chemicals.
   E. This shampoo makes your hair more touchable.

2. Read or watch the special occasion speech by Barack Obama about Egypt, available in Part 7 or through your CourseMate for *The Speaker's Handbook*. Identify the values he appeals to and analyze which ones he seems to prioritize as core values of his listeners. Also, identify the explicit emotional appeals he makes and assess the effectiveness of those appeals.

3. Go to Part 7 or to your CourseMate for *The Speaker's Handbook* to access the sample speeches. How does Dianna Cohen use emotional appeals in her persuasive speech? How does Feisal Abdul Rauf use emotional appeals in his persuasive speech?

4. Of the value dimensions listed in the For Your Benefit box in this chapter, which one or two would you designate as your core values? Which ones do you think are most salient in the value system of the United States today? Which values do you see as having undergone the greatest change in the past few years?

5. Return to the examples in part 1 of this activity above and relate each statement to at least two of the values listed in the For Your Benefit box.

6. Analyze an audience you speak to regularly (speech class, professional association, study group) in terms of their probable responses to a speech on immigration.
   A. What needs could you appeal to?
   B. What core values could you appeal to?
   C. What authority values could you appeal to?
   D. What new value–issue links could you forge?

progress in education. Although your approach in these two cases is different, this does not mean you assume that teachers are impractical or that school board members care nothing about educational progress. The members of both groups probably hold each of these values. However, as a speaker, you make a decision to stress those values likely to be closer to the core in each audience.

Link Issues of Speech to Listeners' Values

The *issues* of your speech are the questions that must be resolved in your listeners' minds before your speech purpose can be met. (See Chapter **6**.) Decisions about what is worth knowing, what should be done, or what touches our spirit often depend on the prior acceptance of certain values. Not only do people differ in what values they hold and how they prioritize them, but they differ in how they perceive connections between particular values and particular issues. Even when listeners share almost identical values and priorities, it is possible for them to perceive links differently. Take two audience members who value creative freedom and efficiency, with efficiency being closer to the core. If your issue is the abolition of tenure, one listener might link that issue to creative freedom and be antagonistic to your speech goal, whereas the other might link it to efficiency and look upon your proposal favorably.

It is not enough, then, to know what values your listeners hold. You must try to discover which values they see as pertinent to your topic. Often, it is necessary to point out value links that are logical but perhaps not readily apparent. As you prepare a speech, clearly develop as many *valid* links to values as you can. One of the less obvious links may be just the connection that strikes through to a core value. Table 20.1 gives some examples.

TABLE 20.1
Issues and value links

ISSUE	OBVIOUS VALUE LINKS	LESS OBVIOUS, BUT PROBABLY VALID, VALUE LINKS
Achieving equality for women and marginalized groups	Justice, fairness, compassion	Increased productivity, avoiding waste, patriotism (world image)
Buying a laptop computer	Efficiency, speed, scientific advancement	Creativity, expressiveness, economy (in the long run)
Deregulating small business	Lack of government interference, pioneer spirit of small entrepreneur	Honesty, trust of fellow citizens, dislike of red tape and paperwork
Welcoming delegation of foreign businesspeople	International harmony, U.S. hospitality, pooling of information	Efficiency, progress, pragmatism

Appeal to Listeners' Sense of Community

Understandably, when people first encounter an issue, they tend to analyze it from a perspective that is close to them in time and space. They ask, "How does this affect me and my immediate circle, now and in the near future?" But one of the most powerful ways public speakers can use motivational appeals is to draw people outward and refocus their awareness on larger frames of reference.

This broader awareness is there and available to be tapped. When the U.S. public really saw and felt the suffering of the Haitian people following the earthquake in 2010, there was an outpouring of financial support. As a speaker, you can create powerful word pictures to remind listeners of their interdependence with other people and creatures, and to transport them into the past and the future. You can use your words to show people the historical and cultural meanings of endangered objects and places. You can take listeners into the future and reveal the effects of our environmental policies or our national debt on unborn generations. Link your speech topic to your audience's values in ways that tie into the broadest sense of community and situate the present in relation to the past and the future.

Check out Speech Studio to see how other students use motivational appeals in their speeches. Or record a speech you're working on, upload it to Speech Studio, and ask your peers for their feedback. What feedback could you use to fine tune your motivational appeals before you give your speech in class?

Avoid Excessive, Inappropriate Motivational Appeals

Throughout this chapter, we have promoted the effective use of appeals to the emotions, needs, and values of your listeners. However, speakers also must be cautious not to overuse or misuse these appeals. A speech with too much emphasis on feelings can embarrass and offend the audience. If listeners perceive that the speaker is playing on their emotions to the exclusion of sense and logic, they can become infuriated. It is always a mistake to underestimate the intelligence of an audience. Aside from the issue of effectiveness (advertisers and politicians show us that often these appeals can be effective), there is the question of ethics. (See Chapter **3**.)

Review, Reconsider, & Act

Summary

Making ideas meaningful sometimes means making ideas *human*. This is accomplished by connecting with audience members' hearts as well as their heads. Effective speakers consider the emotional impact they want to create, or avoid, and they carefully relate their ideas to the needs and values of their listeners. Maslow's hierarchy of needs can help inform a speaker about which needs might be most salient to an audience. Values of audience members can include general values shared in common with others as well as core values that are closely tied to each individual's sense of self. When implemented ethically, appeals to emotions can have powerful effects on audience members' understanding and motivation to act.

Critical Thinking Questions

▷   What value appeals do you find most and least appealing? Why?

▷   How might Maslow's hierarchy of needs help you develop a persuasive speech?

▷   What are the core, authority, and peripheral values of your anticipated audience? How could you find out?

Putting It into Practice

1.   To which core values do the major U.S. political parties appeal? How do you know?

2.   Can you identify what values each U.S. political party appeals to by visiting their websites? To help you determine the answer to this question, visit the official websites for the Democrats and the Republicans, as well any other political websites you wish. You can find quick links to the Democrat and Republican sites by going to your CourseMate for *The Speaker's Handbook* and clicking on **WebLink 20.2** and **WebLink 20.3**.

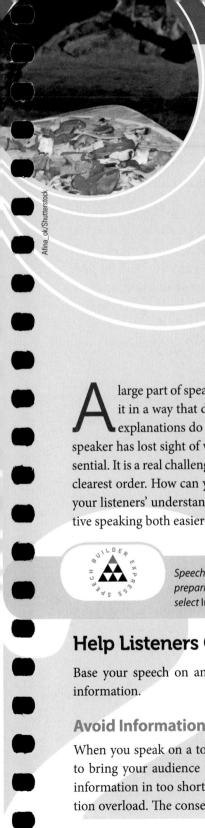

chapter 21
Informative Strategies

For informative speaking, plan a strategy based on information processing. Use clear explanations to aid your audience's comprehension.

A large part of speaking is merely explanation—stating an idea and then restating it in a way that develops or expands on the basic notion. Unfortunately, some explanations do more to confuse than to clarify. Usually, this occurs when the speaker has lost sight of which details from a complex process or idea are the most essential. It is a real challenge to select the most significant details and present them in the clearest order. How can you most economically create the mental picture that will aid your listeners' understanding? Knowledge of the way people learn can make informative speaking both easier and more effective.

Speech Builder Express includes a detailed sequence of prompts for preparing informative speeches. On the Create a New Speech *screen, select* Informative *from the pull-down menu of speech types.*

Help Listeners Grasp the Information

Base your speech on an understanding of how people acquire, process, and retain information.

Avoid Information Overload

When you speak on a topic you know a great deal about, there is a tendency to want to bring your audience up to your level immediately. When you give out too much information in too short a time, the result is a tidal wave of facts and data or information overload. The consequences of this condition—usually in this order—are anxiety, confusion, irritability, anger at the source, and finally, a complete tune-out. Research suggests that the average person can comprehend no more than seven points, plus or minus two.[1] So avoid information overload by limiting yourself to no more than five to nine points, fewer if your topic is complex. This means being selective. You are the expert, and you must pick out the important points for them.

Provide a Framework for Organizing Information

Have you ever tried to put together a jigsaw puzzle without looking at the picture on the box? What you have is a jumble of unrelated pieces. Once you see the big picture, you have some idea of how things are supposed to fit together. This is the same principle that makes you want to look at a map before starting off on a trip or to skim the table of contents before diving into a text. By providing your audience with a sense of the big picture early, you can improve their ability to comprehend how the pieces of your speech fit together as it develops.

Move from Simple to Complex

Even at the risk of temporary oversimplification, it is advisable to lay out the most basic concepts first and introduce qualifiers, exceptions, and interesting tangents later. Think of your listeners as newcomers to town who first want to learn the basic route from home to work; only after mastering that do they want to learn about shortcuts and scenic detours.

Move from Familiar to Unfamiliar

Any group can learn about any subject if you start where its members are and move along at the proper rate. Teachers will attest that learning proceeds best when they are able to adjust the focus of their instruction to a point just beyond the current knowledge level of the group. If the instruction duplicates what the group already knows, the material will not be challenging. If the focus is too many levels beyond them, group members will get discouraged. This fourth principle, even more than the others, ties directly to audience analysis. A creative speaker thinks of examples and analogies that relate directly to the experiences of a particular group of listeners. Connecting listeners to new concepts through familiar concepts will bolster listeners' confidence in their ability to understand the new material.

Go to your *CourseMate for* The Speaker's Handbook *and click on* **WebLink 21.1** *to visit the Biography Channel's website. This site provides great information about people that you might want to give an informative speech about. Also check out* **WebLink 21.2** *to visit a site that provides a lot of ideas for interesting informative topics.*

Use Common Techniques of Clear Explanation

In addition to clear previews and summaries (Chapters **13** and **14**), you will make it much easier for your listeners to understand the points of your speech if you implement the following techniques.

Use Organizers

Provide your listeners with cues on how they should structure the information.

Signposts

One organizer is the signpost. Signposts, like their physical counterparts, point the way you are going and can serve as a reminder of where you've been:

▶ *First,* I'll show you how to make a simple white sauce, and then move on to three more elaborate sauces that start with this basic recipe.

▶ *Finally,* from this short description of one novel and three poems, you can see once again the two themes that permeate Sylvia Plath's work.

Enumeration

Numbering is an obvious organizational cue:

The many steps in building an apartment complex can be grouped into these three phases:

One: Finding attractive sites with the proper zoning.
Two: Negotiating for the purchase of a piece of property.
Three: Contracting with architects and builders.

Acronyms

An acronym is a word formed from the first letters of a series of words and that can be pronounced like a word. For instance, *radar* is an acronym formed from *RA*dio *Detect*ing *A*nd *R*anging. Other examples are *SETI*, for *S*earch for *Extra Terrestrial Intelligence*, and *GIGO*, for *Garbage In, Garbage Out*. An acronym can make a point more memorable, as in the following example:

When you want to show empathy through nonverbal cues, remember to SOFTEN your listening style: [writes on board]
Smile
Open posture
Facial expression
Touch
Eye contact
Nodding

Slogans, Catchwords, and Memorable Phrases

Like acronyms, these types of cues give your listeners a framework for remembering your points:

▶ So, look at those files in your drawer that you haven't used in a year, and assess their real value. Keep in mind Peg Bracken's advice about leftover food: "When in doubt, throw it out."

▶ Try to do something decisive with each piece of mail as you open it. Apply the "Four D's": Drop the item, Delay the item, Delegate the item, or Do the item.

Use Emphasis Cues

Underline and highlight key points with phrases like "this is very important," "if you don't remember anything else . . . ," and "here's what it all comes down to . . . ."

You can also emphasize points by vocal or physical cues. When you want an idea to stand out, speak more loudly or, occasionally, more softly. Pause before and after the big idea. Step forward. Let your facial expression forecast the seriousness of a point.

Use Examples Liberally

When an audience is confused, nothing reassures them like the appearance of a concrete example. You might begin with a simple, even whimsical, example:

> A "win–win" negotiation has occurred when both parties achieve their important goals without perceiving that they have had to make a major sacrifice. Phil and Dave are roommates, and they both think the other needs to do more around the apartment. After talking about it, they agree that Dave will do all the cooking and Phil will do all the cleaning. Each thinks he got off easy.

Next, you could move to a more complex and realistic example:

> Or suppose you have a used car for sale and your neighbor wants to buy it but does not have all the cash now. You offer to carry an interest-free note due in six months if your neighbor will take care of your pets and plants for three weeks while you are on vacation. You are happy because you will receive the asking price for your car and won't have to worry about arranging for a house sitter. Your neighbor is happy because she can have the car now and doesn't have to pay finance charges on a loan.

Finally, you might give an example that is advanced enough for your audience to apply to situations they may actually encounter:

> Now, let's see how these principles apply to negotiating a new job. On this chart you will see the employer's needs and bargaining chips listed in column 1 and your prioritized needs and bargaining chips in column 2. Let's assume an original offer was made of. . . .

It is acceptable to use one example elaborated on throughout an entire presentation to provide unity.

Use Analogies

Continually compare the known to the unknown. You might start with a simple analogy:

> A nuclear power plant is like a steam locomotive. The fireman shovels coal into the furnace, where the heat it gives off turns the water in the boiler into steam. The steam travels through pipes to pistons, where the energy is converted and carried by driving rods to the wheels, pulling long trains of cars down the rails. Substitute a nuclear pile for the coal, a turbine for the pistons, and an electrical generator for the drive wheels, and you have a nuclear power plant.

Then you could clarify the points of dissimilarity:

> Of course, whereas in the locomotive you'd see a grimy engineer squinting at a pressure gauge that has a pop-off valve, in the plant you'd see a large number of scientists and operators presiding over banks of sensors, controls, and computers, each with triple-redundancy safety telltales. The biggest difference, as we know, is that a lump of plutonium contains 240 million times the potential heat energy of a similarly sized lump of coal.

To reinforce points and reach more listeners, draw analogies from many areas: sports, movies, nature, history, culture, and so on.

Use Multiple Channels

Your message will be clearer if you send it through several channels. As you describe a process with words, also use your hands, a visual aid, a chart, or a recording. Appeal to as many senses as possible to reinforce the message. A good rule to follow is this: If a point is very important or very difficult, always use at least one other channel besides the spoken word to get it across.

Use Repetition and Redundancy

People learn and remember what they hear repeatedly. If a principle is important, say it over again, in the same words or different words. Repeat it. Paraphrase it. Reinforce it. Refer back to it. Then mention it again.

Go to your CourseMate for The Speaker's Handbook *and click on* **WebLink 21.3** *for more informative speaking strategies, provided by Colorado State University.*

Check out Speech Studio to see other students' informative speeches. Or record a speech you're working on, upload it to Speech Studio, and ask your peers for their feedback. What feedback could you use to fine tune your informative speech before you give it in class?

CHECKLIST ~ **Helpful Strategies for Informative Speaking**

- ☐ Organize your material so it is clear and memorable.
- ☐ Highlight key points.
- ☐ Plan powerful and plentiful examples and metaphors.
- ☐ Send your message in multiple ways to engage the senses.
- ☐ Repeat important points for emphasis.

Speaker's Workshop 21.1

1. How many analogies and metaphors are used in this chapter? Do they help clarify things?

2. How might you link the familiar and the unfamiliar when speaking about these topics to these groups?
   A. A motorcycle club about nutrition
   B. A group of engineering students about writing a résumé
   C. Elementary school students about endangered species

3. Go to Part 7 or to your CourseMate for *The Speaker's Handbook* and access the sample speeches. Analyze the speeches by Megan Soileau and Brian Sharkey, and identify several different informative strategies used by these speakers.

Review, Reconsider, & Act

Summary

Helping your audience grasp your message is at the heart of every speaker's objective. To achieve this objective, speakers must avoid creating information overload, offer a framework for organizing information, move from the simple to the complex and from the familiar to the unfamiliar, and use common techniques of clear explanation, including signposts, emphasis cues, examples, analogies, multiple message channels, and built-in redundancies.

Critical Thinking Questions

▶ Why is information overload a speaker's concern?

▶ What can a speaker do to avoid overloading an audience with information?

▶ Which common technique of clear explanation do you find most difficult and why?

Putting It into Practice

Review a recent presidential broadcast. Go to your CourseMate for *The Speaker's Handbook* and access **WebLink 12.3** for an archive of White House video broadcasts.

1. How does the president help listeners minimize information overload?

2. How does the president use organizers, emphasis cues, examples, analogies, and other techniques of clear explanation?

chapter 22
Persuasive Strategies

Plan a strategy based on sound logical analysis and an understanding of audience attitudes. Select and arrange your content for maximum persuasion.

How does a person persuade another? What gives one person the right to try to change the attitudes or behavior of another? Answering these questions requires an understanding of how and why people change their minds.

There are many theoretical frameworks for approaching persuasion—from Aristotle's *logos, pathos,* and *ethos;* through post–World War II models of social judgment theory and consistency theories; up to the contemporary cataloging of compliance-gaining strategies. Although an examination of these theories is out of place in a practical handbook, we allude to several of them in the following suggestions.

Regardless of what framework is used, persuasion begins with the need to clearly understand your audience and persuasive objective. By understanding the audience's attitude toward the topic either for, against, or undecided, the speaker can begin to make choices and in the end organize ideas to enhance the persuasive impact of the speech.

Speech Builder Express provides a detailed sequence of prompts for preparing persuasive speeches. On the Create a New Speech *screen, select* Persuasive *from the pull-down menu of speech types.*

Clarify Your Persuasive Goals

A strong grasp of purpose is especially important in persuasive speaking. When you try to change people, and not simply educate or inspire them, you are more likely to run into resistance. It helps establish a realistic target based on what your goals are—and what they are not. (See Chapter **6**.)

Some authorities distinguish between persuasive speeches that seek to change actual behavior and those that merely try to influence beliefs and attitudes. Generally, if you want action, you should set your goals in terms of action and tell the audience what to *do*, not what to *think*. However, you can make an exception to this guideline when you will be speaking to an unfavorable audience. Here, it is better to set a realistic goal of obtaining agreement with your views; you risk losing the audience if you ask for too much too soon. In any persuasive speech, then, ask yourself if you are *primarily* trying to change people's minds or their actions.

It is also important in setting goals to think carefully about the nature and direction of the impact you seek. There is a tendency to characterize persuasion as "getting people to start doing something," such as buy a product or vote for a candidate. This persuasive goal, known as *adoption*, is only one of four. You might also try to persuade a person to stop doing something (*discontinuance*), to keep doing something (*continuance*), or to not start doing something (*deterrence*).[1]

On the general topic of physical fitness, for example, you could choose one of a number of persuasive tacks for your speech, such as persuading your audience to:

▶ *Adopt* an exercise program
▶ *Continue* eating healthful foods
▶ *Stop* eating junk foods
▶ *Avoid* cigarette smoke

Technically, then, persuasion is not always geared toward change. The advocates of continuance or deterrence want to maintain the status quo from what they fear might happen. These two persuasive goals make sense only if there is some jeopardy or pressure from the opposite direction. A football coach might give a persuasive speech to the booster club asking them to *continue* supporting the team. He knows that his audience has other demands on their time and money, and might choose to stop donating to the football team.

Analyze Your Persuasive Goals

Inquiry precedes advocacy for both ethical and practical reasons. Before you can design a persuasive message that will achieve your goal, you need to analyze, or break down, the logical obligations you have taken on. In Chapter **6**, this process was described as finding within your thesis statement the list of questions that absolutely must be answered. In Chapter **16**, the process was discussed in terms of the kind of reasoning needed to provide a link between the evidence you have and the major claim(s) of your speech. Here, we pursue the analytical process more specifically from the direction of understanding the type of proposition you support and identifying the points at issue as you set out to prove your case.

Identify Whether You Need a Proposition of Fact, Value, or Policy

The thesis of a speech and the claim of an argument are also described as propositions— in persuasion, the speaker *proposes* something to the audience. There are three kinds of propositions: the proposition of fact, the proposition of value, and the proposition of policy. Determining which kind of proposition lies at the heart of your speech is essential to identifying your obligations and planning your persuasive strategy.

Proposition of Fact

It may seem that if something is a *fact* there is no need to use persuasion to establish it, but there are issues in the factual domain that cannot be verified directly. For instance, there either is or is not life on other planets. The question is one of fact, but because we lack the means to find out, we must argue from the data we have, drawing the most logical inferences from them. Here are some other examples:

▶   Sparks from a cell phone can ignite gasoline vapors while you fuel your car.

▶   Lack of physical activity increases a person's risk of developing type II diabetes.

▶   Converting to solar energy can save the average homeowner money.

Proposition of Value

Persuasive speakers are often attempting to prove evaluative positions. Their goal is to judge the worth of something, to establish that it is good or bad, wise or foolish, just or unjust, ethical or unethical, beautiful or ugly, competent or incompetent. For example:

▶   It is wrong to try to avoid jury duty.

▶   The free enterprise system is the best economic model for the working class.

▶   Peyton Manning is the best NFL quarterback to ever play the game.

Proposition of Policy

The most common and most complex of the persuasive theses is the proposition of policy, which advocates a specific course of action. Here are some propositions of policy:

▶   The federal government should legalize marijuana for private use.

▶   You should avoid consuming high fructose corn syrup.

▶   You should send your children to a charter school.

When you undertake to prove a thesis statement that is a proposition of policy, you must be very specific about what plan or program should be adopted by what specifically empowered group or agency. Otherwise, although your thesis includes *should* or *should not*, it is really a disguised proposition of value. "Tax loopholes should be closed," for example, is only another way of saying, "The present tax system is bad." To be a proposition of policy, it must read, "Congress should change the present tax structure to reduce oil depletion allowances, home mortgage deductions, and home office deductions."

The thesis of a speech is a claim that, in turn, is supported by subpoints. (See Chapter **16**.) By the same token, notice that the types of propositions are cumulative: The proposition of value assumes certain propositions of fact, and the proposition of policy takes its direction from a proposition of value. Or, proving that something *should/should not* be done depends on proving that something is *good/bad*, which, in turn, requires establishing that something else *is/is not* the case. For instance, to establish this proposition of policy

> Our local government should/should not commence the aerial spraying of malathion to eradicate the Mediterranean fruit fly.

one has to prove at least this proposition of value:

> It is appropriate/inappropriate to risk some danger to human health in order to protect an important agricultural product.

To accept this proposition of value, three propositions of fact need to be established:

> The effect of malathion on human health is/is not minimal or nonexistent.
>
> Malathion is/is not effective in controlling the Mediterranean fruit fly.
>
> The fruit attacked by the fly is/is not important to the agricultural economy of the area.

Propositions of fact: IS/IS NOT
Propositions of value: GOOD/BAD
Propositions of policy: SHOULD/SHOULD NOT

Speaker's Workshop 22.1

1. Identify which of the following are propositions of fact, value, or policy:
    A. The cost of maintaining the International Space Station will be astronomical.
    B. Music on MTV is simplistic and tasteless.
    C. Cats make better pets than dogs.
    D. Children should learn a foreign language before fifth grade.

2. Write a proposition of fact, value, and policy on each of these general topics:
    ▶ Immigration
    ▶ Nutrition
    ▶ Gays in the military

Use Stock Issues to Help You Analyze Your Topic

For some kinds of speeches, well-defined lists of requirements, or stock issues, guide speakers. Propositions of policy lend themselves to formal argumentative analysis, and so referring to a list of stock issues can be helpful. Drawing on pre-established "stock" issues can save you time and effort. For the standard argumentative problem-solving approach, there is no need to reinvent the wheel. Central to understanding stock issue analysis is the concept of burden of proof, which is drawn from the legal system and from formal debate. It means that the individual or side that advocates change has specific responsibilities.

As an extreme example, consider all the burdens on the prosecutor in a murder case in the United States. In U.S. law, murder is defined as: the unlawful (1) killing (2) of a human being (3) with malice (4) aforethought (5).[2] We have numbered each of the five issues the prosecutor must prove. To fail on even one issue is to lose the case. That is, if the defense can show that any *one* of the conditions was not present—for instance, that there was no malice aforethought, or that the killing was not unlawful (as in self-defense),—then murder has not occurred. The burdens on the prosecutor are great, but they are publicly acknowledged and agreed to.

Stock Debate Issues

In a formal debate on a proposition of policy, the speaker advocating a change must provide the audience with satisfactory answers to the following questions:

▶ Is there a compelling need for change?

▶ Is that need inherent in the very structure of the present system?

▶ Will the proposed solution meet the need presented?

▶ Is the proposed solution workable and practical?

▶ Do the advantages of the proposed solution outweigh its disadvantages?

You do not have to be a debater to use these stock issues—they serve as helpful guidelines in analyzing any persuasive topic.

Speaker's Workshop 22.2

Which stock debate issue is being addressed in each of the following points?

▶ Putting more money into the welfare program will not get at its underlying problems.

▶ Adopting a voucher system for the financing of education will allow parents to choose the educational approach that is best for their children.

▶ Violent crime has gotten out of control in our cities.

Stock Issues Against a Change

The examples in the previous paragraph apply to persuasive speeches in which the primary objective is adoption. In a speech that argues against a policy—in which deterrence or discontinuance is the goal—this list of stock issues can be turned around. Because the burden of proof lies with the advocates of change, an opponent of change can succeed by establishing a negative answer to just one key issue.

Adjust Content Based on Audience's Attitudes

Chapter 7 asks you to analyze your listeners' possible reactions to your thesis. Based on surveys, observations, or inference, you can make some determination of their predisposition toward your topic. The following continuum classifies audiences according to that predisposition:

Types of audiences

Unfavorable		Neutral		Favorable		
Strongly disagree	Moderately disagree	Slightly disagree	Neither agree nor disagree	Slightly agree	Moderately agree	Strongly agree

Here are some suggestions on how to deal with such favorable, neutral, or unfavorable audiences.

Favorable Audience

A speaker facing a favorable audience is relieved of a number of burdens. In this situation, as a speaker, you rarely need to establish credibility. Your listeners, perceiving your position as identical to theirs, approve of you and your good taste already. Furthermore, a favorable audience will not raise internal counterarguments for you to deflect or defuse. When speaking to a favorable audience, you can focus on solidifying or strengthening their attitudes, or you can cause them to move from theoretical agreement to positive action.

Use Emotional Appeals to Intensify Your Listeners' Support

The difference between intellectual agreement with and commitment to some purpose, and the difference between commitment and action are usually a function of emotional arousal. Out of the vast number of positions you might agree with, there is a much shorter list of issues that you really *care* about. These issues appeal to your most basic needs, touch on your core values, or have a personal effect on your life.

To get your speech topic on your listeners' short list, make extensive use of appeals to basic values such as patriotism, humanitarianism, and progress; appeals to basic needs such as survival, security, and status; and appeals to basic emotions such as fear, pity, and love. (See Chapter 20.)

Here is one example of how a position can be intensified:

Logical stem
It is only fair to allow groups with which we disagree to exercise their legal constitutional rights.

Emotional intensifier
Where will it stop if we allow selective enforcement of the protection provided by the Bill of Rights? Today, the flag burners or skinheads may be denied their rights as Americans; tomorrow, it may be any of us. [appeal to fear, appeal to core value of civil liberties]

See also the examples in the appropriate sections of Chapter **20**.

When listeners agree with you but are not taking action, they probably do not feel personally involved with the subject. A major task in speaking to a favorable audience is the creation of that personal involvement in two ways. First, be very specific about how their lives are affected. Then, show them that their actions can make a difference:

▶ Your $10 check can feed a Sudanese refugee family for a week.

▶ If you can take that extra second to switch off the lights as you leave the room, you can save yourself $50 a year.

For most audiences, emotional appeals should be handled sparingly and cautiously. But for the favorable audience, you can hardly be too vivid or personalized as long as you avoid bad taste and redundancy.

Get Your Audience to Make a Public Commitment
Invite your listeners to offer suggestions, sign a petition, raise their hands to volunteer, lend their names to a letterhead, or talk to others. People who have made a public commitment—oral, written, or physical—are less likely to change their minds.

Provide Several Specific Alternatives for Action
Make it easy for listeners to take action by offering several specific choices. For example, to people who have shown up at a rally for a candidate, do not say, "Stop by campaign headquarters sometime." Instead, say, "I'd like everyone here either to walk a precinct or to spend an evening making phone calls. Sign-up sheets are being passed around now. If you can't help out in either of these ways, Judy will be standing at the door and can tell you about other things that need to be done to ensure our success." With a favorable audience, do not settle for urging members to do "something." If you want them to write letters, give them addresses; if you want them to reduce their sodium intake, give them low-sodium recipes.

Present Abbreviated Arguments so Audience Members Actively Participate in the Reasoning Process
Because a favorable audience often shares your values and beliefs, it is not always necessary to spell out every step of your reasoning. In fact, classical rhetorical theory suggests that enthymemes (compact lines of argument) are very powerful. When audience members fill in parts of the reasoning you have not spelled out—be it major

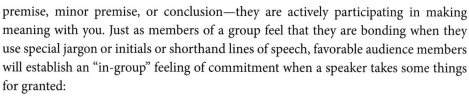

CHECKLIST ~ **For a Favorable Audience**

- Use emotional appeals to solidify agreement.
- Seek a public commitment from listeners.
- Tell your audience exactly what actions they can take.
- Give your listeners ammunition to answer opposing points.
- Create involvement by letting your listeners "fill in the blanks" in your argument.

premise, minor premise, or conclusion—they are actively participating in making meaning with you. Just as members of a group feel that they are bonding when they use special jargon or initials or shorthand lines of speech, favorable audience members will establish an "in-group" feeling of commitment when a speaker takes some things for granted:

▶ If we elect this candidate, it will be like returning to the George W. Bush years. [taking for granted that listeners agree that the George W. Bush years were bad]

▶ We must support this bond issue, for if it fails, there will be no raises for teachers for five years. [assuming the audience agrees that raises for teachers are desirable]

To use these brief enthymematic arguments that create audience involvement, however, you must be sure your listeners really do share your beliefs. Otherwise, the shortcut can backfire.

Prepare Your Audience to Carry Your Message to Others

You can tap the potential of audience members as persuaders in their own right. Each of them may later discuss your topic with coworkers, neighbors, or friends who are neutral or hostile toward it. Give your listeners ammunition for these interactions, and make that material as memorable and quotable as possible. When, in front of a favorable group, you offer examples, arguments, and statistics that support your position, your goal is not to persuade your immediate audience. Rather, you are aiming at the second generation of listeners. This second audience is a reason to avoid relying solely on the compact argument of the enthymeme.

A part of this preparation involves providing your audience with ready answers to refute standard counterarguments. This also serves to inoculate your listeners against the persuasiveness of those counterarguments. Here's an example:

> You may meet people who tell you that the administration's economic policy is designed to help the average worker. Just ask those people why the greatest tax relief goes to the rich. Have them explain to you why a person who earns $300,000 a year will have a 50 percent reduction in taxes, but a person making $18,000 a year will see a reduction of only 6 percent. They may say, "Ah, but we are creating new jobs." Ask them this . . .

Neutral Audience

An audience can be neutral toward your position for one of three reasons: they are *uninterested*, they are *uninformed*, or they are genuinely *undecided*.

Stress Attention Factors with an Uninterested Neutral Audience

Listeners may be uninterested in a topic or position because they do not see how it affects them directly. With this sort of audience, draw on all the attention factors described in Chapter **18**, but give special emphasis to the *vital*. Their interest and attention can be gained only through concrete illustrations of the impact of your subject on their lives:

> A lot of you are probably saying, "So what? So what if somebody across the room lights up a cigarette? It's a free country, and *he's* inhaling the smoke, not me." Would you say, "So what?" if I told you secondhand smoke can blacken your lungs just as badly as if you smoked 2 to 27 cigarettes a day?

Be sure the facts and statistics you use are relevant to your listeners' experience. Sprinkle your speech with humor and human interest. Make a special effort to have a lively and animated delivery and style to stimulate your audience.

Clarify and Illuminate Your Position with an Uninformed Neutral Audience

Before you can expect people to agree with you, they must have some comprehension of the issue. When they lack that essential background, you must spend a significant portion of your speech filling them in, even if it means sacrificing time better spent making points to support your position.

The main concern is clarity: Use explanation, definitions, examples, and restatement. (See Chapter **21**.) Visual aids can be helpful. Keep your language simple and your organization straightforward.

A direct persuasive appeal should be saved until the very end of the speech.

Present New Arguments that Blend Logical and Emotional Appeals for an Undecided Neutral Audience

The undecided neutral audience is both interested in and informed about your topic, but these listeners find the arguments for each side equally compelling. Let them know that you understand their ambivalence. Grant the complexity of the issue, and admit that there is truth on both sides.

Offer yourself as the vehicle for reducing their ambivalence. Establish your credibility by communicating expertise and integrity. As you present the arguments for your side, emphasize any recent evidence or new interpretations that might justify a change in position. By definition, this audience finds sense in some aspects of the opposing arguments. This means you must acknowledge and respond to the main arguments

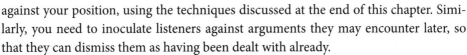

CHECKLIST ~ For a Neutral Audience

- [ ] Use plenty of attention factors.
- [ ] Make sure your point is clear and understandable.
- [ ] Present the most recent evidence and examples you can find.
- [ ] Send your message in multiple ways to engage the senses.
- [ ] Blend logical and emotional appeals.

against your position, using the techniques discussed at the end of this chapter. Similarly, you need to inoculate listeners against arguments they may encounter later, so that they can dismiss them as having been dealt with already.

In short, a well-documented, logical presentation works best for the undecided neutral audience. Appeals to emotions, needs, and values are effective only if used sparingly and clearly interwoven with the logical argument of the speech.

Unfavorable Audience

An unfavorable audience is by no means a belligerent one—remember that *unfavorable* encompasses anything on the "disagree" side of neutral, starting with "slightly disagree." However, the more intensely the audience disagrees with you, the more its members will be predisposed to reject both you and your message. Any idiosyncrasies of appearance and style of delivery will allow them to dismiss you as someone on the lunatic fringe. A single joke that falls flat turns you into a buffoon. A stance expressed with too much conviction brands you as a fanatic.

At the same time, your audience realizes the disadvantage under which you are working. If you handle the situation with grace and aplomb, you might earn their respect. The results can be gratifying when you approach the speech to an unfavorable audience as a challenge to your skill.

Set Realistic Goals for a Single Speech

Do not try to do too much with an unfavorable audience. Attitude change takes place slowly. If most of your audience falls at the "strongly disagree" end of the continuum, do not expect your ten-minute speech to change them to strong agreement. Sometimes, the measure of success is that they throw eggs and not bricks. Even if it means modifying your thesis statement, set a goal that you have a reasonable chance of achieving, such as easing those who strongly disagree over to moderate disagreement, or those who moderately disagree over to neutrality. Do not make an express call for action when such action is highly unlikely. For instance, it would be self-defeating to ask a pro-choice group to contribute money to the campaign coffers of a right-to-life candidate.

Better to ask members to think about the issues you have raised, or to ask them to work together to find a compromise.

Stress Common Ground

However great the difference between you and your audience on any particular issue, there are bound to be places where your opinions and experiences overlap. Ask yourself what goals and values you share with your unfavorable audience. Even an intense disagreement over, say, school busing reveals a common concern for children's education.

Finding common ground is important to every speech, but it is crucial to the speech to the unfavorable audience. Stress it in your introduction and at several points throughout the speech. Make these points of commonality the major premises from which your arguments proceed. (See Chapter **16**.) When you minimize the differences between you and your audience, you create the basis for communication to occur.

Use Sound Logic and Extensive Evidence

The unfavorable audience is skeptical of your position and will reject most emotional appeals as manipulative. Your only chance to persuade these listeners is to build an iron-clad case supported by impeccable, unbiased evidence. With this audience, you must clearly indicate every step of your reasoning—nothing can be taken for granted. Discuss and defend even those assumptions that seem obvious to you. Spell out the logical links and connections that hold your argument together. Do not overstate your points; be careful not to claim more than the data allow. Say, "These examples suggest . . ." rather than "These examples prove . . ."; say, "Smoking is one contributing cause of cancer," rather than "Smoking causes cancer."

Use factual and statistical evidence, and always cite your sources completely. If you mention the results of a survey, for example, tell when, where, and how it was conducted and where it was presented or published. When supporting your points with testimony, quote reluctant experts, if possible, or highly respected unaffiliated authorities. Quotations from your own partisans are hardly worth giving. (See Chapter **15**.)

Directly confront the arguments that are foremost in your listeners' minds. Do not be afraid to concede minor points that do not damage your basic case. State the remaining counterarguments fairly and answer them forcefully, but never stoop to ridicule. In fact, it has been shown to be advantageous to state your opponents' view *even more elegantly than they have*, before proceeding to refute it.

Establish a Credible Image

Nowhere is the careful establishment of good character, good sense, and goodwill more important than in a speech to an unfavorable audience. (See Chapter **19**.) Plan every detail of your speech content and delivery to project an image of a calm, reasonable, fair, well-informed, and congenial person. The judicious use of humor can bolster this image while releasing tension and putting the issue in perspective. Direct the humor at

CHECKLIST ~ **For an Unfavorable Audience**

- Be realistic about what change you ask listeners to make.
- Emphasize common ground.
- Be very thorough in your reasoning and careful with your evidence.
- Build your credibility by being fair and open-minded, and by using humor carefully.

Speaker's Workshop 22.3

Examine Hans Erian's speech transcript, available in Part 7 or through your CourseMate for *The Speaker's Handbook*. Do you think the speaker perceived the audience as unfavorable, neutral, or favorable? What strategic decisions reflected in the speech content justify your conclusion? Name two specific adjustments the speaker should make if presenting this speech to each of the other possible types of audiences.

yourself, your position, a common enemy, or the ironic aspects of the confrontation. Never direct it at your listeners and their beliefs.

Although you do not want to seem combative, you should remain firm in your position. It is fine to build rapport by stressing common ground and granting minor points, but do not waffle or be overly conciliatory. Also resist the temptation to be snide, shrill, defensive, paranoid, outraged, arrogant, sarcastic, facetious, or patronizing.

Do not become defensive or frustrated by heckling or other indications that you are not getting through to the audience. (See Chapter **28**.) Remember that attitude change is a slow process and that by maintaining your dignity and rationality you will not hurt, and may help, your cause in the long run.

Organize Points for Optimal Persuasive Impact

The speech organization patterns discussed in Chapter 10—topical, spatial, and chronological—grow out of analysis of the speech content. Other patterns can form from retracing the reasoning that led you to your conclusion—inductively, deductively, causally, or analogically. (See Chapter **16**.) Yet another way to think about ordering points is to consider how your speech unfolds for your listeners. So, if none of the familiar formats seems strategically adequate, here are some suggestions for alternative arrangements.

Organize Using the Motivated Sequence

Developed by Alan Monroe, the **motivated sequence** is a preferred method for organizing persuasive speeches. This psychologically based format echoes and anticipates the mental stages through which your listeners progress as they hear your speech. Note that it includes the speech introduction and conclusion, unlike the sample outlines in the organization chapters in Part 3.

Attention: The speaker must first motivate the audience to listen to the speech.

Need: Listeners must become aware of a compelling, personalized problem.

Satisfaction: The course of action advocated must be shown to alleviate the problem.

Visualization: Psychologically, it is important that the audience have a vivid picture of the benefits of agreeing with the speaker or the evils of alternatives.

Action: The speech should end with an overt call for the listeners to act.

Here is an example of a speech that follows the motivated sequence:

Thesis statement: We need a light rail system in our county to reduce excessive commuter traffic congestion.

Attention

Introduction: I was on my way to work, having left home earlier than usual so I could be there in plenty of time for my first important presentation. I heard screeching brakes. It turned out to be only a fender-bender a quarter-mile ahead of me. Nevertheless, I sat in my car, and sat, and sat, while my mood progressed from irritation to outrage to despair. I arrived at work an hour and a half late, just as the meeting was breaking up.

Need

I. Excessive reliance on automobile transportation to the county's major employment areas is causing severe problems.
    A. Major traffic jams
    B. Pollution
    C. Stress to commuters

Satisfaction

II. A light rail system should be constructed to alleviate these problems.
    A. (Definition of light rail)
    B. (Proposed route)
    C. (Proposed funding)

Visualization

III. The new system would be a vast improvement.
    A. (Scenario with the light rail system)
    B. (Scenario without the light rail system)

Action

Conclusion: Support the county initiative for a light rail system. Urge your friends to vote for it. Write to members of the county board of supervisors on this issue. Ask your employer to commit to providing free shuttle service from the proposed light rail station to your place of business.

This organization is rather similar to a standard problem–solution speech, but the presence of the visualization step makes all the difference. Instead of merely providing a logical need satisfaction in Main Point II, this speaker has added another psychologically powerful step in Main Point III. Two detailed narratives drive home the case for the listeners. The actual wording of the speech might go something like this:

> If this proposal is adopted, picture yourself parking at a spacious parking lot, dropping your child off at the child-care facility right at the light rail station, and settling back in your comfortable seat. You can enjoy a cup of coffee, read the paper, review materials for your first business meeting, and arrive at work relaxed.
>
> But, if this proposal is not adopted, picture your commute lasting longer and longer until you are spending nearly one working day a week driving to and from work. The smallest incident will cause gridlock. The pollution will become worse. Your stress-related health problems, such as high blood pressure and headaches, will increase.

It is essential that the attention step be engaging and that the action step be concrete. This does not preclude using the other parts of introductions and conclusions discussed in Chapters 13 and 14 if they enhance clarity.

Go to your CourseMate for The Speaker's Handbook *and click on* **WebLink 22.1** *for more on Monroe's motivated sequence.*

Organize through a Comparison of Advantages

Sometimes, your persuasive task boils down to convincing an audience to choose between two alternatives. It may be that the need to do something is acknowledged or that the choice is *go* or *no go*. In any event, your job is to show the comparative advantage of one choice over the other, which more or less dictates that you organize your speech around a sequence of head-to-head comparisons of the components of each proposal. You might have to compare energy policy based on conservation to energy policy based on expanding access to fossil fuel, or compare cost benefits for the long term and the short term. You are not compelled to say that one is perfect and the other awful. Rather, you strive to tip the scale toward your position. That is why a recurrent and highly effective phrase in comparative-advantage persuasive arguments is "on balance."

Place Strongest Points First or Last

Ideally, all of the arguments and support for your thesis statement should be strong. In reality, however, you will find that you must use materials of varying strength. These should not be arranged randomly. Be aware that people will remember best what you say first (the **primacy** principle) and what you say last (the **recency** principle). In light of this, arranging your arguments either from weakest to strongest (climactic) or from strongest to weakest (anticlimactic) will be more effective than placing your best points in the middle (pyramidal).

The research on which one is stronger—primacy or recency—is far from conclusive. It's best to consider the importance of your topic to your listeners, their attitude toward it, and your credibility. Also, remember that previews and summaries are essential in developing any complex argument. If you use these, your listeners will hear all your most significant points both first and last.

Consider Dealing with Opposing Arguments

When time is limited, it is hard to decide whether to present only your own side of an issue or to bring up and refute opposing arguments. In the first instance, you run the risk of appearing to have a weak position. In the second, you sacrifice time to develop your own arguments, and there is always the chance you will introduce a point against your case that would not have occurred to your audience otherwise.

Generally, it is a good idea to address counterarguments. On widely debated topics, these ideas will already be on listeners' minds, and they expect a response. Even on less familiar subjects with which you may have the first word, you probably won't have the last. At the end of a straightforward "pro" speech, your audience may agree with you. But if listeners become aware of powerful opposing arguments a few hours or days later, they may discredit your entire position. Speakers often inoculate their audiences by presenting a few counterarguments and answering them. Then, when these points are brought up later, the listeners will say, "Oh, yes, I was warned about this." Inoculation has created "antibodies" to resist the opposing position.

Address Opposing Arguments Directly with Refutation Techniques

If opposing positions are known, it is both ethical and prudent to address those positions directly with relevant arguments. Studies have shown that when people form opinions based on issue-relevant arguments, as opposed to peripheral cues, they feel more strongly about that issue, they are more likely to act upon their feelings, and are more resistant to counter persuasion.[3]

If you choose to respond to a point, you may follow these steps of refutation:

1. State the opposing view fairly and concisely.
2. State your position on that argument.
3. Document and develop your own position.
4. Summarize the impact of your argument and show how the two positions compare.

Here is a distilled example:

1. Many people argue that flexible work schedules lead to reduced productivity.

2. I challenge the underlying assumption that most people work only for money and will do as little as possible. Employees who are treated like responsible partners take pride in their work and are dependable and productive.

3. There are several research studies that support my point of view: [speaker introduces and explains the studies.]

4. So, these examples refute the position that flextime will lead to decreased productivity. I have shown you how that argument is based on a false assumption about why people work.

Effective refutation can take various forms. In a speech against capital punishment, a speaker might follow the points supporting the thesis with this main point:

IV. Arguments in favor of capital punishment do not justify its continuation.

    A. It is argued that capital punishment deters crime; the facts do not support this.

    B. It is argued that it is very costly to provide life sentences for serious offenders; this is true, but expenditure of money is not a justification for collective murder.

    C. It is argued that dangerous criminals are released on parole and endanger lives; this may be a problem, but we can respond with stricter parole policies rather than execution.

Note that counterarguments may be handled in different ways. Point A is denied directly. Point B is conceded but labeled unimportant. Point C is partly conceded and then analyzed in a different light. Responding to a counterargument does not mean utterly obliterating it. You may concede it, minimize it, dismiss it as irrelevant, or attack the supporting evidence or underlying premise. Even if you grant the existence of a problem, you can differ from your audience on the best solution.

Answer Counterarguments after Developing Your Position

Pro-to-con order is almost always more effective than con-to-pro. The only exception to this rule is when you know audience members are so preoccupied with an opposing position that they may not listen to you. In that case, respond to the audience's opposing point first.

Check out Speech Studio to see other students' persuasive speeches. Or record a speech you're working on, upload it to Speech Studio, and ask your peers for their feedback. What feedback could you use to fine tune your persuasive speech before you give it in class?

© geopaul / iStockphoto 3620311

Speaker's Workshop 22.4

1. Go to Part 7 or to your CourseMate for *The Speaker's Handbook* and access the sample speeches. In her speech, Kayla Strickland uses vivid imagery in her Visualization step to help her audience imagine the impact of ending malaria. Select another of the sample speeches and create an explicit visualization step by developing two or more scenarios of what would happen if change is or is not adopted. Explain how this addition could improve the persuasive impact of the speech.

2. Watch Feisal Abdul Rauf's speech "There Is Everything Right with Being an American Muslim" and describe how he chooses to refute a counterargument directly. Rauf's speech is available in Part 7 or through your CourseMate for *The Speaker's Handbook*.

3. Watch "Let's Move! Launch Anniversary Speech to Parents" by First Lady Michelle Obama available online. A link has been provided on the CourseMate for *The Speaker's Handbook* under **WebLinks** for this chapter. Give an example of where she answers a counterargument, either explicitly or implicitly. Are her attempts effective?

Review, Reconsider, & Act

Summary

One might maintain that *inquiry* is a prerequisite to *advocacy*. You earn a license to persuade by doing your homework about your persuasive topic—researching it fully, thinking about it analytically, and examining the best evidence on both sides. Then and only then are you in a place to recommend your position to someone else. Persuasive strategies work best when matched to the needs and attitudes of the audience. Adjust your content and strategies based on audience attitudes, whether they be favorable, neutral, or unfavorable. Organize your points for optimal impact, placing the strongest points first or last, and consider dealing with opposing views.

Critical Thinking Questions

▶ How should a speaker's audience analysis influence the persuasive strategies he or she employs?

▶ How would an audience in favor of the speaker's position influence the speaker's call to action?

▶ How would an audience in opposition to the speaker's position influence the speaker's organization of ideas?

Putting It into Practice

What strategies or concerns do the following situations suggest? If you were the speaker, how would you develop your speech in each situation?

1. You are trying to persuade a group of high school students to take AP math and science courses.

2. You are trying to persuade the finance committee of a local nonprofit to invest in expensive software to help manage the volunteers efficiently.

3. You are trying to persuade a local school board to hire an additional English as a Second Language (ESL) teacher to serve the needs of a growing group of immigrant families.

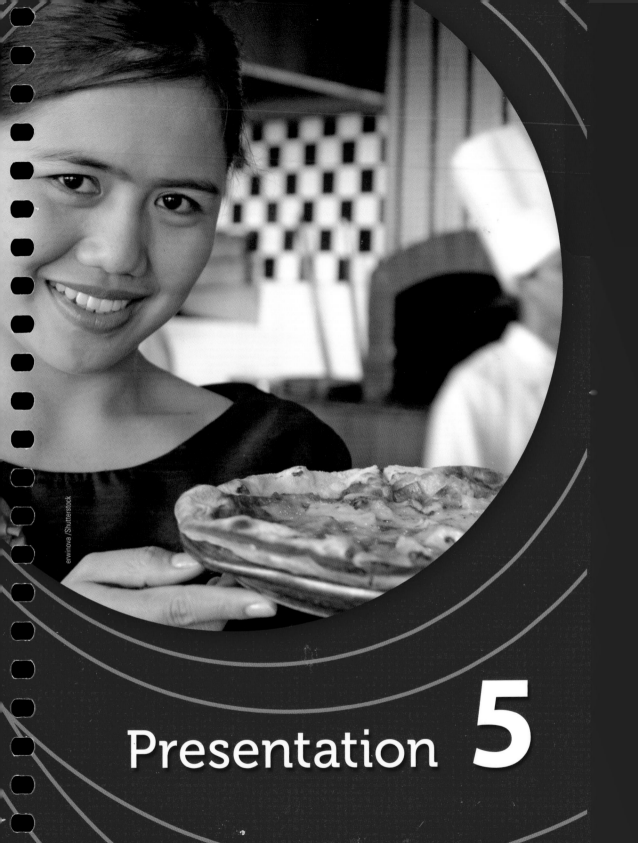

erwinova /Shutterstock

Presentation 5

PART 5
PRESENTATION

INTRODUCTION: THE NATURAL THEORY OF DELIVERY

introduction
The Natural Theory of Delivery

A face-to-face speech puts heavy demands on speakers and listeners. However, "keynote handouts" have not replaced keynote speeches at conventions, nor have memos usurped the role of conference presentations. This is because information transmission is but a small part of the total communicative event. People meet in public spaces to affirm their sense of community and to act collectively. The combination of voice, body, and personality—as well as on-the-spot chemistry—makes speech a form of communication of compelling vitality. It is exciting to listen to a good speaker.

By *good speaker,* we mean someone who has something to say, organizes it well, and says it well. Too often, when people describe a speaker as good or poor, the reference is to the speaker's delivery only. It seems that an audience will listen avidly to a well-delivered speech even if, at the end, they discover there was little substance in it. They will not afford the same consideration to a poorly delivered speech, no matter how exciting or important the content.

As we explained in Chapter **1**, borrowing too directly from the performance-related repertoire of the actor can be inappropriate because being in a play and giving a speech are fundamentally different. As an actor, you assume the role of someone else, speak words written by another person, and strive to perform each line exactly as rehearsed. As a speaker, you present your own personality, speak your own words, and try to adapt to the response you receive. Thus, public speaking is far more like conversation than like acting.

We all have had more practice communicating than performing. The natural theory of delivery is based on the assumption that you communicate well many hours of every day without consciously thinking about speech mechanics. When you are intensely involved in conversation, you do not stop to think, "Now I'll furrow my brow and point my finger." Changes in your voice and actions just happen naturally when you are wrapped up in communicating your message. If you are similarly wrapped up in the content of your speech, your delivery should take care of itself. The single most important delivery goal for any speaker is to internalize this conception of speech as conversation. Once you feel the sense of interaction with an audience—the sort of give-and-take you experience in other conversations—your enjoyment of speaking will increase along with your confidence and skill.

Part 5 of this handbook looks at presentation skills by using a natural theory of delivery focusing on an extemporaneous style. Extemporaneous speeches are practiced in advance, with natural vocal inflection, purposeful physical expression, and support-ive visual aids adapted to the speech situation. They might also include opportunity for questions and answers.

erwinova /Shutterstock

chapter 23
Modes of Delivery

Select a mode of delivery that is appropriate to
your topic, audience, and occasion.

How you deliver your speech drastically affects perceptions of you, your content, and your ability to inform or persuade your listeners. Decide early if your speech will be *extemporaneous* (given from notes), *impromptu* (off-the-cuff), *manuscript* (written out and read), or *memorized* word-for-word. Settle on the predominant mode you will use, but be aware that no speech is purely one mode. As we've seen, each speech is a unique blend of conversation, writing, and performance. Even in an extemporaneous speech, for example, it is often advisable to write out the introduction and conclusion and to commit them mostly to memory. And any speaker who accepts questions or encounters hecklers must be prepared to offer some impromptu retorts.

Extemporaneous Delivery

We advocate an extemporaneous delivery style following a *natural theory of delivery*, which emphasizes speech as an interaction of ideas as opposed to speech as a performance. However, this does not deny the performance aspects of a public speech. It does claim that the performance will be most effective when conceptualized as amplified conversation, rather than as a whole new kind of speaking.

Perhaps you have heard a speaker give a speech presentation stiffly and mechanically and then heave a sigh of relief and ask for questions. Suddenly, a great transformation occurred! In the question-and-answer period, while clarifying points, the speaker had more facial expression, more variety of tone, and more body language. It was as if the speaker thought, "I'm through with my speech. Now I can really talk to these people."

The delivery became much more "listenable" as the speaker's attitude toward the situation shifted from performance to interaction.

Prepare an Extemporaneous Speech in Four Steps

Extemporaneous speaking is the most common mode of delivery and the one you should use in all but a few special cases. This mode is sometimes confused with impromptu speaking. Although it shares some aspects of spontaneity with the impromptu, the extemporaneous mode is considerably more structured. In the **extemporaneous** mode, you prepare extensively, constructing the progression of ideas with the aid of an outline, planning your content thoroughly, and practicing until you are comfortable and conversational. But you never commit yourself to a rigid, exact sequence of words.

Preparing a set of ideas rather than a set of verbatim paragraphs is the only practical and realistic method for most teachers, business managers, trial lawyers, salespersons, and others engaged in speaking for hours at a time or for large portions of the day. But even for the occasional public speaker, the extemporaneous mode, once mastered, offers a sense of power and confidence. You will sound more natural and conversational if you phrase your sentences as you go along. Your mind will be on your ideas and on your audience's reaction to them—you are less likely to go blank than if you are focusing on recalling certain words. You will also find that speaking extemporaneously lets you be flexible and adjust to audience response. If you find your listeners nodding knowledgeably at points you thought would be confusing and in need of clarification, you can drop your extensive examples and move on. Conversely, you can spend more time on points at which you hit unexpected resistance or do not get the response you anticipated.

Prepare an extemporaneous speech in four steps:

1. *Begin with a fully developed outline.* Follow the recommendations in Chapters **9**, **10**, and **11** to arrange your material in a logical and effective manner.

 Speech Builder Express provides extensive help with outlining. For the stage and type of speech preparation discussed in this section of the handbook, select Completing the Speech Outline *from the program's left-hand navigation menu. Also, note that Speech Builder Express includes an "export to Word" button on each screen, so you can move your work into a word-processing environment and have the full range of options for manipulating your text.*

2. *Convert your full-sentence outline into a keyword or key-phrase outline.* The full-sentence outline is a tool to ensure that you develop your speech content adequately and logically. The full-sentence outline is not the written version of the words you will use in your speech, however. The declarative sentences that characterize a full-sentence outline are written English, not spoken English, and if you follow them too closely as you develop

the wording of your speech, the result may be dull and lifeless. In other words, you may find your expressiveness being limited by what you see on the page. For this reason, we suggest you reduce the full-sentence outline to a keyword or key-phrase outline—those words and phrases that convey essential ideas or information. For instance, Main Point IV of the full-sentence outline in Chapter **11** is "During World War II and after, women were used as a dispensable and secondary source of labor." This could be reduced to "WWII—dispensable labor." An outline constructed of such phrases retains the structure derived from the full-sentence outline while enabling you to improvise as you proceed through Step 3.

3. *Word the speech.* Working from your keyword outline, practice putting your ideas into words. Listen to yourself carefully to detect a clumsy sentence or an exciting turn of phrase. The second time through, some of the clumsy phrases will have disappeared (and some of the exciting ones, maybe) as you play with sentence structure, rhythms, and so forth. Third time, fourth time, fifth time through—your topic is becoming more and more familiar, giving you the freedom to relax and to allow yourself to experiment with construction. You will also discover that no one way of expressing a set of thoughts is necessarily better than another: You have said the same thing five times, differently each time, but each of the last three ways works equally well.

4. *Convert your keyword outline to speech notes.* See Chapter **24** for directions on how to transfer your content to a format that provides easy visual cues to which you can refer while you are speaking.

Follow Four Steps for Impromptu Speaking

No one should set out to give an important speech in the impromptu mode—on-the-spot delivery without notes or prior preparation. Those good speakers who seem to be able to speak fluently on the spur of the moment are usually speaking extemporaneously, stringing together practiced "bits" to fit the subjects that have been dropped into their laps. Just as you should not let apprehension about speaking lead you to avoiding preparation, do not assume being spontaneous is possible without prior preparation.

Several scenarios can lead to impromptu speaking.

▶   *No excuse:* A lazy or overconfident speaker may decide to "wing it" even though there has been plenty of time to prepare. The resulting shoddy word choice, lack of organization, repetition, generalities, and unsupported assertions will be a monumental waste of the audience's time.

▶   *Should have seen it coming:* Many impromptu speeches could have been extemporaneous if the speaker had analyzed the requirements and potentials of the situation. The best man at a wedding who has not prepared a toast is guilty of failing to investigate his responsibilities.

▶   *Legitimately unexpected:* There are some instances in which a speaker has no idea that he or she will have to speak. The executive who finds fifty demonstrators in the boardroom can be excused for not having a prepared statement. In a meeting, you might innocently agree to a whispered request to nominate a colleague, and, to your dismay, the chair might then announce, "Now we will have the nominators make statements about their candidate's qualifications."

If you too often find yourself in a no-excuse or should-have-seen-it-coming scenario, the solutions can be found in other chapters of this book, especially Chapters **5, 8**, and **11**. The suggestions that follow pertain to the third, legitimately unexpected, case.

Keep Your Composure

Do not apologize. Knowing the situation is truly a surprise, the audience will understand minor difficulties. You should have realistic expectations of yourself and not fall apart if you fail to deliver your most polished performance. Speak slowly and confidently. Remind yourself that you speak all the time without extensive preparation. In any casual conversation, not only are you speaking, but you are also planning what to say next. You do mental composition *all the time*. Do not let the stress of a speaking situation make you forget that!

By maintaining your composure, you can take full advantage of the few minutes lead time often afforded speaker's walking into a speaking situation. Use the time to do accelerated speech preparation. However short the period, the steps should be the same: pick a theme, an organizational pattern, and a beginning and ending sentence. The more you use these steps the more easily and quickly they come.

Select a Theme

Quickly list several possible approaches to the topic. Do it mentally or, if time permits, with pencil and paper. By thinking beyond the most obvious approach, you may discover a way to link your topic to a subject you are conversant with.

Select an Organizational Framework

You will not have time to make an extensive outline, obviously, but that does not mean you are justified in bouncing erratically from point to point. You can hook your topic to a simple framework like one of the following:

▶ Past–present–future

▶ Pros and cons

▶ Problems and prospects

▶ Concentric rings, with main points progressing from immediate concerns to universal concerns (e.g., in the home, in the school, in the community; or locally, regionally, nationally, internationally)

▶ Domains, developing the different spheres touched by the topic (e.g., political, social, or economic spheres; or practical, theoretical, or moral implications)

After you have divided your topic along the lines of one of these frameworks, find one means of support or development for each idea, such as an explanation, example, story, fact, or statistic.

If time permits, make a rudimentary outline. Even a few keywords on a napkin can reassure you and keep you on track once you have started to speak.

Plan Your First and Last Sentences

The beginning and ending are the most difficult parts of any speech, and this is especially true in impromptu speaking. Even the simplest attention-getter can propel you through that awkward first moment. When you know what your concluding sentence is, you avoid the panicky search for an ending when you run out of steam. One of the authors uses the following quote when appealing to audiences for contributions to an educational charity: "The only way to have is to share, the only way to keep is to give and the only thing worth finding is opportunity" –George Gough Booth. By planning introductory and concluding sentences, you avoid the aimless rambling so characteristic of impromptu speaking.

Speak from a Manuscript Only When Necessary

There is a widespread misconception that manuscript speaking is the easiest and safest mode of delivery ("I'm not an experienced speaker, so I'm going to read my speech"). This is no excuse for avoiding the extemporaneous mode. A bad manuscript speech is much worse than a bad extemporaneous speech. Stilted phrasing, monotonous vocal delivery, and lack of eye contact are all dangerous pitfalls confronting an inexperienced manuscript style speaker.

Limit your use of manuscripts to the following three situations.

1. *The time allotted is specific and inflexible.* This is mostly the case in the broadcast media. Short replies to editorials need to be precise and compact, with only a few seconds of leeway in the scheduling.

2. *The wording is extremely critical.* Many ways of phrasing a thought are acceptable, but there are occasions when slight differences in phrasing are not acceptable. Sometimes, poor word choices can have severe consequences. The most visible examples are the public statements made by world leaders during a crisis. As the crisis deepens, the wording of these statements becomes more and more precise to forestall the misinterpretation that could trigger an escalation of hostility. In other situations, a lack of precision in speaking can lead to lawsuits. On some emotionally charged topics, the consequences of an ill-chosen word can be hurt feelings or loss of business. A speaker is also best advised to use a manuscript for technical reports in which there are a lot of complex data and specialized meanings for many words.

3. *The style is extremely important.* There are occasions when precision is required. The necessity of precision springs from matters not so much of content but of style. It is expected that your language will be more compact, elevated, witty, or elegant than your everyday speech. For instance, though you still want to sound conversational in a major speech of tribute, the desire for the best possible word choice, sentence rhythm, and polished tone might lead you to use a manuscript.

Prepare an Easily Readable Manuscript

Do not let the fact that you are writing out a manuscript lure you away from the tenets of good organization and composition. Work from a full-sentence outline. (See Chapter **11**.) Remember that the sentences of the outline are meant to be logical guides, not the actual wording of the speech.

To get from the outline to the manuscript, "talk" the speech out and onto the paper. You need to check your composition against your ear more than your eye. As you write, and rewrite, keep saying it aloud, listening for the rhythms of oral style. (See Chapter **17**.) A digital voice recorder or voice recorder software is helpful here. Listen to yourself and identify the stiff, unwieldy phrases that need revision. To get a second opinion, have a friend listen.

When you have settled on the final version of your speech, produce the copy you will read from, following these guidelines:

▶ Don't write it out by hand; print it out on a printer, triple-spaced, with large fonts and wide margins.

▶ Use capital and lowercase letters in standard sentence format. Text written in all capitals is more difficult to read.

▶ Print it on heavy paper. Avoid lightweight, crinkly or flimsy paper.

▶ Make sure the letters are dark and legible.

Figure 23.1 gives an example of a manuscript page prepared along these lines. Note that the speaker has included marginal notations to help him find his place and has marked up the text to indicate areas for emphasis.

In some speaking situations, you will not have your manuscript in your hands, but will be reading it from a teleprompter or similar machine. To practice using a web-based teleprompter, click on **WebLink 23.1** *through your CourseMate for* The Speaker's Handbook. *Apps are also available at this site for portable electronic phones and the iPad.*

Become Familiar with Your Manuscript

The two biggest problems in delivering a manuscript speech are a lack of conversational inflection and a lack of eye contact. Even though every word is written out, you should not sight-read. Practice reading your manuscript out loud often enough to become comfortable with it. Do not memorize the words, but become familiar with the concepts and language including the flow and rhythm. If you follow the hints for composing in the oral style, you will avoid slipping into a singsongy cadence or gasping for breath between overlong sentences.

The printed, easy-to-follow page, as shown in Figure 23.1, is essential to maintaining good eye contact during a manuscript speech. The spaces and visual cuing make

FIGURE 23.1
Easy-to-follow manuscript

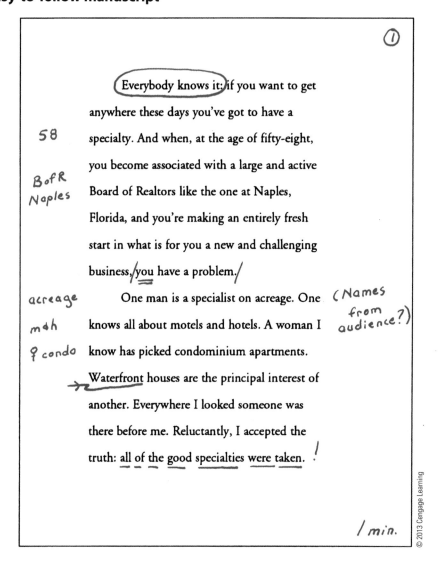

you less likely to lose your place while looking out at the audience regularly. Only through sustained eye contact can you create connections, build credibility and capture feedback. An occasional quick glance up from the page will not provide you with much information about what is going on in the audience, and such jerky movements can be distracting to listeners. If you have practiced your speech enough, you will be comfortable raising your head and engaging the audience with unhurried looks.

Never read your first or last few sentences. Have them memorized so you can begin and end your speech making eye contact with your audience. And never read your punch lines.

Memorize Certain Manuscript Speeches

By definition, giving a memorized speech entails a manuscript speech—without the manuscript. The only times you should give a memorized speech, therefore, are the same as discussed in the previous section, with the added limitations that the speech should be a short one and the situation inappropriate for reading. These occasions are most often ceremonial: giving a toast, presenting a plaque, or accepting an honor.

Memorize Structure First

Learn a few keywords that help you internalize the sequence of ideas. For example, if you are presenting an award to your company's salesperson of the year, you might learn this outline for your brief speech:

    I. Selection process for the award

    II. Chris Welch's sales record for this year

    III. Chris's qualities as a successful salesperson

Or even more simply:

▶ Process

▶ Record

▶ Qualities

Read Speech Aloud Several Times; Then Learn It Paragraph-by-Paragraph

Always keep your mind on the meaning. Do not try to learn sentences in isolation, but rather work on whole paragraphs at a time, reinforcing their logical and conceptual unity.

As You Practice, Visualize Giving the Speech

Avoid thinking of your speech as lines of text in a social vacuum. You do not want to be startled and lose your concentration when you realize you are actually facing a roomful of people.

Speaker's Workshop 23.1

Go to your CourseMate for *The Speaker's Handbook* to access the interactive videos and watch the speeches by Dianna Cohen and Mitt Romney. Classify each speaker's delivery mode as extemporaneous, impromptu, manuscript, or memorized. Did any of these speakers blend more than one mode? The speeches are also available in Part 7.

Don't Go into a Trance When Delivering the Speech

Once again, be comfortably familiar with your material so that you can maintain eye contact and establish a rapport with your audience, instead of having your eyes glaze over and your voice and body tighten with concentration. The audience should not think you are having an "out-of-body experience," but rather, they should sense your presence and connection to the moment. If you happen to forget your lines, the best strategy is to speak along the general lines of the point you know you were trying to make, so you can collect your thoughts and connect back into what you have memorized.

Go to your CourseMate for The Speaker's Handbook *and click on* **WebLink 23.2** *to visit a site that concisely reviews the four delivery modes.*

Check out Speech Studio to see how effectively other students deliver their speeches. Or record a speech you're working on, upload it to Speech Studio, and ask your peers for their feedback. What feedback could you use to fine tune your delivery before you give your speech in class?

Review, Reconsider, & Act

Summary

The four main speech delivery modes are extemporaneous, impromptu, manuscript, and memorized. Although most speeches should be delivered extemporaneously, even an extemporaneous speech might incorporate impromptu and memorized modes. Use a four-step process to develop an effective extemporaneous style. First, fully develop an outline of your speech ideas. Second, create a keyword outline based on your full sentence outline. Third, practice the speech aloud to develop the wording of the speech. Fourth, create speech notes based on your oral practice and keyword outline.

Critical Thinking Questions

▶ Which delivery style is most conducive to developing a conversation with the audience?

▶ How are the impromptu, manuscript, and memorized styles useful to an extemporaneous delivery?

▶ What are the disadvantages of extemporaneous speaking?

Putting It into Practice

 Go to your CourseMate for *The Speaker's Handbook* and click on **WebLink 11.2** (AmericanRhetoric.com) to watch the famous and familiar speeches listed below. Determine the style of delivery employed in each speech.

1. Christine O'Donnell's primary election victory speech
2. Michael Bloomberg's address in support of religious tolerance and New York City mosque
3. Andre Agassi's retirement speech
4. Robert Kennedy's "Remarks on the Assassination of Martin Luther King, Jr."

What are the advantages and disadvantages of each style?

erwinova /Shutterstock

chapter 24
Practice Sessions

Use practice sessions to help compose and polish your speech. Allow time for three stages of practice.

Start practicing your speech aloud well before your presentation. This enables you to finalize your points, get feedback, and polish your delivery. Individual differences and situational constraints will determine how much practice time is necessary. Novice speakers will benefit from five to seven run-throughs; more experienced speakers will find two to three rehearsals sufficient.

Get Effective Feedback

With a little planning, you can increase your chances of getting focused and useful feedback.

Form a Feedback Support Group

Although you can get feedback from a number of sources, the best way is to establish an ongoing relationship with people who have similar goals. In a speech class, this may be a group of classmates who meet to discuss ideas and practice speeches. The value of peer collaboration is acknowledged in business and professional settings and by politicians and citizens' groups. The most effective speakers routinely test their messages with others throughout the phases of development.

Set Guidelines for Feedback

Any group of speakers should establish some ground rules for commenting on each other's speeches, such as offering specific rather than general feedback. See Chapter **2** for a discussion of constructive feedback. Often, the speakers lead these discussions, asking for comments with respect to organization, delivery, message clarity, or other areas of concern.

Allow Time for Three Stages of Practice

It is not necessarily true that more is better. In the case of your speech or report, too much practice may make your delivery stale, and you run the risk of becoming bored with your topic. Most new speakers err in the opposite direction, however, and the result is even more disastrous. To avoid falling into either of these traps, you should plan your practice sessions, write down a timetable of steps and phases, and adhere to it. We recommend three stages of practice: early, middle, and final.

Your speech is not going to be static between these sessions. The creative process, as outlined in Chapter 5, will continue, and the practice timetable should not be so rushed that the periods of incubation between sessions are squeezed out. Doing a stand-up, full-scale practice once in the morning and once in the evening for three days is immeasurably better than running through the speech six times in a row. With your practice sessions spread out, you are more likely to benefit from the illumination and refinement that follow incubation.

There is no one timetable that works for all speeches. Table 24.1 shows possible timetables for three speeches in which the advance notice is different for each. This can be used as a guide to help you create a schedule unique to your circumstances.

A practice timetable can also be influenced by personal differences in speaking ability. For instance, an experienced speaker giving a classroom speech may not need

TABLE 24.1
Practice schedules for different types of speeches

	MAJOR POLICY ADDRESS	CLASSROOM SPEECH	ROUTINE ORAL REPORT IN BUSINESS MEETING
Commitment made to speak	Several weeks before	10 days before	24 hours before
Preliminary analysis, research, and outline completed	1 week before	4 days before	Evening before
Early practice sessions (development)	1–2 weeks before: Discuss ideas with colleagues.	4–10 days before: Talk about speech with friends.	Afternoon or evening before: Talk through basic ideas with friends or colleagues.
	5–6 days before: Talk through speech once a day.	4 days before: Read outline several times; practice aloud twice.	Evening before: Practice aloud 1–3 times.

(continued)

TABLE 24.1
(continued)

	MAJOR POLICY ADDRESS	CLASSROOM SPEECH	ROUTINE ORAL REPORT IN BUSINESS MEETING
Middle practice sessions (feedback)	4 days before: Videotape speech, review with advisors, repeat.	3 days before: Give speech to friendly critic, receive feedback, practice aloud once more.	Morning of meeting: Give report to colleague if possible.
Final practice sessions (refinement)	3 days before: Practice aloud each day; read notes or outline each day. Day of speech: Practice aloud once; review notes just before speaking.	2 days before: Practice aloud 1–3 times each day; read outline and notes several times. Day of speech: Practice aloud once; review notes just before speaking.	Day of presentation: Practice aloud once; review notes just before leaving for meeting.

© 2013 Cengage Learning

three final practices a day—one may suffice. Adapt your timetable based on an honest evaluation of your speaking skills.

Use Early Sessions to Flesh Out Your Outline

During these early developmental sessions, you transform your outline of ideas into a speech by adding the elements of language and delivery to the logical framework erected by your outline.

Begin by internalizing your outline. Read it over a number of times, becoming familiar with the flow of the logic. Sit at your desk or a table and talk your way through the outline. Try to explain the ideas to yourself—part thinking, part talking it out, and part note taking.

At this point, pick a quiet spot and start to put together the speech as it will actually be given. Stand up and give the speech out loud in your speaking voice. Include everything. Do not say to yourself, after making a point, "and then I'll give a few examples"— actually give them. You want to discover awkward phrases and constructions and poor word choices sooner rather than later. Visualize the speech situation and mentally put yourself there. Do not think, "This is a practice session." Instead, make it real—envision the faces out there and talk to them. At this point, do not worry about refining your gestures and vocal inflection.

Sometime during this stage, you will have made the first draft of your speech notes, discussed later in this chapter. Do not carve them in stone. Things will change as you tinker with the wording.

Use Middle Sessions to Get Feedback

After you have become comfortable with your material but before doing the final polishing, seek feedback on your speech. This is usually sometime in the middle of your timetable. If you solicit feedback on content, style, and delivery before you have finished shaping your basic speech, you will miss getting help on those parts that have not yet been crystallized. If the feedback comes too late in the schedule, you will not have time to incorporate the useful information you have received.

Practice in Front of Others and Ask for Their Feedback

Seek a variety of responses from others—colleagues, family members, friends. If possible, move beyond your support group and find critics who are representative of your potential audience. If you are going to speak to a high school audience, for instance, ask your teenage cousin to listen to a practice session. As you rehearse your speech, imagine you are in front of your actual audience, and skip the nervous clowning and friendly informality. Do not leave things out and say, "You've heard this story." Tell the story. **Most importantly, do not talk about your speech. Give your speech aloud, start to finish.**

Ask for honest feedback on content and delivery, but do not necessarily take any single person's comments as the last word. He or she has quirks and prejudices just like everyone else. A group of people is preferable because it gives you a sampling of responses.

You should not ask, "How'd you like my speech?" Answers like "It was nice" or "I thought it was okay" certainly do not help you much. Lead your critics with a few questions and seek clarification of their answers. Here are some specific questions you can ask:

- "What did you see as the single most important thing I was trying to say?"
- "What were the main ideas I was trying to get across?"

Get answers to these two questions before moving on to finer points of development and delivery. If your audience cannot come up with your thesis sentence and main points, then you must look at your structure again. You are speaking for a specific purpose, and everything else is insignificant if your reason for speaking is not being understood. If you are satisfied that your purpose is clear, then you can ask questions along these lines:

- "Did my ideas flow in a logical sequence?"
- "Did the speech hold your attention? What parts were boring? Confusing?"
- "Did I prove my points?"
- "Did my introduction show you where I was going?"
- "Did the conclusion tie the speech together?"
- "Did I sound natural?"
- "Did I have any distracting mannerisms?"

Record Your Practice Session and Analyze Your Performance

A video is the next best thing to a human critic. If you don't own a video camera or have one attached to or part of your computer, you may be able to find one that you can use. If you are taking classes, your school may have equipment you can use. Some speech consultants offer a video recording service. Your company may have video equipment for training or other purposes.

When you view your performance on playback, try to get outside yourself and see the image as that of a stranger. Become the audience and ask yourself the same questions raised previously. You might not believe it when a friend tells you that you start every other sentence with "I mean" and you are always playing with your hair, but the evidence is inescapable when you watch yourself do it on tape. A hazard to avoid here is being too self-critical. Seeing yourself on video can be devastating if you notice only the aspects that need improvement. Look also for things you are doing right. Do not get caught up in examining physical attributes—worrying about the shape of your nose, or the fact that your ears stick out, or that your taped voice sounds strange to you. This is where it can be helpful to watch the tape with a friend or coach who can give you a more balanced perspective.

If a video camera is not available, an audio recorder can be useful for feedback on content, pacing, voice, and so on. Occasionally, you may want to use an audio recorder earlier in the schedule, especially if you are blocked creatively. The recording can help you remember good ideas and possible wordings, and hearing your own ideas and phrasings will complement talking your ideas out with friends.

Practice in Front of a Mirror Only Once, if at All

Practicing in front of a mirror often does more harm than good. Other feedback methods *delay* the feedback: first you speak, then you assess the details of your presentation. With a mirror, however, you are compelled to divide your attention between what you are saying and how you are saying it. If you have no other way to check on the visual impact of your posture, gestures, and facial expressions, it may be worthwhile to practice before a mirror just once. But focus on giving the whole speech. Avoid starting and stopping your delivery and use the mirror as a guide to the amount of eye contact you are currently able to make.

Use Final Sessions for Refinements

By this time, you should be committed to a basic version of your speech while maintaining the flexibility of the extemporaneous mode. You should not be making radical changes.

Make the Final Practice Sessions as Realistic as Possible

If you are going to use visual aids, they should be ready early enough that you can include them in your final practice sessions. The same holds true for the final draft of your notecards. Check yourself against your time limit. Practice your speech, standing up, at the rate and volume you will be using at your presentation. Speaking with rudimentary mechanical amplification to a large audience, for example, will use more breath than will the conversational volume used in early practice. You need to boom out your speech unabashedly in the final practice sessions if that is what it will take to be heard when you actually give the speech.

Continue reading through your notes and outline, but do not think of these activities as a substitute for the formal practice sessions.

Prepare Speech Notes

You should not confuse speech notes with your outline, as they serve different functions. An outline is used to ensure the speech has a logical organization. Speech notes (also called speaker's notes), in contrast, are used as an aid while you are actually speaking.

Like your outline and wording, your notes can go through several drafts. Work on them, doodle on them, and then copy them over. The physical act of copying over your notes is an excellent way to firm up your speech in your mind.

Include Keywords, Phrases, and Material That Is to Be Cited Directly

Unlike your outline—in which points must be parallel, mutually exclusive, and in full sentences—speech notes do not have a regulation format. A point can be represented by a word, a sentence fragment, or a complete sentence or two. What goes into your notes depends on what you find you need during practice.

For example, perhaps one point of your speech, which in your outline was developed to the second level of subordination, with all its accompanying A's and B's and 1's and 2's, is one with which you are so familiar that it can be represented in speech notes resembling those in Figure 24.1.

While practicing, you may also find that you want more than just a keyword reminder to get through an important but tongue-twisting sentence, or to ensure you remember an especially eloquent turn of phrase that has a delicate rhythm. Your notes may also contain material that you will be citing exactly as written out, such as long quotations or complicated statistics.

Keep in mind, however, that your notes should remain *notes*. If you make them too extensive and detailed, you risk moving out of the extemporaneous mode and into the realm of the manuscript speech. Your notes should be referred to, **not read**.

Prepare Speech Notes in a Format That Aids Delivery

Your speaking can occur in many contexts (see Part 6), and these will dictate to some degree the format your notes take. The invited speaker at a world affairs forum may use

FIGURE 24.1
Speech notes

B. Recurring experiments with Protectionism
   1. Just doesn't work
      ――――――――――――
                    -- F Co's absorb, cut profits
   2. Pass to consumer
                    $66 B   Gary Hufbauer
                                   (Prof of finance GT U)
   3. Hurt US Co's
                    15% imports multinat.
                    need cheap F mat'ls & components
   ★ 4. Retaliation
            McFadden (Fortune)
            trade war ――→ recession ――→ depression

                    CHECK TIME *(about 8 min)*

© 2013 Cengage Learning

4×6-inch cards. An attorney in court does not look out of place referring to a legal pad while speaking. A project manager can glance at the PowerPoint note page on her laptop screen covering the content of her slides. For all of these instances, however, our earlier advice on preparing speech notes still applies.

In addition, formatting guidelines apply to notes in any layout. The words and phrases should be large, well spaced, and uncluttered. There should be a lot of visual cues—large card numbers, underlining, indenting, stars, highlighting, different colors—all for the purpose of making it easy to find what you want at a glance. Speech notes should also include written cues for choices you will make during the speech. Time notations are essential. You might write at one point, "If more than eight minutes, skip to [card 6/point 4/slide 10]." You might use a special color to mark optional sections of the speech. Examples highlighted in yellow could mean: "Include this if the audience seems uncertain about my point. Otherwise, omit it."

Preparing Speech Notes on Notecards

Many speakers prefer to put their notes on 4×6-inch cards. As opposed to a large, flimsy $8\frac{1}{2} \times 11$-inch sheet of paper, a few medium-sized notecards in your hand will not distract your listeners as you gesture and move about. Do not be coy about using your notes—refer to them honestly. A surreptitious peek at protectively cupped hands will not fool your listeners into believing that you are speaking without aids.

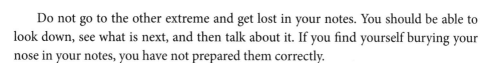

CHECKLIST ~ Formatting Guidelines for Speech Notes

☐ Keep words and phrases large, well spaced, and uncluttered.

☐ Include visual cues (large card numbers, underlining, indenting, stars, highlighting, different colors) to make it easy for you to find what you want at a glance.

☐ Add time notations to keep on track (writing, "If more than 8 minutes, skip to . . . ").

☐ Mark optional sections of the speech, if appropriate (color-coded highlighting to signify importance).

Do not go to the other extreme and get lost in your notes. You should be able to look down, see what is next, and then talk about it. If you find yourself burying your nose in your notes, you have not prepared them correctly.

Preparing Speech Notes with Presentation Software

Presentation software gives you the option of entering notes to accompany the digital slides you create. You can even include the precise data or a short quotation. Adjust the font so that it is easily readable, and feel free to mark up the output with the other visual cues as illustrated in Figure 24.1. Trim excess paper and staple or glue the sheets to your note cards. Chapter **27** provides additional suggestions for preparing and practicing with presentation aids.

Fit Speech into Time Limit

As discussed in Chapter **6**, you must limit your topic according to the time allowed. Often, you cannot tell for sure how much time your speech will take until you have gotten well into the practice sessions. In extemporaneous practice, your speech time will vary as you work with the form of your ideas and the style and rhythm of your speaking. This, again, is where envisioning audience response is helpful. Most first-time speakers practice at a speaking rate faster than the one they find necessary for clarity during the speech itself. The more realistic your practice, the less likely you are to overestimate or underestimate your time.

To clock your speech, do not glue your eyes to the sweep hand of your watch or the changing digits on your watch or cell phone. Merely note the time when you begin and when you finish. Time watching can induce unnatural behavior, such as speaking at twice your normal rate for the last minute if you think you are running long, or, in the opposite case, slowing your delivery to a tired shuffle. There are more sensible ways to address problems of length. The first step is to time the parts of your speech, perhaps by having a helper jot down the times of your main points on your outline as you practice or doing it yourself with an audio recorder.

Look at the relative proportions of your introduction, body, and conclusion. Generally, the body should make up 75 percent of your speech. Does an extended story make the introduction too long? Look, too, at the relative proportions of your main points. Are you spending half your time on only the first main point? Is it worth it?

If Your Speech Is too Long

1. Consider cutting out an entire main point. (Adjust your thesis accordingly.)
2. Eliminate redundant supporting evidence and examples. (But save the ones cut; you might be able to use them for the question-and-answer period.)
3. Turn some of your illustrations into examples; instead of telling the whole story, toss off a one-liner that encapsulates it.
4. Eliminate long stories, jokes, and narrations unless they are absolutely essential.
5. Instead of explaining technical or detailed information, use handouts or visual aids.
6. Polish and tighten your language and phrasing. Speak simply.

If Your Speech Is too Short

1. Consider whether some important ideas are not sufficiently developed in relation to the other points.
2. See if you are too concise for your own good. Remember that the spoken word needs repetition, embellishment, and illustration to bring home your message to every member of the audience.
3. Make sure you have proved all your points. Double-check your evidence to make sure you have not assumed too much or made some logical leaps that are not justified.
4. Do more research. You may have given up too soon at the library.

In a speech class, there may be penalties for not reaching a minimum time limit. In most other settings, no one is going to be awfully upset if you take only 15 out of the 20 minutes you have been given. However, taking 40 minutes when you have been allotted 20 can disrupt the schedules of countless other people.

The experienced speaker always knows the duration of each element of the speech. Even if the first clocking run-throughs show that the speech meets the time requirements, it still helps to have a point-by-point time breakdown. This knowledge makes it easier to adapt to changes that might crop up in the speech situation itself. (See Chapter 28.)

When you reach that point in your practicing at which the speech consistently comes out the same length, mark the cumulative times of the parts in your notes. For example, you might print "2 min" at the bottom right of your notes on the introduction, "4 min" after the first main point, "6 min" after the second, and so on. (See Figure 24.1.)

Here, as examples, are two plausible scenarios in which knowing the timing of the elements of your speech will help you adapt without panic:

First Situation

You planned to spend five minutes on your first main point. Feedback from the audience convinces you to use eight minutes to make certain they are getting it. You decide to drop anecdotes from your second and third points to make up the three minutes.

Second Situation

You are on a program that is running late but can't go over time because of scheduling conflicts. The moderator asks you to trim your presentation from 30 minutes to 10. You begin doing mental arithmetic, subtracting combinations of points until you arrive at a plausible shortened version of the speech.

Some people have internal clocks that are accurate enough that they do not need external cues. If yours is not that well developed (and most people's are not), feel free to take off your watch and lay it where you can see it, use your cell phone's clock feature, or have a colleague in the audience give you prearranged time signals. However, avoid excessive reliance on the clock. Become comfortable with your presentation by practicing and timing your speech.

Do a Final Run-Through

Imagine that you are giving an important speech one evening. You should have planned your practice sessions so that, by the night before, your speech is polished and you are comfortable with it. Remember that it is never a good idea to compress your practice into a few frantic hours. On the morning of the event, allow for one unpressured practice session. As you go about the day's activities, you may want to look over your outline or notes one time. If you feel yourself becoming anxious, try some of the relaxation or visualization techniques recommended in Chapter **4**.

The last quiet, private moment before the speech is the time to go through your notes and outline once again. This could be done just as you leave your home or office or as you sit on a bench outside the building. In the final minutes before your presentation, go through your introduction and conclusion. Visualize the basic structure of the speech, a macro view of the ideas. Think in terms of main points.

Throughout the construction of your speech, you should keep in mind what preparation it will take to get yourself to the podium in a relaxed frame of mind. Take time well before the speech to think about those possible situations that might throw you off your pace, and develop strategies to avoid or dilute them. Try to arrange your day so you are not rushing. If you have a meeting just before the speech, one that you know is usually tense and upsetting, do not go. Be conscious of your idiosyncratic responses to a number of stimuli. If you know you do not function well on a full stomach, do not eat a filling, rich meal. In short, be a little selfish and take care of yourself in the ways you have learned work best. You owe it to your audience and to yourself to be feeling comfortable, confident, and composed when you present the speech you have worked so hard to prepare.

Avoid Common Practice Pitfalls

Here are some pitfalls to watch out for when practicing.

"Mental" Rather Than Oral Practice

Sitting and thinking about your speech, or reading over your outline or notes, is no substitute for rehearsing the speech aloud. Oral practice is essential to get comfortable with phrasing and to check your timing. Do not let your speaking anxiety (Chapter **4**) lead you to put off practicing orally until the last moment. Instead, replace negative messages with positive, affirming statements and visualize yourself being successful.

Too Many Critics

Some speakers seek feedback from everyone they know, and most of these people are happy to oblige. Although it is good to get a variety of opinions, it can be confusing to receive contradictory advice: "Make it longer." "Make it shorter." "You seem too serious." "You seem too casual." It is *your* speech; after receiving comments from a few people whose judgment you trust, decide what advice to take, and move on to finalizing your speech.

Over-Preparation

This is rare, but some speakers rehearse their speech so much that it becomes mechanical. As noted in Chapter **1**, by drawing too heavily on writing or performing or both, speakers can lose all sense of the original meaning of the words and ignore audience reactions. When speaking, do you notice the audience members' facial expressions and are you able to respond to them? You should.

Self-Consciousness Rather Than Audience Consciousness

Except for a few middle practice sessions in which you receive feedback from others or from recordings, try to keep your attention off yourself as a speaker and on your message and the audience response you desire. Remember to visualize *them* when you practice. Again, don't let the performer upstage the conversationalist.

Go to your *CourseMate for* The Speaker's Handbook *and click on*
WebLink 24.1. *Here, Maui Community College gives tips on how to practice a speech.*

Review, Reconsider, & Act

Summary

Adequate practice is paramount to successful speaking. Using beginning, middle, and final practice sessions over several days will lead to reduced anxiousness and a conversational style comforting to both audience and speaker and can offer the additional benefits of illumination and refinement that follow from incubation. Beginning practice sessions should focus on fleshing out the outline. Middle stage practice will help immensely by affording you feedback from support group members, fellow employees, or family members. Proper practice requires careful preparation of speech notes and an effort to fit the speech within time limits. A final run-through the day of your presentation will help to get in the proper frame of mind. Common practice pitfalls can be avoided by practicing aloud with a limited number of critics, while maintaining an audience focus.

Critical Thinking Questions

▶ Why is practicing "mentally" a pitfall?

▶ How many times should you deliver your speech aloud to be fully ready?

▶ How might technology aid the practice phase of speech preparation?

▶ What is your best strategy for effective practice?

Putting It into Practice

Review several online or published articles on speech preparation. Use your favorite online search tool or library database to locate appropriate articles.

1. Which article appears most credible?

2. What do the articles have in common?

3. Where do the articles differ? Why?

chapter 25
Vocal Delivery

Speak clearly, correctly, and conversationally.
Vary your vocal delivery for interest and
emphasis.

As important as preparation, organization, content, and style are, the essence of the speech is still your spoken words. What a waste of time and brainpower if what you have to say cannot be heard or understood by your audience. You must be aware of the mechanics of transmitting sound: articulation, breath control, projection, and so on. At the same time, your most important goal is to develop a style of vocal delivery that sounds natural and conversational. The "orator," who overdramatizes his speech with trilling r's and shuddering pauses, creates distractions and reduces opportunities to create mutual understanding. Except for the stylized chants of the auctioneer and revival minister, most public speech should sound like private speech, only adjusted to fit the size of the audience in the room.

Your way of speaking reveals your ethnic and cultural heritage, as well as your personality. Your "voiceprint" is as distinctive as your fingerprints. In a multicultural society, the sounds of everyday speech are always changing to include new voices. As you develop your public speaking skills, stay attuned to your distinctive sound.

Speak to Be Heard and Understood

How loudly, clearly, and quickly you speak all affect your ability to communicate with your listeners.

Speak Loudly

For the inexperienced speaker, just about *any* volume level will sound too loud. This is understandable. There are few occasions for speaking above a conversational level, and even on such occasions, as when we scream our heads off at a football game, we rarely care if we are being understood. But you'll need to be heard—and understood—by the entire audience, and the only way you'll feel more comfortable speaking more loudly is by practicing. In the early stages of practice, you may have to ignore how loud your voice seems to you, and get feedback from a friend or recording device set some distance away.

What you are aiming for is a louder voice that retains the rhythms and inflections of your normal conversation. You want to be loud, but not be yelling like a drill instructor. As you practice, you will discover that this requires more air for each phrase. You will need to develop breath control to keep your breathing pauses in normal patterns. Think of yourself as broadcasting or propelling your voice to the far corners of the room. You will then begin to do things that naturally aid projection, such as keeping your head up and opening your mouth wide.

Speak at an Average Rate

The average rate of speaking is around 150 words per minute. To check your rate, time yourself for three or four minutes as you read a magazine or newspaper article aloud in a natural, conversational manner. Next, count the number of words in the passage and divide by the number of minutes you read. If you speak more than 200 words per minute or fewer than 100 words per minute, you may not be fully understandable to your audience. Extremely fast speakers expect listeners to decode and process information more rapidly than is their custom. Plodding speakers, who seem to avoid phrases and slowly lay out each word as if it were unrelated to any other, keep listeners in a state of bored suspension as they wait for the words to gel into some sort of context.

Generally, when giving a speech, plan to speak a little more slowly than you do in daily conversation. To be sure you have timed the speech realistically, practice at the rate and volume you will actually use.

Enunciate Your Words

When speaking, either publicly or privately, people rarely enunciate *every* sound in *every* word. The phrase "jeetyet?" can be deciphered as "did you eat yet?" by a friend who has a context for the remark. In public speaking settings, much information can be lost due to the audiences' distance from the speaker and distracting noises. So it is important to work on crisp, precise articulation. Use your tongue, teeth, and lips to pronounce every sound. Be sure you say "government" rather than "goverment" and "hundred" rather than "hunnerd." Do not mumble, run words together, or swallow whole phrases.

You can enunciate properly and still sound natural. It merely takes some practice incorporating precision into your normal conversation. Some people, in a misguided attempt to sound more formal or "literate" during a speech, will overarticulate words or take on exaggerated mannerisms or pronunciations. The result is quite the opposite of what they wish. Rather than sounding well educated, they come across as patronizing, melodramatic, and a little silly. Do not say "thee" in a place where "thuh" is natural when pronouncing *the*. Do not use "would not" where "wouldn't" feels right. (Just be sure to say "wouldn't" rather than "wunt.")

Make Adjustments for an Accent

If you have a regional accent or if you are a nonnative speaker of American English, you may be concerned about being understood. Do not try to eliminate or hide your accent. Your manner of speaking is part of your personality. The differences can add interest and charm to your presentation. However, to ensure that your audience understands you, follow these suggestions:

1. Don't start out with the most important material. Use your introduction to let the audience adjust to the pronunciations and patterns of emphasis that differ from their own. Usually, this will take just a minute or so.

2. Speak more slowly and distinctly than you do in daily conversation.

3. Be very alert to audience feedback. If you see confused faces, repeat ideas slowly. Unclear vocabulary or mispronunciation of one key word may mystify your listeners. Try several synonyms for important words.

4. Consider using more visual presentation aids and gestures with key phrases.

If you are a nonnative speaker of English, you may also find these two simple tips useful in increasing your intelligibility:

1. Prolong your vowel sounds. In contrast to many other languages, spoken American English carries more meaning in vowels than consonants. It will sound odd to you, but make a conscious effort to extend your vowels.

2. Also blend the end of one word into the beginning of the next so that each phrase sounds like one long word. This reduces the perceived choppiness of much accented English.

Nonnative English speakers aren't the only ones who must consider their accents. If you're a native English speaker who must speak to an audience of nonnative English speakers, you also must ensure that you're understood. For tips on communicating effectively with nonnative English speakers, go to your CourseMate for The Speaker's Handbook *and click on* **WebLink 25.1**.

Use Vocal Variety

Speakers who have clear speaking voices devoid of vocal tics waste these good qualities if they speak hypnotically, with no variation in pitch, rate, or volume. Such change and movement of the voice—what's referred to as **vocal variety**—are intrinsically more interesting than the static or predictable. In Chapters **17** and **18**, we stress the importance of variety in word choices and examples in maintaining a high level of audience attention. Vocal variety is equally important, and the need for it goes beyond a mere desire for novelty. Your voice should not simply transmit words; it should underscore and reinforce your message. Suppose your speech on air pollution contained these two sentences:

▶ When the pollution levels are high, my hair feels gritty, and I have to wash it more often.

▶ Every time pollution reaches the Alert level in our city, more people with chronic respiratory problems die.

Delivering these sentences in the same tone of voice could imply that they are of equal importance. Changes in pace and emphasis show your audience what is significant and can signal humor, seriousness, irony, and a range of emotions.

Vary Your Pitch

Speaking in a monotone says to an audience: "I have little interest in the subject or confidence in my ability to interest others in it." A listless vocal performance will negate any dynamism that ordinarily would spring from your word choice and content. Do not be afraid to use the full range of your voice.

Varied inflection, or pitch, implies a high energy level and self-confidence, and generally aids your credibility. The pitch you use for the delivery of a word or phrase can underscore its meaning or imply its opposite. For instance, it is common to indicate disagreement with an assertion or a statement merely by raising the tone of our voice at the end of the statement signaling a question. Try it. Vocalize the following sentence: "You do love me." As a statement your voice drops. As a question your voice rises at the end. This vocal adjustment creates a powerful difference in meaning.

Vary Your Speaking Pace

The average pace of your delivery should be geared toward comfortable listening. However, changes in rate at different times during the speech can be effective in creating interest by establishing moods or adding emphasis. Speaking slowly can make you seem thoughtful and deliberate, and it can also impart a sense of drama. Similarly, an extended pause at the end of a sentence signals to your audience that you consider what you just said important and worth some thought. Rapid delivery shows excitement and activity. A climactic effect is achieved by presenting a series of ideas or examples at a rapid clip, as in the following example:

> [slow] Since we adopted this management system, [fast] absenteeism is down, productivity is up, morale is up, sales are up, profits are up.

This example also demonstrates that the shift in rate (in this case, slow to fast) is as important to creating a climactic effect as the rate itself.

The following passage shows what a fast-to-slow shift can achieve. If you read it aloud, you would speak more quickly through the first sentence, but you would read the second sentence very slowly.

> In the next hour they looked in her room, checked the tree house, went over to the playground, called several of her friends, drove around the block, asked all the neighbors. No one—had seen—Emily—since—she—got off—the school bus.

The accelerating pace of the first sentence communicates mild concern turning to frantic worry, which leads to the climactic moment of fear contained in the measured delivery of the last sentence.

Vary Your Volume

You should speak loudly enough that you can drop your voice for effect and still be audible to the listeners in the far corners. At the same time, you should hold some **volume** or loudness in reserve so that you can raise your voice for emphasis. Consider two examples.

Notice how a drop in volume can pique interest by evoking an air of confidentiality:

> I was having an awful week. Few prospects, no sales. It was hard on a young, eager guy just out of school. On the other hand, I never saw old Jones without a customer at his side or a signed contract in his hand. I guess he saw my hangdog look and took pity on me, because he walked over and said, "Smith, you've got the makings of a great salesman, but you're doing one thing wrong." [in a softer voice] Now, this is what he said: . . .

And notice here how raising one's voice can add emphasis:

> The city council has approved yet another check cashing service. The university is using our streets for its parking lot. The state parole board dumps its parolees downtown. Prostitutes from miles around converge each night on Second Street.
>
> [in a louder voice] Do you want to know what's coming next?

Speaker's Workshop 25.1

1. Locate a video online by a non-native speaker (consider Americanrhetoric.com or YouTube.com) and analyze the speech delivery using the guidelines for nonnative speakers.

2. Go to the interactive videos in your CourseMate for *The Speaker's Handbook* and analyze the presentations of Elizabeth Lopez and Nathanael Dunlavy, identifying ways they reinforce the meaning of their ideas through the use of voice.

Use Standard Pronunciation

Speakers are often unaware of habitual mispronunciations. It's worth the effort to identify such areas of unconscious incompetence (see Chapter 1) and address them.

Identify Words You Habitually Mispronounce

Some differences in the ways people pronounce words are inevitable and cause no problem for public speakers. A person from New England might say, "I went to a pahty," a Pennsylvanian may have "cot a cold," and a Texan may tell you to come "ovah heah." Unless they have strong biases against some part of the country, listeners rarely make negative inferences about the speaker on the basis of regional pronunciations like these. If, however, a person says "warsh" instead of "wash" or "ax" instead of "ask," many listeners will consider this substandard and draw conscious or unconscious conclusions about the speaker's educational level, competence, and intelligence. This sort of linguistic snobbery can be unfair, but it is easier to change some pronunciations than to change everyone else's attitudes.

Look over the list in Table 25.1 and see if you make any of these pronunciation errors. If you find one or two words that you mispronounce, you can easily work on correcting them. If you find five or more, you may need more extensive help in the form of coaching or coursework. Due to factors in your background or perhaps a lazy ear for the finer distinctions of speech, you probably are also mispronouncing several other words and impairing your effectiveness in communicating with certain groups of people. Here, too, feedback from your practice audience can alert you to errors of which you were unaware.

To see additional words that are commonly mispronounced, go to your CourseMate for The Speaker's Handbook *and click on* **WebLink 25.2.**

Check the Pronunciation of Unfamiliar Words

Your vocabulary can include words you frequently see and understand yet rarely speak or hear spoken. Without exposure and feedback, you might develop your own way of mentally pronouncing such a word that involves a mistake like adding a sound or reversing sounds. If you give a whole speech about the Electorial College (instead of Electoral), your listeners might wonder just how knowledgeable you really are. Or they may be confused or amused if you constantly refer to the need for a counselor to listen "emphatically" when you think you are saying "empathically," a word that means something entirely different. Check words you encounter in research, but do not use regularly, to be sure you have them right.

TABLE 25.1
Pronunciation errors

WORD	PROPER PRONUNCIATION	IMPROPER PRONUNCIATION
ask	ask	ax
get	get	git
just	just	jist
across	a cross	a crost
nuclear	nu clee ar	nu cyou lar
perspiration	pers pir a tion	press pir a tion
strict	strict	strick
escape	es cape	ex cape
compulsory	com pul sory	com pul so rary
recognize	rec og nize	reck a nize
library	li brar y	li berry
mischievous	mis che vous	mis chee vious
theater	*thee* a ter	thee *a* ter
picture	pic tchure	pit chure
surprise	sur prise	sup prise
comparable	*com* per able	com *pare* able
larynx	lar inks	lar nix
relevant	rel a vant	rev a lant
drowned	drowned	drown ded
et cetera	et cet era	ek cet era
February	feb roo ary	feb you ary
temperature	temp per achure	temp achure

Place names are always an area for careful investigation. Looking at the word *Beaulieu*, you might expect to say it "Bowl yew." However, the village by that name in Britain is pronounced "Byew lee." Similarly, *Leicester* is "Lester." The Cairo in Egypt we call "Kie row"; the Cairo in Illinois is "Kay row." Houston Street in New York City is "How ston," but Texans have "Hyew ston." The city in Peru is called "Leema," but in Ohio the name is pronounced "Lyma," like the lima bean.

Minor differences in pronunciation can also be troublesome. "*Apricot*" or "*aypri-cot*"? "Har *rass*" or "*har* rass"? Which pronunciation of *Vietnam, Peking,* or *Caribbean*? A dictionary is not much help when there are several correct pronunciations or chang-ing ones, or when words become more or less anglicized, or when unusual proper names like *Nagorno-Karabakh* spring upon the scene. It has been said that the arbiters of the most current acceptable pronunciation are the anchors of national news programs. You are usually safe to follow their lead or that of other such models as the most articulate and respected leaders of your community.

Refer to these sources for questions of pronunciation:

▶ Eva Easton's Authentic American Pronunciation website. To access her site, go to your CourseMate for *The Speaker's Handbook* and click on **WebLink 25.3**.

▶ Jean Yates, *Pronounce It Perfectly in English*, 2nd ed. (with four audio CDs). Hauppauge, NY: Barrons Educational Series, 2005.

Eliminate Distracting Vocal Characteristics

Your reason for speaking is undermined when your listeners begin to pay less attention to what you are saying and more to how you are saying it: "That's the fifteenth time she's said 'quite frankly' " or "Why doesn't he clear his throat?" Your voice and speech style should be unobtrusive vehicles for your ideas.

Distracting speech habits are difficult to identify and even more difficult to change. Vocal mannerisms become so familiar to you and your closest friends that they are often overlooked, but they can be blatant to a new audience. Follow the suggestions in Chapter **24** for receiving feedback. Use video or audio recordings and feedback from knowledgeable friends to get some objective perspectives on your performance. When you isolate a problem, do not view it as simply a public speaking problem. An overused phrase and a shrill voice reduce your daily communication effectiveness. Resolve to correct problems gradually and permanently by modifying your everyday speaking habits.

Identify Voice Quality Problems

The resonant, musical voice you view as an ideal may be beyond your reach, but there is, of course, no one perfect voice for effective speaking. Rather, there is a range of pleasing voices. Although the quality and timbre of your voice are determined to a great extent by your larynx and by the size and shape of your nasal cavities, you can find yourself within that range unless you are hampered by one of the following problems.

Harshness, Hoarseness, or Stridency

These qualities are caused by constriction of the throat or by tension in or damage to the vocal folds. The voice may sound husky, rough, or shrill and so give an impression of anger or gruffness.

Breathiness, Thinness, or Weakness

These qualities are caused by having an inadequate air stream, by releasing excessive air, or by speaking in an unnaturally high falsetto. The result is a soft, childish-sounding voice that lacks authority and power.

Nasality and Denasality

Incorrect flow of air through the nasal passages creates these problems. With nasality, too much air escapes through the nose; with denasality, too little air escapes. These problems primarily affect *m, n,* and *ng* sounds, and produce either whiny or stuffed-up qualities.

Identify Articulation Problems

Many people have speech problems that are not severe enough to be considered disabling, but that are still sufficiently distracting to impede good communication. Stutterers are certainly aware of their condition, but people with lesser problems are usually not conscious of their misarticulations.

Listen closely to your speech for irregularities in articulation—the way you produce consonant sounds or blends of consonants. Many articulation errors take the form of *substitutions*, such as "*tholution*" for "*solution*" or "*dese*" for "*these.*" Also common are sound *distortions*: the slushing, hissing, or whistling *s* or the lazy *l* or *r*. If you discover any of these errors, notice whether they occur every time you make the sound, or only in the initial, middle, or final positions in a word. For instance, a lazy *r* may show up in the middle but not the initial position: you can say "rabbit," but "tu*r*key" comes out as "tuw-key." Also, consonant sounds that you produce well in isolation may tend to be distorted in consonant blends: That same *r* sound may give you trouble only in *cr, gr,* or *dr* combinations. In severe cases it may be necessary to see a speech therapist to relearn how to form these sounds and properly articulate words.

The real distraction caused by these misarticulations is not the minor aural irritation it may arouse in your listeners. Rather, these speech problems can create a contradictory message that works against the credibility you want to project. An audience listening to a speaker who says "wange of pothibilities" will experience conflict between the competence conveyed by the words and what may seem like a lack of maturity due to the way those words are pronounced. Similarly, sound distortions can produce an image of sloppiness that conflicts with an otherwise crisp and concise presentation. Consider the image discord created by the accountant who presents precise facts while slushing his *s*'s in phrases like "the projections for the next fishcal year sheem to shupport our prediction of sholid growth potential." It may seem unfair to associate certain articulation errors with a lack of maturity, but there is an unconscious tendency of listeners to do so.

Identify Irrelevant Sounds and Phrases

Don't be afraid to pause between sentences or thoughts when you speak, but avoid filling those pauses with distracting, meaningless sounds and phrases known as vocalized pauses. When a speaker is nervous, a one-second pause can seem like a ten-second stretch of dead air, and the temptation to fill it with something can be great. Consider these questions:

▶ Do you use vocalized pauses: "uh," "um," "err"?

▶ Do you fill pauses with other nonspeech sounds: lip smacking, tongue clicking, throat clearing, snuffling?

▶ Do you unconsciously insert a giggle after every sentence?

▶ Do you repeat to excess certain words or phrases in nonsensical places?

In the last case, repetition of certain phrases may have originated in requests for feedback. The coherent question "Do you know what I mean?" following a complicated idea turns into "y'know" tossed in whenever the speaker feels uncertain. From there, it is a short step to using it as a pause-filler. Other irrelevant repetitions may develop when individuals feel their communication is less than clear. Tacking on "or whatever" at the end of every sentence is an example.

Check your speech for the use of these words and phrases:

▶ *okay?*

▶ *y'know*

▶ *see*

▶ *like*

▶ *I mean*

▶ *and stuff like that*

▶ *and so on and so forth*

▶ *et cetera*

▶ *in other words*

▶ *so to speak*

▶ *you might say*

▶ *right?*

Identify Repetitious Patterns of Inflection

While growing up and listening to other people, you learned very early that there are logical and natural places in sentences to vary the pitch of your voice. For instance, in English, your voice usually goes higher in pitch at the end of a question or deepens for an emphatic statement. In normal conversation, we use a variety of inflections without having to think about it. In public speaking, however, there can be a tendency to deliver every sentence with the same inflectional pattern regardless of the sentence's meaning or grammatical structure. This happens when the speaker is not thinking about the content of the speech, is nervous, is reading from a manuscript, or is recalling a memorized text. A singsongy, hypnotic pattern of *inflection* can easily lead to drooping eyelids in the audience. Review a recording of your speech for vocalized pauses or repetitious inflection.

Check out Speech Studio to see how other students pronounce words and incorporate vocal variety in their speeches. Or record a speech you're working on, upload it to Speech Studio, and ask your peers for their feedback. What feedback could you use to fine tune your pronunciation and vocal variety before you give your speech in class?

Use a Self-Improvement Program or Get Professional Help

When you identify a problem and your motivation to correct it is strong, the next step is to determine how best to rectify it.

Self-Improvement

In some cases you may devise a simple plan of action, as Demosthenes did in ancient Greece when he was troubled by problems of articulation and enunciation. His solution was to practice being understood while speaking over the roar of the ocean with his mouth full of pebbles. That may seem a bit ridiculous today; we can be thankful that there are other resources to tap. Books and recordings are available that provide exercises in breathing and projection. Some exercises, such as tongue twisters, make apparent the muscle groups used to produce certain sounds properly. You can start with resources such as these:

▶   J. Goldes, *The Dialect Coach*. To access his website, go to your CourseMate for *The Speaker's Handbook* and click on **WebLink 25.4**.

▶   Lyle Vernon Mayer, *Fundamentals of Voice and Articulation*. Boston: McGraw Hill, 2008.

For a deeply ingrained habit, you may choose to map out a program of behavior modification. This approach, which has been quite successful in helping people lose weight or quit smoking, is based on the premise that habits that develop gradually are best eliminated gradually. New behaviors are substituted for old ones, and the new behaviors are rewarded. For many, the result of a changed habit is a sufficient reward. But there's nothing wrong with rewarding yourself with something more tangible (a new shirt, a movie with a friend, etc.) if it will help you stay on track and reach your goal.

Professional Help

Some problems of vocal delivery are difficult to diagnose or solve without professional help. In seeking help, consider the nature and seriousness of your vocal problem, as well as the time and money you are able to commit. Then consult the appropriate professional from the following list:

▶   *Speech therapists* are the best source of help for fairly serious or persistent articulation and voice problems.

▶   *Voice coaches* may be affiliated with theater, radio, or television. They can help you improve voice quality, diction, and pronunciation. If you also want to work on regionalisms or accents and want to develop greater variety and expressiveness, consider a course in voice and diction or oral interpretation. An acting course will help in these areas and improve your physical movement.

▶   *Public speaking teachers* and *consultants* can provide help with voice, articulation, emphasis, and expressiveness within the context of public speaking. Usually, work on speech delivery is integrated with the development of speech content.

© laurent Renault / iStockphoto 14363693

CHECKLIST ~ Steps to Modifying Vocal Behavior on Your Own

☐ Assess your current behavior. Quantify the exact frequency of the distracting habit.

☐ Set a specific, realistic goal. If you say "okay?" after nearly every sentence, perhaps twenty times in a ten-minute speech, resolve to cut down to ten times in a ten-minute speech.

☐ Monitor your behavior. Do not simply estimate your progress. Have a friend tally the occurrences or record each speech yourself. Keep a written chart of your progress.

Review, Reconsider, & Act

Summary

How effectively a person uses his or her voice can be the difference between a great speech and a real snoozer. If you are a nonnative English speaker, you may find vocal delivery to be an issue of great concern. However, many native speakers of English also make mistakes in vocal delivery. Begin by making sure to speak loudly enough to be heard and understood. Develop vocal variety including pitch, rate, and volume. Learn to use standard pronunciation with both familiar and unfamiliar terms. If you are troubled by distracting vocal characteristics, determine their origin and make every effort to correct them either on your own or with the assistance of professionals.

Critical Thinking Questions

▶ What is the danger of speaking too quickly or too slowly?

▶ Should a person eliminate his or her accent in order to be understood more effectively? Why?

▶ How might vocal variety make a speech more "listenable"?

▶ What options are available for individuals interested in improving their voice or diction?

Putting It into Practice

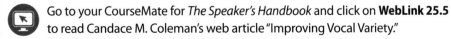 Go to your CourseMate for *The Speaker's Handbook* and click on **WebLink 25.5** to read Candace M. Coleman's web article "Improving Vocal Variety."

1. To what degree do you believe you use a wide vocal range when speaking with friends?

2. How does your vocal range change when you give a speech?

3. What aspects of your delivery could be more varied when you present in front of a group?

erwinova /Shutterstock

chapter 26
Physical Delivery

Use physical delivery to add interest and complement the content of your speech.

Much of how your listeners respond to you is a result of what they see rather than what they hear. The words may be confident, but shaking knees and fidgeting fingers tell another story. Slouching posture and a grim expression can reveal the lie in "I'm so happy to be here!" When practicing and delivering your speech, be aware of the visual image you are creating. As with vocal delivery, the goal of physical delivery is to be natural and to avoid anything that would contradict your verbal message.

Be Conscious of Your Appearance

What kinds of first impressions do people have of you? Are they initially intimidated by you because you are big and burly? Do people dismiss you because you look ten years younger than you are? Obviously, you cannot trade in your body, but if such impressions get in the way of your speech goals, you can try to compensate. Correct false impressions, especially in the opening minutes of your presentation, by using speech content and all those physical characteristics you have control over.

As you get ready for a particular speech, consider what your hairstyle, grooming, clothing, and accessories might communicate to your audience. You do not need, nor do you necessarily want, to mimic the dress of your audience. Regardless of differences in sense of style, however, you should show that you took care in preparing, that you consider the event important enough to expend some energy in trying to look good. Don't make the mistake of looking like you just rolled off your friend's couch.

Ideally, your clothes should provide a tasteful and unobtrusive frame for your personality and your remarks. Be aware of regional, cultural, and occupational norms.

In some parts of the country, and in certain professional or social settings, jeans and a sport jacket may be considered formal enough for a presentation. When in doubt, though, lean toward conservative business attire. "Business casual" may be acceptable in a college speech class. There is no need to be drab, but remember that your audience could be distracted by loud colors, busy patterns, showy jewelry or piercings, visible tattoos, unorthodox combinations of apparel, and any clothing they consider too revealing. Avoid anything that will divert attention from your primary message.

Eliminate Distracting Mannerisms

Distracting mannerisms fall into two categories: those you have all the time (pushing your glasses up on your nose, tucking your hair behind your ear, cracking your knuckles), and those you have only when giving a speech (noisily fanning and squaring up your notecards, rocking back and forth on your heels, tapping your pencil on the lectern). These are physical equivalents of saying "y'know . . . y'know . . . y'know." Few acts are inherently distracting—it is the repetition of some act that becomes distracting. As with vocal mannerisms, you may be unaware of the frequency of the act until someone points it out. Thus, the first step toward eliminating the problem is to become consciously aware of it. Use the practice techniques laid out in Chapters **2** and **24** to get feedback on your delivery; then reduce the frequency of any distracting mannerisms by adapting the behavior modification techniques described in Chapter **25**.

Maintain a Relaxed, Alert Posture

As a general rule, you should stand when speaking. This focuses audience attention on you and gives you a better view of your listeners. There are exceptions, of course. In an intimate setting, such as a circle of a few people, you might choose to remain seated while you speak. As a member of a panel discussion, you may feel constrained to use a lectern if other panelists do so; however, it is permissible to stand away from the lectern or desk for your portion of the presentation even if other panel members don't. It is best to learn to be comfortable speaking without a lectern—with your weight evenly distributed, your notes grasped casually in one hand at waist level, and no props of any kind for support. Appropriate variations might include leaning forward to show deep involvement or sitting on the edge of a desk or table to signal the shift to an informal mood. However, avoid draping yourself across the lectern, slouching, standing with hands at your hips, elbows extended, or rocking back and forth, as these positions are incompatible with the energetic and controlled image of a polished public speaker. You should also avoid an overly rigid stance. Be especially careful not to lock your knees, as you risk becoming light-headed or even fainting.

Make Purposeful, Relevant Movements

You can give a perfectly good and proper speech standing behind a lectern. However, most speeches can be aided by movement at appropriate times. Taking a few steps to the left or right or moving closer to your listeners can add variety and emphasis to your speech. You also establish contact with the segment of the audience that you move toward. If you sense you've lost the attention of one portion of an audience, sometimes movement toward them can regain their attention. Moreover, physical movement during a speech is a constructive way to release tension.

Make your movements purposeful. Pacing nervously around the room is distracting, as are the tentative dance steps of the speaker who cannot really decide whether to move or not. This speaker shuffles, rocks from side to side, and seems to stay in constant motion. If you are going to move, be decisive. Take at least two or three normal paces diagonally or directly forward. When you stop, keep your body orientation and eye contact toward the most concentrated part of your audience.

The timing of your movement can reinforce your ideas. Generally, it is best to remain in one place while explaining complex material or when delivering your most emotional examples or powerful arguments. Physical movement works best at transitional points, where it signals a change in mood, content, or form. A moving transition literally combines physical movement with a transitional statement such as those described in Chapter 12.

Go to your CourseMate for The Speaker's Handbook *and click on* **WebLink 26.1** *to read more about physical movement during speech delivery.*

Make Natural Gestures

Many people have trouble figuring out what to do with their hands while speaking. The solution is actually quite simple. We should use our hands while speaking exactly as we do in normal conversation. For some people, using their hands in this manner means hardly using them at all. For others, it means gesturing a great deal. Whether you gesture a little or a lot, you do it to describe, to point out, to enumerate, to emphasize, to implore, and so on.

There is no need to plan what gestures go with your speech. If you are absorbed with your topic and with communicating it to your listeners, your gestures will emerge spontaneously at the appropriate points. But this will happen only if your hands are free to move. Too many speakers immobilize their hands completely, out of both the panicky need to cling to something and the desire to prevent uncontrolled movement.

Do not lock yourself into any of these gesture-inhibiting stances:

▶ *The bear hug:* Arms across the chest—one of the most common ways of getting a grip on yourself

▶ *Ten-hut!:* Arms stiff, wrists nailed to hips

▶ *The flesh wound:* One arm hanging useless at the side, the other hand serving as a tourniquet above or below the elbow

▶ *The firing squad:* Legs slightly spread, hands clasped behind back

▶ *The choirboy/girl:* Hands clasped at waist level, with fingers entwined

▶ *The supplicant:* Same as the choir, but higher, at chest level

▶ *The fig leaf:* Demurely crossed hands, strategically placed

Actually, all of these are perfectly acceptable *transitory* postures. The problem with them lies not in the position of the limbs, but in the temptation to leave them there, statue-like, while you concentrate on what is coming out of your mouth. As you become more involved in your message and the audience's response to it, your natural gestures will come back to you. When these natural impulses collide with the unnatural posture you have locked yourself into, the results can be bizarre.

So, what *do* you do with your hands? First, do nothing distracting such as nervously shredding notecards, drumming on the table, scratching, or making other kinds of unproductive hand movements:

▶ *The Lady Macbeth:* Hands wrung compulsively and continuously to wash out the "stain" of having to speak

▶ *Happy pockets:* Keys, change, and other pocket contents set to jingling by restless hands, the sound competing with the speaker's voice

Second, do nothing contrived—no rehearsed gestures. A hand can be at your side, holding cards at waist level, resting lightly on the other, *gently* grasping the lectern, or

FOR YOUR BENEFIT: Simply Smile

YOUR NEW CAREER

The one expression that has the same meaning in every culture is the smile. Most public speakers underuse or misuse this powerful tool. A constant, fixed, jaw-aching grin is as bad as a deadpan expression. A smile at a sad or serious moment is inappropriate. However, remind yourself to smile genuinely whenever it can reinforce your message. Begin your speech with direct eye contact and a smile to your audience. It is one of the easiest ways to establish rapport, show your goodwill, and put you and your audience at ease.

Rtimages / www.BigStockPhoto.com

casually resting in a pocket (no change-jingling). What matters most is that your arms, wrists, and fingers are relaxed so that your hands can move naturally as the occasion arises.

Maintain Eye Contact

Be familiar enough with your material that you can look at as many members of your audience as possible, as often as possible. In an American culture, looking into another's face connotes openness and interest, whereas looking away or down is interpreted as a sign of insincerity or shiftiness. People would much rather look at your face than the top of your head. Moreover, it can distract them from what you are saying if you stare fixedly out the window or up at the ceiling. After a while, listeners' attention begins to shift in those directions, and they wonder if cue cards are taped to the rafters or if a major crime is in progress outside. But more essentially, maintaining eye contact allows you to read your listeners' faces to get feedback on how your message is being received. Faking eye contact by looking between heads or just over the heads of the people in the back row misses the whole point.

At the beginning of your speech, find a few listeners who are responding supportively with nods and positive facial expressions. Look at them and use their support to help you through this initially uncomfortable phase. As soon as you start to feel more confident, however, broaden your eye contact to include everyone.

Actually look into the eyes of the individual audience members, and hold that contact for at least three seconds. Do not skim across rows of faces. Move your eye contact randomly throughout the room. Do not fall into a head-bobbing pattern: left, center, right, center, left . . . Have a friend or colleague observe and tell you if you scan mechanically or if you have a tendency to neglect any one segment of the audience.

In any speech, even a manuscript speech, you should have eye contact 85 percent of the time, looking down only to read technical material or to refer briefly to your notes.

Speaker's Workshop 26.1

Go to your CourseMate for *The Speaker's Handbook* to access the interactive videos for this book. Analyze the physical delivery of these speakers in terms of appearance, gestures, movement, and facial expression: Brian Sharkey, Hans Erian, and Julian Treasure. What aspects of their delivery do you find particularly effective or ineffective?

Most important, be sure to maintain eye contact throughout your introduction and conclusion and during the most telling points and pivotal arguments.

Use Facial Expression to Reflect Tone

Do not let the tension of a speaking situation force you into a deadpan face. Your natural facial expressions serve as one more channel for effective communication. Generally, changes in facial expression precede and forecast shifts in tone or mood. Replacing your cheerful countenance with a concerned frown can be a better transition than using that old cliché "but seriously, folks."

You should not plan a series of mugs, smiles, and grimaces—all you need to do is exaggerate slightly those expressions that arise normally. The subtle nuances that work in face-to-face contact will not reach the back row.

Check out Speech Studio to see how other students use physical movement in their speeches. Or record a speech you're working on, upload it to Speech Studio, and ask your peers for their feedback. What feedback could you use to fine tune your physical movement before you give your speech in class?

Review, Reconsider, & Act

Summary

Physical delivery should support and enhance, not distract from, your message. As you practice your speech, be aware of what messages you may be sending via dress and adornments, movement, gestures, and facial expression. Work to eliminate or reduce distracting mannerisms and focus on natural delivery, matching your movement and expression to the mode or tone of the speech.

Critical Thinking Questions

▶ How does physical delivery affect speaker credibility?

▶ How can movement be used to enhance a speech and maintain appropriate attention?

▶ What impact does eye contact have on audience attention and later retention? Why?

▶ What are the worst things a speaker can do with respect to physical delivery?

Putting It into Practice

Watch a live or recorded keynote or business speech, such as Cisco CEO John Chambers's speech on leadership at the University of California, Berkeley, in September 2010. A good site for these types of speeches is the UC Berkeley's site for the Haas School of Business. For easy access to this site, go to your CourseMate for *The Speaker's Handbook* and click on **WebLink 26.2**.

1. What does the speaker do physically to enhance the verbal message?
2. What does the speaker do that detracts from the verbal message?
3. What would you recommend the speaker do differently?

yarnix/Shutterstock

Additional Resources 8

PART 8
ADDITIONAL RESOURCES

INTRODUCTION: JUST IN CASE

GUIDE TO COMMON PRONUNCIATION AND USAGE ERRORS

GLOSSARY OF KEY TERMS

introduction
Just in Case

This last part of the handbook provides two additional resources that you may find helpful as you use this text and prepare speeches: The first is a Guide to Common Pronunciation and Usage Errors, and the second is a Glossary of Key Terms. Both resources are intended to be references—compilations of specific information that you may choose to consult as needed.

We created the Guide to Common Pronunciation and Usage Errors for both native and nonnative speakers of English. Many English words are used and pronounced incorrectly every day, and often we encounter them courtesy of popular media. Because we tend to think that media figures must know how to say things correctly, and because we hear incorrect forms over and over, we sometimes even adjust our usual way—which had been the correct way—of saying things to the incorrect ways that are so prevalent. If you're going to give a public presentation, you may want to play it safe and check this guide to ensure that you are understood and are perceived to be as credible as possible.

If you are uncertain about the pronunciation of words not included in this guide, then you might want to visit the Merriam-Webster website, which provides audio pronunciations for about 105,000 English words. Other online dictionaries also provide audio pronunciation, and you can find guides to English usage online as well. One good source is Paul Brians' Common Errors in English usage, a site sponsored by Washington State University. (Scroll down to the bottom of the site for several links to other good resources.)

To access Merriam-Webster's dictionary online, go to your CourseMate for The Speaker's Handbook and click on **WebLink 17.1** (Merriam-Webster's) and **WebLink 37.1** (Paul Brians' site).

The Glossary of Key Terms pulls together all of the words and phrases that appear in **bold** throughout the chapters. Here, those "key," or essential, terms are presented with definitions of each. Even though we define most terms in the context of using them in the chapters, you may find this alphabetical compilation helpful. A few of the words we use while discussing communication concepts and precepts throughout the book are rather exotic—for example, *enthymeme* and *assonance.* Possibly as challenging are the words that are used in a specialized way when related to communication theory: *rhetoric, style,* and *credibility* are not new words, but the way they are used in everyday conversation may be somewhat different from the way they are used in the context of helping you to prepare and deliver a public speech. We hope you'll consult the glossary for clarification as often as you need to. Also, keep in mind that the CourseMate for *The Speaker's Handbook* includes flashcards and crossword puzzles to help you learn the key terms and the concepts they represent.

Guide to Common Pronunciation and Usage Errors

For a speaker, pronunciation and usage errors are impediments to intelligibility and credibility. Well-reasoned points and lively descriptions can lose their impact if a mispronounced or misused word lands with a clunk to interrupt the concentration and attention of your listeners. Here we list just a few of the common errors that can crop up; references at the end describe many more usage and word-choice snares to which you should be alert. You can find pronunciation references in Chapter **25**.

Problems in Pronunciation

Word	*Proper*	*Improper*
across	a cross	a crost
athlete	ath leet	a thuh leet
comparable	COM per able	com PARE able
compulsory	com pul sory	com pul so rary
drowned	drowned	drown ded
err	ur	air
escape	es cape	ex cape
et cetera	et cet era	ek cet era
February	feb roo ary	feb you ary
get	get	git
just	just	jist
larynx	lar inks	lar nix

library	li brar y	li berry
mischievous	mis che vous	mis chee vious
nuclear	nu clee ar	nu cyou lar
perspiration	pers pir a tion	press pir a tion
picture	pic tchure	pit chure
recognize	rec og nize	reck a nize
relevant	rel a vant	rev a lant
strict	strict	strick
surprise	sur prise	sup prise
temperature	temp per achure	temp achure
theater	THEE a ter	thee A ter

Word-Choice Errors

Wrong Use	*Comments*
adverse/averse	
"I would be adverse to adopting this plan."	Because the speaker is talking about an aversion to something, the proper adjective is "averse." When describing feelings, use "averse"; when describing things, use "adverse"—for example, "Without restructuring, we shall end up working in adverse conditions."
affect/effect	
"The affect of the plan could be very beneficial."	Usually "affect" is a verb. Properly, this sentence should use "effect" in its sense of "result."
bi/semi	
"Under this plan, paychecks will be distributed bimonthly on the first and fifteenth."	"Bi" means "every two" and "semi" means "twice a," so in this case it should be "distributed semimonthly on the first and fifteenth."
comprise/compose	
"Let's look at the three actions that comprise this plan."	A whole comprises its parts, so this sentence is backward; "compose" or "constitute" would be correct. For "comprise" to be correct, the sentence should read: "The plan comprises three actions; let's look at them now." Also, "is comprised of" is not correct.
disinterested/uninterested	
"Some of you may be disinterested in the workings of this plan."	"Disinterested" means having no stake in the outcome or being neutral, as in "a disinterested third party will judge the results." If you instead mean "lack of interest," then use "uninterested."

flaunt/flout

"One thing about this plan is that it makes it less easy for users to flaunt our guidelines."

"Flaunt" means to show off; "flout" means to treat with disregard or scorn. These words are not interchangeable.

i.e./e.g.

"Some parts of this plan, i.e., restructuring, won't take place immediately."

This choice is wrong at two levels. First, "i.e." is an abbreviation of the Latin id est, meaning "that is." It does not mean "for example"—that role is taken by "e.g.," from the Latin exempli gratia. Second, a speaker should not use these abbreviations orally and instead use plain English "that is" and "for example."

imply/infer

"I'm not inferring this plan will solve everything."

"Imply" means to suggest something that has not been stated explicitly, and "infer" means to draw a conclusion from something not stated explicitly. So, correct use would be either "I'm not implying this plan will solve everything," or something like, "You might have inferred that I think this plan will solve everything, but that is not the case."

ironic/coincidental

"It's ironic that, after working on this plan, Alexis and I discovered we both changed our original expositions."

Irony is more than mere coincidence. Irony requires that there be some incongruity rising from a result that was different from the one expected. So, unless the speaker and Alexis had both vowed repeatedly that they were going to be steadfast in their original positions, it would be more accurate to say: "Coincidentally, Alexis and I discovered we both changed our original positions after working on this plan."

less/fewer

"There are less opponents to this plan than supporters."

If something can be counted in discrete units it should be modified by "fewer," not by "less." So, "there are fewer opponents" is correct. Note that changing to "there is less opposition than support" makes the usage correct, too.

nonplussed/nonchalant

"The opponents of this plan seem remarkably nonplussed in their calm acceptance of the status quo."

When one is nonplussed, one is bewildered or perplexed, not "nonchalant" or "calm."

tortuous/torturous

"The torturous logic of the opponents of this plan is hard to fathom."

Because the speaker means "twisted or complex"—not "painful"—in this context, "tortuous" is the correct choice.

Some Grammar and Usage Problems

Wrong use	*Comments*
Dangling/misplaced modifier	
"Having failed twice before, I wouldn't support any more attempts by the Baker committee to come up with a plan."	As constructed, this sentence makes the speaker the one who has failed twice. To be grammatically correct, and certainly less confusing, the sentence could be: "Having failed twice before, the Baker committee won't get my support for any more attempts to come up with a plan," or "I wouldn't support any more attempts by the Baker committee to come up with a plan because they have failed twice before."
Misuse of pronouns in the subjective case	
"The composition of the Baker committee came as a surprise to Alexis and I."	"I" is a subjective pronoun and so is reserved for use as the subject of a sentence: "Alexis and I were surprised by the composition of the Baker committee." For a sentence in which the speaker is the object of the verb, the objective case is appropriate: "The composition of the Baker committee came as a surprise to Alexis and me." A preposition (to, by, from, etc.) is usually a dead giveaway to use the objective case of a pronoun.
Misuse of reflexive pronoun	
"The people who looked over the plan were David, Carla, and myself."	"Myself" is the reflexive form of the pronoun, and the reflexive ordinarily is used only where the object of a sentence is the same as the subject ("I overworked myself on this project"), as an object of a preposition that refers to the subject ("I worked on this project by myself"), or to emphasize the subject ("Although others helped with the research, I wrote the plan myself"). The sentence in this case should use the objective case for the pronoun: "The people who looked over the plan were David, Carla, and me." Be alert to the misuse of other reflexive pronouns like "himself," "herself," "yourself," and "themselves."
Subject–verb disagreement	
"The source of these failures are to be found in the incomplete research done."	"Of these failures" is a phrase that modifies the singular subject of the sentence, "source," and the fact that the noun in the phrase is plural has no effect on the verb. Because the subject is singular, the verb should also be singular: "The source of these failures is to be found in ... "

Glossary of Key Terms

A

acronym A device to aid in memory based on creating a word from the first letters of a phrase.

ad hominem fallacy An error in reasoning that consists of attacking a person identified with a position instead of refuting the position itself.

affirming the consequent The most common form of the faulty reversal of an if–then statement. A person reasons that because *X* necessarily follows *Y*, the opposite is also true. Just because "if there is a rainbow, it is raining," it does not mean that every time it is raining there is a rainbow.

agenda A specific predetermined plan for the conduct of a meeting or a group event. It provides structure for groups and helps minimize conflict over what will be discussed, in what sequence, and, perhaps, for how long.

alliteration A stylistic device that consists of the repetition of a consonant sound. "Big, brutal bullies" will be more memorable and have more impact than "large, mean bullies."

antithesis A stylistic device that consists of two contrasting ideas set up in opposition.

articulation The ability to produce the sounds of speech correctly so that words are understandable.

assonance A stylistic device that consists of the repetition of a vowel sound. "People are dreaming of pie in the sky, by and by" repeats the long I sound and is likely to have an impact.

attention getter The opening one or two sentences of a speech introduction designed to immediately engage the listeners' interest.

B

bar graphs A format for displaying data that compares related items by having them represented by bars of different lengths or heights.

C

causal reasoning The justification for an argument claiming that one thing is the direct result of another. A causal claim should not be confused with mere coincidence or correlation.

cause–effect pattern A way of organizing speech points that begins by discussing the origins of a situation and moves to discussing the consequences that follow those conditions.

central idea A more informal designation for the thesis of a speech. Even if one's major point is not fully developed into a subject–predicate assertion as required for a thesis sentence, this core idea provides a touchstone for developing the speech.

chronological pattern A way of organizing the points of a speech that follows a time order; it might be historical or it might follow steps in a process, for example.

circular reasoning An error in reasoning that occurs when a speaker assumes the truth of the conclusion and uses that as the starting point for developing an argument, instead of building a case for the conclusion by creating a valid line of reasoning.

claim A proposition that a speaker advances as a conclusion. The claim might be the thesis of the speech, a main point, or a subpoint. Typically, a claim is a controversial statement that does not earn automatic acceptance but needs to be proven by the development of an argument.

clearinghouse question An open-ended question asked near the end of an interview segment that allows the interviewee to offer any additional information that may be useful to the interviewer.

clincher The closing sentence of a speech conclusion that gives a sense of finality and has a powerful impact. A carefully thought-out clincher replaces the "trailing off" phenomenon that can ruin a good speech.

cognitive restructuring A treatment for communication apprehension that involves discovering the underlying statements that are driving one's fear, analyzing the logic of these, and replacing them with more realistic statements. Regularly repeating the more realistic statements can eventually restructure the way you think about speaking.

concept mapping An organizational technique for marshalling ideas. Before a speaker settles on main points, it is often helpful to use circle diagrams or movable components to pull similar ideas together and show how clusters relate to one another.

conclusion The final section of a speech, which generally restates the thesis and main points and often attempts to establish logical and psychological closure for the speech.

context The features that surround the core message of a speech and shape its meaning. General contextual features involve time, space, degree of formality, and the like. Specific contexts such as the workplace or the political sphere have sets of norms and expectations that shape speaking in those settings.

coordinate points Points of equal importance that cannot be nested under one another. For example, points I, II, and III are coordinate to each other. Points A, B, and C under each of these are also coordinate to one another.

credibility The perception that a certain speaker is believable, over and above the logical message and the emotional impact. The persuasive power of credibility comes from being able to project qualities such as competence, trustworthiness, concern, and dynamism. Other things being equal, speakers perceived as having these qualities will be more persuasive.

D

data Verifiable information often in numerical form, such as statistics used in a speech to support a specific point or line of reasoning.

deduction A form of reasoning that demonstrates how the relationships among established premises lead to a necessary conclusion.

definition by authority Explaining the meaning of a word by calling on an expert in the field or by some authoritative ruling, such as in a court.

definition by example Explaining the meaning of a word by giving familiar instances of the concept.

definition by negation or opposition Explaining the meaning of a word by contrasting it to its opposite or telling what it is not.

denying the antecedent A form of faulty reasoning that is related to but less common than affirming the consequent. It assumes that, because *X* necessarily follows from *Y*, the absence of *Y* means the absence of *X*. However, there may be other causes for *Y*. (If a major premise states "if and only if *Y* is present, *X* will be present," then denying the antecedent is not fallacious.)

E

enhanced conversation A way of thinking about public speaking that encourages speakers to rely heavily on the same resources they use daily in conversation but to amplify these, project them more enthusiastically, and pay a bit more attention to crafting details of style and organization.

enthymemes The classical term for the more informal, conversational, often shortened form that reasoning takes in actual persuasion. For example, a complete logical syllogism might state: "Anything our president does is in the national interest. This policy is initiated by our president. This policy is in the national interest." An enthymeme would be shorter and more natural sounding, such as: "Of course this is in the national interest; the president introduced it." Enthymemes are harder to dissect and analyze. However, they can be powerful in that they call on the listeners to "fill in the blanks" and thus involve them in making the case.

etymological definition A way of explaining the meaning of a term by looking at the historical roots of the word or at its linguistic origins.

evocative A speech with the purpose of evoking is designed to call forth an emotion or shared feeling. This is sometimes called the speech to entertain, but evocative speaking is a broader term that can include arousing feelings of sympathy or grief as well as feelings of happiness or amusement.

extemporaneous A mode of delivery that consists of preparing the organization of a speech and becoming familiar with the structure and some of the phrases where language is important, but not writing out or memorizing the speech. It is delivered in a conversational manner from general notes. This is the most common form of delivery.

F

factual examples Specific instances used to illustrate a more general point. Brief examples are used when the audience is assumed to be familiar with the case, such as "it hurts about as much as a pinprick." Extended examples are used when the audience is not familiar with the case, so more details are required to make the point, such as "let me tell you about my Uncle George's experience . . . . "

fallacies Errors in reasoning that make a particular argument or position invalid.

fallacy of the absurd extreme An error in reasoning that makes a potentially sound argument appear groundless by extending it to a point where it can be easily ridiculed.

false dichotomy An error of reasoning that results from assuming that there are only two clear-cut alternatives in a situation when there are, in fact, many intermediate alternatives.

full-sentence outline A detailed logical plan for a speech that states each main point and at least the first level of subpoints in complete subject–predicate sentences. This attention to detail provides a test to be sure that every part of the speech is logically related to each other. The outline is an important planning tool but it is not the same as a speech manuscript or as speaking notes.

G

GANTT A project management tool (named for its developer Henry Laurence Gantt) used to establish the timeline of a project by offering a visual representation of when each task occurs and how long it will take.

H

hasty generalization An error in inductive reasoning that results from making a premature inductive leap and basing a generalization on insufficient data.

historical definition Explaining the meaning of a term by tracing how it has been used in the past, perhaps showing how the meaning has evolved.

holistic listening Listening to another person in an open, nonjudgmental way—not just analyzing his or her points, but trying to take in all the verbal and nonverbal cues, silences, and omissions to get some sense of the full message that is available to be interpreted.

hypothetical example A plausible story created by the speaker to illustrate a point. As with factual examples, these may be either brief or extended. In contrast to factual examples, though, hypothetical examples can be used only to clarify a point, not to prove it.

I

impromptu A mode of speaking that does not allow for any formal preparation but requires the speaker to speak "off the cuff." Impromptu speaking can still draw on many of the principles of other kinds of speaking, such as having a clear first and last sentence, involving the audience, and using lots of examples.

inductive reasoning A pattern of reasoning that consists of combining a series of specific observations that lead to a probable general conclusion.

internal preview At some point after the first point has been developed, a speaker forecasts the remaining points to be covered.

internal summary At some point before the last point is developed, a speaker restates the points that have been covered so far.

introduction The opening section of a speech that serves to get attention and orient the audience before beginning to develop the first main point.

J

jargon Informal or technical terms that relate to a particular activity or group; the use of jargon sets apart the practitioners or group members.

K

keyword or key-phrase outline A preliminary organizational tool that consists of just words and phrases to be used. It is more developed than brainstorming tools like concept mapping, but less elaborate than a topic outline or a full-sentence outline.

L

line graphs A format for displaying data that uses points connected by lines to indicate changes over time or distance.

listening A complex and active process of receiving, processing, and evaluating an oral message. It includes the reception of stimuli, their organization into usable chunks of sound, the identification of comprehensible words or phrases, and the interpretation of meanings.

logical definition The most common and precise way of defining terms, which begins by placing the term in its broad category (genus), and then listing the qualities that differentiate the term from all other members of that category (species).

logical orientation A section of the introduction that provides the intellectual framework for the speech, often stating the thesis sentence and previewing the main points.

M

main points Primary ideas, those that are central and indispensable to the development of the thesis.

major premise The basic assumption that underlies a line of deductive argument. If the argument is laid out as a formal syllogism, then the major premise is the first statement and it lays out an absolute relationship such as either/or, if/then, or the classic "all men are mortal."

manuscript speaking   A mode of delivery that involves writing out a speech fully (in the oral style preferably) and then practicing it until it is familiar and sounds conversational when delivered.

Maslow's hierarchy of needs   A systematic arrangement of human needs based on the assumption that people will give priority to more basic needs and fill these at a minimal level before attending to higher needs. The hierarchy proceeds from security needs to belongingness needs to esteem needs to self-actualization needs.

meaning   The complex mutual understanding of communication co-created by senders and receivers within a given social, contextual, and contingent situation.

memorized   A mode of delivery that involves writing out a speech fully (in the oral style preferably) and then practicing it until it can be delivered word for word from memory.

metaphor   A stylistic device that uses language as if there were an identity between two things that belong to different categories—for example, "my job is a nightmare."

minor premise   The part of a deductive argument that introduces some data about the actual state of affairs into the reasoning. In an either/or or if/then syllogism, for example, it asserts that one of the alternatives is or is not true. In a categorical syllogism, the minor premise places a specific case into a general category, as in "Socrates is a man."

motivated sequence   An organizer for persuasion that echoes the mental stages through which listeners progress as they hear a speech.

mutuality of concern   A give-and-take between a speaker and a listener that develops over time into a meaningful exchange of ideas.

O

operational definition   A way of explaining the meaning of a term by explaining how it works or what it does.

P

persuasive speaking   Speech that has the purpose of changing behavior or attitudes of the listeners.

PERT   A project management tool used to organize a project by visually establishing the required order of steps needed to complete the task.

PERT stands for Program Evaluation and Review Technique.

pictorial reproductions   Presentation aids that use a visual depiction (e.g., a photograph, sketch, or video) of an object in two dimensions.

pictorial symbols   Presentation aids that consist of representations of abstract concepts.

pie chart   A format for displaying data that compares related items by having them represented by pie segments, all of which add up to 100 percent of some category.

pitch   How high or low a speaker's voice is. It is helpful to find a pitch that is natural and also to vary one's pitch.

post hoc fallacy   The error in reasoning that results from assuming that, because one event followed another event, it is caused by that event. The tests of causation must be met or the relationship might be coincidental or correlational.

presentation aid   An object or thing that adds another communication dimension beyond a speaker's content and delivery.

presentation software   Computer software specialized for creating presentation aids.

preview   An organization tool that gives listeners a road map of what is to follow: "Today I will cover these three points."

primacy   The persuasive effect that sometimes comes from placing a point first or early in a speech to give it greater impact or make it memorable.

primary audience outcome   The most important result that a speaker wants to achieve, phrased in terms of what the audience will actually do after the speech.

probability   The condition that exists when a conclusion is likely to be true but cannot be established with absolute certainty. In psychological and social matters, most claims are discussed in terms of some degree of probability. When speakers try to persuade listeners on these topics, the task is to show the likelihood of certain costs and benefits coming about so that the "odds" favor the speaker's position.

problem–solution pattern   A way of arranging the main points of a speech that begins with creating an awareness of some issue requiring change and then moves to explaining what should be done to remedy the concerns raised.

project proposal   A kind of workplace presentation in which a speaker or a group provides a plan that should be undertaken and then gives the rationale for this approach. These presentations can range from a research proposal to a sales presentation to a proposal for undertaking some technical project.

project status report A kind of workplace presentation that updates listeners of the progress being made on a project that is already under way. This sort of interim report serves to reassure colleagues or customers about what is being done, to alert them to any problems encountered, and to seek feedback.

proposition of fact A claim that something is or is not true.

proposition of policy A claim that a certain course of action should or should not be adopted.

proposition of value A claim that something is good or bad (in the broadest sense).

PSR statement A problem–solution–result (PSR) statement is a brief but memorable personal success story that states a problem, describes a solution, and lists the results; it should be delivered in 90 seconds or less.

public speaking A communication setting in which one person has primary control and direction of the resources of communication. It may happen in a formal or informal setting, but it involves preparation and the focus is on the speaker for at least much of the time.

Q

question-and-answer period A time allotted after the conclusion of the main speech in which audience members can ask for clarification or elaboration on the speaker's position.

R

rate The speed or pace at which one speaks. Ideally, rate must be fast enough to hold attention, slow enough to be understood, and varied to emphasize meaning.

reasoning by analogy A form of reasoning in which people can draw conclusions about unknown events based on what is known about similar events.

recency The persuasive effect that sometimes comes from placing a point last or late in a speech to give it greater impact or make it memorable.

refutation A structured challenge to an opposing point of view that consists of showing exactly how the evidence and reasoning are faulty. One can refute a point in a debate where another speaker

is present or refute a position that is widely held in society and that audience members may have heard about.

rhetoric The art of finding the available means of persuasion in any given situation. The emphasis is on the thoughtful decisions speakers make in adapting their points to audiences. This classical use contrasts with some contemporary suggestions that "mere rhetoric" is superficial or tricky persuasion.

S

secondary orality Sound-based communication that, unlike the primary orality of preliterate cultures, is based in literacy and finds its outlet in electronic media.

semantic fallacy An error in reasoning that occurs when a word is used in different senses in different parts of the argument.

signposts Organizational techniques that keep the listener informed about how the speech is unfolding. They tell what has been covered, what remains to be covered, and when changes in direction are occurring.

simile A stylistic device that compares two things from different categories, such as "managing a group of scientists is like herding cats."

slang Nonstandard words and expressions.

slippery slope fallacy An error in reasoning that claims the first step in some direction must result in going to dangerous lengths in that direction.

spatial pattern A way of organizing the main points of a speech according to some relationship in space. This might be by geographical regions or by rooms in a museum, for example.

speech or speaker's notes These are working notes designed for quick reference and easy readability during a speech. They are not the same as a manuscript or a full-sentence outline, but they contain key words, phrases, organizational cues, and perhaps some specific details that must be cited exactly.

statistical evidence Data that has been systematically collected and coded in numerical form so that speakers can capture a broad number of cases or make formal comparative statements.

stock issues A set of standardized questions to which a speaker can refer in order to be sure that a proposition has been fully established. These can be the basis of building a strong persuasive case or they can be points of refutation for a speaker who opposes a proposition. The stock issues vary in context—such as the legal context, where each kind of charge raises particular points of controversy—but in a general policy proposition the stock issues are: Is there a need? Is the need inherent to the current system? Does the proposal meet the need? Is the proposal workable? Does the plan have disadvantages that outweigh the advantages?

straw figure fallacy   An error in reasoning that stems from stating an argument in a much weaker form than is fair to those advocating the view and then proceeding to demolish that weak argument.

style   The use of language to make speech effective. Style consists of being clear and concise and also of using various devices to enhance the impact of language.

subordinate points   The lesser points that fall beneath main points of a speech—either to elaborate on the main points or to support them.

supporting materials   The parts of a speech that expand on or prove the claims made in main points or subpoints. These examples, definitions, statistics, and testimony serve as the actual building blocks of a speech.

T

team presentation   A speech given by a small group of presenters who have worked collaboratively to prepare a unified statement and to make sure that all the requirements of an effective speech are present. Presumably, the presenters all bring some special expertise or perspective to the presentation.

testimony   A form of supporting material that reports the experience or opinions of another person. The testimony is most helpful when the person cited either is an expert or has direct experience with the topic.

text   A message captured in words. Thus, all the nonverbal, psychological, and cultural factors that surround this core message and help shape its meaning are called the context.

topic outline   An outline that identifies the points to be covered and the relationships among them but that may not spell out all of the logical connections that would be present in a full-sentence outline.

topical pattern   A way of organizing the main points of a speech that grows naturally out of what is being talked about and is not arranged according to sequential, spatial, or logical rules.

training presentation   A form of informative speaking that is in an extended and focused format. Associated with the workplace, it will often take the form of a series of workshops or seminars in which the goal is to help people learn a rather specific set of skills or body of knowledge.

V

vocal variety   Altering the tone and pitch of one's voice to provide for interest and emphasis. It's the opposite of a monotone.

vocalized pauses   Filler phrases such as "um," "er," "y'know," and "like" that break the fluency of speaking and can be distracting to listeners.

volume   The loudness (or softness) with which one speaks.

W

warrant   The part of an argument that links the evidence to the claim. Because the same data can be used to prove multiple (even opposite) points, a speaker must show explicitly the reasoning that links data to a particular conclusion.

whiteboard   A board with an erasable shiny surface for making temporary markings, such as drawings or words.

Notes

Chapter 1

1. Daniel J. Boorstin, "Dissent, Dissension, and the News," in *The Decline of Radicalism: Reflections on America Today* (New York: Random House, 1960). Retrieved from the Columbia World of Quotations, http://www.bartleby.com/66/80/7780.html, on June 28, 2008.

2. J. William Fulbright, Speech to the American Newspaper Publishers Association, April 28, 1966. Retrieved from the Columbia World of Quotations, http://www.bartleby.com/66/56/24156.html, June 28, 2008.

3. W. J. Ong, *Rhetoric, Romance, and Technology: Studies in the Interaction of Expression and Culture* (Ithaca, NY: Cornell University Press, 1971).

4. Marshall McLuhan, *Understanding Media: The Extensions of Man* (New York: McGraw-Hill Book Co., 1964).

5. Claude E. Shannon and Warren Weaver, *The Mathematical Theory of Communication* (Urbana, IL: University of Illinois Press, 1949).

6. Sonja K. Foss and Cindy L. Griffin, "Beyond Persuasion: A Proposal for an Invitational Rhetoric," *Communication Monographs* 62 (March 1995): 2–18.

7. Patrik Jonsson, "Shirley Sherrod: Does She Have a Case against Andrew Breitbart?" *Christian Science Monitor* 29 July 2010. Retrieved from EBSCOhost Academic Search Complete database on August 2, 2010.

Chapter 3

1. Adapted from Alfred McClung Lee and Elizabeth Briant Lee, *The Fine Art of Propaganda* (New York: Harcourt and Institute for Propaganda Analysis, 1939), 23–24.

Chapter 4

1. H. Thomson, "What is the function of mirror neurons?" *New Scientist* 205, no. 2754 (2010): 28–29. Retrieved from EBSCOhost Academic Search Complete database on May 9, 2011.

2. V. Cunningham, M. Lefkoe, and L. Sechrest, "Eliminating fears: An intervention that permanently eliminates the fear of public speaking," *Clinical Psychology & Psychotherapy* 13 no. 3 (2006): 183–193, doi:10.1002/cpp.487.

Chapter 5

1. Based on Catherine Patrick, *What Is Creative Thinking?* (New York: Philosophical Library, 1955), 1–48. Patrick's work is based on G. Wallas, *The Art of Thought* (New York: Harcourt, Brace, 1926). This theory has been further advanced by Sébastien Hélie and Ron Sun, "Incubation, Insight, and Creative Problem Solving: A Unified Theory and a Connectionist Model," *Psychological Review* 117, 3 (2010): 994–1024. Retrieved from EBSCOhost Academic Search Complete database on September 12, 2010.

Chapter 6

1. Arne Duncan, "The Quiet Revolution," *Vital Speeches of the Day* 76, no. 10 (October 2010): 455–459. Retrieved from EBSCOhost Academic Search Complete database on December 3, 2010.

2. Hillary Rodham Clinton, "Women's Progress Is Human Progress," *Vital Speeches of the Day* 76, no. 5 (May 2010): 199–203. Retrieved from EBSCOhost Academic Search Complete database on December 3, 2010.

3. Muhtar Kent, "Are We Ready for Tomorrow, Today?" *Vital Speeches of the Day* 76, no. 3 (March 2010): 117–121. Retrieved from EBSCOhost Academic Search Complete database on December 3, 2010.

4. Barack Obama, "Educated Citizens in a Changing World," *Vital Speeches of the Day* 76, no. 8 (August 2010): 364–366. Retrieved from EBSCOhost Academic Search Complete database on December 3, 2010.

5. John M. McCardell Jr., "From Tentative Twig to Mighty Branch," *Vital Speeches of the Day* 76, no. 11 (November 2010): 492–495. Retrieved from EBSCOhost Academic Search Complete database on December 3, 2010.

Chapter 7

1. Izzy Gesell, "How to Lead When the Generation Gap Becomes Your Everyday Reality," *Journal for Quality & Participation* 32, no. 4 (January 2010): 21–24. Retrieved from EBSCOhost Academic Search Complete database on December 5, 2010.

2. Sidney Lowe and Susie Skarl, "Talkin'' bout My Generation." *College & Research Libraries News 70, no. 7* (July): 400–403. Retrieved from

http://crln.acrl.org/content/70/7/400.full.
pdf+html on December 5, 2010.

3. Definition of "ethnicity" from the *American Heritage New Dictionary of Cultural Literacy,* 3rd ed. (Boston: Houghton Mifflin Co., 2005). Retrieved from Dictionary.com, http://dictionary.reference.com/browse/ethnicity, August 3, 2008.

4. Barack Obama '08, "Meet the Candidate." Retrieved from http://www.barackobama.com/learn/meet_barack.php on May 25, 2008.

Chapter 12

1. Barack Obama, "The World that America Seeks." *Vital Speeches of the Day* 76, no. 11 (November 2010): 508–512. Retrieved from EBSCO*host* Academic Search Complete database on December 10, 2010.

Chapter 13

1. Kayla Strickland, "Malaria." Personal outline for Effective Public Speaking class at Sinclair Community College (November 2010).

2. Robert M. Gates, "What Must Change in the U.S. Military." *Vital Speeches of the Day* 76, no. 7 (July 2010): 310–314. Retrieved from EBSCO*host* Academic Search Complete database on December 10, 2010.

3. Lisa Kudrow, "The Biology Major Who Became a Friend." *Vital Speeches of the Day* 76, no. 8 (August 2010): 367–370. Retrieved from EBSCO*host* Academic Search Complete database on December 10, 2010.

4. Glenn Beck, "It Is Still Morning in America." *Vital Speeches of the Day* 76, no. 4 (April 2010): 167–173. Retrieved from EBSCO*host* Academic Search Complete database on December 10, 2010.

5. Dan Brutto, "Globalization 4.0 and the New Logistics." *Vital Speeches of the Day* 76, no. 11 (November 2010): 512–514. Retrieved from EBSCO*host* Academic Search Complete database on December 11, 2010.

6. Carol W. Kinsley, "What Is Community Service Learning?" *Vital Speeches of the Day* 61, no. 2 (November 1, 1994): 40–42.

Chapter 14

1. Kayla Strickland, "Malaria," Personal outline for Effective Public Speaking class at Sinclair Community College (November 2010).

2. Peter M. Gerhart, "The Future of the Legal Profession," *Vital Speeches of the Day* 60, no. 11 (March 15, 1994): 347–352.

Chapter 15

1. Bureau of Labor Statistics, "Usual Weekly Earnings of Wage and Salary Workers News Release," retrieved from http://www.bls.gov/news.release/archives/wkyeng_07162009.htm on December 12, 2010.

2. Department of Rehabilitation and Correction, "Frequently Asked Questions," retrieved from http://www.drc.ohio.gov/web/FAQ.htm on December 12, 2010.

3. Ohio Literacy Network, "Donate," retrieved from http://www.ohioliteracynetwork.org/donate.html on December 12, 2010.

4. Laura Walter, "EHS Today: Why We Need to Hang Up on Our Distracted Driving Addiction." LexisNexis® Academic & Library Solutions, June 1, 2010, page 35. Retrieved from http://www.lexisnexis.com.sinclair.ohionet.org/hottopics/lnacademic/ on December 13, 2010.

5. Regina Brett, "Making your car a no-phone zone," *Cleveland Plain Dealer,* Metro Final edition, May 2, 2010, page B1. Retrieved from http://www.lexisnexis.com.sinclair.ohionet.org/hottopics/lnacademic/ on December 13, 2010.

Chapter 16

1. David Zarefsky, "Argumentation" in *Encyclopedia of Rhetoric,* edited by Thomas Sloan, October 2001, Oxford University Press. Retrieved from http://rave.ohiolink.edu/ebooks/ebc/t223 on May 22, 2011.

Chapter 17

1. Michael E. Eidenmuller, "Personification," American Rhetoric: Rhetorical Figures in Sound Web site, http://www.americanrhetoric.com/speeches/bobbyjindallouisianagovvictory.htm. Accessed on May 22, 2011.

2. Michael E. Eidenmuller, "Alliteration," American Rhetoric: Rhetorical Figures in Sound Web site, http://www.americanrhetoric.com/figures/alliteration.htm. Accessed on May 22, 2011.

3. Michael E. Eidenmuller, "Assonance," American Rhetoric: Rhetorical Figures in Sound, http://www.americanrhetoric.com/figures/assonance.htm. Accessed on May 22, 2011.

Chapter 18

1. Kathleen German, Bruce E. Gronbeck, Douglas Ehninger, and Alan H. Monroe, *Principles of Speech Communication*, 17th ed. (New York: Allyn and Bacon, 2010).

Chapter 19

1. David Abney, "Preparing American Students to Succeed in a Global Era of Change," *Vital Speeches of the Day* 74, no. 4 (April 2008): 178–181. Retrieved from EBSCO*host* Academic Search Complete database on December 11, 2010.

Chapter 20

1. "Malaria-Topic Overview: What Is Malaria?" WebMD website, http://www.webmd.com/a-to-z-guides/malaria-topic-overview.

2. "Malaria-Topic Overview: What Are the Symptoms of Malaria?" WebMD website, http://www.webmd.com/a-to-z-guides/malaria-topic-overview.

3. Abraham Maslow, *Motivation and Personality*, 2nd ed. (New York: Harper & Row, 1970), 35–58.

4. One resource for poll information is the Inter-University Consortium for Political and Social Research (ICPSR) databank in Ann Arbor, MI (www.icpsr.umich.edu). Another resource for poll information is the Roper Center for Public Opinion Research, http://www.ropercenter.uconn.edu/about_roper.html.

5. Simeon Chow and Sarit Amir, "The Universality of Values: Implications for Global Advertising Strategy." *Journal of Advertising Research* 46, no. 3 (September 2006): 301–314. Retrieved from EBSCOhost Academic Communication & Mass Media Search Complete database on December 14, 2010.

6. This approach to values is adapted from Milton Rokeach's method of classifying beliefs by their centrality: Rokeach, in collaboration with Richard Bonier and others, *The Open and Closed Mind* (New York: Basic Books, 1960).

Chapter 21

1. Nelson Cowan, Troy D. Johnson, and J. Scott Saults, "Capacity Limits in List Item Recognition: Evidence from Proactive Interference," *Memory* 13, no. 3/4 (2005): 293–299. Retrieved September 26, 2008, from Academic Search Complete, EBSCOhost.

Chapter 22

1. Wallace C. Fotheringham, *Perspectives on Persuasion* (Boston: Allyn & Bacon, 1966), 32.

2. United States Code: Title 18,1111. Murder | LII / Legal Information Institute. Retrieved from http://www.law.cornell.edu/uscode/uscode18/usc_sec_18_00001111----000-.html on February 16, 2010.

3. Richard E. Petty and John T. Cacioppo, *Communication and Persuasion: Central and Peripheral Routes to Attitude Change* (New York: Springer-Verlag, 1986), 5.

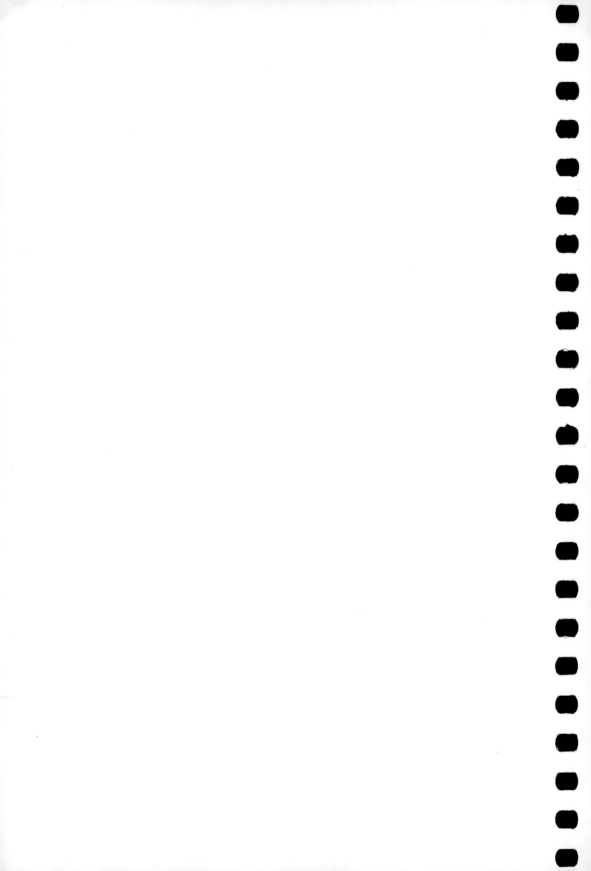

Index

Pages followed by t *indicate tables and* f *indicate figures.*

FIGURES AND TABLES

FIGURES

TABLES